American Military History

American Military History

A Documentary Reader

Second Edition

Brad D. Lookingbill

Registered Office(s)
John Wiley & Sons, Inc., 111 River Street, Hoboken, NJ 07030, USA

Editorial Office
101 Station Landing, Medford, MA 02155, USA

For details of our global editorial offices, customer services, and more information about Wiley products
visit us at www.wiley.com.

Wiley also publishes its books in a variety of electronic formats and by print-on-demand. Some content that
appears in standard print versions of this book may not be available in other formats.

Library of Congress Cataloging-in-Publication data applied for

[Paperback] 9781119335986

Cover image: © AHDesignConcepts/iStockphoto
Cover design by Wiley

Set in 10/12pt Warnock by SPi Global, Pondicherry, India

10   9   8   7   6   5   4   3   2   1

Contents

List of Illustrations *ix*
Acknowledgments *xi*

Introduction *1*

1 **An Uncommon Defense** 7
1.1 Powhatan Describes War among the Natives (1607) *7*
1.2 John Mason Campaigns against the Pequot (1637) *9*
1.3 Elizabeth Bacon Observes Skirmishes in Virginia (1676) *11*
1.4 Benjamin Church Plans for Action in New England (1704) *13*
1.5 James Oglethorpe Strikes Spanish Outposts (1739–1741) *15*
1.6 Robert Rogers Provides Rules for the Rangers (1757) *17*
1.7 An Unknown Soldier Sings "Yankee Doodle" (1775) *20*

2 **War for Independence** *23*
2.1 James Monroe Goes to War (1776) *23*
2.2 Albigence Waldo Treats Soldiers at Valley Forge (1777) *26*
2.3 Jeffrey Brace Fights for Liberty (1778) *28*
2.4 John Paul Jones Captures a British Frigate (1779) *30*
2.5 A French Officer Draws the Continental Line (1781) *32*
2.6 Deborah Sampson Wears a Uniform (1782) *34*
2.7 George Washington Bids Farewell to the Army (1783) *36*

3 **Establishing the Military** *41*
3.1 Alexander Hamilton Considers National Forces (1787) *41*
3.2 Henry Knox Arranges the Militia (1790) *44*
3.3 Anthony Wayne Prevails at Fallen Timbers (1794) *46*
3.4 Thomas Truxtun Recruits Seamen for the Quasi-War (1798) *48*
3.5 Congress Passes the Military Peace Establishment Act (1802) *51*
3.6 William Eaton Arrives on the Shores of Tripoli (1805) *52*
3.7 James Wilkinson Faces a Court Martial (1811) *55*

4   Mr. Madison's War   *59*
4.1   James Madison Calls for War (1812)   *59*
4.2   Lydia Bacon Enters Fort Detroit (1812)   *62*
4.3   Michel Felice Cornè Portrays the U.S.S. *Constitution* (1812)   *64*
4.4   Black Hawk Takes the War Path (1813)   *65*
4.5   Oliver Hazard Perry Defends Lake Erie (1813)   *68*
4.6   Francis Scott Key Pens "Defence of Fort McHenry" (1814)   *71*
4.7   Andrew Jackson Triumphs at New Orleans (1815)   *72*

5   The Martial Republic   *77*
5.1   John C. Calhoun Proposes an Expansible Army (1820)   *77*
5.2   The National Guard Parades in New York (1825)   *80*
5.3   John Downes Sails to Sumatra (1832)   *82*
5.4   Ethan Allen Hitchcock Patrols in Florida (1836)   *84*
5.5   Juan Seguín Remembers the Alamo (1837)   *86*
5.6   Michael H. Garty Serves on the U.S.S. *Somers* (1842)   *88*
5.7   Henry W. Halleck Lectures on War (1846)   *90*

6   The Forces of Manifest Destiny   *95*
6.1   James K. Polk Calls for War (1846)   *95*
6.2   James K. Holland Marches into Mexico (1846)   *98*
6.3   Zachary Taylor Describes Buena Vista (1847)   *101*
6.4   Winfield Scott Lands at Veracruz (1847)   *103*
6.5   James Walker Views the Storming of Chapultepec (1847)   *105*
6.6   Matthew C. Perry Steams to Japan (1852)   *106*
6.7   Elizabeth C. Smith Petitions for Bounty Land (1853)   *109*

7   The Blue and the Gray   *113*
7.1   Abraham Lincoln Issues Proclamations (1861)   *114*
7.2   Julia Ward Howe Composes "The Battle Hymn of the Republic" (1862)   *116*
7.3   Samuel Dana Greene Operates an Ironclad (1862)   *117*
7.4   Francis Lieber Promulgates Rules for War (1863)   *119*
7.5   Joshua Lawrence Chamberlain Defends Little Round Top (1863)   *121*
7.6   Sam R. Watkins Survives Chickamauga (1863)   *123*
7.7   James Henry Gooding Protests Unequal Pay (1863)   *126*
7.8   Robert E. Lee Requests Additional Troops (1864)   *128*
7.9   Phoebe Yates Pember Nurses at Chimborazo (1864)   *130*
7.10   Ulysses S. Grant Prevails at Appomattox (1865)   *132*

8   Twilight of the Indian Wars   *137*
8.1   William T. Sherman Discusses Indian Policy (1868)   *137*
8.2   Elizabeth B. Custer Camps with the Cavalry (1873)   *139*
8.3   Making Medicine Sketches Warriors and Soldiers (1877)   *142*
8.4   Emory Upton Evaluates Military Policy (1880)   *143*
8.5   The *Soldier's Handbook* Gives Healthy Advice (1884)   *145*
8.6   Henry W. Lawton Pursues the Apache (1886)   *148*
8.7   Nelson A. Miles Remembers Wounded Knee (1890)   *150*

9   A Rising Power   *155*
9.1   Alfred Thayer Mahan Advocates Sea Power (1890)   *155*
9.2   William McKinley Calls for War (1898)   *157*
9.3   Frank W. Pullen Charges in Cuba (1898)   *160*
9.4   Clara Barton Visits a Field Hospital (1898)   *162*
9.5   Frederick N. Funston Operates in the Philippines (1901)   *165*
9.6   The Committee on Naval Affairs Investigates Submarines (1902)   *167*
9.7   Dan Dugal Tours the World (1907–1909)   *169*

10   The War to End all Wars   *173*
10.1   Woodrow Wilson Calls for War (1917)   *173*
10.2   George M. Cohan Composes "Over There" (1917)   *176*
10.3   Congress Passes the Selective Service Act (1917)   *177*
10.4   John J. Pershing Commands the AEF (1917)   *180*
10.5   Howard Chandler Christy Publicizes the Navy (1917)   *183*
10.6   Ida Clyde Clarke Supports the Troops (1918)   *184*
10.7   Ben Hur Chastaine Reaches the Front (1918)   *186*

11   Out of the Trenches   *191*
11.1   The American Legion Rallies Veterans (1919)   *191*
11.2   George S. Patton Ponders the Next War (1922)   *194*
11.3   Billy Mitchell Advocates Air Power (1927)   *196*
11.4   Holland M. Smith Studies Marine Landings (1932)   *198*
11.5   Charles E. Humberger Joins the CCC (1933)   *200*
11.6   George C. Marshall Speaks to Historians (1939)   *202*
11.7   Harold R. Stark Recommends Plan Dog (1940)   *204*

12   Fighting World War II   *209*
12.1   Franklin D. Roosevelt Calls for War (1941)   *210*
12.2   Raymond A. Spruance Defends Midway (1942)   *211*
12.3   Charles C. Winnia Flies in the South Pacific (1943)   *214*
12.4   Hiro Higuchi Volunteers for Service (1943)   *216*
12.5   Dwight D. Eisenhower Invades Normandy (1944)   *218*
12.6   Congress Passes the GI Bill (1944)   *221*
12.7   Bill Mauldin Draws Willie and Joe (1944)   *223*
12.8   Melvin E. Bush Crosses the Siegfried Line (1945)   *224*
12.9   Jacqueline Cochran Praises the WASPs (1945)   *227*
12.10   B-29s Drop Atomic Bombs on Japan (1945)   *229*

13   A Cold War Begins   *233*
13.1   James V. Forrestal Manages the Pentagon (1948)   *233*
13.2   Omar Bradley Discusses Desegregation (1949)   *236*
13.3   Harry S. Truman Intervenes in Korea (1950)   *238*
13.4   Douglas MacArthur Addresses Congress (1951)   *240*
13.5   Spike Selmyhr Maneuvers in Korea (1951)   *243*
13.6   Maxwell D. Taylor Suggests a Flexible Response (1955)   *245*
13.7   Presidential Candidates Debate the Cold War (1960)   *248*

14   The Tragedy of Vietnam *251*
14.1   Herbert L. Ogier Patrols in the Tonkin Gulf (1964) *251*
14.2   Lyndon Johnson Escalates the War (1965) *254*
14.3   Sarah L. Blum Encounters Casualties (1967) *256*
14.4   William C. Westmoreland Reacts to Tet (1968) *258*
14.5   George T. Olsen Hunts the Enemy (1969) *260*
14.6   The Gates Commission Proposes an All-Volunteer Force (1970) *262*
14.7   George J. Eade Assesses the Christmas Bombings (1972) *265*

15   A New Military *269*
15.1   N. W. Ayer Rebrands the Army (1981) *269*
15.2   Ronald Reagan Envisions SDI (1983) *271*
15.3   Colin L. Powell Evaluates National Security (1989) *274*
15.4   H. Norman Schwarzkopf Defends the Persian Gulf (1990) *276*
15.5   Daniel L. Davis Sees Action in Desert Storm (1991) *278*
15.6   Congress Approves "Don't Ask, Don't Tell" (1993) *281*
15.7   Richard I. Thornton Readies the Marines (1999) *283*

16   Global War on Terror *287*
16.1   George W. Bush Calls for War (2001) *287*
16.2   Jessica Lynch Soldiers in Iraq (2003) *290*
16.3   Craig M. Mullaney Deploys to Afghanistan (2003) *292*
16.4   David H. Petraeus Counters an Insurgency (2007) *295*
16.5   Sean Householder Shares "The Warrior Song" (2009) *297*
16.6   William H. McRaven Commands SEALs (2011) *299*
16.7   The Pentagon Secures Cyberspace (2015) *301*

Full Chronology *305*
Sources and Credits *313*
Index *325*

List of Illustrations

2.5 Jean-Baptiste Antoine de Verger, "American Foot Soldiers during the Yorktown Campaign, 1781," Anne S. K. Brown Military Collection, Brown University Library.

4.3 "Action between USS *Constitution* and HMS *Guerriére*, 19 August 1812: Oil on canvas, by Michel Felice Cornè," Photo # K-26254, Naval History and Heritage Command, Department of the Navy, Washington, DC.

6.5 The Storming of Chapultepec, 1847, Prints and Photographs Division, Library of Congress.

8.3 Detail from U.S. Cavalry and Native American Indians by Making Medicine (Cheyenne), 17.5 × 33.3 cm, Book of Sketches made at Fort Marion, St. Augustine, Fla., ca. 1875–1878, Manuscript collection, Massachusetts Historical Society.

10.5 Gee!! I Wish I were a Man, 1917, Prints and Photographs Division, Library of Congress.

12.7 "Don't hurry for me, son. I like to see young men take an interest in their work," 1944. Bill Mauldin Cartoon Collection, 45th Infantry Division Museum, Oklahoma City, Oklahoma. © 1944 Bill Mauldin. Courtesy of Bill Mauldin Estate LLC.

15.1 N. W. Ayer & Son Advertising Records, Archives Center, National Museum of American History, Smithsonian Institution.

Acknowledgments

Many individuals helped me with this textbook. First and foremost, I would like thank my son, Augustus, and my daughter, Beatrice. Because they are my greatest teachers, I dedicate this work to them.

I am able to do this work because of the American military. While pursuing an education in 1988, I joined the Army National Guard and received G.I. Bill benefits. I was recognized as an honor graduate of my Army basic training unit at Fort Sill and later earned honors at the Primary Leadership Development Course for noncommissioned officers. I was a member of the historic 45th Division from Oklahoma, and my service in the field artillery included time as the gun chief on a M110 howitzer. Proud to call myself a "Thunderbird," my intellectual devotion to the history of the armed forces is personal as well as professional. In a sense, the men and women in uniform remain a part of my extended family.

I also appreciate the immeasurable support of colleagues and friends. Roger Bromert, Gerald Thompson, Charles Glaab, and Robert Freeman Smith passed away before the completion of this work, but I am indebted to each for mentoring me during my career as well as for their service in the military. Many individuals helped to locate documents, including Michael E. Gonzalez, curator for the 45th Infantry Division Museum in Oklahoma City, Oklahoma. Carl S. Richardson sent me a copy of a Marine pilot's diary, which had been entrusted to his care. At Columbia College of Missouri, Michael Polley shared his research on World War II. Terry Smith critiqued an early draft of the introduction. Academic Affairs funded various stages of my research. I am indebted to individuals at Stafford Library, namely Janet Caruthers, Cynthia Cole, Mary Batterson, Lucia D'Agostino, Peter Neely, Nason Throgmorton, and Vandy Evermon. I was assisted by work-study students, Sara Hurst and Craig Rush. Finally, the undergraduates enrolled in HIST 370 helped to hone my thinking about the primary sources. If I have failed to list a name deserving acknowledgment, then please accept my apology and my gratitude.

I am very grateful for the support of the professionals at Wiley-Blackwell. I benefited enormously from the expertise and advice of anonymous reviewers. Linda Auld and Caroline Richards copy-edited the manuscript. Furthermore, Galen Smith guided me throughout the publication process. In my opinion, there is no better editor in the publishing business than Peter Coveney. He understood from the beginning what the textbook offered to instructors and students alike. I am privileged to work with such a great team of professionals.

In preparing the second edition, I have profited from the assistance of many others. Andrew Davidson at Wiley-Blackwell recommended updating the textbook. Haze

Humbert, Maddie Koufogazos, Jennifer Manias, and Kelley Baylis kept everything on track. Janani Govindankutty managed the production and the permissions. Katherine Carr provided copy editing. Aneetta Antony handled production editing. Beth Bailey at the University of Kansas and Kara Dixon Vuic at Texas Christian University shared new materials with me. Major Andrew J. Forney at the United States Military Academy aided me as well.

I will conclude by giving thanks to Deidra, my amazing wife. She gave me her criticisms and suggestions. She gave me her empathy, too. Simply stated, I owe her everything.

In spite of all the advice and guidance I have received while working on the textbook, I alone am responsible for any errors.

Introduction

"To fight out a war, you must believe something and want something with all your might," declared Oliver Wendell Holmes, a wounded veteran of the American Civil War and later an associate justice on the United States Supreme Court. His words before a Memorial Day audience in 1884 expressed something elemental about American military history. The former Lieutenant Colonel spoke of those who were near and dear to him, "not because their lives have become historic," but because "their lives are the type of what every soldier has known and seen" in war. He called them "the army of the dead," who swept before the nation wearing "wounds like stars." He remembered his comrades with great reverence: "I speak of those whom I have seen." With a gesture to the audience, he mused: "But you all have known such; you, too, remember!"[1]

No one should forget the millions of Americans, who have fought in wars large and small. They embody what endures at the heart of military affairs, that is, the will to fight for something greater than the self. For centuries, they provided for the common defense. The history of the American military offers a framework through which the people and the nation can be analyzed. At the dawn of a new millennium, acts of war still permit individuals to dedicate themselves to a cause in life as well as in death. Because so many have fought with all their might, I ask the readers of this textbook to consider the historical question: What did American warriors believe and want?

What they said has survived in scores of documents, which I sample in the following pages as broadly as possible. A number consider the role and the use of the armed forces in relation to the social, cultural, economic, political, and territorial development of the United States. Some feature commentary on strategic initiatives, combat operations, force structure, public policy, and home fronts. Others offer the firsthand testimony of extraordinary men and women in uniform. Most reveal the connections between combatants and the societies that spawned them. Thanks to an abundance of documentary materials, I present excerpts from diaries, memoirs, letters, speeches, songs, posters, memoranda, reports, manuals, laws, debates, petitions, reviews, and articles.

Attentive to diversity in the American military, I present not one point of view but many. The sampling of extracts makes for an eclectic mix, but not infinitely so. The result may be described as a reconnaissance of a historical field. The point is not to go left or right to engage the past. Rather, it is to dig deeper and to reach wider in the effort to grasp what happened and why. Whether part of the U.S. Army, Navy, Air Force, Marine Corps, National Guard, or Coast Guard, Americans from all walks of life served with honor and dignity. Even while facing the prospect of death, they remained focused

American Military History: A Documentary Reader, Second Edition. Brad D. Lookingbill.
© 2019 John Wiley & Sons, Inc. Published 2019 by John Wiley & Sons, Inc.

on accomplishing their missions in theaters around the world. In the process, their experiences became entangled with thematic issues common to each historical era. To help readers recognize the most prevalent themes of the documents, my aims in this textbook are threefold.

My first aim is to trace America's ways of war. Beginning in 1607, the approaches to combat in North America appeared as varied and as ambiguous as each individual. In a sense, each was fighting his or her own battles. Over time, the use of the armed forces by the United States revealed patterns of design and purpose. Although war often created a momentum of its own, Americans mastered strategies for attrition as well as tactics for defense, concentration, maneuver, and assault. Combat included not only strategic and tactical aspects but also social and intellectual thrusts. In other words, operations involved fighting as well as thinking. What distinguished American warriors was not just the logistics of their military campaigns. It was also their passion for the literature, music, and art of war. The face of battle elicited extreme emotional responses, which resonated with the lingering effects of stress and trauma. At the same time, the nation expressed a great deal of pride about the profession of arms. The ways of war involved a private and public sense of civic virtue, collective anxieties, and shared memories.

Of course, there never was a single or simple way of war. Warfare involved extraordinary actions, which combatants often remembered differently. Whether charging or retreating, no one observed everything on the battlefield. Lies, falsehoods, distortions, and exaggerations appear at times in the spoken and the written accounts of individuals. Thus, language itself may seem inadequate for the task of recovering the whole story from partial and fragmentary narratives. Even so, the recollections and the commemorations of war illustrate the martial spirit at home and abroad. Veterans told stories about adventures that astonished and perplexed. They recalled experiences marked by horror and misery. The most vivid and compelling tales give a sense of combat, thereby providing the next best—or worst—thing to having been there. Once recorded, the reports of eyewitnesses convey far more than words alone can possibly say. Their voices deserve amplification, because they have come to terms with the incontrovertible fact that death remains the end of all war. Engaging with the primary sources permits readers to study the ways of war in a raw and unfiltered form.

My second aim is to study leadership in military affairs. Time and again, commissioned and noncommissioned officers led others through the fog of war. They made tough choices in order to achieve military objectives, whether or not they fully recognized all the obstacles before them. In spite of the risks to life and limb, they persuaded their comrades in arms to follow them up hills or into caves. While setting courageous examples, they drove the rank and file across dark skies and stormy waters. They endeavored to seize the initiative in a struggle, which on many occasions placed them in the crossfire. Their sway turned motley crews into cohesive units. Their foresight made teamwork successful. To be sure, combat operations were punctuated with accidents and surprises. Even the best laid plans for action faltered in the absence of adequate resources, proper training, high morale, or public support. From boot camps to battle stations, however, leaders often adapted and overcame. Many of the challenges they met in the past continue to pose challenges to men and women in uniform today. With respect to decision-making, the following pages will expose readers to models of military leadership at all levels of service.

Without a doubt, a number of martial figures in the United States possessed a genius for leadership. More than simply trumpeting their military accomplishments, many leaders wrote reflectively about how they worked major problems. The best and the brightest studied innovative concepts to improve the readiness of the armed forces. Searching for determining factors in war, they obsessed over losses as well as victories. They carefully analyzed elements of battle—from both the ground up and the inside out. They assessed outcomes to better understand their own strengths and weaknesses rather than merely to second-guess the choices made by others. They benefited from the privileges of hindsight, which enabled them to identify historical parallels instructive to future generations. Lively and open-ended discussions about the lessons learned tended to educate their senses. Insights born out of wisdom provoked and enlightened not simply by pleasing guardians of a set of ideological assumptions or by refighting each battle from the last campaign. Rather, great military leaders developed a pragmatic style that privileged performance and results over orthodoxies and doctrines.

Thirdly, my aim is to reveal the vitality of civil–military relations in the United States. Since the Age of Enlightenment, standing armies and navies represented nothing if not state-organized instruments of violence. The founders of the American republic established the military based—at least in theory—on the notion that service constituted an obligation of all citizens. The U.S. Constitution permitted Congress to draw largely from the preexisting militia system while building a new nation. Moreover, each Commander in Chief tried to strike a delicate balance. On the one hand, the military establishment seemed at odds with the most liberal impulses of community life. On the other hand, global empires on the march made the world unsafe for democracy. Consequently, a professional military with trained regulars prepared for peace as well as for war. Civilian authorities used them in constabulary roles across the continent and deployed them in contingency operations overseas. During the draft era, the federal government forged a massive war machine to stop the aggression of totalitarian regimes. With the introduction of nuclear arms and guided missiles, the American military became a mighty tool for national security.

For the sake of national security, the United States continues to marshal its military power to meet the challenges of globalization. Blood is still shed on land, at sea, and in air, but battles also rage in cyberspace. Wars have been won and lost in Washington, DC, where the Commander in Chief works closely with the military brass inside the Pentagon. With Congressional appropriations for procurement, pay, and benefits, civilian control over the military establishment endures. However, American society no longer considers military service an obligation of citizenship. Instead, the Department of Defense now depends upon an all-volunteer force structure. Thanks to public policies that have revolutionized military affairs, the armed forces destroy enemies on battlefields with as little risk to civilians as possible. Ironically, defense experts want the best military on the planet in order to give peace a chance. Hence, a number of the documents will invite readers to engage in an ongoing national dialogue about the common defense. Each reader undoubtedly will recognize something vital to the American republic in the relationship between civilians and the military.

In sum, my aims complicate the dominant narrative without necessarily changing it. Critics have dismissed the phrase "freedom fighters," but the American military effectively liberated people under tyranny. Whatever their races, classes, and genders, men and women in uniform fought oppression around the world. Experiencing no easy days or nights, they considered war not only in theory but also in practice. Of course, they often disagreed about the meanings of their encounters with each other and with their enemies. They suffered and sacrificed, but they were not silenced. However socially or culturally constructed, ideas mattered to them as much as bullets or bombs. Whether they carried a flintlock musket or piloted an A-4 *Skyhawk*, they battled for a vast country. They remained as much a part of the fabric of the United States as any other thread. The implications of war differed for individuals, yet all service members knew something personal about American military history. The documentary evidence conveys what no one should forget about their stories. Everywhere they went they fulfilled the nation's fondest hopes of what America was, is, and should be.

To be sure, there are things absent from this kind of a textbook. Obviously, the documents give only fleeting glimpses of the contingencies in war. By focusing upon the contest between the English colonists and the indigenous populations, the early chapters offer no comparative viewpoints from Spanish, Dutch, or French outposts on the continent. Likewise, the later chapters ignore the clandestine operations, nuclear umbrellas, and defense contractors of the Cold War. Although campaigns appear in every chapter, they lack the "drum-and-bugles" of battle histories that some historians may prefer. Historians seeking details regarding logistics, manpower, and arsenals may be uninterested in the linguistic turns of the documents. Missing are excerpts that illustrate the full extent to which staff rides, war games, military fiction, or social media shaped expectations about combat. More might be said about the evolving definitions of wounds, disabilities, and bodies. The key to any textbook on American military history, nonetheless, is to not be so far off the mark or too narrow in focus that it becomes irrelevant once the future is revealed.

To the greatest extent possible, I have tried to preserve the richness of the primary sources in this textbook through careful editing. With only minimal refinements to the language, the quaint spellings, curious acronyms, and archaic renderings appear unaltered. By retaining most of their original forms, the passages convey a sense of the past. Nevertheless, words that pass through the hands of several scribes occasionally require polishing to ensure readability in the present. From time to time, edits to typography, capitalization, punctuation, and grammar have clarified awkward prose. Ellipses indicate redactions; brackets contain additions. The margins are not cluttered with annotations, because excessive editorial commentary tends to distract from what was actually said. Given the completeness of the citations, readers will be able to consult the primary sources to find the full texts of the edited excerpts.

I have arranged the edited excerpts chronologically into 16 chapters. From English colonization to current globalization, they align with major periods of American military history. As a frame of reference, a timeline of key events opens each chapter. Each closes with a list of suggested sources for further reading. Introduced with information on people, places, and actions, a head-note places the excerpt within a historical context. To provide a scaffold for working with the blocks of text, three questions appear after each excerpt. They range from a basic query for inviting literal responses to an advanced one for making appropriate inferences. In regard to the history of the American military, the scope of coverage reveals the "big picture" from various angles of vision.

In the final analysis, American military history teaches us about the human element in war. In the words of one wounded veteran, American warriors believed something and wanted something with all their might. Because their "hearts were touched with fire," he said, they had learned that "life is a profound and passionate thing."[2] They forever will remain the subjects of historical epics, because their jobs by definition involved matters of life and death. Though battle itself is never glorious, their devotion to the greater good is full of glory. Their bravery through the ages resonates with the narrative of the United States as a whole. It is an incredible saga, which began long ago on the North American seaboard and continues even now near another shore.

Notes

1 Oliver Wendell Holmes, Jr., *Dead, Yet Living: An Address Delivered At Keene, NH, Memorial Day, May 30, 1884* (Boston: Ginn, Heath, and Company, 1884), 3–10.
2 Holmes, *Dead, Yet Living*, 11–12.

1

An Uncommon Defense

Chronology

1492	Europeans invade the Americas
1565	The Spanish establish Saint Augustine
1607	The English establish Jamestown
1608	The French found Quebec
1609–1613	First Anglo-Powhatan War in Virginia
1614	The Dutch erect Fort Nassau
1620	The Pilgrims settle Plymouth
1636–1637	The Pequot War in New England
1644–1646	Second Anglo-Powhatan War in Virginia
1675–1676	King Philip's War in New England
	Bacon's Rebellion in Virginia
1698	King William's War
1702–1712	Queen Anne's War
1715–1716	Yamasee War in South Carolina
1739–1748	King George's War (War of Jenkins' Ear)
1754–1763	Great War for Empire (French and Indian War)
1770	Boston Massacre
1774	Parliament Adopts the Coercive Acts

1.1   Powhatan Describes War among the Natives (1607)

As the seventeenth century dawned in North America, European empires staked their claims to the continent. They established outposts in distant corners of North America: the Spanish at Saint Augustine and Santa Fe, the French at Quebec, the Dutch at Fort Nassau, and, most significantly for the future United States, the English at Jamestown. Arriving in 1607, the English colonists of Virginia included a few military veterans such as Captain Christopher Newport and Captain John Smith. They encountered a powerful chieftain named Powhatan, who governed the Native people along the James River through tribute, diplomacy, and trade. Called a Werowance, or great ruler, he asserted supremacy over a host of Algonquian-speaking tribes. They were loosely affiliated in what rather grandly came to be known as Powhatan's Confederacy. Their

American Military History: A Documentary Reader, Second Edition. Brad D. Lookingbill.
© 2019 John Wiley & Sons, Inc. Published 2019 by John Wiley & Sons, Inc.

warriors practiced a mode of combat that accentuated "skulking" tactics such as the ambush. Powhatan initially considered the strangers from England as potential allies in a struggle to extend his power around the Chesapeake Bay. In addition to their loyalty, he desired to acquire their technologically advanced swords, guns, and powder. However, relations between the Natives and the newcomers in Virginia grew increasingly violent over the years, especially once the starving English colonists began raiding indigenous food supplies.

Document

Yet Captaine Smith, sayth the King, some doubt I have of your comming hither, that makes me not so kindly seeke to relieve you as I would: for many doe informe me, your comming hither is not for trade, but to invade my people, and possesse my Country, who dare not come to bring you corne, seeing you thus armed with your men. To free us of this feare, leave aboord your weapons, for here they are needlesse, we being all friends, and for ever *Powhatans* […]

Captaine Smith, you may understand that I having seene the death of all my people thrice, and not any one living of these three generations but my selfe; I know the difference of peace and warre better then any in my Country. But now I am old and ere long must die, my brethren, namely *Opitchapam, Opechancanough*, and *Kekataugh*, my two sisters, and their two daughters, are distinctly each others successors. I wish their experience no lesse then mine, and your love to them no lesse then mine to you. But this bruit from *Nandsamund*, that you are come to destroy my Country, so much affrighteth all my people as they dare not visit you.

What will it availe you to take that by force you may quickly have by love, or to destroy them that provide you food? What can you get by warre, when we can hide our provisions and fly to the woods? Whereby you must famish by wronging us your friends. And why are you thus jealous of our loves seeing us unarmed, and both doe, and are willing still to feede you, with that you cannot get but by our labours?

Thinke you I am so simple, not to know it is better to eate good meate, lye well, and sleepe quietly with my women and children, laugh and be merry with you, have copper, hatchets, or what I want being your friend: then be forced to flie from all, to lie cold in the woods, feede upon acornes, rootes, and such trash, and be so hunted by you, that I can neither rest, eate, nor sleepe; but my tyred men must watch, and if a twig but breake, every one cryeth there commeth Captaine Smith: then must I fly I know not whether: and thus with miserable feare, end my miserable life, leaving my pleasures to such youths as you, which through your rash unadvisednesse may quickly as miserably end, for want of that, you never know where to finde. Let this therefore assure you of our loves, and every yeare our friendly trade shall furnish you with corne; and now also, if you would come in friendly manner to see us, and not thus with your guns and swords as to invade your foes […]

Captaine Smith, I never use any *Werowance* so kindely as your selfe, yet from you I receive the least kindnesse of any. Captaine Newport gave me swords, copper, cloathes, a bed, towels, or what I desired; ever taking what I offered him, and would send away his gunnes when I intreated him: none doth deny to lye at my feet, or refuse to doe what I desire, but onely you; of whom I can have nothing but what you regard not, and yet you will have whatsoever you demand. Captaine Newport you call father, and so you call me; but I see for all us both you will doe what you list, and we must both seeke to content you.

But if you intend so friendly as you say, send hence your armes, that I may beleeve you; for you see the love I beare you, doth cause me thus nakedly to forget my selfe […]

I gladly accept your salute of love and peace, which while I live, I shall exactly keepe, his pledges thereof I receive with no lesse thanks, although they are not so ample as formerly he had received; but for my daughter, I have sold her within this few daies to a great *Werowance*, for two bushels of *Rawrenoke*, three daies journie from me […] I desire no former assurance of his friendship, than the promise hee hath made, from me he hath a pledge, one of my daughters, which so long as she lives shall be sufficient, when she dies, he shall have another: I hold it not a brotherly part to desire to bereave me of my two children at once. Farther, tell him though he had no pledge at all, hee need not distrust any injurie from me or my people; there have beene too many of his men and mine slaine, and by my occasion there shall never be more, I which have power to performe it, have said it, although I should have just cause, for I am now old, & would gladly end my daies in peace; if you offer me injurie, my countrie is large enough to goe from you: Thus much I hope will satisfie my brother.

Now because you are wearie, and I sleepie, wee will thus end.

Source: John Smith, *The Generall Historie of Virginia, New England, and the Summer Isles,* Volume 1 (London, 1624; rpt. New York: Macmillan, 1907), 157–161, 225–226.

Questions for Consideration

1) What, according to Powhatan, were the essential differences between "peace and warre" under his rule?
2) Why did he dread fighting against the English in particular?
3) How did he propose to prevent more fighting in the future?

1.2 John Mason Campaigns against the Pequot (1637)

The colonists of New England established a militia system to defend new settlements, to act as a police force, and to secure the backcountry. In contrast to the stylized and ritualistic combat common to Native Americans, the English governments sanctioned wars of extirpation. From 1636 to 1637, tensions over trade relations exploded into New England's first major Anglo-Indian war. The Pequot Indians constituted a polity whose location at the mouth of the Connecticut River enabled them to deal with Dutch traders from Manhattan and English colonists in the Massachusetts Bay. The death of two traders sparked fears among the English that the Pequot planned an uprising. Militia companies from New England towns and allied warriors from the Mohegan and the Narragansett tribes assailed the Pequot along the Mystic River. On May 26, 1637, Captain John Mason urged the English militiamen and their Indian allies to torch Fort Mystic and to kill those gathered behind the palisades. They burned wigwams, shot fleeing warriors, captured women and children, and divided the spoils. They killed as many as 700 at Fort Mystic. Some survivors were forced into "praying towns" for religious conversion. Others were sold to Caribbean slave traders. The Pequot name was outlawed in New England thereafter.

Document

In Matters of War, those who are both able and faithful should be improved; and then bind them not up into too narrow a Compass: For it is not possible for the wisest and ablest Senator to foresee all Accidents and Occurrents that fall out in the Management and Pursuit of a War: Nay although possibly he might be trained up in Military Affairs; and truly much less can he have any great Knowledge who hath had but little Experience therein. What shall I say? GOD led his People thro' many Difficulties and Turnings; yet by more than an ordinary Hand of Providence he brought them to Canaan at last [...]

We then Marching on in a silent Manner, the Indians that remained fell all into the Rear, who formerly kept the Van; (being possessed with great Fear) we continued our March till about one Hour in the Night: and coming to a little Swamp between two Hills, there we pitched our little Camp; much wearied with hard Travel, keeping great Silence, supposing we were very near the Fort [Mystic] as our Indians informed us; which proved otherwise: The Rocks were our Pillows; yet Rest was pleasant: The Night proved Comfortable, being clear and Moon Light: We appointed our Guards and placed our Sentinels at some distance; who heard the Enemy Singing at the Fort, who continued that Strain until Midnight, with great Insulting and Rejoycing [...]

In the Morning, we awaking and seeing it very light, supposing it had been day, and so we might have lost our Opportunity, having purposed to make our Assault before Day; rowsed the Men with all expedition, and briefly commended ourselves and Design to GOD, thinking immediately to go to the Assault; the Indians shewing us a Path, told us that it led directly to the Fort. We held on our March about two Miles, wondering that we came not to the Fort, and fearing we might be deluded: But seeing Corn newly planted at the Foot of a great Hill, supposing the Fort was not far off, a Champion Country being round about us; then making a stand, gave the Word for some of the Indians to come up: At length ONKOS and one WEQUOSH appeared; We demanded of them, Where was the Fort? They answered: On the Top of that Hill: Then we demanded, Where were the Rest of the Indians? They answered, Behind, exceedingly affraid: We wished them to tell the rest of their Fellows, That they should by no means Fly, but stand at what distance they pleased, and see whether ENGLISH MEN would now Fight or not. Then Captain Underhill came up, who Marched in the Rear; and commending our selves to GOD divided our Men: There being two Entrances into the Fort, intending to enter both at once: Captain Mason leading up to that on the North East Side; who approaching within one Rod, heard a Dog bark and an Indian crying *Owanux! Owanux!* which is Englishmen! Englishmen!

We called up our Forces with all expedition, gave Fire upon them through the Pallizado; the Indians being in a dead indeed their last Sleep: Then we wheeling off fell upon the main Entrance, which was blocked up with Bushes about Breast high, over which the Captain passed, intending to make good the Entrance, encouraging the rest to follow. Lieutenant Seeley endeavoured to enter; but being somewhat cumbred, stepped back and pulled out the Bushes and so entred, and with him about sixteen Men: We had formerly concluded to destroy them by the Sword and save the Plunder.

Whereupon Captain Mason seeing no Indians, entred a Wigwam; where he was beset with many Indians, waiting all opportunities to lay Hands on him, but could not prevail. At length William Heydon espying the Breach in the Wigwam, supposing some English might be there, entred; but in his Entrance fell over a dead Indian; but speedily recovering himself, the Indians some fled, others crept under their Beds: The Captain going out of the Wigwam saw many Indians in the Lane or Street; he making towards them, they fled, were pursued to the End of the Lane, where they were met by Edward Pattison, Thomas Barber, with some others; where seven of them were Slain, as they said. The Captain facing about, Marched a slow Pace up the Lane he came down, perceiving himself very much out of Breath; and coming to the other End near the Place where he first entred, saw two Soldiers standing close to the Pallizado with their Swords pointed to the Ground: The Captain told them that We should never kill them after that manner: The Captain also said, WE MUST BURN THEM; and immediately stepping into the Wigwam where he had been before, brought out a Fire-Brand, and putting it into the Matts with which they were covered, set the Wigwams on Fire. Lieutenant Thomas Bull and Nicholas Omsted beholding, came up; and when it was throughly kindled, the Indians ran as Men most dreadfully Amazed.

And indeed such a dreadful Terror did the ALMIGHTY let fall upon their Spirits, that they would fly from us and run into the very Flames, where many of them perished. And when the Fort was thoroughly Fired, Command was given, that all should fall off and surround the Fort; which was readily attended by all; only one Arthur Smith being so wounded that he could not move out of the Place, who was happily espied by Lieutenant Bull, and by him rescued. The Fire was kindled on the North East Side to windward; which did swiftly over-run the Fort, to the extream Amazement of the Enemy, and great Rejoycing of our selves. Some of them climbing to the Top of the Pallizado; others of them running into the very Flames; many of them gathering to windward, lay pelting at us with their Arrows; and we repayed them with our small Shot: Others of the Stoutest issued forth, as we did guess, to the Number of Forty, who perished by the Sword.

Source: John Mason, *A Brief History of the Pequot War* (Boston: Printed by S. Kneeland and T. Green, 1736), 1–9.

Questions for Consideration

1) What were the Pequot doing when Captain Mason and his militia first arrived at the fort?
2) Who provided the intelligence regarding the fort?
3) How did he justify his command decisions in the field?

1.3   Elizabeth Bacon Observes Skirmishes in Virginia (1676)

The English tradition of militia trainbands and watch patrols influenced colonial affairs in the Chesapeake. Though Governor Sir William Berkeley of Virginia proposed erecting a series of forts along the western frontier, he refused to permit the new settlers to bear their arms in attacks on Native Americans. The militia thus turned to a 29-year-old planter named Nathaniel Bacon, who settled in Virginia during 1674. Writing a letter to a sister in June of 1676, his wife Elizabeth observed the frequent skirmishes in the backcountry that prompted him to take command of the militia. He demanded a commission from the governor and, without waiting for it, launched sorties against Indian communities. When the governor refused to grant the commission, Bacon then led his forces to seize Jamestown. The governor, who traded ammunition and powder to the Appomattox Indians, eventually issued the commission, though he ordered "General" Bacon to cease his operations. The officer chased the governor from the capital and torched it. The militia spread havoc in Virginia for weeks. On October 26, Bacon suddenly died of dysentery. Meanwhile, the governor marshaled cannons and crews from merchant ships to crush the rebellion. After regaining control of Virginia by 1677, he hanged more than 20 of Bacon's lieutenants.

Document

Dear Sister,

I pray God keep the worst Enemy I have from ever being in such a sad condition as I have been in [...] occasioned by ye troublesome Indians, who have killed one of our Overseers at the outward plantation which wee had, and we have lost a great stock of cattle, which wee had upon it, and a good crop that wee should have made there, such plantation Nobody durst come nigh, which is a very great losse to us.

If you had been here, it would have grieved your heart to hear the pitiful complaints of the people, The Indians killing the people daily the Governour not taking any notice of it for to hinder them, but let them daily doe all the mischief they can: I am sure if the Indians were not cowards, they might have destroied all the upper plantations, and killed all the people upon them; the Governour so much their friend, that hee would not suffer any body to hurt one of the Indians; and the poor people came to your brother to desire him to help against the Indians, and hee being very much concerned for the losse of his Overseer, and for the losse of so many men and women and children's lives every day, hee was willing to doe them all the good hee could; so hee begged of the Governour for a commission in severall letters to him, that hee might goe out against them, but hee would not grant one, so daily more mischief done by them, so your brother not able to endure any longer, he went out without a commission.

The Governour being very angry with him put out high things against him, and told mee that he would most certainly hang him as soon as hee returned, which hee would certainly have done; but what for fear of the Governour's hanging him, and what for fear of the Indians killing him brought mee to this sad condicon, but blessed be God hee came in very well, with the losse of a very few men; never was known such a fight in Virginia with so few men's losse. The fight did continue nigh a night and a day without any intermission. They did destroy a great many of the Indians, thanks bee to God, and might have killed a great many more, but the Governour were so much the Indian's friend and our enemy, that hee sent the Indians word that Mr. Bacon was out against them, that they might save themselves. After Mr. Bacon was come in hee was forced to keep a guard of soldiers about his house, for the Governour would certainly have had his life taken away privately, if he would have had opportunity; but the country does so really love him, that they would not leave him alone anywhere; there was not anybody against him but the Governour and a few of his great men, which have gott their Estates by the Governour; surely if your brother's crime had been so great, all the country would not have been for him, you never know any better beloved than hee is.

I doe verily believe that rather than hee should come to any hurt by the Governour or anybody else they would most of them willingly loose their lives. The Governour has sent his Lady into England with great complaints to the King against Mr. Bacon, but when Mr. Bacon's and all the people's complaints be also heard, I hope it may be very well. Since your brother came in hee hath sought to the Governour for commission, but none would be granted to him, so that ye Indians have had a very good time, to doe more mischief.

They have murdered and destroied a great many whole families since, and the men resolving not to goe under any but yor brother, most of the country did rise in Armes, and went down to the Governour, and would not stir till hee had given a commission to yor brother which hee has now done. He is made General of the Virginia Warr, and now I live in great fear, that hee should loose his life amongst them. They are come verry nigh our Plantation where wee live.

Source: "Bacon's Rebellion," *William and Mary Quarterly* 9 (July 1900), 1–10.

Questions for Consideration

1) Which functions of the militia seemed most important to Elizabeth Bacon?
2) What official commission did her husband receive from the governor?
3) Why was she so alarmed by the skirmishes in Virginia?

1.4 Benjamin Church Plans for Action in New England (1704)

From King Philip's War to Queen Anne's War, provincials honed their strategies and tactics in the woodlands. To encourage Indian alliances, authorities paid bounties for enemy scalps. Colonial arms trading with Indians, though officially outlawed, lessened the technological advantages that the English militia initially possessed against Native warriors. The latter learned to master the flintlock musket and became quite skilled at utilizing firearms in deadly "hit-and-run" raids. Likewise, the former grew to appreciate the use of mobile units on multiple fronts to harass an enemy in hiding. Chief among the English veterans of these wars, Colonel Benjamin Church was born in the Plymouth colony and later resided in Massachusetts and Rhode Island. While successfully penetrating forests and swamps, he commanded an "Army of the United Colonies" during 1676. His expedition killed the belligerent Wampanoag chieftain known as King Philip, although sporadic fighting continued in New England for decades. English antagonism drove many Algonquian-speakers into the arms of the French. During 1704, Massachusetts Governor Joseph Dudley requested that Colonel Church draw up a plan of action to fight the French and the Indians. Thereafter, he conducted special operations in Maine, Canada, and Acadia. By the time of his death in 1718, the Europeans were engaged in a fierce struggle for dominion over North America.

Document

According to your request, when I was last with yourself, and in obedience thereunto, I present you with these following lines, that concern the preparation for next spring's expedition, to attack the enemy. According to my former direction; for it is good to have a full stroke at them first, before they have opportunity to run for it. For the first of our action will be our opportunity to destroy them, and to prevent their running away, in waylaying every passage, and make them know we are in good earnest. And so we being in a diligent use of means, we may hope for a blessing from the Almighty, and that he will be pleased to put a dread in their hearts, that they may fall before us and perish. For my advice is,

First. That ten or twelve hundred good able soldiers, well equipped, be in a readiness fit for action, by the first of April at farthest; for then will be the time to be upon action.

Secondly. That five and forty or fifty, good whaleboats be had ready, well fitted with five good oars and twelve or fifteen good paddles to every boat. And upon the wale of each boat, five pieces of strong leather be fastened on each side to slip five small ashbars through; that so, whenever they land, the men may step overboard, and slip in said bars across, and take up said boat that she may not be hurt against the rocks. And that two suitable brass kettles be provided to belong to each boat to dress the men's victuals in to make their lives comfortable.

Thirdly. That four or five hundred pairs of good Indian shoes be made ready, fit for the service for the English and Indians, that must improve the whale boats and birch canoes; for they will be very proper and safe for that service. And let there be a good store of cow hides well tanned, for a supply of such shoes, and hemp to make thread, and wax to mend and make more such shoes when wanted, and a good store of awls.

Fourthly. That there be an hundred large hatchets, or light axes, made pretty broad, and steeled with the best steel that can be got, and made by workmen, that [they] may cut very well, and hold, that the hemlock knots may not break or turn them, to widen the landing place up the falls. For it may happen that we may get up with some of our whale boats to their falls or headquarters.

Fifthly. That there be a suitable quantity of small bags, or wallets provided, that every man that wants may have one to put up his bullets in, of such a size as will fit his gun, (and not be served as at Casco.) That every man's bag be so marked that he may not change it. For if so, it will make a great confusion in action. That every man's store of ball be weighed to him, that so he may be accountable and may not squander it away and also his store of powder, that so he may try his powder and gun before action. And that every particular company may have a barrel of powder to themselves and so marked that it may by no means be changed. That men may know beforehand, and may not be cheated out of their lives, by having bad powder, or not knowing how to use it. And this will prove a great advantage to the action.

Sixthly. That Colonel John Gorham, if he may be prevailed with, may be concerned in the management of the whale boats, he having been formerly concerned in the eastern parts and experienced in that affair. And whalemen then will be very serviceable in this expedition, which having a promise made to them, that they shall be released in good season, to go home a whaling in the fall, your excellency will have men enough.

Seventhly. That there may be raised for this service three hundred Indians at least, and more if they may be had; for I know certainly, of my own knowledge that they exceed most of our English in hunting and skulking in the woods, being always used to it. And it must be practised if ever we intend to destroy those Indian enemies.

Eighthly. That the soldiers already out eastward in the service, men of known judgment, may take a survey of them and their arms, and see if their arms be good and they know how to use them in shooting right, at a mark, and that they be men of good reason and sense to know how to manage themselves in so difficult a piece of service as this Indian hunting is, for bad men are but a clog and hinderance to an army, being a trouble and vexation to good commanders, and so many mouths to devour the country's provision, and a hinderance to all good actions.

Ninthly. That special care be had in taking up the whaleboats that they be good, and fit for that service, so that the country be not cheated as formerly in having rotten boats and as much care that the owners may have good satisfaction for them.

Tenthly. That the tenders or transports, vessels to be improved in this action, be good decked vessels, not too big because of going up several rivers having four or six small guns apiece for defence, and the fewer men will defend them, and there are enough such vessels to be had.

Eleventhly. To conclude all, if your excellency will be pleased to make yourself great and us a happy people, as to the destroying of our enemies and easing of our taxes, &c., be pleased to draw forth all those forces now in pay in all the eastward parts, both at Saco and Casco bay, for those two trading houses never did any good nor ever will, and are not worthy the name of Queen's forts; and the first building of them had no other effect but to lay us under tribute to that wretched pagan crew; and I hope will never be wanted for that they were first built; but sure it is, they are very serviceable to them; for they get many a good advantage of us to destroy our men and laugh at us for our folly, that we should be at so much cost and trouble to do a thing that does us so much harm, and no manner of good: but to the contrary when they see all our forces drawn forth, and in pursuit of them they will think that we begin to be roused up, and to be awake and will not be satisfied with what they have pleased to leave us, but are resolved to retake from them that they took formerly from us, and drive them out of their country also. The which being done, then to build a fort at a suitable time, and in a convenient place, and it will be very honourable to your excellency, and of great service to Her Majesty, and to the enlargement of Her Majesty's government (the place meant being at Portroyal).

Source: Benjamin Church, *The Entertaining History of King Philip's War. As Also of Expeditions More Lately Made Against the Common Enemy, and Indian Rebels, in the Eastern Parts of New-England* (Boston, 1716; rpt. Newport, RI: Solomon Southwick in Queen Street, 1772), 245–249.

Questions for Consideration

1) What kinds of weapons did Colonel Church requisition from the governor for this expedition?
2) Did his plans suggest that he was foolhardy, brave, or lucky?
3) Why do you think he called for the service of "three hundred Indians at least, and more if they may be had"?

1.5 James Oglethorpe Strikes Spanish Outposts (1739–1741)

Seeking a military buffer against the Spanish, French, and Indians near South Carolina, Great Britain created the colony of Georgia in 1732. James Oglethorpe, a British army officer serving as royal protector of the colony, received an appointment as commander in chief of His Majesty's forces in both Georgia and South Carolina. The general assumed command in 1736. He dealt peaceably with scores of Native bands and confederacies, especially the Creek, Cherokee, Chickasaw, and Choctaw in the interior. In 1739, General Oglethorpe traveled with his regiment to a grand Indian assembly at

Coweta. While pausing in Augusta, he received instructions from Great Britain to "annoy" the Spanish in Florida. He was delighted to contribute to what was declared the War of Jenkins' Ear. Gathering 500 Indians, 400 South Carolina militia, 500 regulars, 400 Rangers and Scottish Highlanders, and several British naval vessels, he conducted a siege of Fort San Marcos in Saint Augustine. He eventually abandoned the effort, because his cannonading failed to penetrate its walls. In 1743, he struck it again to no avail. He returned to London that year to answer charges by a regimental officer and to impress upon Parliament the necessity of defending the Georgia coast.

Document

July the 24th. The General set out with about twenty Five Persons in Company and some Indians all well Armed, it being very Necessary so to be, for not long before a Party of the Choctau Indians came down to the General who gave them Presents and they staid amongst the English as Friends, but did not prove so, for in their Return home, they met two English Men who traded among the Indians, one of these they killed and shot three of the others Fingers off, however he made his Escape to a Town of the lower Creeks, Who upon hearing his Relation of what the Choctau's had done, imediately armed themselves and went in pursuit of the Choctau's whom they find encamped round a Fire; The Creeks imediately charged them, killed a great many and took the rest Prisoners. The General had also at this time two of the Choctau Indians with him who had put themselves under his Protection for fear of the People of the Creek Nation who would have killed them for the Barbarity of their Countrymen to the two English Traders. But now I return to our Journey, which we Continued being Supplied with Venison by the Indian Hunters, and also Wild Honey of which they took Plenty [...]

Septr. the 13th. This day arrived advices to the General of a Declaration of War with Spain, at noon the General gave the Cherokee Indians their Presents they took their leave of him and returned very well Satisfied.

Septr. 16th. The General set out from Fort Augusta and about Seven or Eight Miles from thence we stoped at a Fort belonging to Carolina which saluted the General with 15 Guns, the General staid and Dined there, this Fort is situate on a Hill and Commands two rivers; near the Fort are about one hundred Houses.

Septr. 17th. We set out from this Fort and as we were going down the River we met a Trading Boat going to Fort Augusta, the People on board her told us the Negroes in Carolina had raised up in Arms and killed about forty White People. We went to the Uchee Town and from thence to Fort Prince George where we found thirty men come from Purysburg to Strengthen the Fort [...]

December the 3d. His Excellcy General Oglethorpe set out for the Spanish Look out to observe the motions of the Spaniards and see what preparations they were making, taking a body of two hundred men with him; but they discovered us before they could Land and fled to Augustine leaving us the House built for a Look out. We marched along the Beach and came within 25 Miles of the Town of St. Augustine, where we discovered a Party of Don Pedro's Horse with some Indians and Negroes but as soon as they saw us they made the Utmost speed to the Town of St. Augustine and our Indians pursued them till they came to Diego Fort, in the Pursuit they killed one Negroe as he was going into Diego Fort and brought his Scalp to the Genl. Who rewarded them very well [...]

May the 3d. The General set out for the siege of St. Augustine with a Body of 600 Men also giving me orders to attend him. We [had] also 150 Indians of Different Nations the Main Body of them being to follow us as Soon as possible with provisions and other Stores.

May the 8th. At night we landed at the Spanish Look-out on the Florida side of St. Juan's River [and] here we lay very quiet 'till about four o'th' Clock the next morning, then we sent out a party of about 50 Indians on the Scout who returned at night with a Spanish Negroe who they had taken Prisoner they also pursued six other Spaniards as far as the Fort from which the Spaniards fired several Cannon shot at them but did no Execution, this day arrived two sloops and four Schooners from Charlestown with provisions and men for the Siege.

May the 10th. The men being landed we proceeded in order To attack a Fort about twenty three Miles distance from St. Augustine [...]

June the 5th. The General went with a Body of 800 Men along the Sea Beach to See if the Spaniards would venture out and hazard a Battle. He marched as far as Moosa a Small Fort about 2½ Mile Distant from St. Augustine and found it Deserted by the Spaniards who on their discovering our Troops fled to St. Augustine. We displayed Six Stand of English Colours on the Ramparts to try if we could Provoke the Spaniards to come out and give us Battle but all would not do, so we set Fire to the Fort and returned to Diego, struck the Tents and put them on board the Vessels in order to go to St. Augustine Barr.

June the 11th. Came up with the Men of War who lay off The Barr of St. Augustine to assist at the Siege.

June the 12th. The General landed on the Island of St. Eustatia over against the Castle of St. Augustine [and] the Captains of the Men of War landed 400 Men at the same time, a Party of our Indians came up with a party of Spanish Horsemen and killed four [...]

August 15th, 1741. General Oglethorpe preparing to Cruize on the Spanish Privateers that sculk'd along shore from Saint Augustine ordered me to attend him. He set out on board the St. Philip Guard Sloop, the Schooner Norfolk and Sloop Faulcon in Company and about 200 Men on board.

Source: "A Ranger's Report of Travels with General Oglethorpe in Georgia and Florida, 1739–1742," in *Travels in the American Colonies*, ed. Newton D. Mereness (New York: Macmillan, 1916), 215–236.

Questions for Consideration

1) Where did General Oglethorpe and his regiment search for a Spanish lookout?
2) How did the Indians near Diego Fort earn a "reward" from him?
3) What was his primary military objective in Saint Augustine?

1.6   Robert Rogers Provides Rules for the Rangers (1757)

Between 1754 and 1763, European states clashed in the Great War for Empire. British colonists in North America called it the French and Indian War. One volunteer company of irregulars from New Hampshire was commanded by Captain Robert Rogers, who dubbed them the Rangers. Whatever his questionable reputation, Rogers took responsibility for mustering, equipping, and leading them. His Rangers trained at an island fortress identified today as Rogers Island, which was situated in the Hudson River across from Fort Edward. They prepared to maneuver undetected, to scout locations, to capture prisoners, and to gather intelligence. Disrespected by many British regulars, they represented one of the few non-Indian forces able to overcome harsh conditions and mountainous terrain. They undertook long and seemingly impossible winter marches, trekking with crude snowshoes across frozen waters. In 1759, General Jeffrey Amherst dispatched Rogers, then a major, to sack the Indian town of Saint Francis. Provincials in British America celebrated the sacking while also rejoicing over the fall of Quebec. The French and the Indians at Fort Detroit surrendered to Rogers in a ceremony on November 29, 1760, solidifying the British hold over the vast territory along the Great Lakes. Rogers' Rangers took command of the western outpost and raised the British flag in triumph.

Document

All Rangers are to be subject to the rules and articles of war; to appear at roll-call every evening on their own parade, equipped each with a firelock, sixty rounds of powder and ball, and a hatchet, at which time an officer from each company is to inspect the same, to see they are in order, so as to be ready on any emergency to march at a minute's warning; and before they are dismissed the necessary guards are to be drafted, and scouts for the next day appointed.

Whenever you are ordered out to the enemy's forts or frontiers for discoveries, if your number be small, march in a single file, keeping at such a distance from each other as to prevent one shot from killing two men, sending one man, or more, forward, and the like on each side, at the distance of twenty yards from the main body, if the ground you march over will admit of it, to give the signal to the officer of the approach of an enemy, and of their number, &c.

If you march over marshes or soft ground, change your position, and march abreast of each other, to prevent the enemy from tracking you till you get over such ground, and then resume your former order, and march till it is quite dark before you encamp, which do, if possible, on a piece of ground that may afford your sentries the advantage of seeing or hearing the enemy at some considerable distance, keeping one half of your whole party awake alternately through the night [...]

If you are obliged to receive the enemy's fire, fall, or squat down, till it is over, then rise and discharge at them. If their main body is equal to yours, extend yourselves occasionally; but if superior, be careful to support and strengthen your flanking parties, to make them equal with theirs, that if possible you may repulse them to their main body, in which case push upon them with the greatest resolution, with equal force in each flank and in the center, observing to keep at a due distance from each other, and advance from tree to tree, with one half of the party before the other ten or twelve yards. If the enemy push upon you, let your front fire and fall down, and then let your rear advance thro' them and do the like, by which time those who before were in front will be ready to discharge again, and repeat the same alternately, as occasion shall require; by this means you will keep up such a constant fire, that the enemy will not be able easily to break your order, or gain your ground.

If you oblige the enemy to retreat, be careful, in your pursuit of them, to keep out your flanking parties, and prevent them from gaining eminences, or rising grounds, in which case they would perhaps be able to rally and repulse in their turn.

If you are obliged to retreat, let the front of your whole party fire and fall back, till the rear has done the same, making for the best ground you can; by this means you will oblige the enemy to pursue you, if they do it at all, in the face of a constant fire.

If the enemy is so superior that you are in danger of being surrounded by them, let the whole body disperse, and every one take a different road to the place of rendez-vous appointed for that evening, which must every morning be altered and fixed for the evening ensuing, in order to bring the whole party, or as many of them as possi-ble, together, after any separation that may happen in the day; but if you should happen to be actually surrounded, form yourselves into a square, or if in the woods, a circle is best, and, if possible, make a stand till the darkness of the night favours your escape [...]

At the first dawn of day, awake your whole detachment; that being the time when the savages choose to fall upon their enemies, you should by all means be in readiness to receive them.

If the enemy should be discovered by your detachments in the morning, and their numbers are superior to yours, and a victory doubtful, you should not attack them till the evening; as then they will not know your numbers, and if you are repulsed, your retreat will be favoured by the darkness of the night.

Before you leave your encampment, send out small parties to scout round it, to see if there be any appearance or track of an enemy that might have been near you during the night.

When you stop for refreshment, choose some spring or rivulet if you can, and dispose your party so as not to be surprised, posting proper guards and sentries at a due distance, and let a small party waylay the path you came in, lest the enemy should be pursuing.

If, in your return, you have to cross rivers, avoid the usual fords as much as possible, lest the enemy should have discovered, and be there expecting you.

If you have to pass by lakes, keep at some distance from the edge of the water, lest, in case of an ambuscade, or an attack from the enemy, when in that situation, your retreat should be cut off.

If the enemy pursue your rear, take a circle till you come to your own tracks, and there form an ambush to receive them, and give them the first fire.

When you return from a scout, and come near our forts, avoid the usual roads, and avenues thereto, lest the enemy should have headed you, and lay in ambush to receive you, when almost exhausted with fatigues.

When you pursue any party that has been near our forts or encampments, follow not directly in their tracks, lest you should be discovered by their rear guards, who, at such a time, would be most alert; but endeavour, by a different route, to head and meet them in some narrow pass, or lay in ambush to receive them when and where they least expect it.

If you are to embark in canoes, bateaux, or otherwise by water, choose the evening for the time of your embarkation, as you will then have the whole night before you, to pass undiscovered by any parties of the enemy, on hills, or other places, which command a prospect of the lake or river you are upon.

In paddling or rowing, give orders that the boat or canoe next the sternmost, wait for her, and the third for the second, and the fourth for the third, and so on, to prevent separation, and that you may be ready to assist each other on any emergency.

Appoint one man in each boat to look out for fires, on the adjacent shores, from the numbers and size of which you may form some judgment of the number that kindled them, and whether you are able to attack them or not.

If you find the enemy encamped near the banks of a river, or lake, which you imagine they will attempt to cross for their security upon being attacked, leave a detachment of your party on the opposite shore to receive them, while, with the remainder, you surprise them, having them between you and the lake or river.

If you cannot satisfy yourself as to the enemy's number and strength, from their fire, &c. conceal your boats at some distance, and ascertain their number by a reconnoitring party, when they embark, or march, in the morning, marking the course they steer, &c. when you may pursue, ambush, and attack them, or let them pass, as prudence shall direct you [...]

Such in general are the rules to be observed in the Ranging service; there are, however, a thousand occurrences and circumstances which may happen that will make it necessary in some measure to depart from them and to put other arts and stratagems in practice; in which cases every man's reason and judgment must be his guide, according to the particular situation and nature of things; and that he may do this to advantage, he should keep in mind a maxim never to be departed from by a commander, viz. to preserve a firmness and presence of mind on every occasion.

Source: Robert Rogers, *Journals of Major Robert Rogers* (London: J. Millan, 1765), 43–51.

Questions for Consideration

1) How, according to Robert Rogers, should the Rangers respond to being surrounded?
2) What circumstances did he say might "make it necessary in some measure" to depart from his rules?
3) Why do you think his rules appeared to be repetitious?

1.7 An Unknown Soldier Sings "Yankee Doodle" (1775)

A song native to the colonial era was variously titled "A Visit to Camp," "The Lexington March," and even "Doodle Dandy." It is known today as "Yankee Doodle." In all likelihood, no original documentary source for its verses exists. Rather, it entered the oral tradition at different times and places, eventually worked by broadside printers into a composite. Folk circulation began as early as 1745, though no published copy of the stanzas appeared until approximately 1775. Certain lines were attributable to Richard Shuckburgh, an army surgeon for a British regiment stationed in New York. Clearly, the chorus offered a derisive epithet for the militiamen. "Yankee" probably derived from a Dutch nickname for the provincials, whereas "doodle" in English denoted playful, shiftless, or menial activities. Given a martial beat with fife and drums, the cadences resonated with colonials during the 1760s. Festivals, fairs, and parades featured the air.

Its performance involved dancing, gesturing, mocking, and frolicking. Its lyrics contained innuendo, jokes, parody, and nonsense. The printed versions often expurgated the most irreverent parts, particularly the crude references to masturbation and scatology. They questioned authority with a mix of satire and irony, which insinuated that the regular officers, not the citizen soldiery, were the foolish ones.

Document

Father and I went down to camp, along with Captain Gooding,
And there we saw the men and boys, as thick as hastypudding.

And there we saw a thousand men, as rich as 'Squire David;
And what they wasted every day, I wish it could be saved.

The 'lasses they eat every day, would keep an house a winter;
They have as much that I'll be bound they eat it when they're a mind to.

And there we saw a swamping gun, large as a log of maple,
Upon a deucid little cart, a load for father's cattle.

And every time they shoot it off, it takes a horn of powder;
And makes a noise like father's gun, only a nation louder.

Cousin Simon grew so bold, I thought he would have cock'd it;
It scar'd me so, I shrink'd it off, and hung by father's pocket.

And Captain Davis had a gun, he kind of clap'd his hand on't,
And stuck a crooked stabbing iron upon the little end on't.

And there I see a pumpkin shell as big as mother's bason,
And every time they touch'd it off, they scamper'd like the nation.

I see a little barrel too, the heads were made of leather,
They knock'd upon't with little clubs, and called the folks together.

And there was Captain Washington, and gentlefolks about him,
They say he's grown so tarnal proud, he will not ride without 'em.

He got him on his meeting clothes, upon a slapping stallion,
He set the world along in rows, in hundreds and in millions.

The flaming ribbons in his hat, they look'd so tarring fine ah,
I wanted pockily to get, to give to my Jemimah.

I see another snarl of men a digging graves, they told me,
So tarnal long, so tarnal deep, they 'tended they should hold me.

It scar'd me so, I hook'd it off, nor stop'd, as I remember,
Nor turn'd about 'till I got home, lock'd up in mother's chamber.

Yankee Doodle, keep it up, Yankee Doodle dandy,
Mind the music and the step, and with the girls be handy.

Source: "Father and I Went Down to Camp," in *Report on "The Star-Spangled Banner," "Hail Columbia," "America," "Yankee Doodle,"* comp. Oscar Sonneck (Washington, DC: Library of Congress, 1909), 134–137, 195.

Questions for Consideration

1) What types of weaponry did the militia display in camp?
2) Which verse humorously described a martial drum?
3) Why do you think the lyrics mentioned "a snarl of men a digging graves"?

Suggested Readings

Anderson, Fred. *Crucible of War: The Seven Years War and the Fate of Empire in British North America, 1754–1766.* New York: Knopf, 2000.

Cave, Alfred A. *The Pequot War.* Amherst: University of Massachusetts Press, 1996.

Cohen, Eliot A. *Conquered into Liberty: Two Centuries of Battles along the Great Warpath that Made the American Way of War.* New York: Free Press, 2011.

Dederer, John Morgan. *War in America to 1775: Before Yankee Doodle.* New York: New York University Press, 1990.

Ferling, John E. *Struggle for a Continent: The Wars of Early America.* Arlington Heights, IL: Harlan Davidson, 1993.

Grenier, John. *The First Way of War: American War Making on the Frontier, 1607–1814.* Cambridge: Cambridge University Press, 2005.

Keegan, John. *Fields of Battle: The Wars for North America.* New York: Knopf, 1996.

Leach, Douglas Edward. *Arms for Empire: A Military History of the British Colonies in North America, 1607–1763.* New York: Macmillan, 1973.

Lepore, Jill. *The Name of War: King Philip's War and the Origins of American Identity.* New York: Random House, 1998.

Malone, Patrick M. *The Skulking Way of War: Technology and Tactics Among New England Indians.* Lanham, MD: Madison Books, 2000.

Peckham, Howard H. *The Colonial Wars, 1689–1762.* Chicago: University of Chicago Press, 1964.

Ross, John F. *War on the Run: The Epic Story of Robert Rogers and the Conquest of America's First Frontier.* New York: Bantam Books, 2009.

Shea, William L. *The Virginia Militia in the Seventeenth Century.* Baton Rouge: Louisiana State University Press, 1983.

Silver, Peter. *Our Savage Neighbors: How Indian War Transformed Early America.* New York: W. W. Norton, 2008.

Starkey, Armstrong. *European and Native American Warfare, 1675–1815.* Norman: University of Oklahoma Press, 1998.

2

War for Independence

Chronology

1775	Battles of Lexington and Concord
	Battle of Bunker Hill (Breed's Hill)
	The Continental Army and Navy formed
1776	Declaration of Independence
	Battle of New York
	Battle of Trenton
1777	Battle of Princeton
	Battle of Brandywine
	Battle of Germantown
	Battle of Saratoga
1778	Battle of Monmouth
	France allies with the United States
1779	John Paul Jones captures the *Serapis*
	Battle of Stony Point
1780	Battle of Waxhaws
	Battle of Camden
	Battle of King's Mountain
1781	Battle of Cowpens
	Battle of Guilford Courthouse
	Battle of Yorktown
1783	Treaty of Paris signed
	General George Washington retires

2.1 James Monroe Goes to War (1776)

With Americans turning against the British Empire, the Continental Congress met in the city of Philadelphia. On June 14, 1775, the delegates created a Continental Army. A few days later, George Washington of Virginia became the Commander in Chief. James Monroe, an 18-year-old student at the College of William and Mary, left his books and joined the Third Virginia Regiment in early 1776. Graded in Captain John Thornton's company, Monroe was named a lieutenant. The raw recruits stumbled while defending New York that year. They fled into New Jersey and crossed the Delaware

American Military History: A Documentary Reader, Second Edition. Brad D. Lookingbill.
© 2019 John Wiley & Sons, Inc. Published 2019 by John Wiley & Sons, Inc.

River, prompting Thomas Paine, an American pamphleteer with the army, to lament the "summer soldier and sunshine patriot." On Christmas night, Monroe was among the Continentals recrossing the icy Delaware for a surprise attack at Trenton. He was hit in the left shoulder by a musket ball, which severed an artery. He recovered from his nearly fatal wounding and returned to the field in the battles of Brandywine, Germantown, and Monmouth. When he wrote of these events in his autobiography, he often spoke of himself in the third person. Monroe later became the fifth President of the United States—the only one to have been wounded by enemy fire in combat.

Document

As the war then pressed on New York and there were few regular regiments in the army, the Third Virginia Regiment, commanded by Colonel Weedon, was ordered there, which it reached by rapid marches immediately after the battle of Long Island, in which Smallwood's and Haslet's regiments were nearly cut to pieces. Weedon's regiment was posted on Harlem Heights, where the troops that were drawn together in that quarter, to oppose the enemy who soon afterwards landed on York Island, took possession of the city, and menaced Fort Washington. Three companies of that regiment, Thornton's in which Mr. Monroe was a lieutenant, Chilton's, and Ashby's, under the command of Major Leitch, and a like number of troops from Connecticut, under Colonel Knolton, were detached in advance of the army, across the valley, at Harlem, to meet them. This small corps met the head of a column of the enemy at the edge of a wood, through which it passed bordering on the valley, and fighting gallantly, checked its career. Knolton and Leitch both fell, and their wounds being mortal, died. Such was the good conduct of this small detachment in that encounter that the commander, in reviewing the occurrence in the general orders of the succeeding day, bestowed on it the highest commendation.

Checked at that point, the enemy passed up the Sound, with the intention to fall in the rear of the troops, which were collected around Fort Washington. This movement drew our army to the White Plains, where something like a general action ensued, in which the enemy gained the advantage. They then moved down towards the fort, and in the disposition which was made of our force, the Third Regiment was ordered into Jersey to support Fort Lee, which was erected on the south side of the Hudson, opposite to Fort Washington. That regiment took its position at Newark. Both those forts fell, and immediately afterwards General Washington drew the few remaining troops back in that quarter to the same point. The enemy, knowing how inconsiderable his forces were, pressed on him, and thus commenced through Jersey a retreat which will be forever celebrated in the annals of our country for the patient suffering, the unshaken firmness, and gallantry of this small band when brought to action, of which the army consisted, and of the great and good qualities of the commander. We passed the Delaware at Trenton and occupied the commanding ground contiguous to it on the opposite shore. Soon after this, the winter having commenced, the enemy retired to winter quarters, stationing their troops in the different towns through Jersey from the Delaware to New York [...]

The success of the enemy in the battles of Long Island and the White Plains, with the capture of Forts Washington and Lee, and the retreat of our army through Jersey, put fairly at issue with the nation the great question whether they were competent and resolved to support their independence, or would sink under the pressure. The councils of the union exhibited a firmness which showed that they were equal to the crisis. The

Congress of the United States and the legislatures of all the states were in session, and not the slightest symptom of hesitation was seen in either of those public bodies. The most active efforts were made by all, and with the most faithful cooperation between them, each performing its appropriate duties, to raise and support a force which would meet and defy the enemy in the field the next campaign. General Washington was equally attentive to his duties. He perceived that the British Commander, by the disposition which he had made of his troops, had estimated his success beyond their merit: that he considered the country essentially conquered. The opportunity for profiting of that error, of depressing the British power, and elevating the hopes and spirits of his country, was favorable, and he resolved to take advantage of it. The force at Trenton was small, but believed by the British commander to be superior to any that he could bring to bear on it. His other troops in Jersey were dispersed through the towns in a line from the Delaware to the Hudson, and Princeton, New Brunswick, Elizabethtown, and Newark.

The first attack was to be made on Trenton, on the result of which everything would depend. This was arranged in a general council, on great consideration, and with consummate judgment. The command of the vanguard, consisting of 50 men, was given to Captain William Washington, of the Third Virginia Regiment, an officer whose good conduct had already been noticed. This appointment having been communicated to the other officers by Colonel Weedon, Lieutenant Monroe promptly offered his services to act as a subaltern under him, which was promptly accepted. On the 25th of December, 1776, they passed the Delaware in front of the army, in the dusk of the evening, at Coryell's Ferry, ten miles above Trenton, and hastened to a point, about one and one-half miles from it, at which the road by which they descended intersected that which led from Trenton to Princeton, for the purpose, in obedience to orders, of cutting off all communication between them and from the country to Trenton. The night was tempestuous, as was the previous day, and made more severe by the heavy fall of snow. Captain Washington executed his orders faithfully. He soon took possession of the point to which he was ordered, and holding it through the night, intercepted and made prisoners of many who were passing in directions to and from Trenton.

At the dawn of the day, our army approached with the Commander in Chief at its head. Captain Washington then moved with the vanguard in front, attacked the enemy's picket, shot down the commanding officer, and drove in before him. A general alarm then took place among the troops in town. The drums were beat to arms, and two cannons were placed in the main street to bear on the head of our column as it entered. Captain Washington rushed forward, attacked, and put the troops around the cannon to flight, and took possession of them. Moving on afterwards, he received a severe wound and was taken from the field. The command then devolved on Lieutenant Monroe, who advanced in like manner at the head of the corps, and was shot down by a musket ball which passed through his breast and shoulder. He also was carried from the field. Our troops, then entering the town in several columns and attacking the enemy as they formed, soon overcame and made prisoners of them. Lieutenant Monroe was taken to the same room to which Captain Washington had been carried, and their wounds were dressed by Dr. Cochrane, the Surgeon General of the army, and Dr. Riker, who had quartered with them in the country and accompanied them in the vanguard in the attack on the picket and advance in the city.

In the great events of which I have spoken, Mr. Monroe, being a mere youth, counted for nothing in comparison with those distinguished citizens who had the direction of public affairs. In adverting to the epoch of his commencement, I have thought it proper, and have taken delight in noticing in appropriate terms, the high character of that epoch and of those into whose hands its destiny fell. Taken together, they formed a school of practical instruction, for many successful purposes, of which it is believed that history has furnished no equal example. It was a school of practical instruction in the knowledge of mankind, in the science of government, and what is of still great importance, for inculcating on the youthful mind those sound moral and political principles on which the success of our system depends.

Source: James Monroe, *Autobiography of James Monroe*, ed. S. G. Brown (Syracuse: Syracuse University Press, 1959), 22–26. Used with permission of Syracuse University Press.

Questions for Consideration

1) How, according to Lieutenant Monroe, was the enemy "checked" near Harlem?
2) Where were the two cannons placed in Trenton?
3) What formed a "school of practical instruction" for citizens?

2.2 Albigence Waldo Treats Soldiers at Valley Forge (1777)

The Continental Army stood at a crossroads in 1777. British General John Burgoyne with 8,000 troops advanced southward from Canada to the Hudson River. His slow trek through the wilderness permitted General Horatio Gates to rally the Continentals and the militia, forcing General Burgoyne to surrender at Saratoga on October 17. Nevertheless, General Howe outmaneuvered General Washington to capture Philadelphia. As Congress fled to York, the residual forces huddled in the Pennsylvania countryside. Already exhausted from strenuous campaigning, long marches, and sparse supplies, they camped at Valley Forge that December. The high ground of Mount Joy and Mount Misery combined with the Schuylkill River to make the camp defensible from an attack. The valley, however, offered little forage. The diary of a Connecticut surgeon, Dr. Albigence Waldo, testified to the low morale of the rank and file. They suffered from insufficient food, clothing, and shelter. They battled disease, hunger, and boredom. They left bloody footprints in the snow. Even the most steadfast reached a breaking point. Thousands deserted or perished. With the help of a former Prussian officer, Friedrich Wilhelm von Steuben, General Washington insisted on regimental training and camp discipline. Even though their numbers grew smaller, they were forged into a more respectable army in the valley.

Document
December 21. Preparations made for hutts. Provisions Scarce. Mr. Ellis went homeward— sent a Letter to my Wife. Heartily wish myself at home, my Skin & eyes are almost spoil'd with continual smoke. A general cry thro' the Camp this Evening among the Soldiers, "No Meat! No Meat!"—the Distant vales Echo'd back the melancholly sound—"No Meat! No Meat!" Immitating the noise of Crows & Owls, also, made a part of the confused Musick. What have you for your Dinners Boys? "Nothing but Fire Cake & Water, Sir." At night,

"Gentlemen the Supper is ready." What is your Supper Lads? "Fire Cake & Water, Sir." Very poor beef has been drawn in our Camp the greater part of this season. A Butcher bringing a Quarter of this kind of Beef into Camp one day who had white Buttons on the knees of his breeches, a Soldier cries out—"There, there Tom is some more of your fat Beef, by my soul I can see the Butcher's breeches buttons through it."

December 22. Lay excessive Cold & uncomfortable last Night—my eyes are started out from their Orbits like a Rabbit's eyes, occasion'd by a great Cold & Smoke. What have you got for Breakfast, Lads? "Fire Cake & Water, Sir." The Lord send that our Commissary of Purchases may live [on] Fire Cake & Water, 'till their glutted Gutts are turned to Pasteboard. Our Division are under Marching Orders this morning. I am ashamed to say it, but I am tempted to steal Fowls if I could find them, or even a whole Hog, for I feel as if I could eat one. But the Impoverish'd Country about us, affords but little matter to employ a Thief, or keep a Clever Fellow in good humour. But why do I talk of hunger & hard usage, when so many in the World have not even fire Cake & Water to eat. The human mind is always poreing upon the gloomy side of Fortune, and while it inhabits this lump of Clay, will always be in an uneasy and fluctuating State, produced by a thousand Incidents in common Life, which are deemed misfortunes, while the mind is taken off from the nobler pursuit of matters in Futurity. The sufferings of the Body naturally gain the Attention of the Mind, and this Attention is more or less strong, in greater or lesser souls, altho' I believe that Ambition & a high Opinion of Fame, makes many People endure hardships and pains with that fortitude we after times Observe them to do. On the other hand, a despicable opinion of the enjoyments of this Life, by a continued series of Misfortunes, and a long acquaintance with Grief, induces others to bear afflictions with becoming serenity and Calmness. It is not in the power of Philosophy however, to convince a man he may be happy and Contented if he will, with a *Hungry Belly*. Give me Food, Cloaths, Wife & Children, kind Heaven! and I'll be as contented as my Nature will permit me to be. This Evening a Party with two field pieces were order'd out. At 12 of the Clock at Night, Providence sent us a little Mutton, with which we immediately had some Broth made, & a fine Stomach for same. Ye who Eat Pumkin Pie and Roast Turkies, and yet Curse fortune for using you ill, Curse her no more, least she reduce your Allowance of her favours to a bit of Fire Cake, & a draught of Cold Water, & in Cold Weather too.

December 23. The Party that went out last evening not Return'd to Day. This evening an excellent Player on the Violin in that soft kind of Musick, which is so finely adapted to stirr up the tender Passions, while he was playing in the next Tent to mine, these kind of soft Airs it immediately called up in remembrance all the endearing expressions, the Tender Sentiments, the sympathetic friendship that has given so much satisfaction and sensible pleasure to me from the first time I gained the heart & affections of the tenderest of the Fair. A thousand agreeable little incidents which have Occurr'd since our happy connection, and which would have pass'd totally unnoticed by such who are strangers to the soft & sincere passion of Love, were now recall'd to my mind, and filled me with these tender emotions, and Agreeable Reflections, which cannot be described, and which in spite of my Philosophy forced out the sympathetic tear. I wish'd to have the Musick Cease, and yet dreaded its ceasing, least I should loose sight of these dear Ideas, which gave me pain and pleasure at the same instant. Ah Heaven why is it that our harder fate so often deprives us of the enjoyment of what we most wish to enjoy this side of thy brighter realms. There is something in this strong passion of Love far more agreeable than what we can derive from any of the other Passions and which Duller Souls & Cheerless minds are insensible of, & laugh at—let such fools laugh at me.

December 24. Party of the 22d not returned. Hutts go on Slowly—Cold & Smoke make us fret. But mankind are always fretting, even if they have more than their proportion of the Blessings of Life. We are never Easy, allways repining at the Providence of an Allwise & Benevolent Being, Blaming Our Country or faulting our Friends. But I don't know of anything that vexes a man's Soul more than hot smoke continually blowing into his Eyes, & when he attempts to avoid it, is met by a cold and piercing Wind.

December 25, Christmas. We are still in Tents—when we ought to be in huts—the poor Sick, suffer much in Tents this cold Weather. But we now treat them differently from what they used to be at home, under the inspection of Old Women and Doct. Bolus Linctus. We give them Mutton & Grogg and a Capital Medicine once in a While, to start the Disease from its foundation at once. We avoid Piddling Pills, Powders, Bolus's Linctus's Cordials and all such insignificant matters whose powers are Only render'd important by causing the Patient to vomit up his money instead of his disease. But very few of the sick Men Die.

Source: "The Diary of Surgeon Albigence Waldo of the Connecticut Line," in *Pennsylvania Magazine of History and Biography*, Volume 21 (Philadelphia: Historical Society of Pennsylvania, 1897), 309–313.

Questions for Consideration

1) What, according to the doctor, were the soldiers at Valley Forge served for meals?
2) How did they spend Christmas day?
3) Do you believe that he understood both the mental and physical aspects of soldiering?

2.3 Jeffrey Brace Fights for Liberty (1778)

Manpower shortages within the Continental Army necessitated the acceptance of an evolving force structure. Doubting the persistence of citizen soldiers, Congress gradually organized a "standing army" for hire. At General Washington's request, they increased the bounties, bonuses, pay, and benefits. They promised those who would serve for the war's duration a hundred acres of land. Recruiters targeted a landless pool that included transients, immigrants, debtors, laborers, and slaves. United by their poverty, volunteers bonded with others who were willing and able to show deference toward line officers. Service in the armed forces opened a path for upward mobility or outright freedom, that is, if independence was won. Jeffrey Brace, who was also known as Boyrereau Brinch, served with comrades from Stanford to Hackensack. Born in western Africa around 1742, he was captured at age 16 and shipped to the Caribbean island of Barbados. Sold into slavery, he eventually arrived in Connecticut for sale again. In 1777, he enlisted in an infantry regiment and fought against the British forces until 1783. He was honorably discharged and, thanks to his meritorious service, earned emancipation from slavery. He moved to Vermont, obtained landed property, started a family, and shared war stories that attracted the attention of prominent abolitionists.

Document

Nothing of consequence took place that related to me till spring [of 1778], when we moved to Hackensack in the Jerseys. Soon after our arrival there, the enemy stole some cattle from our lines. Capt. Granger with twenty chosen men was sent in pursuit of them, with orders to go about two miles to a place called Hackensack-four-corners. I was one of the number, but when we arrived at the destined place, we discovered that they had passed with the cattle; one Ahiel Bradley, a sergeant in the company said if myself and one Adam Waggonor, would accompany him, he would go and find them, as he believed that they were driven to a certain meadow back from the road, which meadow he was acquainted with.

The Captain consented and we pursued our course upon the track, to a pasture fronting the meadow, into which we discovered they had been driven. We came to a small hill or rise of land over which they must have passed. This rise being covered with bushes, it was thought prudent that I should wait upon the hither side of the hill while they went over and examined into the fact, whether the cattle were actually in the meadow or not, and at the same time, to keep a look out for the enemy.

While I stood there anxiously waiting for their return, I suddenly discovered a man riding up to me not more than eight rods distant on full speed with a pistol in his hand, and ordered me to lay down my arms. But not being so instructed by my officers you may well suppose that I did not. At first I thought he was a Jerseyman and was attempting to fool me, as they had played some such pranks before upon some of the soldiers belonging to our line—therefore in return I demanded to whom I was to surrender and by what authority he demanded it. He said I must surrender to him who demanded me in the name of the King His Majesty of Great Britain. I then plainly told him that neither him nor his King's majesty would get my arms unless he took them by force. He immediately cocked his pistol and fired; I fell flat upon the ground in order to dodge his ball, and did so effectually do it that he missed me. I rose, he drew his sword and rode up to me so quick that I had no time to take aim before he struck my gun barrel with his cutlass, and cut it almost one third off—also cut off the bone of my middle finger on my hand. As he struck the horse jumped before he could wheal upon me again. Altho' my gun barrel was cut, I fired and killed him. As he fell I caught his horse and sword. He was a British light horseman in disguise.

I mounted immediately, and that instant discovered four men on horseback approaching me from a different direction. I fled, passed one man, just before I came to a stone wall. Both of our horses were upon the full run. He fired and missed me. My horse leaped the wall like a deer; they all pursued me. When we got into the road, they were joined by many more; and all with swords in hand pursued me in full career. I drove my horse as fast as possible, stabbed him with my sword and gun, kicked my heels in his side, but having no spurs, and not being so good a horseman they gained upon me. I looked forward and saw my Capt. in full view, almost a mile distant. This encouraged me, and the long-shanked negro soldier with a leather cap, mounted on an elegant English gelding light horse, made all whistle again. When I came in about twenty or thirty rods, I heard the Captain say, "There come one of our leather caps, and it is Jeffrey. Reserve your fire so as not to kill him." However the men fired, and three balls cut my garments, one struck my coat sleeve, the next hit my bayonet belt, and the third went through the back side of my leather-cap. They were so close upon me that the same fire killed four of the British and five horses—and wounded some more. I did not stop for this salute, but pulled on for head quarters. When our men fired the enemy were within two or three jumps of me; but being so handsomely saluted upon surprise, as our men were concealed from their view, they made the best retreat possible.

I made no halt until I arrived within our Camp. When I dismounted tied my horse and went to set up my gun, I found I could not open my hand which was the first time that I discovered that I was wounded. Slight fear and precipitation had turned me almost as white as my fellow soldiers. In consequence of my wounds, I was unfit for duty again for almost three months. But after all the poor simple Negro was cheated out of his horse; as I sold horse, saddle and bridle, holsters, pistols and sword, to Col. Roger Sherman for his contract of two hundred and fifty dollars, who thought proper never to pay the same. Yet I felt more gratitude towards the horse than regret for the loss of him, as he with the assistance of divine providence saved my life.

And here I will observe that I can give no other reason why the enemy did not fire upon me, only I presume they chose to take me alive, which they had full faith in, as they when our men fired upon them were fast approaching me—and what caused me to form this opinion, I had been one of the standing sentry upon the outposts for some time, therefore I presume they concluded that I would acquaint them with the state of our army. Perhaps the soldiers thought I might be sold by them and enrich their coffers; as these mercenary beings seem rather more inclined to deal in human flesh and blood than in fighting.

I belonged to one Capt. Baker's company when the attack was made upon us at Hackensack. I was on the flank and the charge was made there; we gave them a warmer salute, and lost many brave Yankee-boys. Our Battalion was charged by their light horse, and we beat them off with our bayonets.

After this battle, we heard that the enemy were making their way to Stanford. We marched there immediately, and arrived before them. A party marched down into some meadows to watch their motion; on discovering their superior force, we fired upon them and ran off fully believing that he who fights and runs away, may live to fight another day.

Source: Jeffrey Brace, *The Blind African Slave.* © 2005 The Board of Regents of the University of Wisconsin System. Reprinted by permission of The University of Wisconsin Press.

Questions for Consideration

1) How did Jeffrey Brace respond to the enemy's attack on his party in the meadow?
2) Did he reveal any patterns of racial distinctions within his regiment?
3) Why do you think he said that "he who fights and runs away, may live to fight another day"?

2.4   John Paul Jones Captures a British Frigate (1779)

The Franco-American alliance of 1778 offered prospects for foreign aid, coordinated campaigns, and naval operations. A French declaration of war on Great Britain that year was followed by a Spanish declaration in 1779 and by a Dutch declaration in 1780. Thus began a world war that in the long term overstretched British military resources. Any "privateer" who secured a letter of marque from one of the states or from Congress could attempt to raid enemy ships. Congress also authorized the Continental Navy and the Continental Marines, but their daring efforts barely challenged the Royal Navy's blockade of the Atlantic seaboard. Once opened to the United States, the French ports invited Continental officers such as Captain John Paul Jones to sail near British shores. Jones, who famously preyed upon British commerce aboard the *Ranger*, commanded several vessels. During 1779, the French provided the courageous captain with the *Duc de Duras*, which he refitted and renamed the *Bonhomme Richard* to honor Benjamin Franklin, whose nom de plume was Poor Richard. On September 23, the *Bonhomme Richard* confronted a British frigate, the *Serapis*, in one memorable clash. Asked to surrender by the British commodore, Jones reportedly barked: "I have not yet begun to fight!" Jones actually captured the prize, although his own warship sank two days later.

Document

The battle being thus begun was continued with unremitting fury. Every method was practiced on both sides to gain an advantage and rake each other. And I must confess that the enemy's ship, being much more manageable than the *Bonhomme Richard*, gained thereby several times an advantageous situation in spite of my best endeavours to prevent it. As I had to deal with an enemy of greatly superior force, I was under the necessity of closing with him to prevent the advantage which he had over me in point of manoeuvre. It was my intention to lay the *Bonhomme Richard* athwart the enemies bow; but as that operation required great dexterity in the management of both sails and helm, and some of our braces being shot away, it did not exactly succeed to my wish. The enemy's bowsprit, however, came over the *Bonhomme Richard*'s poop by the mizzen-mast, and I made both ships fast together in that situation, which by the action of the wind on the enemy's sails, forced her stern close to the *Bonhomme Richard*'s bow, so that the ships lay square alongside of each other, the yards being all entangled, and the cannon of each ship touching the opponent's side. When this position took place, it was eight o' clock, previous to which the *Bonhomme Richard* had received sundry eighteen-pound shot below the water, and leaked very much.

My battery of twelve-pounders, on which I had placed my chief dependence, being commanded by Lieutenant Dale and Colonel Weibert, and manned principally with American seamen and French volunteers, was entirely silenced and abandoned. As to the six old eighteen-pounders that formed the battery of the lower gun-deck, they did no service whatever, except firing eight shot in all. Two out of them burst at the first fire and killed almost all the men who were stationed to manage them. Before this time, too, Colonel de Chamillard, who commanded a party of twenty soldiers on the poop, had abandoned that station after having lost some of his men.

I had now only two pieces of cannon (nine-pounders), on the quarter-deck, that were not silenced, and not one of the heavier cannon was fired during the remainder of the action. The purser, Mr. Mease, who commanded the guns on the quarter deck, being dangerously wounded in the head, I was obliged to fill his place, and with great difficulty rallied a few men, and shifted over one of the lee quarter deck guns, so that we afterwards played three pieces of nine-pounders upon the enemy. The tops alone seconded the fire of this little battery and held out bravely during the whole action, especially the main top, where Lieutenant Stack commanded. I directed the fire of one of the three cannon against the main-mast, with double headed shot, while the other two were exceedingly well served with grape and canister shot, to silence the enemy's musketry and clear her decks, which was at last effected. The enemy were, as I have since understood, on the instant of calling out for quarters, when the cowardice or treachery of three of my under officers induced them to call to the enemy. The English commodore asked me if I demanded quarter, and I having answered him in the most determined negative, they renewed the battle with redoubled fury. They were unable to stand the deck; but the fire of their cannon, especially the lower battery, which was entirely formed of ten-pounders, was incessant. Both ships were set on fire in various places, and the scene was dreadful beyond the reach of language [...]

This prize proved to be the British ship of war the *Serapis*, a new ship of forty-four guns, built on their most approved construction, with two complete batteries, one of them of eighteen-pounders, and commanded by the brave Commodore Richard Pearson. I had yet two enemies to encounter, far more formidable than the Britons, I mean, fire and water. The *Serapis* was attacked only by the first, but the *Bonhomme Richard* was assailed by both. There was five feet of water in the hold, and though it was moderate from the explosion of so much gun powder, yet the three pumps that remained could with difficulty only keep the water from gaining. The fire broke out in various parts of the ship, in spite of all the water that could be thrown in to quench it, and at length broke out as low as the powder magazine and within a few inches of the powder. In that dilemma, I took out the powder upon deck, ready to be thrown overboard at the last extremity, and it was ten o'clock the next day, the 24th, before the fire was entirely extinguished. With respect to the situation of the *Bonhomme Richard*, the rudder was cut almost entirely off, the stern frame and transoms were almost entirely cut away, and the timbers by the lower deck, especially from the main-mast towards the stern, being greatly decayed with age, were mangled beyond my power of description, and a person must have been an eyewitness to form a just idea of the tremendous scenes of carnage, wreck, and ruin, which everywhere appeared. Humanity cannot but recoil from the prospect of such finished horror and lament that war should be capable of producing such fatal consequences.

Source: John Paul Jones, "Official Account," in *Life and Correspondence*, comp. Janette Taylor (New York: D. Fanshaw, 1830), 180–187.

Questions for Consideration

1) What two enemies did Captain Jones consider more formidable than the British?
2) Who did he accuse of "cowardice or treachery" while battling the *Serapis*?
3) How effective were the quarter-deck cannons aboard the *Bonhomme Richard*?

2.5   A French Officer Draws the Continental Line (1781)

British armed forces were widely dispersed by 1780, when they launched a major offensive to win the war in the American South. General Charles Cornwallis, the British commander, marched inland from the coast. Fighting between "partisans" spread across the backcountry. Continentals under General Gates fled the field at Camden in South Carolina, which prompted General Washington to dispatch General Nathanael Greene to replace him. General Greene undermined British attempts to secure bases while disrupting their supply lines. Unable to capture or to destroy Greene's nimble corps, General Cornwallis relocated his 7,500 troops to the Chesapeake Bay during 1781. Awaiting provisions and reinforcements at Yorktown in Virginia, the British mistakenly assumed that naval superiority would protect them. Comte de Grasse, who commanded the French fleet in the West Indies, sailed northward to drive the British fleet from the Chesapeake. During September, General Washington and Comte de Rochambeau marched their allied armies overland to the tidewater. They besieged Yorktown with 7,800 Frenchmen, 5,700 Continentals, and 3,200 militiamen. Jean-Baptiste Antoine de Verger, a sublieutenant in a French regiment, drew a colorful "snapshot" of the Continental line for his diary. He noted a successful siege. Faced with direct fire from allied field artillery, General Cornwallis signed official surrender papers on October 19.

Document

Source: Jean-Baptiste Antoine de Verger, "American Foot Soldiers during the Yorktown Campaign, 1781," Anne S. K. Brown Military Collection, Brown University Library.

Questions for Consideration

1) What types of weaponry did the soldiers carry?
2) What can you discern about the identity of the profiled soldier approaching the two standing at attention?
3) Why do you suppose that the French officer depicted each soldier in a different uniform at Yorktown?

2.6 Deborah Sampson Wears a Uniform (1782)

During the final years of the war, the United States struggled to keep an army in the field. Not only was the government virtually bankrupt, but Congress repudiated many financial obligations to the men in uniform. Behind the lines, female patriots offered vital assistance. Esther DeBerdt Reed, an officer's wife, formed the Philadelphia Ladies Association. In 1780, its members began a fund-raising drive to support the troops. They sewed at least 2,200 shirts. They also penned broadsides, circulated letters, and drafted declarations. Numerous "campfollowers" accompanied the army and managed the cooking, cleaning, laundering, nursing, and entertaining. Of course, more than a few craved adventure or drifted from camp to camp in search of income. Others became spies, scouts, and couriers. Several accounts tell of women wearing uniforms. Deborah Sampson, for instance, enlisted on May 20, 1782, in the Fourth Massachusetts Regiment under the alias "Robert Shurtliff." She was discharged from service the next year and received a veteran's pension decades later. She collaborated with Herman Mann, a writer, who composed her dramatic memoir as well as a theatrical address. Dressed on stage to recite her oration, the American heroine performed a soldier's manual exercise of arms. Whatever the embellishments on the tour, audiences applauded the telling of her story.

Document

FOR several years I looked on these scenes of havoc, rapacity and devastation, as one looks on a drowning man, on the conflagration of a city—where are not only centered his coffers of gold, but with them his choicest hopes, friends, companions, his all—without being able to extend the rescuing hand to either.

WROUGHT upon at length, you may say, by an enthusiasm and phrenzy, that could brook no control—I burst the tyrant bands, which held my *sex in awe*, and clandestinely, or by stealth, grasped an opportunity, which custom and the world seemed to deny, as a natural privilege. And whilst poverty, hunger, nakedness, cold and disease had dwindled the *American Armies* to a handful—whist universal terror and dismay ran through our camps, ran through our country—while even WASHINGTON himself, at their head, though like a god, stood, as it were, on a pinnacle tottering over the abyss of destruction, the last prelude to our falling a wretched prey to the yawning jaws of the monster aiming to devour —not merely for the sake of gratifying a facetious curiosity, like that of my reputed Predecessor, in her romantic excursions through the garden of bliss—did I throw off the soft habiliments of *my sex*, and assume those of the *warrior* already prepared for battle.

THUS I became an actor in that important drama, with an inflexible resolution to persevere through the last scene; when we might be permitted and acknowledged to enjoy what we had so nobly declared we would possess, or lose with our lives— FREEDOM and INDEPENDENCE!—when, the philosopher might resume his researches unmolested—the statesman be disembarrassed by his distracting theme of national politics—the divine find less occasion to invoke the indignation of heaven on the usurpers and cannibals of the inherent rights and even existence of man—when the son should again be restored to the arms of his disconsolate parent, and the lover to the bosom of her, for whom indeed he is willing to jeopardy his life, and for whom alone he wishes to live!

A NEW scene, and, as it were, a new world now opened to my view; the objects of which now seemed as important as the transition before seemed unnatural. It would, however, here be a weakness in me to mention the tear of repentance, or of that temerity, from which the stoutest of my sex are, or ought not to be, wholly exempt on extreme emergencies, which many times involuntarily stole into my eye, and fell unheeded to the ground: And that too before I had reached the embattled field, the ramparts, which protected its internal resources—which shield youth, beauty, and the delicacy of that sex at home, which perhaps I had forfeited in turning volunteer in their defense. *Temeritis*— when reflections on my former situation, and this new kind of being, were daggers more frightful, than all the implements of war—when the rustling of every leaf was an omen of danger, the whisper of each wind, a tale of woe! If then the poignancy of thought stared me thus haggardly in the face, found its way to the endmost recess of my heart thus forcibly in the commencement of my career—what must I not have anticipated before its close!

THE curtain is now up—a scene opens to your view; but the objects strike our attention less forcibly, and less interestingly, than they then did, not only my own eyes, but every energetic sensation of my soul. What shall I say further? Shall I not stop short, and leave to your imaginations to pourtray the tragic deeds of war? Is it not enough that I here leave it even to inexperience to fancy the hardships, the anxieties, the dangers, even of the best life of a soldier? And were it not improper, were it not unsafe, were it not indelicate, and were I certain I should be entitled to a pardon, I would appeal to the soft bosom of my own sex to draw a parallel between the perils and sexual inconveniences of a girl in her teens, and not only in the armour, but in the capacity, at any rate, obliged to perform the duties in the field—and those who go to the camp without a masquerade, inconsequently subject only to what toils and sacrifices they please; Or, will a conclusion be more natural from those, who sometimes take occasion to complain by their own domestic fire-sides; but who, indeed, are at the same time in affluence, cherished in the arms of their companions, and sheltered from the storms of war by the rougher sex in arms?

MANY have seen, and many can contemplate, in the field of imagination, battles and victories amidst garments rolled in blood: but it is only one of my own sex, exposed to the storm, who can conceive of my situation.

Source: Deborah Sampson Gannet, *An Address, Delivered with Applause, at the Federal Street Theatre, Boston, Four Successive Nights of the Different Plays, Beginning March 22, 1802* (Dedham, MA: Printed and sold by H. Mann, 1802), 11–16.

Questions for Consideration

1) How did Deborah Sampson explain her initial decision to "masquerade" as a male soldier?
2) In what ways did she speak of military service as a natural right?
3) Why do you think she delivered her oration while wearing a soldier's uniform?

2.7 George Washington Bids Farewell to the Army (1783)

For eight years, General Washington battled rivalries, betrayals, cabals, and mutinies in addition to the British armed forces. During 1782, he redeployed regiments from Yorktown to New York. From his headquarters in Newburgh, he kept a vigilant eye on enemies inside and outside the lines. Despite key losses in the war, the British maintained thousands of troops within North America. They decided to begin a gradual withdrawal and agreed to peace talks with the Americans in Paris. After Congress reviewed the final wording, the Treaty of Paris was signed on September 3, 1783. Congress ratified it the following January. Before disbanding the "standing army," a cadre of Continental officers demanded back pay, outstanding pensions, and further entitlements from Congress. Some formed the Society of the Cincinnati, which selected General Washington as their "president." Considered the embodiment of the revolution, he reinforced the republican mythology about a veteran's return to the plow after wartime. Once news of honorable discharges arrived, he calmed restless and footloose soldiers by reinforcing civilian authority over the military. At Rocky Hill, New Jersey, he issued farewell orders on November 2, 1783. They were read from Annapolis to West Point. He surrendered his sword and his commission to Congress the next month and then retired to Mount Vernon.

Document

A contemplation of the complete attainment (at a period earlier than could have been expected) of the object for which we contended, against so formidable a power, cannot but inspire us with astonishment and gratitude—The disadvantageous circumstances on our part, under which the War was undertaken, can never be forgotten—The singular interpositions of Providence in our feeble condition were such, as could scarcely escape the attention of the most unobserving, while the unparalleled perseverance of the Armies of the United States, through almost every possible suffering and discouragement, for the space of eight long years, was little short of a standing Miracle.

It is not the meaning nor within the compass of this Address, to detail the hardships peculiarly incident to our Service, or to describe the distresses which in several instances have resulted from the extremes of hunger and nakedness, combined with the rigors of an inclement season. Nor is it necessary to dwell on the dark side of our past affairs. Every American Officer and Soldier must now console himself for any unpleasant circumstances which may have occurred, by a recollection of the uncommon scenes in which he has been called to act, no inglorious part; and the astonishing Events of which he has been a witness—Events which have seldom, if ever before, taken place on the stage of human action, nor can they probably ever happen again. For who has before seen a disciplined Army formed at once from such raw materials? Who that was not a witness could imagine, that the most violent local prejudices would cease so soon, and that Men who came from the different parts of the Continent, strongly disposed by the habits of education, to despise and quarrel with each other, would instantly become but one patriotic band of Brothers? Or who that was not on the spot can trace the steps by which such a wonderful Revolution has been effected, and such a glorious period put to all our Warlike toils?

It is universally acknowledged that the enlarged prospect of happiness, opened by the confirmation of our Independence and Sovereignty, almost exceeds the power of description. And shall not the brave Men who have contributed so essentially to these inestimable acquisitions, retiring victorious from the Field of War, to the Field of Agriculture, participate in all the blessings which have been obtained? In such a Republic, who will exclude them from the rights of Citizens and the fruits of their labours? In such a Country so happily circumstanced, the pursuits of Commerce and the cultivation of the Soil, will unfold to industry the certain road to competence. To those hardy Soldiers, who are actuated by the spirit of adventure, the Fisheries will afford ample and profitable employment, and the extensive and fertile Regions of the West will yield a most happy Asylum to those, who fond of domestic enjoyment, are seeking for personal independence. Nor is it possible to conceive that any one of the United States will prefer a National Bankruptcy and a dissolution of the Union, to a compliance with the requisitions of Congress and the payment of its just debts—so that the Officers and Soldiers may expect considerable assistance in recommencing their civil occupations from the sums due to them from the Public, which must and will most inevitably be paid.

In order to effect this desirable purpose, and to remove the prejudices which may have taken possession of the Minds of any of the good People of the States, it is earnestly recommended to all the Troops that with strong attachments to the Union, they should carry with them into civil Society the most conciliating dispositions; and that they should prove themselves not less virtuous and usefull as Citizens, than they have been persevering and victorious as Soldiers. What tho' there should be some envious Individuals who are unwilling to pay the Debt the public has contracted, or to yield the tribute due to Merit, yet let such unworthy treatment produce no invective, or any instance of intemperate conduct, let it be remembered that the unbiased voice of the Free Citizens of the United States has promised the just reward, and given the merited applause; let it be known and remembered that the reputation of the Federal Armies is established beyond the reach of Malevolence, and let a consciousness of their achievements and fame, still incite the Men who composed them to honorable Actions; under the persuasion that the private virtues of economy, prudence, and industry will not be less amiable in civil life, than the more splendid qualities of valour, perseverance, and enterprise were in the Field: Every one may rest assured that much, very much of the future happiness of the Officers and Men, will depend upon the wise and manly conduct which shall be adopted by these, when they are mingled with the great body of the Community. And, altho' the General has so frequently given it as his opinion in the most public and explicit manner, that unless the principles of the Federal Government were properly supported, and the Powers of the Union increased, the honor, dignity, and justice of the Nation would be lost forever; yet he cannot help repeating on this occasion, so interesting a sentiment, and leaving it as his last injunction to every Officer and every Soldier, who may view the subject in the same serious point of light, to add his best endeavours to those of his worthy fellow Citizens towards effecting these great and valuable purposes, on which our very existence as a nation so materially depends.

The Commander in Chief conceives little is now wanting to enable the Soldiers to change the Military character into that of the Citizen, but that steady and decent tenor of behaviour which has generally distinguished, not only the Army under his immediate Command, but the different Detachments and separate Armies, through the course of the War; from their good sense and prudence he anticipates the happiest consequences; And while he congratulates them on the glorious occasion which renders their Services in the Field no longer necessary, he wishes to express the strong obligations he feels himself under, for the assistance he has received from every Class—and in every instance. He presents his thanks in the most serious and affectionate manner to the General Officers, as well for their Counsel on many interesting occasions, as for their ardor in promoting the success of the plans he had adopted—To the Commandants of Regiments and Corps, and to the other Officers for their great Zeal and attention in carrying his orders promptly into execution—To the Staff for their alacrity and exactness in performing the duties of their several Departments—And to the Non-commissioned Officers and private Soldiers, for their extraordinary patience in suffering, as well as their invincible fortitude in Action—To the various branches of the Army, the General takes this last and solemn opportunity of professing his inviolable attachment & friendship—He wishes more than bare professions were in his power, that he were really able to be useful to them all in future life; He flatters himself however, they will do him the justice to believe, that whatever could with propriety be attempted by him has been done.

And being now to conclude these his last public Orders, to take his ultimate leave, in a short time, of the Military Character, and to bid a final adieu to the Armies he has so long had the honor to Command—he can only again offer in their behalf his recommendations to their grateful country, and his prayers to the God of Armies. May ample justice be done them here; and may the choicest of heaven's favors both here and hereafter attend those, who under the divine auspices have secured innumerable blessings for others; With these wishes, and this benediction, the Commander in Chief is about to retire from Service—The Curtain of separation will soon be drawn—and the Military Scene to him will be closed for ever.

Source: "Washington's Farewell Address to the Army, 2 November 1783," *Founders Online*, National Archives. http://founders.archives.gov/documents/Washington/99-01-02-12012 (accessed 4 May 2017).

Questions for Consideration

1) Where, according to General Washington, could discharged veterans find "a most happy Asylum" after the war?
2) How did he address the discontent of officers during this farewell?
3) Do you agree that the war's outcome was "little short of a standing Miracle"?

Suggested Readings

Breen, T. H. *American Insurgents, American Patriots: The Revolution of the People*. New York: Hill and Wang, 2010.

Carp, E. Wayne. *To Starve the Army at Pleasure: Continental Army Administration and American Political Culture, 1775–1783*. Chapel Hill: University of North Carolina Press, 1984.

Cox, Caroline. *A Proper Sense of Honor: Service and Sacrifice in George Washington's Army*. Chapel Hill: University of North Carolina Press, 2004.

Ferling, John. *Almost a Miracle: The American Victory in the War of Independence*. New York: Oxford University Press, 2007.

Fowler, William M. *Rebels under Sail: The American Navy during the Revolution*. New York: Scribner, 1976.

Frey, Sylvia R. *Water from the Rock: Black Resistance in a Revolutionary Age*. Princeton: Princeton University Press, 1991.

Hibbert, Christopher. *Redcoats and Rebels: The American Revolution through British Eyes*. New York: W. W. Norton, 2002.

Higginbotham, Donald. *The War of Independence*. New York: Macmillan, 1983.

Lengel, Edward G. *General George Washington: A Military Life*. New York: Random House, 2005.

Martin, James Kirby, and Mark Edward Lender. *A Respectable Army: The Military Origins of the Republic, 1763–1789*. Third Edition. Malden, MA: Wiley Blackwell, 2015.

Mayer, Holly A. *Belonging to the Army: Camp Followers and Community during the American Revolution*. Columbia: University of South Carolina Press, 1999.

Middlekauff, Robert. *The Glorious Cause: The American Revolution, 1763–1789*. Revised and Expanded Edition. New York: Oxford University Press, 2005.

Morrison, Samuel Eliot. *John Paul Jones: A Sailor's Biography*. Boston: Little, Brown, 1959.

Royster, Charles. *A Revolutionary People at War: The Continental Army and American Character, 1775–1783*. Chapel Hill: University of North Carolina Press, 1979.

Saunt, Claudio. *West of the Revolution: An Uncommon History of 1776*. New York: W. W. Norton, 2014.

Shy, John. *A People Numerous and Armed: Reflections on the Military Struggle for American Independence*. New York: Oxford University Press, 1976.

Young, Alfred F. *Masquerade: The Life and Times of Deborah Sampson, Continental Soldier*. New York: Random House, 2004.

3

Establishing the Military

Chronology

1786	Shays' Rebellion
1787	Constitutional Convention
1788	The Constitution ratified
1791	The Bill of Rights ratified
1792	Congress Passes the Uniform Militia Act
	The Legion of the United States formed
1794	Whiskey Rebellion
	Battle of Fallen Timbers
	Jay's Treaty
1795	Pinckney's Treaty
1798	The Quasi-War against France begins
	Navy Department created
	Marine Corps created
1799	George Washington dies
1800	Convention of Mortefontaine
1802	Congress Passes the Military Peace Establishment Act
1803	Tripolitan War begins
	The Louisiana Purchase
1804–1806	The Lewis and Clark Expedition
1805	Battle of Derne
1807	Aaron Burr Trial
	The Chesapeake–Leopard Affair

3.1   Alexander Hamilton Considers National Forces (1787)

The framers of the Constitution divided civilian authority between a legislative branch, an executive branch, a judicial branch, and the various states. In deference to popular anxieties about military establishments, however, they carefully limited the powers of the federal government regarding national forces. Alexander Hamilton, who previously served as an artillery officer and aide-de-camp to General Washington, was one of the most ardent militarists. While a delegate to the Philadelphia convention, Hamilton

American Military History: A Documentary Reader, Second Edition. Brad D. Lookingbill.
© 2019 John Wiley & Sons, Inc. Published 2019 by John Wiley & Sons, Inc.

pursued reforms to what the preamble called the "common defence." Along with James Madison and John Jay, he composed essays that came to be known as the Federalist Papers. They drove the public debate for the ratification of the Constitution. Hamilton made the largest contribution to that collective effort, writing 51 of the 85 essays. For example, Federalist No. 24 appeared in the *Independent Journal* on December 19, 1787. Addressed to the people of New York, Hamilton signed it with the pseudonym "PUBLIUS." It eloquently justified the building of a permanent army and navy in order to confront internal and external threats to the nation. Consequently, Hamilton served as the first Secretary of the Treasury in the administration of President George Washington. Wounded during a duel, Hamilton died on July 12, 1804, in New York.

Document

To the powers proposed to be conferred upon the federal government, in respect to the creation and direction of the national forces, I have met with but one specific objection, which, if I understand it right, is this, that proper provision has not been made against the existence of standing armies in time of peace; an objection which, I shall now endeavor to show, rests on weak and unsubstantial foundations.

It has indeed been brought forward in the most vague and general form, supported only by bold assertions, without the appearance of argument; without even the sanction of theoretical opinions; in contradiction to the practice of other free nations, and to the general sense of America, as expressed in most of the existing constitutions. The propriety of this remark will appear, the moment it is recollected that the objection under consideration turns upon a supposed necessity of restraining the LEGISLATIVE authority of the nation, in the article of military establishments; a principle unheard of, except in one or two of our State constitutions, and rejected in all the rest.

A stranger to our politics, who was to read our newspapers at the present juncture, without having previously inspected the plan reported by the convention, would be naturally led to one of two conclusions: either that it contained a positive injunction, that standing armies should be kept up in time of peace; or that it vested in the EXECUTIVE the whole power of levying troops, without subjecting his discretion, in any shape, to the control of the legislature.

If he came afterwards to peruse the plan itself, he would be surprised to discover, that neither the one nor the other was the case; that the whole power of raising armies was lodged in the *legislature*, not in the *executive*; that this legislature was to be a popular body, consisting of the representatives of the people periodically elected; and that instead of the provision he had supposed in favor of standing armies, there was to be found, in respect to this object, an important qualification even of the legislative discretion, in that clause which forbids the appropriation of money for the support of an army for any longer period than two years a precaution which, upon a nearer view of it, will appear to be a great and real security against the keeping up of troops without evident necessity [...]

Though a wide ocean separates the United States from Europe, yet there are various considerations that warn us against an excess of confidence or security. On one side of us, and stretching far into our rear, are growing settlements subject to the dominion of Britain. On the other side, and extending to meet the British settlements, are colonies and establishments subject to the dominion of Spain. This situation and the vicinity of the West India Islands, belonging to these two powers create between them, in respect to their American possessions and in relation to us, a common interest. The savage tribes on our Western frontier ought to be regarded as our natural enemies, their natural allies, because they have most to fear from us, and most to hope from them. The improvements in the art of navigation have, as to the facility of communication, rendered distant nations, in a great measure, neighbors. Britain and Spain are among the principal maritime powers of Europe. A future concert of views between these nations ought not to be regarded as improbable. The increasing remoteness of consanguinity is every day diminishing the force of the family compact between France and Spain. And politicians have ever with great reason considered the ties of blood as feeble and precarious links of political connection. These circumstances combined, admonish us not to be too sanguine in considering ourselves as entirely out of the reach of danger.

Previous to the Revolution, and ever since the peace, there has been a constant necessity for keeping small garrisons on our Western frontier. No person can doubt that these will continue to be indispensable, if it should only be against the ravages and depredations of the Indians. These garrisons must either be furnished by occasional detachments from the militia, or by permanent corps in the pay of the government. The first is impracticable; and if practicable, would be pernicious. The militia would not long, if at all, submit to be dragged from their occupations and families to perform that most disagreeable duty in times of profound peace. And if they could be prevailed upon or compelled to do it, the increased expense of a frequent rotation of service, and the loss of labor and disconcertion of the industrious pursuits of individuals, would form conclusive objections to the scheme. It would be as burdensome and injurious to the public as ruinous to private citizens. The latter resource of permanent corps in the pay of the government amounts to a standing army in time of peace; a small one, indeed, but not the less real for being small. Here is a simple view of the subject that shows us at once the impropriety of a constitutional interdiction of such establishments, and the necessity of leaving the matter to the discretion and prudence of the legislature.

In proportion to our increase in strength, it is probable, nay, it may be said certain, that Britain and Spain would augment their military establishments in our neighborhood. If we should not be willing to be exposed, in a naked and defenseless condition, to their insults and encroachments, we should find it expedient to increase our frontier garrisons in some ratio to the force by which our Western settlements might be annoyed. There are, and will be, particular posts, the possession of which will include the command of large districts of territory, and facilitate future invasions of the remainder. It may be added that some of those posts will be keys to the trade with the Indian nations. Can any man think it would be wise to leave such posts in a situation to be at any instant seized by one or the other of two neighboring and formidable powers? To act this part would be to desert all the usual maxims of prudence and policy.

If we mean to be a commercial people, or even to be secure on our Atlantic side, we must endeavor, as soon as possible, to have a navy. To this purpose there must be dock-yards and arsenals; and for the defense of these, fortifications, and probably garrisons. When a nation has become so powerful by sea that it can protect its dock-yards by its fleets, this supersedes the necessity of garrisons for that purpose; but where naval establishments are in their infancy, moderate garrisons will, in all likelihood, be found an indispensable security against descents for the destruction of the arsenals and dock-yards, and sometimes of the fleet itself.

Source: "The Federalist No. XXIV," in *The Federalist: A Commentary on the Constitution of the United States* (New York: M. W. Dunne, 1901), 158–163.

Questions for Consideration

1) What were the concerns about "standing armies" expressed by the newspapers that Hamilton read?
2) Did he describe how these concerns were addressed by the relevant articles of the Constitution?
3) Why did he say that military establishments would be "indispensable" to the security of the United States?

3.2 Henry Knox Arranges the Militia (1790)

One of President Washington's most trusted military advisors was Henry Knox, the former chief of the Continental artillery and a founder of the Society of the Cincinnati. The corpulent Knox headed the War Department after 1789. Respecting the sentiments of the Commander in Chief and other retired officers, he worked to formalize the "dual-army" tradition of America. While he wanted to make the Legion of the United States into the nation's primary national force, the Second Amendment to the Constitution presumed a "well regulated Militia" at the state level. He drafted a sweeping plan for the "General Arrangement of the Militia of the United States" and submitted it to Congress in January of 1790. After much deliberation, Congress passed the Uniform Militia Act on May 8, 1792. As the basic militia law for more than a century, it required all able-bodied men from the ages of 18 to 45 to enroll for service. Even though the law incorporated much of Knox's plan, it revealed several shortcomings. It permitted states to add numerous exemptions for militia service. It did not provide for a select corps from each state, as Knox had envisioned, or for federal control of officer training. Whatever its failings, the militia helped to quell the Whiskey Rebellion in 1794.

Document

It is the intention of the present attempt to suggest the most efficient system of defense which may be compatible with the interests of a free people—a system which shall not only produce the expected effect, but which, in its operations, shall also produce those habits and manners which will impart strength and desirability to the whole government.

The modern practice of Europe, with respect to the employment of standing armies, has created such a mass of opinion in their favor, that even philosophers and the advocates for liberty have frequently confessed their use and necessity in certain cases. But whoever seriously and candidly estimates the power of discipline, and the tendency of military habits, will be constrained to confess, that, whatever may be the efficacy of the standing army in war, it cannot in peace be considered as friendly to the rights of human nature. The recent instance in France cannot with propriety be brought to overturn the general principle, built upon the uniform experience of mankind. It may be found, on examining the causes that appear to have influenced the military of France, that, while the springs of power were wound up in the nation to the highest pitch, the discipline of the army was proportionably relaxed. But any argument on this head may be considered as unnecessary to the enlightened citizens of the United States.

A small corps of well disciplined and well informed artillerists and engineers, and a legion for the protection of the frontiers and the magazines and arsenals, are all the military establishment which may be required for the present use of the United States. The privates of the corps to be enlisted for a certain period, and after the expiration of which returned to the mass of the citizens. An energetic national militia is to be regarded as the *capital security* of a free republic, and not a standing army, forming a distinct class in the community. It is the introduction and diffusion of vice, and corruption of manners, into the mass of people, that renders a standing army necessary. It is when public spirit is despised, and avarice, indolence, and effeminacy of manners predominate, and prevent the establishment of institutions which would elevate the minds of the youth in the paths of virtue and honor, that a standing army is formed and riveted forever [...]

Youth is the time for the State to avail itself of those services which it has a right to demand, and by which it is to be invigorated and preserved; in this season, the passions and affections are strongly influenced by the splendor of military parade. The impressions the mind receives will be retained through life. The young man will repair with pride and pleasure to the field of exercise; while the head of a family, anxious for its general welfare, and perhaps its immediate subsistence, will reluctantly quit his domestic duties for any length of time.

The habits of industry will be rather strengthened than relaxed, by the establishment of the annual camps of discipline, as all the time will be occupied by the various military duties. Idleness and dissipation will be regarded as disgraceful, and punished accordingly. As soon as the youth attain the age of manhood, a natural solicitude to establish themselves in the society, will occur in its full force. The public claims for military service will be too inconsiderable to injure their industry. It will be sufficiently stimulated to proper exertions, by the prospects of opulence attending on the cultivation of a fertile soil, or the pursuits of a productive commerce.

It is presumed that thirty days annually during the eighteenth and nineteenth, and ten days during the twentieth year, is the least time that ought to be appropriated by the youth to the acquisition of military art. The same number of days might be added during the twentieth as during the two preceding years, were not the expense an objection.

Every means will be provided by the public to facilitate the military education of the youth, which it is proposed shall be an indispensable qualification of a free citizen, therefore they will not be entitled to any pay. But the officers, being of the main corps, are in a different predicament; they are supposed to have passed through the course of discipline required by the law, and to be competent to instruct others in the military art. As the public will have but small claims for personal services on them, and as they must incur considerable expenses to prepare themselves, to execute properly their respective offices, they ought to be paid while on actual duty.

As soon as the service of the youth expires in the advanced corps, they are to be enrolled in the main corps. On this occasion, the republic receives disciplined and free citizens, who understand their public rights, and are prepared to defend them. The main corps is instituted to preserve and circulate throughout the community the military discipline acquired in the advanced corps; to arm the people, and fix firmly, by practice and habit, those forms and maxims, which are essential to the life and energy of a free government. The reserved corps is instituted to prevent men being sent to the field, whose strength is unequal to sustain the severities of an active campaign. But by organizing and rendering them eligible for domestic service, a greater proportion of the younger and robust part of the community may be enabled in cases of necessity to encounter the more urgent duties of war [...]

It is conceded that people, solicitous to be exonerated from their proportion of public duty, may exclaim against the proposed arrangement as an intolerable hardship. But it ought to be strongly impressed that, while society has its charms, it also has its indispensable obligations. That, to attempt such a degree of refinement as to exonerate the members of the community from all personal service, is to render them incapable of the exercise, and unworthy of the characters of freemen.

Every State possesses, not only the right of personal service from its members, but the right to regulate the service on principles of equality for the general defense. All being bound, none can complain of injustice, on being obliged to perform his equal proportion. Therefore, it ought to be a permanent rule, that those who in youth decline or refuse to subject themselves to the course of military education, established by the laws, should be considered as unworthy of public trust or public honors, and be excluded therefrom accordingly.

If the majesty of the laws should be preserved inviolate in this respect, the operations of the proposed plan would foster a glorious public spirit, infuse the principles of energy and stability into the body politic, and give a high degree of political splendor to the national character.

Source: Henry Knox, "Plan submitted to Congress, January 1790," in U.S. Congress, *American State Papers: Military Affairs*, Volume 1 (Washington, DC: Gales and Seaton, 1832), 6–14.

Questions for Consideration

1) What form did Secretary Knox plan for the permanent establishment of the militia to take?
2) Which age groups of servicemen did he presume would require annual training in military camps for at least 30 days?
3) Do you agree with him in that individuals avoiding service should be deemed "unworthy of public trust or public honors"?

3.3   Anthony Wayne Prevails at Fallen Timbers (1794)

Foreign powers watched the Northwest Territory of the United States with great interest. A group of Indian nations there formed the Miami Confederacy and refused to negotiate with agents of the War Department. They soundly defeated two separate military expeditions under Generals Josiah Harmer and Arthur St. Clair. To command a new and improved Legion of the United States, Secretary Knox promoted General Anthony Wayne in 1792. Called "Mad Anthony," he trained and equipped around 4,600 soldiers for the field. During the summer of 1794, General Wayne and the Legion reached the confluence of the Auglaize and Maumee Rivers, where they erected Fort Greenville. At a clearing near Fort Miamis, which was still occupied by the British, they broke through a line of Indian warriors and Canadian militia on

August 20. They marched around Fort Miamis, insulting the British officers inside. To complete the mission, they proceeded to raze Indian villages and to destroy food supplies. Eight days later, General Wayne dispatched to Secretary Knox his official report on the battle. The next year, Indian leaders ceded the land by signing the Treaty of Greenville. Thanks to a smashing victory in the Battle of Fallen Timbers, Wayne's Legion secured federal control over the Northwest Territory.

Documents

The legion was immediately formed in two lines, principally in a close, thick wood, which extended for miles on our left; and for a very considerable distance in front, the ground being covered with old fallen timber, probably occasioned by a tornado, which rendered it impracticable for the cavalry to act with effect; and afforded the enemy the most favorable covert for their savage mode of warfare. They were formed in three lines, within supporting distance of each other, and extending near two miles, at right angles with the river.

I soon discovered, from the weight of the fire, and extent of their lines, that the enemy were in full force in front, in possession of their favorite ground, and endeavoring to turn our left flank. I therefore gave orders for the second line to advance, to support the first, and directed Major-General Scott to gain and turn the right flank of the savages, with the whole of the mounted volunteers, by a circuitous route. At the same time I ordered the front line to advance with trailed arms, and rouse the Indians from their coverts, at the point of the bayonet; and, when up, to deliver a close and well directed fire on their backs, followed by a brisk charge, so as not to give time to load again. I also ordered Captain Miss Campbell, who commanded the legionary cavalry, to turn the left flank of the enemy next the river, and which afforded a favorable field for that corps to act in.

All those orders were obeyed with spirit and promptitude; but such was the impetuosity of the charge by the first line of infantry, that the Indians and Canadian militia and volunteers were driven from all their coverts in so short a time, that although every exertion was used by the officers of the second line of the legion, and by Generals Scott, Todd, and Barbee, of the mounted volunteers, to gain their proper positions, yet but a part of each could get up in season to participate in the action; the enemy being driven, in the course of one hour, more than two miles, through the thick woods already mentioned, by less than one-half their numbers.

From every account, the enemy amounted to 2,000 combatants; the troops actually engaged against them, were short of 900. This horde of savages, with their allies, abandoned themselves to flight, and dispersed with terror and dismay; leaving our victorious army in full and quiet possession of the field of battle, which terminated under the influence of the guns of the British garrison, as you will observe by the enclosed correspondence between Major Campbell, the commandant, and myself, upon the occasion [...]

In fact, every officer and soldier who had an opportunity to come into action displayed that true bravery which will always insure success. And here permit me to declare, that I never discovered more true spirit and anxiety for action, than appeared to pervade the whole of the mounted volunteers; and I am well persuaded that had the enemy maintained their favorite ground but for one half hour longer, they would have most severely felt the prowess of that corps.

But whilst I pay this just tribute to the living, I must not forget the gallant dead; among whom we have to lament the early death of those worthy and brave officers, Captain Miss Campbell, of the dragoons, and Lieutenant Towles, of the light infantry of the legion, who fell in the first charge.

Enclosed is a particular return of the killed and wounded. The loss of the enemy was more than double that of the Federal army. The woods were strewed, for a considerable distance, with the dead bodies of Indians and their white auxiliaries; the latter armed with British muskets and bayonets.

We remained three days and nights on the banks of the Miamis, in front of the field of battle; during which time all the houses and cornfields were consumed and destroyed for a considerable distance, both above and below Fort Miamis, as well as within pistol-shot of that garrison, who were compelled to remain tacit spectators of this general devastation and conflagration; among which were the houses, stores, and property of Colonel M'Kee, the British Indian agent, and principal stimulator of the war now existing between the United States and the savages.

The army returned to this place on the 27th by easy marches, laying waste the villages and corn-fields for about fifty miles on each side of the Miamis. There remains yet a number of villages, and a great quantity of corn, to be consumed or destroyed upon Au Glaize and the Miamis above this place, which will be effected in the course of a few days. In the interim, we shall improve Fort Defiance, and as soon as the escort returns with the necessary supplies from Greenville and Fort Recovery, the army will proceed to the Miami villages, in order to accomplish the object of the campaign.

It is, however, not improbable that the enemy may make one more desperate effort against the army, as it is said that a reinforcement was hourly expected at Fort Miamis, from Niagara, as well as numerous tribes of Indians living on the margins and islands of the lakes. This is a business rather to be wished for than dreaded, whilst the army remains in force. Their numbers will only tend to confuse the savages, and the victory will be the more complete and decisive, and which may eventually insure a permanent and happy peace.

Source: "Letter to the Secretary of War, 28 August 1794," in Horatio Newton Moore, ed., *The Life and Services of General Anthony Wayne* (Philadelphia: John B. Perry, 1845), 190–197.

Questions for Consideration

1) What did the Battle of Fallen Timbers demonstrate about General Wayne's training of the soldiers?
2) How did the British garrison at Fort Miamis react to his operations in the field?
3) Why did the report highlight the "gallant dead" among the officers?

3.4 Thomas Truxtun Recruits Seamen for the Quasi-War (1798)

President John Adams, a Federalist leader and Washington's successor, believed that the U.S. faced serious threats after 1797. The French government refused to meet his envoys, claiming that a "bribe" was required. France closed its ports to neutral shipping and declared any vessels carrying trade with the British to be subject to capture. Congress appropriated substantial funding for harbor fortifications and cannon foundries. They created a "provisional army," organized the Marine Corps, armed merchant ships, and abrogated previous French treaties. To provide the nation with "wooden walls," they established a Navy Department. Benjamin Stoddert, a merchant of Georgetown, was appointed its first Secretary. As war clouds gathered across the Atlantic Ocean, a fleet of warships was necessary to protect American shores. Although the six original frigates were authorized a few years earlier, the Navy expanded to 50 ships and more than 5,000 officers and sailors under the Adams administration. Beginning in April of 1798, Captain Thomas Truxtun instructed his lieutenants to recruit sailors for service on board the U.S. frigate *Constellation*. American and French ships soon clashed in an undeclared "Quasi-War" upon the high seas. Naval strength proved critical in achieving peace with France, which ended hostilities by signing the Convention of Mortefontaine in 1800.

Document

You are hereby directed to open a Rendezvous at the house of Mr. Cloney, at Fells Point in the City of Baltimore, For the purpose of entering one hundred and thirty able Seamen, and Ninety ordinary Seamen, to Serve in the Navy of the United States, and for the present, on board the Ship under my command.

These men must be engaged for the term of Twelve calendar months, unless sooner discharged by order of the President of the United States.

The pay of the able Seamen, is to be Fifteen Dollars per month, and the ordinary Seamen ten dollars, and each class may have two months pay in advance on giving good and Sufficient Security, for their repairing on board, when order'd with their Clothes and bedding—or on their repairing on board and their names being returned to you that they are actually on board with their effects.

None but able bodied, robust healthy men are to be entered, and the Surgeon or his Mate, must Certify that they are So: as well as of their being free from Scorbutic or Consumptive affections if any are entered and paid their advance without the Officer So entering them, producing Certificates as aforesaid, it will be at his risk & Charge. A return must be made to me without fail every Saturday evening of the number of men you have enter'd, and Such as have been delivered over to the Ship, and a duplicate return sent by post to the Secretary of War.

Shou'd any of these Seamen or others attempt to run away after having Signed the Articles received the advance & taken the Oath, you must immediately give information to the Secretary of War, describe the man minutely, using at the Same tune all your endeavours to apprehend and lodge in jail Such runaway until Further orders from me. Mr. Garretson the Purser is to act as Pay Master to the Ship. He will consequently make a requisition and provide money Sufficient to accomplish all the business with which you are charged, and you must produce to him the Vouchers he shall require for the Settlement of his accounts.

The Agents Messrs. Sam & Ja Sterett will provide Victuals on board the Pilot Boat for the men you enter (say 1 1/2 lbs. of beef & 1 lb. of Bread with 1/2 a pint of Rum for each man until he joins the Ship) and whenever you can collect ten or more men with their clothes, you are to Dispatch the boat under the Charge of a Midshipman or Some other trusty Person.

Every expence attending the rendezvous for fire, candle, Liquor, house rent, &c &c, must not exceed one dollar for every man actually entered & received on board—you must come to a clear understanding with Mr. Cloney on this subject, before you open the rendezvous, a reasonable allowance will be made you for music to indulge and humour the Johns in a farewell frolic;

In order to encourage the entering of Seamen, you may agree to pay to Mr. Cloney, one dollar for every Seaman he procures that is healthy and able to do his duty like a man, which Sum is to be paid him, when our Complement is complete, and the Ship ready to Sail from the Chesapeake Bay—it is absolutely necessary notwithstanding the Certificate required of the Surgeon and his Mates, that you pay particular attention in examining the men you enter, So that none but hale hearty men compose the Crew of this Ship, and the more real natives you can procure the better.

I understand that Captain Moore is well acquainted with the attending of Rendezvous. You must Call on Mr. Sterett, and let him make some agreement with him, to aid you in this business. The Compensation must in all cases be so much per man, but you must take care, that it is not paid to two people, for procuring one man.

The form which you and every officer & man must take is as follows to wit—

I, AB. — — do Solemnly Swear to bear true allegiance to the United States of America and to Serve them faithfully and honestly against all their enemies or opposers Whomsoever, and to observe and obey the orders of the President of the United States of America and the orders of all the officers appointed over me according to the Articles of War, and that I will Support the Constitution of the United States. So help me God.

Sworn before me this day of — —

You must be very particular and Oblige every man that offers, of the description I have mentioned to take the Oath as well as to sign the articles; before he receives a Single Cent, or that you attempt to Send him on board.

You must be very civil and good humour'd with everybody, and endeavour to attach them to the Service, by pointing out the rations &c &c allowed.

You will make every exertion in your power to complete the number of men required, in as short a time as possible.

This service, will require your devoting your whole time & attention to it, in fact you must be at the rendezvous night and day, until the object of your mission is completed.

Source: Naval Documents Related to the Quasi-War Between the United States and France: Naval Operations From February 1797 to October 1798 (Washington, DC: Government Printing Office, 1935), 49–50.

Questions for Consideration

1) What did Captain Truxtun stipulate for pay and benefits to "ordinary Seamen"?
2) How was the health of each recruit to be determined?
3) Why do you think the oath obliged all sailors "to bear true allegiance to the United States of America"?

3.5 Congress Passes the Military Peace Establishment Act (1802)

Coming to power at a critical moment of Republican enthusiasm, President Thomas Jefferson sought to reform the institutions of national defense. Congress passed the Military Peace Establishment Act on March 16, 1802, which permitted critics of past military expenditures to cut the federal budget. While slightly reducing the operational strength of the military, it eliminated around one-third of the officer corps. What was justified as an attempt to depoliticize the corps actually served as a subtle means to pursue ideological ends. President Jefferson and Secretary of War Henry Dearborn proceeded to relieve some of the most visible Federalists previously commissioned by the Adams administration. They recruited young Republicans to fill the new junior rank of ensign and courted the senior leadership by reintroducing the rank of colonel. The law also created a military academy at West Point, New York, which existed to provide a continuous supply of loyal cadets for commissioned service. Following the Louisiana Purchase of 1803, the War Department used Army personnel to promote Indian trade, to build interior roads, to conduct scientific expeditions, and to police western borders. Ironically, the Jefferson administration resolved to perpetuate the military establishment of the Federalists as a way to advance the peacetime goals of the Republicans.

Document

Be it enacted by the Senate and House of Representatives of the United States of America in Congress assembled, that the military peace establishment of the United States, from and after the 1st of June next, shall be composed of one regiment of artillerists, and two regiments of infantry, with such officers, military agents, and engineers, as are hereinafter mentioned.

SEC. 2. That the regiment of artillerists shall consist of one colonel, one lieutenant-colonel, four majors, one adjutant, and twenty companies, each company to consist of one captain, one first lieutenant, one second lieutenant, two cadets, four sergeants, four corporals, four musicians, eight artificers, and fifty-six privates: to be formed into five battalions: *Provided always*, That it shall be lawful for the President of the United States to retain, with their present grade, as many of the first lieutenants, now in service, as shall amount to the whole number of lieutenants required; but that, in proportion as vacancies happen therein, new appointments be made to the grade of second lieutenants, until their number amount to twenty; and each regiment of infantry shall consist of one colonel, one lieutenant-colonel, one major, one adjutant, one sergeant-major, two teachers of music, and ten companies; each company to consist of one captain, one first and one second lieutenant, one ensign, four sergeants, four corporals, four musicians, and sixty-four privates.

SEC. 3. That there shall be one brigadier-general, with one aid-de-camp, who shall be taken from the captains or subalterns of the line; one adjutant and inspector of the army, to be taken from the line of field officers; one paymaster of the army, seven paymasters, and two assistants, to be attached to such districts as the President of the United States shall direct, to be taken from the line of commissioned officers, who, in addition to their other duties, shall have charge of the clothing of the troops; three military agents, and such number of assistant military agents, as the President of the United States shall deem expedient, not exceeding one to each military post; which assistants shall be taken from the line; two surgeons, twenty-five surgeon's mates, to be attached to the garrisons or posts, and not to corps [...]

SEC. 26. That the President of the United States is hereby authorized and empowered, when he shall deem it expedient, to organize and establish a corps of engineers, to consist of one engineer, with the pay, rank, and emoluments of a major; two assistant engineers, with the pay, rank, and emoluments of captains; two other assistant engineers, with the pay, rank, and emoluments of first lieutenants: two other assistant engineers, with the pay, rank, and emoluments of second lieutenants; and ten cadets, with the pay of sixteen dollars per month, and two rations per day: and the President of the United States is, in like manner, authorized, when he shall deem it proper, to make such promotions in the said corps, with a view to particular merit, and without regard to rank, so as not to exceed one colonel, one lieutenant-colonel, two majors, four captains, four first lieutenants, four second lieutenants, and so as that the number of the whole corps shall, at no time, exceed twenty officers and cadets.

SEC. 27. That the said corps, when so organized, shall be stationed at West Point, in the State of New York, and shall constitute a military academy; and the engineers, assistant engineers, and cadets of the said corps, shall be subject, at all times, to do duty in such places, and on such service, as the President of the United States shall direct.

SEC. 28. That the principal engineer, and in his absence the next in rank, shall have the superintendence of the said military academy, under the direction of the President of the United States; and the secretary of war is hereby authorized, at the public expense, under such regulations as shall be directed by the President of the United States, to procure the necessary books, implements, and apparatus for the use and benefit of the said institution.

SEC. 29. That so much of any act or acts now in force, as comes within the purview of this act, shall be, and the same is hereby, repealed; saving, nevertheless, such parts thereof as relate to the enlistments, or term of service, of any of the troops which by this act are continued on the present military establishment of the United States.

Source: "An Act Fixing the Military Peace Establishment of the United States," in *Military Laws of the United States*, comp. John F. Callan (Philadelphia: Henry B. Ashmead, 1863), 141–149.

Questions for Consideration

1) How many first lieutenants, according to the law, could the President of the United States retain within an artillery regiment?
2) Who was designated as the superintendent of the military academy at West Point?
3) Why do you suppose Section 26 mentioned "particular merit" with respect to promotions in the corps?

3.6   William Eaton Arrives on the Shores of Tripoli (1805)

For almost thirty years, the US battled against piracy in the Mediterranean Sea. The North African regencies of Tripoli, Morocco, Tunis, and Algiers regularly demanded tribute in exchange for allowing commercial ships to pass, but President Jefferson refused to pay. Instead, he ordered naval squadrons to the Barbary Coast. They operated in 1803 near Tripoli, where Lieutenant Stephen Decatur and Commodore Edward Preble earned national acclaim for their valor. Because of his ability to speak fluent Arabic, William Eaton, a former Army captain, received an appointment in 1804 as a special agent for the Navy. He made a pact with a deposed leader of Tripoli and began recruiting hundreds of foreign mercenaries in Egypt. Accompanied by a detachment of eight marines and two midshipmen, they trekked for six weeks across the Libyan Desert. Supported by Captain Isaac Hull of the *Argus*, the joint operation converged at Tripoli's easternmost port, Derne. After the Battle of Derne on April 27, 1805, Eaton reported the triumph to Captain Samuel Barron. The Pasha of Tripoli quickly agreed to sign a treaty with the US. The good news from the shores of Tripoli reinforced President Jefferson's fascination with gunboats, which American tars operated in the shallow North African waters.

Document

Owing to impediments too tedious to detail, but chiefly to delinquency in our Quarter Master's department, which I had confided to Richard Farquhar, I did not leave Alexandria 'till the third of last month. The host of Arabs, who accompanied the [Hamet] Bashaw from that place and joined him on the route, moving chiefly with their families & flocks, render'd our progress through the desert slow & painful; add to this the ungovernable temper of this marauding Militia, and the frequent fits of despondency, amounting sometimes to mutiny, occasion'd by information almost every day meeting us of formidable re-enforcements from the enemy for the defence of this place, and it will not seem unaccountable that it was not till the fifteenth instant we arrived at Bomba. We had now been twenty five days without meat, and fifteen without bread, subsisting on rice.

Happily the next morning, discover'd the *Argus*, to whom I made signals by smoke, which were discovered and answered. The *Hornet* soon after appeared. Capt. Hull sent off a boat. I went on board, & had the honor and inexpressible satisfaction of receiving your communications of 22nd ulto. The timely supplies that came forward in these vessels gave animation to our half famished people; and no time was lost in moving forward on the morning of the 25th. We took post on an eminence in the rear of Derne. Several chiefs came out to meet the Bashaw with assurances of fealty and attachment. By them I learn'd that the city was divided into three departments, two of which were in the interest of the Bashaw, and one in opposition. This department, 'tho fewest in numbers, was strongest in position & resources, being defended by a battery of eight guns, the blind walls of the houses, which are provided in all directions with loop holes for musketry, and by temporary parapets thrown up in several positions not covered by the battery, this department is the nearest the sea and the residence of the Bey.

On the morning of the 26th, terms of amity were offered the Bey on condition of allegiance and fidelity. The flag of truce was sent back to me with this laconic answer, "My head or yours!" At 2 P. M. discover'd the *Nautilus* & spoke her at six. In the morning of the 27th the *Argus* and *Hornet* appeared & stood in. I immediately put the Army in motion, and advanced towards the city. A favorable land breeze enabled the *Nautilus* and *Hornet* to approach the shore, which is a steep & rugged declivity of rocks. With much difficulty we landed and drew up the precipice one of the field pieces; both were sent in the boat for the purpose, but the apprehension of losing this favorable moment of attack induced me to leave one on board. We advanced to our position. Lieut. Evans stood in and, anchoring within one hundred yards of the battery, opened a well directed fire. Lieut. Dent dropped in and anchor'd in a position to bring his guns to bear on the battery and city. Capt. Commandant Hull brought the *Argus* to anchor a little south of the *Nautilus*, so near as to throw her 24 pd. shot quite into the town. A detachment of six American marines, a company of 24 cannoniers, and another of 26 Greeks including their proper officers, all under the immediate command of Lieut. O'Bannon, together with a few Arabs on foot, had a position on an eminence opposite to a considerable party of the enemy, who had taken post behind their temporary parapets and in a ravine at the S. E. quarter of the town. The Bashaw seized an old castle which overlook'd the town on the S. S. W. disposing his cavalry upon the plains in the rear. A little before 2 P. M. the fire became general in all quarters where Tripolitans and Americans were opposed to each other. In three quarters of an hour the battery was silenced, but not abandoned; 'tho most of the enemy withdrew precipitately from that quarter and joined the party opposed to the handful of Christians with me, which appeared our most vulnerable point. Unfortunately the fire of our field piece was relaxed by the rammer being shot away.

The fire of the enemy's musketry became too warm, and continually augmenting. Our troops were thrown into confusion, and undisciplined as they were, it was impossible to reduce them to order. I perceived a charge—our dernier and only resort. We rushed forward against a host of savages more than ten to our one. They fled from their coverts, irregularly, firing in retreat from every palm tree and partition wall in their way. At this moment I received a ball through my left wrist, which deprived me of the use the hand and of course of my rifle. Mr. O'Bannon, accompanied by Mr. Mann of Annapolis, urged forward with his marines, Greeks, and such of the cannoniers as were not necessary to the management of the field piece, pass'd through a shower of musketry from the walls of houses, took possession of the battery, planted the American flag upon its ramparts, and turned its guns upon the enemy, who being now driven from their outposts, fired only from their houses, from which they were soon dislodged by the whole fire of the vessels, which was suspended during the charge being directed into them. The Bashaw soon got possession of the Bey's palace; his cavalry flank'd the flying enemy, and a little after four o'clock we had complete possession of the town. The action lasted about two hours & a half. The Bey took refuge, first in a mosque, & then in a Hiram, the most sacred of sanctuaries among the Turks, and is still there. But we shall find means to draw him thence. As he is the third man in rank in the kingdom, he may perhaps be used in exchange for Capt. Bainbridge.

I have fixed my post in the battery, raised parapets and mounted guns towards the country, to be prepar'd against all events, 'tho I have no serious apprehensions of a counterrevolution. The moment of gaining Derne has been peculiarly fortunate, as the camp, which long since left Tripoli for its defence, were within two days, fourteen hours march, the day of our attack; of which we had information in the morning, and from which circumstance, it was with much difficulty I could prevail on the Bashaw's Army to advance to the city & to obey my dispositions. The camp will probably take up a retrograde march.

Of the few Christians who fought on shore, I lost fourteen killed and wounded; three of whom are marines, one dead and another dying; the rest chiefly Greeks, who, in this little affair, well supported their ancient character.

Source: Naval Documents Related to the United States Wars with the Barbary Powers, Volume 5 (Washington, DC: Government Printing Office, 1939), 553–555.

Questions for Consideration

1) What examples did William Eaton give of "impediments" to his arrival at Derne?
2) Which actions taken by Lieutenant Pressley O'Bannon were observed by Eaton?
3) What assumptions about the combatants of the Tripolitan War were revealed by Eaton in his report?

3.7 James Wilkinson Faces a Court Martial (1811)

Rogue elements in the Army and the Navy contributed in various ways to filibusters, that is, private military ventures organized to seize territory from foreign powers. While in uniform, General James Wilkinson participated in an array of ambitious schemes and secret affairs. A veteran officer of the Continental Army, he founded the community of Frankfort in Kentucky after the American Revolution. While Americans debated the Constitution, he established commercial ties with associates in New Orleans. He became known to Spanish officials as "Agent 13." He remained on Spain's payroll, even after he became the senior officer of the U.S. Army. Entrusted as the governor of the newly acquired Louisiana territory, he dispatched military expeditions into the borderlands. He discussed with Aaron Burr, a former officer who was also the Vice-President, a proposal to invade Spanish lands west of the Mississippi River. After Burr was arrested and charged with treason, General Wilkinson testified at the trial during 1807. His own conspiracies invited numerous inquiries, including a court-martial convened by President James Madison on September 2, 1811. Pleading not guilty, he was acquitted of all eight charges leveled against him. The general returned to his command for three years until the Madison administration finally relieved him from active duty. He died in Mexico City a decade later.

Document
CHARGE 1. That the said James Wilkinson, while in the military service, and holding the commission of Brigadier-General in the army of the United States, did corruptly stipulate to receive, and by virtue of such stipulation did actually receive, by way of pension or stipend, diverse sums of money from the officers and agents of a foreign power; that is to say, from the Spanish officers and agents, concerned in the administration of the late provincial government of Louisiana and its dependencies, for the intent and purpose of combining and co-operating with that power, in designs adverse to the law and policy, and hostile to the peace, interest, and union of these states; contrary to his duly and allegiance as an officer and a citizen.

Specification 1. Two mule loads of money, (the amount unknown) being received at New Orleans by one Joseph Ballinger, for the use, and by the authority, of him, the said James Wilkinson, on account of the said pension, and delivered by the bands of one John Ballinger to him, the said James Wilkinson, at Frankfort, Kentucky, some time in the month of December, 1789.

Specification 2. Two other mule or horse loads of money, (the amount unknown) being received by him, the said James Wilkinson, assisted by one Philip Nolan, at

New Orleans, some time in the autumn of the year 1789, also on account of the said pension.

Specification 3. Four thousand dollars and upwards, being received by one La Cassagna, at New Orleans, some time in the year 1793, or in the year 1794, for the use, and by the authority, of him, the said James Wilkinson, also on account of the said pension.

Specification 4. Six thousand dollars, being received by one Henry Owens, at New Orleans, some time in the summer of the year 1794, for the use, and by the authority, of him, the said James Wilkinson, also on account of the said pension.

Specification 5. Six thousand dollars and upwards, that is to say, from six thousand three hundred and thirty-three, to eleven thousand dollars, or thereabouts, being received by one Joseph Collins, at New Orleans, some time in the summer of the year 1795, for the use, and by the authority, of him, the said James Wilkinson, also on account of the said pension.

Specification 6. Six thousand five hundred and ninety dollars, being received for the use, and by the authority, of him, the said James Wilkinson, at New Orleans, by some person unknown, some time prior to the date of a letter, from the said James Wilkinson, to one John Adair; in which letter, dated the 7th of August, 1795, the receipt of that sum is mentioned, also on account of said pension.

Specification 7. Nine thousand six hundred and forty dollars, being sent by the Baron de Carondelet, Governor-general of Louisiana, from New Orleans, some time in the month of January, 1796, and by his direction, deposited at New Madrid, for the use, and subject to the order, of him, the said James Wilkinson; and afterwards, some time in the summer of 1796, taken by one Thomas Power from New Madrid to Louisville, and by him delivered over to one Philip Nolan, by the direction and authority, and for the use, of him, the said James Wilkinson, also on account of the said pension; he, the said Power, retaining out of the said sum of money, six hundred and forty dollars, for defraying his expenses, and receiving the instructions of him, the said James Wilkinson, to secure for him the reimbursement of the same from the Spanish government.

Specification 8. Ten thousand dollars, or thereabouts, being received by him, the said James Wilkinson, at New Orleans, some time between the 7th of December, 1803, and the 21st of April, 1804, on account of the said pension.

Specification 9. He, the said James Wilkinson, (in consideration of having so corruptly engaged himself with the Spanish government) receiving at diverse other places, as yet unknown, and on diverse other days and times, between the first day of January, in the year 1789, and the 21st of April, in the year 1804, by diverse secret ways and means, a pension, stipend, or gratuity, from the officers and agents of that government.

Specification 10. He, the said James Wilkinson, did, some time in the month of October, in the year 1798, at the camp at Loftus Heights, in a secret conference there with one Daniel Clark, set up a claim to ten thousand dollars, as a balance due him, the said James Wilkinson, from the Spanish government, on account of his pension or stipend; and did, then and there, request the said Daniel Clark, to propose to the Spanish Governor Gayoso, that the latter should, in consideration of the said balance of ten thousand dollars, due to the said James Wilkinson, from the Spanish treasury, transfer to him the said James Wilkinson, a plantation near the Natchez, then belonging to the said Gayoso.

Source: "Copy of the Charges, 7 July 1811," in James Wilkinson, *Memoirs of My Own Times*, Volume 2 (Philadelphia: Abraham Small, 1816), 35–41.

Questions for Consideration

1) What type of misconduct was alleged in the first charge against General Wilkinson?
2) Which of the specifications for this charge against him seemed vague?
3) To what extent did the court martial proceedings insinuate the motivation for his misconduct?

Suggested Readings

Bird, Harrison. *War for the West, 1790–1813*. New York: Oxford University Press, 1971.

Crackel, Theodore J. *Mr. Jefferson's Army: Political and Social Reform of the Military Establishment, 1801–1809*. New York: New York University Press, 1987.

Cress, Lawrence Delbert. *Citizens in Arms: The Army and the Militia in American Society to the War of 1812*. Chapel Hill: University of North Carolina Press, 1982.

Daughan, George C. *If By Sea: The Forging of the American Navy from the American Revolution to the War of 1812*. New York: Basic Books, 2008.

Fowler, William M. *Jack Tars and Commodores: The American Navy, 1783–1815*. Boston: Houghton Mifflin, 1984.

Gaff, Alan. *Bayonets in the Wilderness: Anthony Wayne's Legion in the Old Northwest*. Norman: University of Oklahoma Press, 2004.

Hogeland, William. *The Whiskey Rebellion: George Washington, Alexander Hamilton, and the Frontier Rebels Who Challenged America's Newfound Sovereignty*. New York: Scribner, 2006.

Kohn, Richard H. *Eagle and Sword: Federalists and the Creation of the American Military Establishment in America, 1783–1802*. New York: Free Press, 1975.

Lambert, Frank. *The Barbary Wars: American Independence in the Atlantic World*. New York: Hill and Wang, 2005.

Linklater, Andro. *An Artist in Treason: The Extraordinary Double Life of General James Wilkinson*. New York: Walker & Co., 2009.

Myers, Minor. *Liberty without Anarchy: A History of the Society of the Cincinnati*. Charlottesville: University Press of Virginia, 1983.

Owsley, Frank L., and Gene A. Smith. *Filibusters and Expansionists: Jeffersonian Manifest Destiny, 1800–1821*. Tuscaloosa: University of Alabama Press, 1997.

Palmer, Michael A. *Stoddert's War: Naval Operations during the Quasi-War with France, 1798–1801*. Columbia: University of South Carolina Press, 1987.

Puls, Mark. *Henry Knox: Visionary General of the American Revolution*. New York: Palgrave Macmillan, 2008.

Skelton, William B. *An American Profession of Arms: The Officer Corps, 1784–1861*. Lawrence: University Press of Kansas, 1999.

Whipple, A. B. C. *To the Shores of Tripoli: The Birth of the U.S. Navy and Marines*. New York: William Morrow, 1991.

4

Mr. Madison's War

Chronology

1811   Battle of Tippecanoe
1812   Declaration of War
        Surrender of Forts Mackinac, Detroit, and Dearborn
        U.S.S. *Constitution* sails
        Battle of Queenston Heights
1813   River Raisin Massacre
        Battle of York
        Battle of Sacket's Harbor
        Battle of Lake Erie
        Battle of the Thames
        Battle of Chrysler's Farm
        Battle of Chateauguay
1814   The Second Niagara Campaign
        Battle of Bladensburg
        Battle of Plattsburgh Bay
        Battle of Baltimore
        Treaty of Ghent
1815   Battle of New Orleans
        Battle of the Sinkhole

4.1   James Madison Calls for War (1812)

During the Napoleonic Wars, the United States pledged neutrality toward the key belligerents, France and Great Britain. Nevertheless, the Royal Navy stopped and boarded American ships bound for European ports. It impressed, or forced into service, sailors from American crews after seizing them. In fact, it captured well over 500 ships and impressed as many as 6,000 sailors. President Thomas Jefferson signed the Embargo Act of 1807 to coerce European regimes disrespecting neutral rights. His successor, President James Madison, urged Congress to pass the Non-Intercourse Act of 1809 and Macon's Bill Number 2 in 1810, which refined the measures withholding trade from Great Britain. None proved effective in forcing the British to withdraw their Orders in

American Military History: A Documentary Reader, Second Edition. Brad D. Lookingbill.
© 2019 John Wiley & Sons, Inc. Published 2019 by John Wiley & Sons, Inc.

uncil. Meanwhile, Americans blamed the British in Canada for inciting Indian esistance to western settlement, pointing to the arms trade along the Great Lakes. Denouncing the British Empire, prominent "War Hawks" in Congress lobbied the Madison administration to take action. Westerners and Southerners tended to support war, whereas New Englanders expressed opposition. President Madison sent a fiery speech to Congress on June 1, 1812. On June 18, the House and Senate voted to declare war against Great Britain.

Document

I communicate to Congress certain documents, being a continuation of those heretofore laid before them on the subject of our affairs with Great Britain.

Without going back beyond the renewal in 1803 of the war in which Great Britain is engaged, and omitting unrepaired wrongs of inferior magnitude, the conduct of her Government presents a series of acts hostile to the United States as an independent and neutral nation.

British cruisers have been in the continued practice of violating the American flag on the great highway of nations, and of seizing and carrying off persons sailing under it, not in the exercise of a belligerent right founded on the law of nations against an enemy, but of a municipal prerogative over British subjects. British jurisdiction is thus extended to neutral vessels in a situation where no laws can operate but the law of nations and the laws of the country to which the vessels belong, and a self-redress is assumed which, if British subjects were wrongfully detained and alone concerned, is that substitution of force for a resort to the responsible sovereign which falls within the definition of war. Could the seizure of British subjects in such cases be regarded as within the exercise of a belligerent right, the acknowledged laws of war, which forbid an article of captured property to be adjudged without a regular investigation before a competent tribunal, would imperiously demand the fairest trial where the sacred rights of persons were at issue. In place of such a trial these rights are subjected to the will of every petty commander.

The practice, hence, is so far from affecting British subjects alone that, under the pretext of searching for these, thousands of American citizens, under the safeguard of public law and of their national flag, have been torn from their country and from everything dear to them; have been dragged on board ships of war of a foreign nation and exposed, under the severities of their discipline, to be exiled to the most distant and deadly climes, to risk their lives in the battles of their oppressors, and to be the melancholy instruments of taking away those of their own brethren.

Against this crying enormity, which Great Britain would be so prompt to avenge if committed against herself, the United States have in vain exhausted remonstrances and expostulations, and that no proof might be wanting of their conciliatory dispositions, and no pretext left for a continuance of the practice, the British Government was formally assured of the readiness of the United States to enter into arrangements such as could not be rejected if the recovery of British subjects were the real and the sole object. The communication passed without effect.

British cruisers have been in the practice also of violating the rights and the peace of our coasts. They hover over and harass our entering and departing commerce. To the most insulting pretensions they have added the most lawless proceedings in our very harbors, and have wantonly spilt American blood within the sanctuary of our territorial jurisdiction. The principles and rules enforced by that nation, when a neutral nation, against armed vessels of belligerents hovering near her coasts and disturbing her commerce are well known. When called on, nevertheless, by the United States to punish the greater offenses committed by her own vessels, her Government has bestowed on their commanders additional marks of honor and confidence [...]

In reviewing the conduct of Great Britain toward the United States our attention is necessarily drawn to the warfare just renewed by the savages on one of our extensive frontiers—a warfare which is known to spare neither age nor sex and to be distinguished by features peculiarly shocking to humanity. It is difficult to account for the activity and combinations which have for some time been developing themselves among tribes in constant intercourse with British traders and garrisons without connecting their hostility with that influence and without recollecting the authenticated examples of such interpositions heretofore furnished by the officers and agents of that Government.

Such is the spectacle of injuries and indignities which have been heaped on our country, and such the crisis which its unexampled forbearance and conciliatory efforts have not been able to avert. It might at least have been expected that an enlightened nation, if less urged by moral obligations or invited by friendly dispositions on the part of the United States, would have found its true interest alone a sufficient motive to respect their rights and their tranquility on the high seas; that an enlarged policy would have favored that free and general circulation of commerce in which the British nation is at all times interested, and which in times of war is the best alleviation of its calamities to herself as well as to other belligerents; and more especially that the British cabinet would not, for the sake of a precarious and surreptitious intercourse with hostile markets, have persevered in a course of measures which necessarily put at hazard the invaluable market of a great and growing country, disposed to cultivate the mutual advantages of an active commerce.

Other counsels have prevailed. Our moderation and conciliation have had no other effect than to encourage perseverance and to enlarge pretensions. We behold our seafaring citizens still the daily victims of lawless violence, committed on the great common and highway of nations, even within sight of the country which owes them protection. We behold our vessels, freighted with the products of our soil and industry, or returning with the honest proceeds of them, wrested from their lawful destinations, confiscated by prize courts no longer the organs of public law but the instruments of arbitrary edicts, and their unfortunate crews dispersed and lost, or forced or inveigled in British ports into British fleets, whilst arguments are employed in support of these aggressions which have no foundation but in a principle equally supporting a claim to regulate our external commerce in all cases whatsoever.

We behold, in fine, on the side of Great Britain, a state of war against the United States, and on the side of the United States a state of peace toward Great Britain.

Whether the United States shall continue passive under these progressive usurpations and these accumulating wrongs, or, opposing force to force in defense of their national rights, shall commit a just cause into the hands of the Almighty Disposer of Events, avoiding all connections which might entangle it in the contest or views of other powers, and preserving a constant readiness to concur in an honorable re-establishment of peace and friendship, is a solemn question which the Constitution wisely confides to the legislative department of the Government. In recommending it to their early deliberations I am happy in the assurance that the decision will be worthy the enlightened and patriotic councils of a virtuous, a free, and a powerful nation.

Source: James Madison, "Special Message to Congress," in *The Writings of James Madison*, Volume 8, ed. Gaillard Hunt (New York: G.P. Putnam's Sons, 1908), 192–200.

Questions for Consideration

1) How, according to President Madison, was Great Britain responsible for the maritime disputes with the U.S.?
2) What did he accuse the British of doing on the "extensive frontiers" of North America?
3) Do you agree with his assertion that Great Britain was in "a state of war" against the U.S.?

4.2 Lydia Bacon Enters Fort Detroit (1812)

With British armed forces committed to the European theater, the Madison administration decided to invade Canada. General William Hull, governor of the Michigan Territory, organized the Army of the Northwest for the invasion. He gathered 2,500 regulars and militiamen on the shores of Lake Erie. Lydia Bacon's husband, Josiah, was among them. She trekked with his regiment from Vincennes to Fort Detroit. She recorded her arrival in a diary. On July 12, 1812, General Hull's invasion commenced. Upon receiving news of the British capture of Fort Michilimackinac, however, he abandoned the effort. His troops quickly retreated from Canada back to Michigan soil. British regulars, Canadian militiamen, and Indian warriors under General Isaac Brock pursued them. Without firing a shot in defense, General Hull surrendered Fort Detroit on August 16, 1812. On Lake Michigan's southern shore, Fort Dearborn soon followed suit. With the Army of the Northwest in disarray, the British advanced southward to the Maumee River. Justifying surrender, General Hull complained that he possessed only a month's worth of provisions. He also worried that a long siege would permit the Indians in the Michigan Territory to raid the non-Indian population. Two years later, he was court-martialed and convicted of cowardice. Although sentenced to death, he received a pardon from President Madison.

Document

August 12th. Our troops have vacated Sandwich, and returned to Detroit. Since then the enemy have been very busy building, as we suppose, a battery upon the opposite shore. The ends project beyond a large dwelling which conceals them while they work. At night we can hear them throw their cannon-balls, from a boat on to the land [...]

August 15th. A summons has been sent today, from General Brock to General Hull, demanding the surrender of Detroit and the army to the English! This our general has not seen fit to comply with. Every preparation is now making for a bombardment. The British soldiers are very busy in pulling down the large house which conceals the battery which they have been so industriously constructing. If I were not so terrified at the idea of a siege, I could laugh to see their hurry. Never did a building come down faster in a raging fire than in the hands of these bloodthirsty fellows. The women and children are to go into the fort as the only place of security against the savage Indians, and the bombs, shells, and shot of the English. The officers who came with the summons have left us to return, and as soon as they arrive upon the opposite shore, the firing will commence. So I must lay aside my pen and escape to the place of safety, not knowing what shall befall me [...]

Soon as the morning of the 16th arose the cannon commenced to roar with apparently tenfold fury; and alas! It did not continue long without doing execution. The enemy's bombs and shot began to enter the fort. Some of the ladies were employed in making cylinders, viz: bags to hold powder for the cannon. Others were scraping lint, that it might be ready in case of necessity, to dress the wounds of the injured soldiers. While thus engaged, a twenty-four pound shot entered the room next to where we were sitting. Two officers who were standing in the room were cut entirely in two, their bowels gushing out as they fell. The same ball, after doing such horrid execution, passed through the wall into another room where a number of persons were standing. Here it took off both the legs of one man and sliced the flesh off the thigh of another. The man who lost both his legs died very soon. Thus *one* of these angry messengers killed three men and wounded a fourth in a moment of time.

One of the gentlemen who was killed was a captain of the regulars, who had been previously taken prisoner and released upon parole. He was now in the fort *for safety,* not being allowed to take up arms until he was exchanged. But death met him where he least expected it. Soon after this another ball of equal size entered the hospital room. A poor fellow who lay sick upon his bed, and was asleep, had his head instantly severed from his body; and his attendant was killed by the same blow, the shot striking him in his breast. The enemy had got the range of the fort so completely that it was now judged unsafe for the women and children to remain any longer in it. So we were all hurried to the root-house, which was on the opposite side of the fort, and was bomb proof. Never shall I forget my sensations as I crossed the parade ground to gain this place of safety [...]

On looking from the door of the root-house to the quarters opposite I saw a ball knock down one of the chimneys, and was afterwards told that the same shot killed a man who was on duty upon the parapet the other side of the building. About this time the enemy effected a landing on our side, under cover of their armed vessels. Of these they had a sufficiency to demolish Detroit if they chose, while we had not a boat in order to carry a single gun. General Brock's effective force was also double ours, and the Indians were now let loose on the inhabitants. In addition to this our supply of provisions and ammunition was extremely small, and a part of General H[ull]'s most efficient troops were at this juncture at some distance from Detroit, having been sent away on duty a short time previous to the summons to surrender. Under these circumstances General H[ull], after consultation with Colonel Miller, thought it best to capitulate, and obtained the best terms he could. A white flag was accordingly displayed upon the parapet as a signal for the cessation of hostilities.

Immediately the cannon ceased to roar, and all was still. General Brock then sent to ascertain for what purpose the white flag was displayed, and learned the determination of General H[ull] to surrender. Our soldiers were then marched on to the parade ground in the fort, where they stacked their arms, which were then delivered to the enemy. The American stars and stripes were then lowered from the flag-staff, and replaced with English colors. A royal salute was now fired with the very cannon which the Americans had taken from the British in the Revolutionary war, and their music played their national tune, "God save the King." How shall I tell you our grief and mortification at this triumph of our foes? A thousand emotions struggled in my breast, too numerous for utterance, too exquisitely painful to be described!

The poor fellows who were shot in this contest were all buried in one grave. After the surrender those who had fled to the fort for safety returned to their respective abodes. The little girl of whom I had charge at the commencement of the siege was with me until the close. When she saw the fine uniform of the British officers, after they had taken possession, she expressed great delight and admiration, pointing at them and exclaiming in broken language, (for she was too young to speak plainly,) "Pretty, pretty!" Poor child! She little realized what sorrow the transactions of that day caused to her family, her friends, and her country.

August 19th. The prisoners were put on board his Majesty's vessels to-day. They are to be sent to Niagara and from thence to Montreal, on their way to Quebec. Thus a second time in the short space of six weeks am I a prisoner. I fear I shall not be so easily released this time, as my husband is with me; and a man is of more consequence to the enemy as a prisoner than a woman. Whether my husband obtains a parole or not, one thing is certain: I shall not leave him unless I am compelled to.

Source: Biography of Mrs. Lydia B. Bacon (Boston: Massachusetts Sabbath School Society, 1856), 60–70.

Questions for Consideration

1) When did Lydia Bacon begin to hear the British cannonades?
2) What did her diary reveal about the way the war impacted military families?
3) Why did she write: "A thousand emotions struggled in my breast, too numerous for utterance, too exquisitely painful to be described"?

4.3 Michel Felice Cornè Portrays the U.S.S. *Constitution* (1812)

To the astonishment of the world, American success on the open seas undermined the dominance of the Royal Navy. The U.S.S. *Constitution*, a wooden-hulled, three-masted heavy frigate with more than 44 guns, won illustrious battles during the war. She famously escaped from a British squadron after a 57-hour chase and defeated several British warships, including two on one day. On August 19, 1812, she encountered the H.M.S. *Guerriére* off the coast of Nova Scotia. The *Constitution*'s commanding officer, Captain Isaac Hull, pressed sail to get his vessel alongside his enemy. Although the smaller British frigate opened fire, the shots seemed to rebound off the *Constitution*'s hull. The two ships closed to 25 yards, as the Americans fired a full broadside. During repeated collisions, the *Guerriére*'s bowsprit became entangled with the *Constitution*'s rigging. When they pulled apart, the force of extraction damaged the *Guerriére*'s rigging. Her foremast collapsed, taking the mainmast down in a crash. British Commander James Dacres surrendered his wreck. The victory earned the *Constitution* the nickname, "Old Ironsides." Afterward, Captain Hull commissioned Michel Felice Cornè of Salem, Massachusetts, to portray the event with oil on canvas. As a potent national symbol, the *Constitution* remains afloat in active service at the Charlestown Navy Yard in Massachusetts.

Document

Source: "Action between USS *Constitution* and HMS *Guerriére*, 19 August 1812: Oil on canvas, by Michel Felice Cornè," Photo # K-26254, Naval History and Heritage Command, Department of the Navy, Washington, DC. http://www.history.navy.mil/our-collections/photography/numerical-list-of-images/nara-series/80-g-k/80-G-K-20000/80-g-k-26254.html (accessed 2 June 2017).

Questions for Consideration

1) How did Michel Felice Cornè's painting identify the *Constitution*?
2) Did his painting suggest the cause of the *Guerriére*'s defeat?
3) Why do you think his painting featured gun smoke so prominently?

4.4   Black Hawk Takes the War Path (1813)

During the War of 1812, Indian war leaders raised the British flag over the Mississippi Valley. Colonel Robert Dickson, a British trader, recruited Black Hawk, a Sauk, to command an allied force of Native warriors amassed at Green Bay. In addition to weaponry and provisions, Black Hawk received a service medal and a brevet rank of Brigadier General. On January 22, 1813, he watched British and Indian forces at the River Raisin massacre American prisoners of war. Later that year, they besieged Fort Meigs and Fort Stephenson without success. They postponed plans to attack St. Louis, however. Seeing the contest as a long war against American occupation, Black Hawk dismissed European tactics of warfare. Whenever aggrieved, chieftains took the war path only to seek reparations or revenge "to cover the dead." Raiding parties risked the loss of their "war medicine" if they failed to act honorably. Black Hawk renewed his fight in 1814 and in 1815, joining the final land engagement of the war known as the Battle of the Sinkhole. Almost two decades later, he clashed with non-Indian settlers along the Mississippi River in what was called the Black Hawk War. After Americans wrested away his homeland, he died from illness on October 3, 1838.

Document

In the encampment I found a great number of Kickapoos, Ottawas, and Winnbagoes. I visited all their camps and found them in high spirits. They had all received new guns, ammunition, and a variety of clothing [...]

The next day arms and ammunition, knives, tomahawks, and clothing were given to my band. We had a great feast in the evening, and the morning following I started with about five hundred braves to join the British army. We passed Chicago and observed that the fort had been evacuated by the Americans, and their soldiers had gone to Fort Wayne. They were attacked a short distance from the fort and defeated. They had a considerable quantity of powder in the fort at Chicago, which they had promised to the Indians, but the night before they marched away they destroyed it by throwing it into a well. If they had fulfilled their word to the Indians, they doubtless would have gone to Fort Wayne without molestation. On our arrival, I found that the Indians had several prisoners, and I advised them to treat them well.

We continued our march, joining the British below Detroit, soon after which we had a battle. The Americans fought well, and drove us back with considerable loss. I was greatly surprised at this, as I had been told that the Americans would not fight.

Our next movement was against a fortified place. I was stationed with my braves to prevent any person going to, or coming from the fort. I found two men taking care of cattle and took them prisoners. I would not kill them, but delivered them to the British war chief. Soon after, several boats came down the river full of American soldiers. They landed on the opposite side, took the British batteries, and pursued the soldiers that had left them. They went too far without knowing the strength of the British and were defeated. I hurried across the river, anxious for an opportunity to show the courage of my braves, but before we reached the scene of battle all was over.

The British had taken many prisoners and the Indians were killing them. I immediately put a stop to it, as I never thought it brave, but base and cowardly to kill an unarmed and helpless foe. We remained here for some time. I can not detail what took place, as I was stationed with my braves in the woods. It appeared, however, that the British could not take this fort, for we marched to another, some distance off. When we approached it, I found a small stockade, and concluded that there were not many men in it. The British war chief sent a flag of truce. Colonel Dixon [Dickson] carried it, but soon returned, reporting that the young war chief in command would not give up the fort without fighting. Colonel Dixon [Dickson] came to me and said, "you will see to-morrow, how easily we will take that fort." I was of the same opinion, but when the morning came I was disappointed. The British advanced and commenced the attack, fighting like true braves, but were defeated by the braves in the fort, and a great number of our men were killed. The British army was making preparations to retreat. I was now tired of being with them, our success being bad, and having got no plunder. I determined on leaving them and returning to Rock River, to see what had become of my wife and children, as I had not heard from them since I left home. That night I took about twenty of my braves, and left the British camp for home.

On our journey we met no one until we came to the Illinois River. Here we found two lodges of Pottawattomies. They received us in a very friendly manner, and gave us something to eat. I inquired about their friends who were with the British. They said there had been some fighting on the Illinois River, and that my friend, the Peoria trader, had been taken prisoner. "By Gomo and his party?" I immediately inquired. They replied, "no, but by the Americans, who came up with boats. They took him and the French settlers prisoners, and they burned the village of Peoria." They could give us no information regarding our friends on Rock River.

In three days more we were in the vicinity of our village, and were soon after surprised to find that a party of Americans had followed us from the British camp. One of them, more daring than his comrades, had made his way through the thicket on foot, and was just in the act of shooting me when I discovered him. I then ordered him to surrender, marched him into camp, and turned him over to a number of our young men with this injunction: "Treat him as a brother, as I have concluded to adopt him in our tribe."

A little while before this occurrence I had directed my party to proceed to the village, as I had discovered a smoke ascending from a hollow in the bluff, and wished to go alone to the place from whence the smoke proceeded to see who was there. I approached the spot, and when I came in view of the fire, I saw an old man sitting in sorrow beneath a mat which he had stretched over him [...]

In a feeble voice he said, "Soon after your departure to join the British, I descended the river with a small party, to winter at the place I told you the white man had asked me to come to. When we arrived I found that a fort had been built, and the white family that had invited me to come and hunt near them had removed to it. I then paid a visit to the fort to tell the white people that my little band were friendly, and that we wished to hunt in the vicinity of the fort. The war chief who commanded there, told me that we might hunt on the Illinois side of the Mississippi, and no person would trouble us. That the horsemen only ranged on the Missouri side, and he had directed them not to cross the river. I was pleased with this assurance of safety, and immediately crossed over and made my winter's camp. Game was plenty. We lived happy, and often talked of you. My boy regretted your absence and the hardships you would have to undergo. We had been here about two moons, when my boy went out as usual to hunt. Night came on and he did not return. I was alarmed for his safety and passed a sleepless night. In the morning my old woman went to the other lodges and gave the alarm and all turned out to hunt for the missing one. There being snow upon the ground they soon came upon his track, and after pursuing it for some distance, found he was on the trail of a deer, which led toward the river. They soon came to the place where he had stood and fired, and near by, hanging on the branch of a tree, found the deer, which he had killed and skinned. But here were also found the tracks of white men. They had taken my boy prisoner. Their tracks led across the river and then down towards the fort. My friends followed on the trail, and soon found my boy lying dead. He had been most cruelly murdered. His face was shot to pieces, his body stabbed in several places and his head scalped. His arms were pinioned behind him."

The old man paused for some time, and then told me that his wife had died on their way up the Mississippi. I took the hand of my old friend in mine and pledged myself to avenge the death of his son. It was now dark, and a terrible storm was raging. The rain was descending in heavy torrents, the thunder was rolling in the heavens, and the lightning flashed athwart the sky. I had taken my blanket off and wrapped it around the feeble old man. When the storm abated I kindled a fire and took hold of my old friend to remove him nearer to it. He was dead! I remained with him during the night. Some of my party came early in the morning to look for me, and assisted me in burying him on the peak of the bluff. I then returned to the village with my friends. I visited the grave of my old friend as I ascended Rock River the last time.

On my arrival at the village I was met by the chiefs and braves and conducted to the lodge which was prepared for me. After eating, I gave a full account of all that I had seen and done. I explained to my people the manner in which the British and Americans fought. Instead of stealing upon each other and taking every advantage to kill the enemy and save their own people as we do, which, with us is considered good policy in a war chief, they march out in open daylight and fight regardless of the number of warriors they may lose. After the battle is over they retire to feast and drink wine as if nothing had happened. After which they make a statement in writing of what they have done, each party claiming the victory, and neither giving an account of half the number that have been killed on their own side. They all fought like braves, but would not do to lead a party with us. Our maxim is: "Kill the enemy and save our own men." Those chiefs will do to paddle a canoe but not to steer it. The Americans shot better than the British, but their soldiers were not so well clothed, nor so well provided for.

Source: Black Hawk, *Autobiography of Ma-ka-tai-me-she-kia-kiak, or Black Hawk*, ed. J. B. Patterson (St. Louis, MO: Continental Printing Co., 1882), 33–39.

Questions for Consideration

1) How, according to Black Hawk, had the British and the Indians behaved in a "base and cowardly" way?
2) What did he pledge to his old friend at Rock River?
3) Do you agree with his maxim: "Kill the enemy and save our own men"?

4.5   Oliver Hazard Perry Defends Lake Erie (1813)

The Battle of Lake Erie provided a turning point to the War of 1812. During the spring of 1813, Commodore Oliver Hazard Perry supervised the construction of an American naval squadron at Presque Isle. On September 10, his squadron of nine sailed near Put-in-Bay to challenge a British squadron of six under Commander Robert H. Barclay. His brig, the U.S.S. *Lawrence*, hoisted a blue ensign, which declared: "Don't give up the ship." His motto derived from the final words of Captain James Lawrence, the namesake for the flagship. After the last gun on the *Lawrence* became unusable, however, Commodore Perry rode a boat a half-mile through intense gunfire to the U.S.S. *Niagara*. Once aboard, he renewed his attack. He noted the outcome in a brief dispatch to General William Henry Harrison, which read: "We have met the enemy and they are ours." With U.S. control of Lake Erie secured, Commodore Perry paved the way for General Harrison's Army of the Northwest to recover Detroit. Nearly a month later, the Shawnee leader, Tecumseh, was killed in Canada at the Battle of the Thames. Commodore Perry's flag later went on display at the U.S. Naval Academy, where it has inspired generations of midshipmen.

Document

On the morning of the tenth inst., at sunrise, they were discovered from Put-in-Bay, where I lay at anchor with the squadron under my command. We got under way, the wind light at S. W., and stood for them. At 10 A. M., the wind hauled to S. E. and brought us to windward; formed the line and brought up. At 15 minutes before 12 the enemy commenced firing; at 5 minutes before 12 the action commenced on our part. Finding their fire very destructive, owing to their long guns, and its being mostly directed to the *Lawrence*, I made sail, and directed the other vessels to follow, for the purpose of closing with the enemy. Every brace and bowline being shot away, she became unmanageable, notwithstanding the great exertions of the sailing-master. In this situation she sustained the action for upwards of two hours, within canister shot distance, until every gun was rendered useless, and a greater part of the crew either killed or wounded. Finding she could no longer annoy the enemy, I left her in charge of Lieut. Yarnall, who, I was convinced, from the bravery already displayed by him, would do what would comport with the honor of the flag. At half past 2, the wind springing up, Captain Elliott was enabled to bring his vessel, the *Niagara*, gallantly into close action; I immediately went on board of her, when he anticipated my wish by volunteering to bring up the schooners, which had been kept astern by the lightness of the wind, into close action.

It was with unspeakable pain that I saw, soon after I got on board the *Niagara*, the flag of the *Lawrence* come down, although I was perfectly sensible that she had been defended to the last, and that to have continued to make a show of resistance would have been a wanton sacrifice of the remains of her brave crew. But the enemy was not able to take possession of her, and circumstances soon permitted her flag again to be hoisted. At 45 minutes past two, the signal was made for "close action;" the *Niagara* being very little injured, I determined to pass through the enemy's line—bore up and passed ahead of their two ships and a brig, giving a raking fire to them from the starboard guns, and to a large schooner and a sloop, from the larboard side, at half-pistol shot distance. The smaller vessels, at this time, having got within grape and canister distance, under the direction of Captain Elliott, and keeping up a well-directed fire, the two ships, a brig, and a schooner surrendered; a schooner and a sloop making a vain attempt to escape.

Those officers and men, who were immediately under my observation, evinced the greatest gallantry, and, I have no doubt, that all others conducted themselves as becoming American officers and seamen. Lieut. Yarnall, first of the *Lawrence*, although several times wounded, refused to quit the deck. Midshipman Forrest (doing duty as Lieutenant), and Sailing-master Taylor, were of great assistance to me. I have great pain in stating to you the death of Lieut. Brook, of the marines, and Midshipman Laub, both of the *Lawrence*, and Midshipman Clark, of the *Scorpion*; they were valuable officers. Mr. Hamilton, purser, who volunteered his services on deck, was severely wounded, late in the action. Midshipmen Claxton, and Swartwout, of the *Lawrence*, were severely wounded. On board of the *Niagara*, Lieutenants Smith and Edwards, and Midshipman Webster (doing duty as sailing-master), behaved in a very handsome manner. Captain Brevoort, of the army, who acted as a volunteer in the capacity of a marine officer, on board that vessel, is an excellent and brave officer, and with his musketry did great execution. Lieut. Turner, who commanded the *Caledonia*, brought that vessel into action in the most able manner, and is an officer that in all situations may be relied on.

The *Ariel*, Lieut. Packett, and the *Scorpion*, Sailing-master Champlin, were enabled to get early into the action, and were of great service. Captain Elliott speaks of the highest terms of Mr. Magrath, purser, who had been dispatched in a boat on service, previous to my getting on board the *Niagara*; and, being a seaman, since the action has rendered essential service in taking charge of one of the prizes.

Of Captain Elliott, already so well known to the government, it would be almost superfluous to speak. In this action, he evinced his characteristic bravery and judgment; and, since the close of the action, has given me the most able and essential assistance. I have the honor to enclose you a return of the killed and wounded, together with a statement of the relative force of the squadrons. The Captain and 1st Lieutenant of the *Queen Charlotte*, the 1st Lieut. of the *Detroit*, were killed. Captain Barclay, senior officer, and the commander of the *Lady Prevost*, severely wounded. The commander of the *Hunter* and *Chippewa*, slightly wounded. Their loss, in killed and wounded, I have not yet been able to ascertain; it must, however, have been very great.

I have caused the prisoners, taken on the 10th inst. to be landed at Sandusky; and have requested Gen. Harrison to have them marched to Chillicothe, and there wait, until your pleasure shall be known respecting them.

The *Lawrence* has been so entirely cut up, it is absolutely necessary she should go into a safe harbor; I have, therefore, directed Lieut. Yarnall to proceed to Erie, in her, with the wounded of the fleet; and dismantle, and get her over the bar, as soon as possible.

The two ships, in a heavy sea, this day, at anchor, lost their masts, being much injured in the action. I shall haul them into the inner bay, at this place, and moor them for the present. The *Detroit* is a remarkably fine ship; sails well, and is very strongly built; the *Queen Charlotte* is a much superior vessel to what has been represented; the *Lady Prevost* is a large, line schooner.

I also beg your instructions, respecting the wounded; I am satisfied, sir, that whatever steps I might take, governed by humanity, would meet your approbation; under this impression, I have taken upon myself to promise Capt. Barclay, who is very dangerously wounded, that he shall be landed as near Lake Ontario as possible; and, I had no doubt, you would allow me to parole him; he is under the impression, that nothing but leaving this part of the country will save his life. There is, also, a number of Canadians among the prisoners, many who have families.

Source: Herman Allen Fay, ed., Collection of the Official Accounts, in Detail, of all the Battles Fought by Sea and Land, between the Navy and Army of the United States and the Navy and Army of Great Britain, during the Years 1812, 13, 14, & 15 (New York: Printed by E. Conrad, 1817), 122–125.

Questions for Consideration

1) Who commanded the *Niagara* before Commodore Perry boarded?
2) Did his report indicate the reason "the enemy was not able to take possession" of the *Lawrence*?
3) Why did he refer to the "honor of the flag" in the report?

4.6 Francis Scott Key Pens "Defence of Fort McHenry" (1814)

With the defeat of Napoleonic France, Great Britain launched major offensives against the United States during the late summer of 1814. British forces advanced southward from Canada to Lake Champlain, where Captain Thomas Macdonough on September 11 repulsed them at Plattsburgh Bay. However, their offensive in the Chesapeake Bay proved more effective. British forces prevailed at Bladensburg on August 24 and marched into Washington, DC, that same day. They looted and burned the executive mansion and several public buildings. Beginning at dusk on September 13, British warships bombarded Fort McHenry at Baltimore. They were able to sail close enough to fire rockets and mortars, but the bombardment produced little damage. On the morning of September 14, they ceased firing and began withdrawing. Francis Scott Key, a Washington lawyer seeking to negotiate the release of a civilian prisoner of war, spotted Fort McHenry from a nearby truce ship. When Key saw its flag waving at dawn, he began to compose a poem of commemoration. Titled "Defence of Fort McHenry," the stanzas appeared in print on September 21 in the *Baltimore American*. Generations of Americans sang them to the tune of an air called "To Anacreon in Heaven." On March 3, 1931, a resolution by Congress declared "The Star-Spangled Banner" to be the national anthem.

Document
O say can you see by the dawn's early light What so proudly we hail'd at the twilight's last gleaming? Whose broad stripes and bright stars thru the perilous fight O'er the ramparts we watch'd, were so gallantly streaming? And the rocket's red glare, the bombs bursting in air, Gave proof through the night that our flag was still there O, say does that star-spangled banner yet wave O'er the land of the free and the home of the brave? On the shore dimly seen through the mists of the deep, Where the foe's haughty host in dread silence reposes, What is that which the breeze, o'er the towering steep, As it fitfully blows, half conceals, half discloses? Now it catches the gleam of the morning's first beam In full glory reflected now shines in the stream 'Tis the star-spangled banner! O long may it wave O'er the land of the free and the home of the brave! And where is that band who so vauntingly swore, That the havoc of war and the battle's confusion A home and a Country should leave us no more? Their blood has wash'd out their foul footsteps' pollution No refuge could save the hireling and slave

From the terror of flight or the gloom of the grave,
And the star-spangled banner in triumph doth wave
O'er the land of the free and the home of the brave.

O thus be it ever when freemen shall stand
Between their loved home and the war's desolation!
Blest with vict'ry and peace may the heav'n rescued land
Praise the power that hath made and preserved us a nation!
Then conquer we must, when our cause it is just.
And this be our motto: "In God is our trust."
And the star-spangled banner in triumph shall wave
O'er the land of the free and the home of the brave.

Source: "The Star Spangled Banner," in *Report on "The Star-Spangled Banner," "Hail Columbia," "America,"
"Yankee Doodle,"* comp. Oscar Sonneck (Washington, DC: Library of Congress, 1909), 7–37.

Questions for Consideration

1) What did the flag at Fort McHenry symbolize to Francis Scott Key?
2) How were the British forces described in the third stanza?
3) Do you agree with Key that American troops were poised to "conquer" in 1814?

4.7   Andrew Jackson Triumphs at New Orleans (1815)

General Andrew Jackson became America's most celebrated military figure after the war ended. Soldiers under his command said that he was "tough as old hickory." As commander of the Tennessee militia, he fought Creek Indians in bloody battles from 1813 to 1814. The War Department rewarded him with a commission as Major General in the U.S. Army, which resulted in more campaigning along the Gulf of Mexico. After seizing a Spanish fort in Pensacola, General Jackson marched his corps to New Orleans. He learned that a large British fleet in the Gulf was preparing to land at the mouth of the Mississippi River. They advanced while an American delegation negotiated the Treaty of Ghent, although the peace accord signed on December 24, 1814, was not ratified until nearly two months later. The defense of New Orleans began on December 14, 1814, and culminated on January 8, 1815. An expeditionary force under Lieutenant General Sir Edward Pakenham assaulted General Jackson's main line at the Rodriguez Canal. After triumphing over the British, General Jackson stood proudly before his corps on January 21 to thank them for their service. They were a motley crew—regulars, Choctaw Indians, free blacks, frontiersmen, Creoles, and buccaneers. The outcome of the Battle of New Orleans influenced the way Americans remembered the war.

Document

Citizens and fellow soldiers,

The enemy has retreated, and your general has now leisure to proclaim to the world what he has noticed with admiration and pride—your undaunted courage, your patriotism, and patience under hardships and fatigues. Natives of different states, acting together for the first time in this camp, differing in habits and in language, instead of viewing in these circumstances the germ of distrust and division, you have made them a source of honourable emulation, and from the seeds of discord itself, have reaped the fruits of an honourable union [...]

The new year was ushered in with the most tremendous fire his whole artillery could produce; a few hours only, however, were necessary for the brave and skillful men who directed our own, to dismount his cannon, destroy his batteries, and effectively silence his fire. Hitherto, my brave friends, in the contests on our lines, your courage had been passive only; you stood with coolness, a fire that would have tried the firmness of a veteran, and you anticipated a nearer contest with an eagerness which was soon to be gratified.

On the 8th of January, the final effort was made. At the dawn of day the batteries opened, and the columns advanced. Knowing that the volunteers from Tennessee and the militia from Kentucky were stationed on your left, it was there they directed their chief attack. Reasoning always from false principles, they expected no opposition from men whose officers even were not in uniform, who were ignorant of the rules and dress, and who had never been caned into discipline—fatal mistake! A fire incessantly kept up, directed with calmness and with unerring aim, strewed the field with the bravest officers and men of the column which slowly advanced, according to the most approved rules of European tactics, and was cut down by the untutored courage of American militia. Unable to sustain this galling and unceasing fire, some hundreds nearest the entrenchments called for quarter, which was granted; the rest retreating, were rallied at some distance, but only to make them a surer mark for the grape and canister shot of our artillery, which, without exaggeration, mowed down whole ranks at every discharge; and at length they precipitately retired from the field.

Our right had only a short contest to sustain with a few rash men, who, fatally for themselves, forced their entrance into the unfinished redoubt on the river. They were quickly dispossessed, and this glorious day terminated with the loss to the enemy of their commander in chief and one major general killed, another major general wounded, the most experienced and bravest of their officers, and more than *three thousand men*, killed, wounded and missing; while our ranks, my friends, were thinned only by the loss of six of our brave companions killed and seven disabled by wounds—*Wonderful interposition of heaven! Unexampled event in the history of war!*

Let us be grateful to the God of battles who has directed the arrows of indignation against our invaders, while he covered with his protecting shield the brave defenders of their country.

After this unsuccessful and disastrous attempt, their spirits were broken, their force was destroyed, and their whole attention was employed in providing the means of escape. This they have effected, leaving their heavy artillery in our power, and many of their wounded to our clemency. The consequences of this short but decisive campaign are incalculably important. The pride of our arrogant enemy humbled, his forces broken, his leaders killed, his insolent hopes of our disunion frustrated, his expectation of rioting in our spoils and wasting our country changed in to ignominious defeat, shameful flight, and reluctant acknowledgment of the humanity and kindness of those whom he had doomed to all the horrors and humiliation of a conquered state.

On the other side, unanimity established, disaffection crushed, confidence restored, your country saved from conquest, your property from pillage, your wives and daughters from *insult* and *violation*, the union preserved from dismemberment, and perhaps a period put by this decisive stroke to a bloody and savage war. These, my brave friends, are the consequences of the efforts you have made, and the success with which they have been crowned by heaven.

These important results have been effected by the united courage and perseverance of the army; which the different corps, as well as the individuals that compose it, have vied with each other in their exertions to produce. The share they have respectively had will be pointed out in the general order accompanying this address. But the gratitude, the admiration of their country, offers a fairer reward than that which any praise of the general can bestow, and the best is that of which they can never be deprived, the consciousness of having done their duty, and of meriting the applause they will receive.

Source: "General Jackson's Address," in Official Letters of the Military and Naval Officers of the United States, during the War with Great Britain in the Years 1812, 13, 14, & 15, *ed. John Brannan (Washington, DC: Way & Gideon, 1823), 474–476.*

Questions for Consideration

1) What, according to General Jackson, was the "fatal mistake" made by the British on January 8, 1815?
2) Did his address indicate that the battle was romantic, tragic, or unnecessary?
3) Why do you think he recounted the battle in an address to the corps who actually fought it?

Suggested Readings

Barbuto, Richard V. *Niagara 1814: America Invades Canada.* Lawrence: University Press of Kansas, 2000.

Borneman, Walter. *1812: The War that Forged a Nation.* New York: Harper Collins, 2004.

Daughan, George C. *1812: The Navy's War.* New York: Basic Books, 2011.

Elting, John R. *Amateurs to Arms!: A Military History of the War of 1812.* Chapel Hill: Algonquin Books, 1991.

Hickey, Donald R. *The War of 1812: A Forgotten Conflict.* Urbana: University of Illinois Press, 1989.

Hickey, Donald R. *Don't Give Up the Ship!: Myths of the War of 1812.* Urbana: University of Illinois Press, 2006.

Horseman, Reginald. *The War of 1812.* New York: Knopf, 1969.

Latimer, Jon. *1812: War with America.* Cambridge: Harvard University Press, 2007.

Nichols, Roger L. *Black Hawk and the Warrior's Path.* Arlington Heights, IL: Harlan Davidson, 1992.

Owsley, Frank L. *Struggle for the Gulf Borderlands: The Creek War and the Battle of New Orleans, 1812–1815*. Gainesville: University of Presses of Florida, 1981.

Quimby, Robert S. *The U.S. Army in the War of 1812: An Operational and Command Study*. East Lansing: Michigan State University Press, 1997.

Remini, Robert V. *The Battle of New Orleans: Andrew Jackson and America's First Military Victory*. New York: Viking, 1999.

Skeen, C. Edward. *Citizen Soldiers in the War of 1812*. Lexington: University Press of Kentucky, 1999.

Stagg, J. C. A. *Mr. Madison's War: Politics, Diplomacy, and Warfare in the Early American Republic, 1783–1830*. Princeton: Princeton University Press, 1983.

Taylor, Alan. *The Civil War of 1812: American Citizens, British Subjects, Irish Rebels, and Indian Allies*. New York: Knopf, 2010.

Watts, Stephen. *The Republic Reborn: War and the Making of Liberal America, 1790–1820*. Baltimore: Johns Hopkins University Press, 1987.

5

The Martial Republic

Chronology

1815	Army Reduction Act
1816	Naval Expansion Act
	The Fortifications Board formed
1819	The Long Expedition
1824	General Survey Act
	The National Guard designated in New York
	Artillery School established at Fort Monroe
1826	Infantry School established at Jefferson Barracks
1829	U.S.S. *Vincennes* sailed from New York
1830	Indian Removal Act
1832	Black Hawk War
	U.S.S. *Potomac* intervenes in Sumatra
1835–1842	The Second Seminole War
1836	The Creek War
	The Cherokee Trail of Tears
	The Texas Revolution
1838	Army Topographical Corps established
1838–1842	The United States Exploring Expedition
1842	U.S.S. *Mississippi* and U.S.S. *Missouri* launched
	U.S.S. *Somers* mutiny
	Navy Observatory established
1843	U.S.S. *Princeton* launched
1845	U.S. Naval Academy established

5.1   John C. Calhoun Proposes an Expansible Army (1820)

The American republic entered an era of extraordinary national security. During 1817, President James Monroe tapped John C. Calhoun to head the War Department. As Secretary of War, Calhoun helped to bring order to a military establishment in the throes of demobilization. Organized into a Northern and a Southern Division, the regulars inherited the daunting task of defending almost two million square miles of territory. Gradually, Congressional expenditures improved the fortifications and coastal

American Military History: A Documentary Reader, Second Edition. Brad D. Lookingbill.
© 2019 John Wiley & Sons, Inc. Published 2019 by John Wiley & Sons, Inc.

defenses. Constrained by financial panic after 1819, Congress directed Secretary Calhoun to reduce the number of soldiers by a third. On December 12, 1820, he responded to Congress with an innovative plan. He posited that the profession of arms was indispensable to the United States. Furthermore, the U.S. Army needed to maintain the complete organization of companies and regiments along with the full complements of both line and staff officers. However, he proposed reductions to the quantity of enlisted men in active service. In the event of war, a skeleton force could be doubled in size by increasing numbers without organizing new units. Thus, a force structure appropriate for wartime remained in place during peacetime, albeit at a downsized level. Even if Congress ignored elements of Calhoun's plan, the concept of an "expansible army" endured.

Document

However remote our situation from the great powers of the world, and however pacific our policy, we are, notwithstanding, liable to be involved in war; and, to resist, with success, its calamities and dangers, a standing army in peace, in the present improved state of the military science, is an indispensable preparation. The opposite opinion cannot be adopted without putting to hazard the independence and safety of the country. I am aware that the militia is considered, and in many respects justly, as the great national force; but, to render them effective, every experienced officer must acknowledge, that they require the aid of regular troops. Supported by a suitable corps of trained artillerists, and by a small but well-disciplined body of infantry, they may be safely relied on to garrison our forts, and to act in field as light troops. In these services, their zeal, courage, and habit of using firearms, would be of great importance, and would have their full effect. To rely on them beyond this, to suppose our militia capable of meeting in the open field the regular troops of Europe, would be to resist the most obvious truth, and the whole of our experience as a nation. War is an art, to attain perfection in which much time and experience, particularly for the officers, are necessary.

It is true, that men of great military genius occasionally appear, who, though without experience, may, when an army is already organized and disciplined, lead it to victory; yet I know of no instance, under circumstances nearly equal, in which the greatest talents have been able, with irregular and undisciplined troops, to meet with success those regularly trained. Genius, without much experience, may command, but it cannot go much further. It cannot at once organize or discipline an army, and give it that military tone and habit which only, in the midst of imminent danger, can enable it to perform the most complex evolutions with precision and promptitude. Those qualities which essentially distinguish an army from an equal assemblage of untrained individuals, can only be acquired by the instruction of experienced officers. If they, particularly the company and regimental officers, are inexperienced, the army must remain undisciplined; in which case, the genius, and even experience of the commander, will be of little avail.

The great and leading objects, then, of a military establishment in peace ought to be to create and perpetuate military skill and experience; so that, at all times, the country may have at its command a body of officers, sufficiently numerous, and well instructed in every branch of duty, both of the line and staff; and the organization of the army ought to be such as to enable the Government, at the commencement of hostilities, to obtain a regular force adequate to the emergencies of the country, properly organized and prepared for actual service. It is thus only that we can be in the condition to meet the first shocks of hostilities with unyielding firmness, and to press on an enemy, while our resources are yet unexhausted. But if, on the other hand, disregarding the sound dictates of reason and experience, we should in peace neglect our military establishment, we must, with a powerful and skillful enemy, be exposed to the most distressing calamities. Not all the zeal, courage, and patriotism of our militia, unsupported by regularly trained and disciplined troops, can avert them. Without such troops, the two or three first campaigns would be worse than lost. The honor of our arms would be tarnished, and the resources of the country uselessly lavished; for, in proportion to the want of efficiency, and a proper organization, must, in actual service, be our military expenditures. When taught by sad experience, we would be compelled to make redoubled efforts, with exhausted means, to regain those very advantages which were lost for the want of experience and skill. In addition to the immense expenditure which would then be necessary, exceeding manifold what would have been sufficient to put our peace establishment on a respectable footing, a crisis would be thus brought on of the most dangerous character. If our liberty should ever be endangered by the military power gaining the ascendency, it will be from the necessity of making those mighty and irregular efforts to retrieve our affairs, after a series of disasters, caused by the want of adequate military knowledge; just as, in our physical system, a state of the most dangerous excitement and paroxysm follows that of greatest debility and prostration. To avoid these dangerous consequences, and to prepare the country to meet a state of war, particularly at its commencement, with honor and safety, much must depend on the organization of our military peace establishment; and I have, accordingly, in a plan about to be proposed for the reduction of the army, directed my attention mainly to that point, believing it to be of the greatest importance.

To give such an organization, the leading principles in its formation ought to be, that, at the commencement of hostilities, there should be nothing either to new model or to create. The only difference, consequently, between the peace and the war formation of the army, ought to be in the increased magnitude of the latter; and the only change in passing from the former to the latter, should consist in giving to it the augmentation which will then be necessary.

It is thus, and thus only, the dangerous transition from peace to war may be made without confusion or disorder; and the weakness and danger, which otherwise would be inevitable, be avoided. Two consequences result from this principle. First, the organization of the staff in a peace establishment ought to be such, that every branch of it should be completely formed, with such extension as the number of troops and posts occupied may render necessary; and, secondly, that the organization of the line ought, so far as practicable, to be such that, in passing from the peace to the war formation, the force may be sufficiently augmented without adding new regiments or battalions; thus raising the war on the basis of the peace establishment, instead of creating a new army to be added to the old, as at the commencement of the late war.

Source: John C. Calhoun, "Report on the Reduction of the Army, 12 December 1820," *The Works of John C. Calhoun*, Volume 5, ed. Richard K. Crallé (New York: D. Appleton and Company, 1874), 80–85.

Questions for Consideration

1) What, according to Calhoun, ought to be the only difference between "the peace and the war formation of the army"?
2) How did he intend to use the militia as a component of the national force?
3) Why did he prefer experienced officers over "men of great military genius" during wartime?

5.2 The National Guard Parades in New York (1825)

The volunteer militia movement became a distinguishing feature of social life in antebellum America. As the industrial revolution transformed towns and cities, militia companies provided associations for civilians to affirm their sense of patriotism, camaraderie, and honor. Unit armories provided weaponry to the dues-paying members. Extravagant uniforms enabled gentlemen of property and standing to display their martial spirit in public. Indeed, the elected officers viewed their eminent positions as avenues for political advancement. One organized unit in New York was the first military association to adopt the title of "National Guard." Their use of the name began in 1824 with a visit to New York by the Marquis de Lafayette, the French hero of the American Revolution. His honor guard included volunteers from the 2nd Battalion, 11th Regiment of Artillery, who voted afterward to denominate their unit the "Battalion of the National Guards." The next year, they were redesignated the 2nd Regiment. The recorded minutes from their parade on August 5, 1825, testified to fully equipped and splendidly uniformed fellowship, even if their military proficiency seemed more fictive than real. The volunteer militia companies exulted in the pomp and circumstance, but the enrolled militia system and its compulsory service requirements all but faded from memory.

Document

Line was formed under command of Major Prosper M. Wetkore, of the Second Regiment, at 7 A. M., (Lieutenant Charles B. Spicer, of the 5th Company, acting as Adjutant) and marched to the foot of Roosevelt Street, where it embarked in good order on board the steamboat *John Marshall*, for Bloomingdale, where preparations had been made for the exercises of the day. The landing was effected opposite Barnet's Mansion-House in beautiful style—the steamboat was moored within a few yards of the wild, rocky shore, and an extempore bridge constructed, *a la pontoon*, of the small boats and gang-planks, over which the Battalion marched to land in the most perfect order. The scene was singularly picturesque and beautiful as the troops filed across the slight bridge, over the rocky and uneven shore, and moved up the steep bank, through a wild and rural footpath, to the lawn in front of the Mansion-House; the Battalion was there formed for review. General Benedict received the marching salute as the troops proceeded to the ground selected for the firing, where the companies were dismissed, for the special duties of the day, to the command of their respective officers.

    After the firing was completed, the Battalion was reformed and marched to the House, and dismissed for recreation.

Among the officers who accompanied the expedition were General Benedict (Commander of the Brigade) and staff, Colonel Brown and Lieut.-Col. Kumbel (both late of Eleventh Regiment), Lieut.-Col. Stone (Editor of the *Commercial Advertiser),* and Major Noah (Editor of the *National Advocate),* Lieut.-Colonel Hopkins, of Eleventh Regiment, Commissary-General Muir, and a number of others.

It was observed that Barnet, commander in chief of the Mansion-House, had been, during the early part of the day, actively engaged with his whole army of cooks, barmaids, waiters, scullions, &c., in constructing extensive works in the orchard to the left of his house; and when the roll of the "spirit(s)-stirring drum" was heard summoning the men to their duty, it was understood at once that an assault upon Barnet's works was contemplated by our leader; and from the reputed skill of the engineers and artificers who had directed the operations of Barnet, a "warm" reception was expected.

The active duties in which our men had been engaged during the morning had prepared their "appetites for slaughter," so that they moved to the charge with a firm, undaunted step, the band playing a stomach-inspiring tune, which the men (snuffing the air) pronounced to be "Roast Beef," or something that sounded (or smelt) vastly like it.

By a skillful movement to our right, Barnet was taken in flank, and the whole of his formidable array was surrounded and pronounced an easy conquest, as his garrison appeared to be scantily provided with "provant" and deficient in destructive weapons. At a given signal the assault commenced at all points simultaneously, and never since the Battle of Waterloo (or the last target-firing dinner) has there been seen such carnage and slaughter; nothing could withstand the charge—neither age nor sex, rank nor condition, was spared—duck and drake, pigs, poultry, beef and mutton—all, all, met a common doom, and disappeared [...]

Our gallant Major conducted himself with the greatest deliberation and bravery. At the commencement of the operations he "took the chair" in the most elevated and exposed position, and was surrounded by a gallant band of officers of different corps, the veterans of many a well-spread dinner, who all appeared to perform with alacrity the exercises in which they had been invited to join.

At length the conflict ceased—there is an end appointed for all things, especially for dinner-scenes peculiarly circumstanced as this was—a liberal supply of the "generous juice" was brought forth, which had a marvelous effect upon the spirits of the men [...]

After the prizes were presented to the different successful marksmen, the Battalion was marched to the shore, where the steamer was in waiting. In consequence of the lowness of the tide she could not approach sufficiently near the shore to construct the bridge; the men were therefore conveyed to her in boats.

The embarkation was effected in perfect order and regularity, and presented a scene particularly striking; as the Battalion descended the bank through an obscure and irregular footpath to the margin of the river—the groups of officers and men upon the rocks on the shore, the boats plying in rapid succession filled with soldiers, the rays of the setting sun glancing from their glittering arms—all conspired to form a scene of rare beauty and magnificence, and strikingly *a la militaire.*

The expedition terminated about 8 o'clock, the Battalion being dismissed at that hour at the Park; and thus ended the Annual Target-Firing Excursion, which had been looked forward to for many weeks with such high expectations of enjoyment, and in many instances with strong hopes of individual distinction in the competition for the prizes.

Source: Asher Taylor, *Recollections of the Early Days of the National Guard* (New York: J. M. Bradstreet & Son, 1868), 41–45.

Questions for Consideration

1) What happened immediately after the completion of the firing exercise?
2) Who conducted himself with the greatest "deliberation and bravery" among the officers?
3) Why did you suppose the minutes recorded the distribution of "generous juice" to the Battalion?

5.3 John Downes Sails to Sumatra (1832)

Naval expeditions throughout the antebellum period extended the scale and the scope of American power. Squadrons of ships operated in the Pacific, in the Caribbean and Mediterranean Seas, along both coasts of South America, and along the East African coast. Patrols suppressed the transatlantic slave trade. Sailing in 1829 from New York, the U.S.S. *Vincennes* became the first American naval vessel to circumnavigate the globe. The first naval intervention in Asia by the U.S. occurred in response to an act of piracy during 1831. Outraged by an attack on an American merchant ship, the *Friendship*, President Andrew Jackson vowed revenge. He dispatched Commodore John Downes, who commanded the Pacific Squadron, to the coast of Sumatra with 260 marines. The U.S.S. *Potomac* arrived at Quallah-Battoo, Sumatra, on February 5, 1832. Downes ordered landing parties ashore to strike four forts along the coast. The marines and the sailors surprised their targets with a combination of hand-to-hand combat and cannon barrages. No defenders of the forts survived. The village of Quallah-Battoo was left in ruins. While suffering two dead and eleven wounded, the Americans conducted a stunning sea and land operation. They killed as many as 200 natives, although Downes failed to locate the original perpetrators of the piracy.

Document

I anchored off Quallah-Battoo, distant about three miles; my object in so doing being to prevent discovery of the character of the ship, which I had taken care previously to disguise, and so effectually, that a number of fishermen who came on board after I had anchored, did not discover that she was other than a merchant ship, until they came over the side. They were detained on board till after the capture of Quallah-Battoo.

Finding no vessels on the coast, I could obtain no information in addition to that already possessed respecting the nature of the government, the piratical character of the population, or the flagrant circumstances of the injury done to the *Friendship*.

No demand of satisfaction was made previous to my attack, because I was satisfied, from what knowledge I had already of the character of the people, that no such demand would be answered, except by refusals, and that such refusals would proceed from want of ability, as well as from inclination, it being a habit generally among this people to spend their money as soon as obtained.

Soon after anchoring, Lieutenants Shubrick, Pinkham, Hoff, Ingersoll, and Edson of marines, together with passed-midshipman Totten, went on shore in the whale-boat, for the purpose of learning the situation of the town and forts; but everything being built in close concealment, they were unable to arrive at any satisfactory result, except as to one of the forts erected immediately at the place of landing.

No precautions were taken to cut off the opportunity of escape from any inhabitants of the town, the nature of the place rendering it absolutely impossible, situated as it is, in the midst of wood and jungle, impenetrable, except by private passages, known only to the natives.

As soon as it became sufficiently dark to prevent our movements from discovery by the people on shore, the boats were hoisted out, and every preparation made for landing, which was effected about daybreak of the sixth instant. The party under the command of Lieutenant Shubrick consisted of two hundred and fifty men.

I adopted this mode of enforcing our demands, in hopes of getting possession of the rajahs, by surrounding and surprising the forts in which they usually reside, and thus, most probably, inducing the payment of money for their ransom. I regret to say, however, that in consequence of their desperate fighting, neither giving nor receiving quarter, no prisoners were made, nor was any property found belonging to the *Friendship*, save the medicine chest.

Lieutenant Shubrick has my warmest acknowledgments for the able and gallant manner in which he conducted the expedition, and I enclose herewith that gentleman's report, wherein he gives a detailed account of the attack, together with other particulars.

The midshipmen who were on shore and engaged in the action, but named by Lieutenant Shubrick, were William May, in the first division under Lieutenant Pinkham; Messrs. Alonzo B. Davis, James G. Stanley, and Charles W. Morris, of the second division, commanded by Lieutenant Hoff; and of the third division under command of Lieutenant Ingersoll, Messrs. Charles Hunter, Eugene Boyle, and James L. Parker, with Midshipman George T. Sinclair in the launch.

Their gallantry and good conduct in the action are spoken of as deserving the highest praise. In consequence of the fort situated south of the river having fired upon our men while attacking Quallah-Battoo, I ran in with the ship and fired about three broadsides into it, when a white flag was hoisted; upon this I ceased firing, soon after got under way, and stood for this anchorage, where I am taking on board wood and water.

While lying here, a flag of truce has been sent off from Quallah-Battoo; and I was informed by the bearer of the same, that a great many had been killed on shore, and that all the property had been destroyed. He begged that I would grant them peace. I stated to him that I had been sent to demand restitution of the property taken from the *Friendship*, and to insist on the punishment of those persons who were concerned in the outrage committed on the individuals of that ship.

Finding it impossible to effect either object, I said to him, that I was satisfied with what had already been done, and I granted them the peace for which they begged. I at the same time assured him, that if forbearance should not be exercised hereafter from committing piracies and murders upon American citizens, other ships of war would be dispatched to inflict upon them further punishment […]

While making arrangements to open a communication with the chiefs, and to make a formal demand of indemnification, I felt it to be my imperative duty to take such steps at the same time as would cut off the retreat of those who had participated in the piracy of the *Friendship*; and while in the execution of the only feasible plan by which these objects could be effected, our divisions were fired on, and our strength put at defiance; the action was thus unavoidably commenced; and, as to its result, I need only refer you to my previous communication.

I ascertained, after the attack, that the whole inhabitants of Quallah-Battoo were concerned in the plunder of the *Friendship*, and that the character of the transaction agreed substantially with that furnished by the department, marked A and B. The specie and opium had been divided between the four principal rajahs; and all the other articles taken from the ship were distributed among the people of Quallah-Battoo.

All the intercourse I had with the natives while lying at Soo-soo confirmed me in the correctness of the course adopted; and also that the chastisement inflicted on Quallah-Battoo, though severe, was unavoidable and just; and that it will be the means of giving a permanent security to our commerce for a long time to come.

Source: John Downes, "Official Documents," in Jeremiah N. Reynolds, *Voyage of the United States Frigate Potomac* (New York: Harper & Brothers, 1835), 114–120.

Questions for Consideration

1) What did Commodore Downes demand from the inhabitants of Quallah-Battoo before his attack?
2) How did he ascertain that they had plundered the *Friendship*?
3) Do you agree with him in that the naval actions provided "permanent security to our commerce for a long time to come"?

5.4 Ethan Allen Hitchcock Patrols in Florida (1836)

With oceans helping to protect the North American continent, U.S. forces conducted military operations to secure the interior. In the absence of external threats, the Jackson administration tasked citizens in uniform with managing Indian affairs and with performing garrison duty. They functioned mostly as a constabulary, that is, an armed police force in the frontier. The War Department, which extolled a paternalistic attitude toward American Indian nations, carried out the Indian Removal Act of 1830. It required tribal populations to relocate under military supervision to Indian Territory. Over the years, soldiers escorted the Choctaw, the Creek, and the Chickasaw westward. Secretary of War Lewis Cass played a controversial role in the removal of the Cherokee in 1836, when inadequate supplies and miserable conditions on the Trail of Tears resulted in countless deaths. After the United States obtained Florida from Spain in 1819, the War Department authorized a series of bloody wars against the Seminole. Major Ethan Allen Hitchcock, a graduate of West Point, led troops in what became known as the Second Seminole War. On January 20, 1836, he recorded an account of a patrol gone awry in the swamps. Congress transferred Indian affairs from the War Department to the Interior Department in 1849.

Document

Our advanced guard had passed the ground without halting, when the General and his staff came upon one of the most appalling scenes that can be imagined. We first saw some broken and scattered boxes; then a cart, the two oxen of which were lying dead, as if they had fallen asleep, their yokes still on them; a little to the right, one or two horses were seen. We then came to a small enclosure, made by felling trees in such a manner as to form a triangular breastwork for defence. Within the triangle, along the north and west faces of it, were about thirty bodies, mostly mere skeletons, although much of the clothing was left upon them. These were lying, almost every one of them, in precisely the position they must have occupied during the fight—their heads next to the logs over which they had delivered their fire, and their bodies stretched with striking regularity parallel to each other. They had evidently been shot dead at their posts, and the Indians had not disturbed them, except by taking the scalps of most of them. Passing this little breastwork we found other bodies along the road, and by the side of the road, generally behind trees which had been resorted to for covers from the enemy's fire.

Advancing about 200 yards further we found a cluster of bodies in the middle of the road. These were evidently the advanced guard, in the rear of which was the body of Major Dade, and to the right, that of Captain Fraser. These were all doubtless shot down on the first fire of the Indians, except, perhaps, Captain Fraser, who must, however, have fallen very early in the fight. Those in the road and by the trees fell during the first attack. It was during a cessation of the fire that the little band still remaining, about thirty in number, threw up the triangular breastwork, which, from the haste with which it was constructed, was necessarily defective, and could not protect the men in the second attack.

We had with us many of the personal friends of the officers of Major Dade's command, and it is gratifying to be able to state that every officer was identified by undoubted evidence. They were buried, and the cannon, a six-pounder that the Indians had thrown into a swamp, was recovered and placed vertically at the head of the grave, where it is to be hoped it will long remain. The bodies of the non-commissioned officers and privates were buried in two graves, and it was found that every man was accounted for. The command was composed of eight officers and one hundred and two non-commissioned officers and privates. The bodies of eight officers and ninety-eight men were interred, four men having escaped; three of whom reached Tampa Bay; the fourth was killed the day after the battle [...]

A proof that the Indians had done this deed reluctantly is the fact that very little of the clothing of the men had been removed and few had been scalped—these, probably, by the negroes, as Clark recalled their movements. The wolf had not made them his prey: the vulture only had visited them. We buried them all, and, at my suggestion, the cannon, a six-pounder, was placed over the graves. The officers' features could not be discerned, but they were identified by various articles found upon them, which, strange to say, the Indians had left. A breastpin was found on Lieutenant Fraser, a finger ring on Lieutenant Mudge, a pistol upon Lieutenant Keais, a stock on Doctor Gatlin, a map on Captain Gardiner, and a net shirt on Lieutenant Bassinger. Major Dade and Lieutenant Henderson were known by their teeth. The divisions of our little column were allowed to move up in succession and view the melancholy scene [...]

Nothing of importance occurred within the next three or four days when, in the evening, the camp was hailed from the south side of the river, and the Indians, through Abram and other negroes who spoke English, expressed a wish to have a talk with General Gaines. They were told to come next day. At ten o'clock in the morning some half a dozen of them approached the camp from its rear, unarmed and under a white flag, and I was directed by General Gaines to meet them. I took an orderly and went to the interview.

Among the visitors I found Osceola, Alligator, and a chief called Jumper who did the talking for the Indians. He said the Indians did not want fighting; they wanted peace; enough men had been killed. If white men came to plant, they said, they wished to know it; but they wanted the troops to go away. I tried to persuade them to go into the camp and talk with the General, but they declined. He must come out and meet them on neutral ground, they said. When I asked them to come the next day, they expressed a wish to make peace at once, and not put it off, a smart negro suggesting that we might have armed friends coming, and they too might have friends out, and these would fire on each other, and "there have been enough killed" they kept repeating. I reported to the General, who told me to state explicitly the large force coming and the certainty of their being crushed if they persisted.

I went out and made a long talk, enlarging on the merits of General Gaines, his willingness to do them justice, the bleeding of his heart for their sufferings, etc., telling them that 5,000 soldiers were coming, some from one place, some from another, with supplies of all kinds that had been massing on the borders of their country for two months, and that any Indian found with a rifle in his hand would be shot. I then soothed them a little by adding, what, indeed, I believed, that no doubt they thought they had suffered great wrong, but that, if so, they had had satisfaction. Osceola spoke up and said, "I am satisfied," and this was all he said in the council. The fact is, they *have* been abused. They listened very attentively to my talk, and their appearance indicated their entire sincerity.

Source: Ethan Allen Hitchcock, *Fifty Years in Camp and Field* (London: G. P. Putnam's Sons, 1909), 86–95.

Questions for Consideration

1) Where did Major Hitchcock locate the body of Major Dade?
2) Did Hitchcock's account suggest that Dade's party was foolhardy, brave, or unlucky?
3) Why do you think Hitchcock agreed with the Seminole at the council that they had been "abused" by the U.S.?

5.5 Juan Seguín Remembers the Alamo (1837)

Along the southern border of the U.S., the Mexican government permitted Anglo-American immigrants to settle within the state of Coahuila y Texas. General Antonio López de Santa Anna, a military hero who helped to secure Mexican independence from Spain, won election to the presidency but became a dictator. During 1835, Anglos and Tejanos in the Texas district joined together to declare their independence from Mexico. To suppress the rebellion, General Santa Anna marched his army northward. Although not strategically vital, approximately 150 defenders of the Alamo died after a siege on March 6, 1836. Juan Nepomuceno Seguín, a prominent Tejano and captain in the Texas cavalry, carried dispatches from the Alamo before it fell. He organized a corps of Tejanos supporting General Sam Houston in the Battle of San Jacinto, which ended in the defeat of General Santa Anna. Afterward, Seguín accepted the Mexican surrender of San Antonio de Béxar. In a letter written to General Albert Sidney Johnston on March 13, 1837, he described the memorial services for the Alamo dead. Afterward, Seguín served in the Senate of the Lone Star republic and became mayor of San Antonio de Béxar. Seguín and his family fled to Mexico before the United States annexed Texas during 1845.

Document

The bearer of this is John A. Zambrano Adjutant of this corps, whom I despatch [sic] to those Head Quarters for the purpose of obtaining supplies for my command according to the requisition with which he is furnished.

In accordance with your orders and the tenor of my communication of the 9th inst., I have proceeded thus far on my retreat, a point defensible and comparatively safe until I may be advised by my scouts in Bexar and westward of it of the probable immediate approach of the enemy. I am well aware that commander as I am of a corps, being an integral part of the army of Texas the whole of which is under your command, I am bound to obey all your orders to the very letter. Finding myself nevertheless at a point so distant from you, and having discretionary powers not only of a former but of a very recent date from his Excellency Sam Houston Prest. of this Repc., and being in a section of our country where I must in all human probability obtain the earliest information of the movements of the enemy and my only object being the purest of motives to render the greatest service to my country in whatever situation I may be placed to these considerations be pleased to add that of my men being chiefly on foot, naked and barefoot and the probability there is of mounting them, here I hope you will not take offence nor charge me with the remotest intention of disobeying your orders should I remain yet awhile on this side of the River Guadalupe, that is should it meet your entire approbation after taking into consideration the reasons for my delay as I have just set them forth.

Should these reasons however not have sufficient weight with you and should you still wish me to effect an immediate retreat with my command [upon] the slightest intimation from you the subject shall be instantly obeyed, and I beg leave to reiterate my assurances of my great esteem for you as my General and as a friend and of my highest respect for yourself and the orders you may be pleased to communicate.

I crave of you to have the goodness to cause the Quarter Master at Hd Quarters to furnish transportation for the supplies I now require as far as Gonzales, I shall either meet them there or have means to transport them to my camp wherever it may be.

In conformity with the orders from Genl. Felix Huston dated some time back, I caused the honors of war to be paid to the remains of the Heroes of Alamo on the 25th of February last. The ashes were found in three heaps. I caused a coffin to be prepared neatly covered with black, the ashes from the two smallest heaps were placed therein and with a view to attach additional solemnity to the occasion were carried to the Parish Church in Bexar whence it moved with the procession at 4 O'Clock on the afternoon of the day above mentioned. The Procession passed through the principal street of the city, crossed the River and passing through the principal avenue arrived at the spot whence part of the ashes had been collected, the procession halted, the coffin was placed upon the spot, and three volleys of musquetry wer

[sic] discharged over it by one of the companies, proceeding onwards to the second spot from whence the ashes were taken where the same honors were done and thence to the principal spot and place of interment [sic], the coffin was then placed upon the large heap of ashes when I addressed a few words to the Battalion and assemblage present in honor of the occasion in the Castillian language as I do not possess the English. Major Western then addressed the concourse in the latter tongue, the coffin and all the ashes were then interred and three volleys of musquetry were fired over the grave by the whole Battallion with an accuracy that would do honor to the best disciplined troops. We then marched back to quarter in the city with music and colors flying. Half our guns were not fired because I had no powder for the purpose, but every honor was done within the reach of my scanty means. I hope as a whole my efforts may meet your approbation.

The cattle I alluded to in my former respects are on the march and you may expect them shortly, and more shall be collected as soon as possible circumstance permitting.

Source: Juan N. Seguín to Albert Sidney Johnston, 13 March 1837, in *A Revolution Remembered: The Memoirs and Selected Correspondence of Juan N. Seguín*, ed. Jesús F. de la Teja (Austin: Texas State Historical Association, 2002), 161–162. Used with permission of the Texas State Historical Association, Denton.

Questions for Consideration

1) What, according to Seguín, were the supply needs of his Tejano corps?
2) When did he provide the "honors of war" to the Alamo defenders?
3) Why did his letter to General Albert Sidney Johnston reiterate the "highest respect for yourself and the orders you may be pleased to communicate"?

5.6 Michael H. Garty Serves on the U.S.S. *Somers* (1842)

The U.S. Navy offered sailors little more than misery at sea. Motley crews suffered rough justice under the high-handed authority of commanders, who administered floggings, lashings, rationings, and hangings. Maritime education and training remained inadequate, because it relied mostly upon an apprentice system. In 1842, the inadequacies of the system became apparent on board the U.S.S. *Somers*, a naval brig acting as an experimental school ship. Sailing from New York on September 13, it was commanded by Captain Alexander Slidell MacKenzie. It carried 110 men and boys on a cruise to the coast of Africa, although its design comfortably accommodated no more than 75. On the return voyage, MacKenzie executed midshipman Philip Spencer, petty officer Elisha Small, and boatswain's mate Samuel Cromwell for plotting a mutiny. After the brig reached New York without further incident, a court martial exonerated MacKenzie of wrongdoing. Marine Sergeant Michael H. Garty, an Irish immigrant, testified at the trial. Regardless of doubts about the handling of the case, the *Somers* affair marked the first mutiny in U.S. naval history. It led to the reassessment of shipboard training and disciplinary procedures by the Navy Department. Three years later, Congress appropriated funds establishing what would become the U.S. Naval Academy at Annapolis.

Document

Q. What is your name, your age, your rank? Were you on board the *Somers* on her last cruise?

A. My name is Michael H. Garty, my age 29 next September; I was on board of the *Somers* in her last cruise as orderly sergeant of the marine corps, doing the duty of master-at-arms.

Q. How soon after the arrest of Mr. Spencer did you see Cromwell and Small? Where were they then, and what was their demeanor?

A. They were forward of the mainmast, rather on the starboard side, on the berth-deck; they were in close conversation; when I went aft they separated; this was between three fourths of an hour and an hour.

Q. Have you ever had any conversation with Mr. Spencer with regard to taking the *Somers*?

A. Yes, sir; he had a conversation with me; I was sitting on the forehatch. Mr. Spencer came to me, and asked me, if I was to go ashore to do duty, if I would not be reduced to the ranks again. I told him, not unless I committed a crime. He asked me if I was not made sergeant for the purpose of going aboard to do duty as master-at-arms. I told him I was; and he changed his discourse by saying she was a fine vessel; I told him she was. He said he could take her with six men; I told him he would not do it with three times six. He said he would secure the captain and officers first, take possession of the arms, and turn up the crew, and when they saw his men in arms, he made no doubt that they would give in immediately. I said, after he had taken possession of the arms and turned up the crew, we could make a rush on him; there might not be more than six killed, and we could throw him and his six men overboard; that he must think us a very poor crew, that he could take us with six men. "Oh, no," says he, or something to that effect, as he went off.

Q. Did Mr. Spencer ever say anything to you about the place where the keys of the arm-chest were kept?

A. Yes, sir; he said he could take the vessel, provided he knew where everything lay as well as I did, particularly the key of the arm-chest.

Q. Did Mr. Spencer ever say anything to you about soon having a vessel of his own?

A. Yes, sir; it was about the 20th of November; I was sitting on the combings of the forescuttle; Mr. Spencer was sitting near me. There were a number of the crew near; they were talking about one thing or another, and the army was introduced. I asked Mr. Spencer if it was not better for him to join the army than the navy. He said his father told him he would get him a lieutenant's commission in the dragoons: he thought he would not like it; that he was not going to be long in the navy; that he was going to have a vessel of his own shortly.

Q. Did Mr. Spencer ever ask you anything about the condition of the small arms?

A. Yes, sir; I think it was on the 19th of November Mr. Gansevoort sent one of the boys to call me out of my hammock; I went up and reported myself to him on the quarter-deck; he ordered me to take out the arms and load them; I believe it was 23 muskets and 28 pistols that were loaded, but not primed—that was done by me and one of the gunner's mates. It was a day or two after this that Mr. Spencer asked me if all the arms were loaded; I said all but six or seven muskets; he asked me why they were not loaded; I told him that, if they were all loaded and pointed aft, they would not fit in the arm-chest; he asked me then the situation of them in the chest; I told him those that were loaded were pointing aft, and those that were not, forward. Two days after that he asked me about the arms again; I told him the same as I did before, and he made the remark, that they were not primed; I told him not. I recollect of no other conversation with Mr. Spencer […]

Q. Whom did you first hear of the mutiny from?

A. I can't exactly say who; I heard it on the berth-deck from the boys; I was in my hammock; it was on the evening of the 29th of November.

Q. What did you hear then?

A. I heard the boys say Mr. Spencer was going to take the brig and turn her into a pirate.

Q. Was it said how he intended to do it?

A. I did not hear that evening; the next day I heard that they were to kick up a sham fight on the forecastle: Mr. Spencer was to take them aft, call the officer of the deck and throw him overboard, and then go into the cabin and kill the captain; and from that to the wardroom, and kill the wardroom officers; then slew the two after-guns round, and turn up the crew. He was to select from the crew such persons as he wanted, and make the rest walk the plank.

Source: *Proceedings of the Naval Court Martial in the Case of Alexander Slidell Mackenzie, A Commander in the Navy of the United States, &c.: Including the Charges and Specifications of Charges Preferred Against him by the Secretary of the Navy: To Which is Annexed, an Elaborate Review, by James Fennimore [sic] Cooper* (New York: Henry G. Langley, 1844), 119–124.

Questions for Consideration

1) What prompted Sergeant Garty to say that the mutineers "must think us a very poor crew"?
2) How did Spencer intend to dispose of the unwanted sailors?
3) Which questions did the marine seem to have the most difficulty answering?

5.7 Henry W. Halleck Lectures on War (1846)

During the early nineteenth century, the study of Napoleonic warfare profoundly influenced the education of American military officers. The U.S. Military Academy at West Point constituted the center of gravity for martial thought. Instructors introduced cadets to the doctrines of Antoine Henri Jomini, a major general on Napoleon's staff, although the curriculum remained dedicated to science and mathematics. Superintendent Sylvanus Thayer exposed them to the European literature on strategy and tactics before he resigned in 1833. His protégé, Denis Hart Mahan, studied in France previous to joining the West Point faculty. His classes included examinations of fortifications, engineering, and logistics as well as lectures about the impact of warfare on statecraft. Lieutenant Henry Halleck, a Mahan student appointed assistant professor of engineering, was the first West Point officer to author a text on warfare. Published in 1846, his text borrowed heavily from lectures that resonated with Jominian doctrines. It surveyed the concentration of armed forces on decisive points in the battlefield. However, it betrayed a cautious tone with respect to offensive campaigning. Accordingly, the primary role of soldiers remained to defend American soil against foreign attack. It undoubtedly earned him the nickname "Old Brains" before his eventual elevation to General in Chief during the American Civil War.

Document

We shall begin with *infantry*, as the most important arm on the battlefield. There are four different ways of forming infantry for battle: 1st, as tirailleurs, or light troops; 2d, in deployed lines; 3d, in lines of battalions, deployed on the central division of each battalion, or formed in squares; 4th, in deep masses.

These different modes of formation are reduced to four separate systems: 1st, the thin formation of two deployed lines; 2d, a line of battalions in columns of attack on the centre, or in squares by battalions; 3d, a combination of these two, or the first line deployed, and the second in columns of attack; and 4th, the deep formation of heavy columns of several battalions. The tirailleurs are merely accessories to the main forces, and are employed to fill up intervals, to protect the march of the columns, to annoy the enemy, and to maneuver on the flanks [...]

Troops should be habituated to all these formations, and accustomed to pass rapidly from one to another in the daytime or at night. None, however, but disciplined troops can do this: hence the great superiority of regulars on the field of battle, where skillful maneuvers frequently effect more than the most undaunted courage.

The arm next in importance on the battlefield is *cavalry*. The principal merit of this arm consists in its *velocity* and *mobility*. Cavalry has little solidity, and cannot of itself defend any position against infantry; but in connection with the other arms, it is indispensable for beginning a battle, for completing a victory, and for reaping its full advantage by pursuing and destroying the beaten foe [...]

Cavalry may be brought to a charge—1st, in columns; 2d, in line; and 3d, in route, or at random. These may also be varied by charging either at a trot or a gallop. All these modes have been employed with success. In a regular charge in line the lance offers great advantages; in the mêlée the saber is the best weapon; hence some military writers have proposed arming the front rank with lances, and the second with sabers. The pistol and the carbine are useless in the charge, but may sometimes be employed with advantage against convoys, outposts, and light cavalry; to fire the carbine with any effect, the troop must be at a halt. In all charges in line, especially against cavalry, the fast trot is deemed preferable to the gallop, on account of the difficulty of keeping up the alignment when the speed is increased. Lances are utterly useless in a mêlée, and in employing troops armed in this way, it is of the greatest importance to keep them in order and in line. In charging with the saber against artillery the gallop may sometimes be employed, for velocity here may be more important than force.

We will now consider the formation and use of *artillery* on the field of battle. It may be laid down as a fundamental principle, that the fire of artillery should be directed on that part of the enemy's line which we design to pierce; for this fire will not only weaken this point, but will also aid the attack of the cavalry and infantry when the principal efforts are directed towards the intended point.

In the defence, the artillery is usually distributed throughout the whole line, on ground favorable for its fire; but the reserve should be so placed that it can easily be brought to bear on the point where the enemy will be most likely to direct his principal attack.

Artillery placed on a plain, or with ground slightly inclined in front, and using the point-blank or ricochet fire, is the most effective; very high points are unfavorable. If possible, the concentric fire should be employed against the enemy's columns of attack. The position of the English artillery on the field of Waterloo, and the use of the concentric fire, furnishes one of the best examples for the imposition of this arm to be found in modern military history.

The proper use of artillery on the battlefield is against the enemy's infantry and cavalry, consequently only a small part of it should be employed to respond to the fire of the enemy's batteries; not more than one third at most can be spared for this object. If possible, batteries should be established so as to take the enemy's line in flank, either by an oblique or enfilading fire. A direct fire against columns of attack, with a few light pieces thrown out to take it in flank at the same time, will always be advantageous [...]

The order of succession in which the different arms are engaged in a battle, depends upon the nature of the ground and other accidental circumstances and cannot be determined by any fixed rules. The following, however, is most frequently employed, and in ordinary cases may be deemed good.

The attack is first opened by a cannonade; light troops are sent forward to annoy the enemy, and, if possible, to pick off his artillerists. The main body then advances in two lines: the first displays itself in line as it arrives nearly within the range of grape-shot; the second line remains in columns of attack formed of battalions by division, at a distance from the first sufficient to be beyond the reach of the enemy's musketry, but near enough to support the first line, or to cover it, if driven back. The artillery, in the meantime, concentrates its fire on some weak point to open a way for the reserve, which rushes into the opening and takes the enemy in flank and rear. The cavalry charges at the opportune moment on the flank of the enemy's columns or penetrates an opening in his line, and cutting to pieces his staggered troops, forces them into retreat, and completes the victory. During this time the whole line of the enemy should be kept occupied, so as to prevent fresh troops from being concentrated on the threatened point.

Source: Henry W. Halleck, *Elements of Military Art and Science: Or, Course of Instruction in Strategy, Fortification, Tactics of Battles, Etc.* (New York: D. Appleton and Company, 1846), 121–132.

Questions for Consideration

1) Which troops, according to Halleck, form the "most important arm on the battlefield"?
2) What did he consider to be a "fundamental principle" regarding the artillery?
3) Do you agree with him in that some elements of warfare "cannot be determined by any fixed rules"?

Suggested Readings

Ambrose, Stephen E. *Duty, Honor, Country: A History of West Point.* Baltimore: Johns Hopkins University Press, 1966.

Browning, Robert S. *Two If By Sea: The Development of American Coastal Defense Policy.* Westport, CT.: Greenwood Press, 1983.

Cunliffe, Marcus. *Soldiers and Civilians: The Martial Spirit in America, 1775–1865.* New York: Little, Brown, 1968.

Doubler, Michael D. *Civilian in Peace, Soldier in War: The Army National Guard, 1636–2000.* Lawrence: University Press of Kansas, 2003.

Goetzmann, William H. *Army Exploration in the American West, 1803–1863.* New Haven, CT: Yale University Press, 1959.

Hagan, Kenneth J. *This People's Navy: The Making of American Sea Power.* New York: Free Press, 1991.

Hall, John W. *Uncommon Defense: Indian Allies in the Black Hawk War.* Cambridge: Harvard University Press, 2009.

Heidler, David S., and Jeanne T. Heidler. *Old Hickory's War: Andrew Jackson and the Quest for Empire.* Baton Rouge: Louisiana State University Press, 2003.

Kaufmann, J. E., and H. W. Kaufmann. *Fortress America: The Forts that Defended America, 1600 to the Present.* New York: Da Capo Press, 2004.

Langley, Harold D. *Social Reform in the United States Navy, 1798–1862.* Urbana: University of Illinois Press, 1967.

Mahon, John K. *History of the Second Seminole War, 1839–1842.* Gainesville: University of Florida Press, 1985.

Melton, Buckner F. *A Hanging Offense: The Affair of the Warship Somers.* New York: Free Press, 2003.

Prucha, Francis P. *The Sword of the Republic: The United States Army on the Frontier, 1783–1846.* New York: Macmillan, 1969.

Remini, Robert. *Andrew Jackson and His Indian Wars.* New York: Penguin, 2001.

Skelton, William B. *An American Profession of Arms: The Officer Corps, 1784–1861.* Lawrence: University Press of Kansas, 1999.

Watson, Samuel J. *Peacekeepers and Conquerors: The Army Officer Corps on the American Frontier, 1821–1846.* Lawrence: University Press of Kansas, 2013.

6

The Forces of Manifest Destiny

Chronology

1842–1846	The Frémont Expeditions
1846	U.S. troops ambushed in Texas
	Battle of Palo Alto
	Battle of Resaca de la Palma
	Congress passes the War Bill
	New Mexico and California occupied
	Battle of San Pascual
1847	Battle of San Gabriel
	Battle of Sacramento
	Battle of Buena Vista
	Veracruz captured
	Battle of Cerro Gordo
	Battle of Contreras
	Battle of Churubusco
	Battle of Molino del Rey
	Battle of Chapultepec
	The Occupation of Mexico City
1848	Treaty of Guadalupe Hidalgo
	U.S. troops depart Mexico
1849	California Gold Rush
1853–1854	The Perry Expedition

6.1   James K. Polk Calls for War (1846)

An American compulsion for national expansion placed the armed forces of the United States in harm's way. The Army Topographical Corps produced maps for migrants considering the overland trek. Along the 49th parallel, Great Britain and the United States rattled sabers but agreed to divide the Oregon country peacefully. Mexico, which controlled vast stretches of territory west of the Rocky Mountains, hindered what Americans imagined to be their "Manifest Destiny." The phrase gave voice to the notion that God had chosen the United States to spread its dominion from the Atlantic Ocean to the Pacific Ocean. Meanwhile, the annexation of Texas

American Military History: A Documentary Reader, Second Edition. Brad D. Lookingbill.
© 2019 John Wiley & Sons, Inc. Published 2019 by John Wiley & Sons, Inc.

prompted Mexico to cease diplomatic relations with Washington, DC. President James K. Polk offered to settle the boundary dispute regarding the Nueces and the Rio Grande Rivers. As negotiations failed, he ordered General Zachary Taylor to lead 1,500 troops into the disputed border area. A small group of Mexican soldiers attacked his dragoons on April 25, 1846, killing 11 Americans during the clash. On May 11, President Polk sent a special message to Congress asserting that a state of war existed between the United States and Mexico. Two days later, Congress passed a bill declaring war. Claims that the Commander in Chief misled Congress eventually gave rise to the nickname, "Polk the Mendacious."

Document
The existing state of the relations between the United States and Mexico renders it proper that I should bring the subject to the consideration of Congress. In my message at the commencement of your present session the state of these relations, the causes which led to the suspension of diplomatic intercourse between the two countries in March, 1845, and the long-continued and unredressed wrongs and injuries committed by the Mexican Government on citizens of the United States in their persons and property were briefly set forth.
As the facts and opinions which were then laid before you were carefully considered, I can not better express my present convictions of the condition of affairs up to that time than by referring you to that communication.
The strong desire to establish peace with Mexico on liberal and honorable terms, and the readiness of this Government to regulate and adjust our boundary and other causes of difference with that power on such fair and equitable principles as would lead to permanent relations of the most friendly nature, induced me in September last to seek the reopening of diplomatic relations between the two countries. Every measure adopted on our part had for its object the furtherance of these desired results. In communicating to Congress a succinct statement of the injuries which we had suffered from Mexico, and which have been accumulating during a period of more than twenty years, every expression that could tend to inflame the people of Mexico or defeat or delay a pacific result was carefully avoided. An envoy of the United States repaired to Mexico with full powers to adjust every existing difference. But though present on the Mexican soil by agreement between the two Governments, invested with full powers, and bearing evidence of the most friendly dispositions, his mission has been unavailing. The Mexican Government not only refused to receive him or listen to his propositions, but after a long-continued series of menaces have at last invaded our territory and shed the blood of our fellow-citizens on our own soil [...]
But no open act of hostility was committed until the 24th of April. On that day General Arista, who had succeeded to the command of the Mexican forces, communicated to General Taylor that "he considered hostilities commenced and should prosecute them." A party of dragoons of 63 men and officers were on the same day dispatched from the American camp up the Rio del Norte, on its left bank, to ascertain whether the Mexican troops had crossed or were preparing to cross the river, "became engaged with a large body of these troops, and after a short affair, in which some 16 were killed and wounded, appear to have been surrounded and compelled to surrender."

The grievous wrongs perpetrated by Mexico upon our citizens throughout a long period of years remain unredressed, and solemn treaties pledging her public faith for this redress have been disregarded. A government either unable or unwilling to enforce the execution of such treaties fails to perform one of its plainest duties.

Our commerce with Mexico has been almost annihilated. It was formerly highly beneficial to both nations, but our merchants have been deterred from prosecuting it by the system of outrage and extortion which the Mexican authorities have pursued against them, whilst their appeals through their own Government for indemnity have been made in vain. Our forbearance has gone to such an extreme as to be mistaken in its character. Had we acted with vigor in repelling the insults and redressing the injuries inflicted by Mexico at the commencement, we should doubtless have escaped all the difficulties in which we are now involved.

Instead of this, however, we have been exerting our best efforts to propitiate her good will. Upon the pretext that Texas, a nation as independent as herself, thought proper to unite its destinies with our own she has affected to believe that we have severed her rightful territory, and in official proclamations and manifestoes has repeatedly threatened to make war upon us for the purpose of reconquering Texas. In the meantime we have tried every effort at reconciliation. The cup of forbearance had been exhausted even before the recent information from the frontier of the Del Norte. But now, after reiterated menaces, Mexico has passed the boundary of the United States, has invaded our territory and shed American blood upon the American soil. She has proclaimed that hostilities have commenced, and that the two nations are now at war.

As war exists, and, notwithstanding all our efforts to avoid it, exists by the act of Mexico herself, we are called upon by every consideration of duty and patriotism to vindicate with decision the honor, the rights, and the interests of our country.

Anticipating the possibility of a crisis like that which has arrived, instructions were given in August last, "as a precautionary measure" against invasion or threatened invasion, authorizing General Taylor, if the emergency required, to accept volunteers, not from Texas only, but from the States of Louisiana, Alabama, Mississippi, Tennessee, and Kentucky, and corresponding letters were addressed to the respective governors of those States. These instructions were repeated, and in January last, soon after the incorporation of "Texas into our Union of States," General Taylor was further "authorized by the President to make a requisition upon the executive of that State for such of its militia force as may be needed to repel invasion or to secure the country against apprehended invasion." On the 2d day of March he was again reminded, "in the event of the approach of any considerable Mexican force, promptly and efficiently to use the authority with which he was clothed to call to him such auxiliary force as he might need." War actually existing and our territory having been invaded, General Taylor, pursuant to authority vested in him by my direction, has called on the governor of Texas for four regiments of State troops, two to be mounted and two to serve on foot, and on the governor of Louisiana for four regiments of infantry to be sent to him as soon as practicable.

In further vindication of our rights and defense of our territory, I invoke the prompt action of Congress to recognize the existence of the war, and to place at the disposition of the Executive the means of prosecuting the war with vigor, and thus hastening the restoration of peace. To this end I recommend that authority should be given to call into the public service a large body of volunteers to serve for not less than six or twelve months unless sooner discharged. A volunteer force is beyond question more efficient than any other description of citizen soldiers, and it is not to be doubted that a number far beyond that required would readily rush to the field upon the call of their country. I further recommend that a liberal provision be made for sustaining our entire military force and furnishing it with supplies and munitions of war.

The most energetic and prompt measures and the immediate appearance in arms of a large and overpowering force are recommended to Congress as the most certain and efficient means of bringing the existing collision with Mexico to a speedy and successful termination.

In making these recommendations I deem it proper to declare that it is my anxious desire not only to terminate hostilities speedily, but to bring all matters in dispute between this Government and Mexico to an early and amicable adjustment; and in this view I shall be prepared to renew negotiations whenever Mexico shall be ready to receive propositions or to make propositions of her own.

Source: James K. Polk, "Message to the Senate and House, 11 May 1846," in *Messages and Papers of the Presidents, 1789–1907*, Volume 4, ed. James D. Richardson (New York: Bureau of National Literature and Art, 1908), 437–443.

Questions for Consideration

1) How, according to President Polk, did the Mexican government respond to his envoy's negotiations?
2) What immediate military action did he authorize once Mexico "shed American blood upon the American soil"?
3) Why was it necessary for Congress "to call into the public service a large body of volunteers" in 1846?

6.2   James K. Holland Marches into Mexico (1846)

The Polk administration hoped that offensive campaigning would compel the Mexican government to negotiate a quick end to the war. To that end, U.S. forces prevailed in the battles of Palo Alto and Resaca de la Palma near the Rio Grande. After May 18, 1846, they drove their enemy westward from Matamoras to Monterrey. General Taylor advanced overland with around 3,000 regulars and more than 3,000 volunteers. Captain James K. Holland documented that long, hot summer in Mexico. He was born in Tennessee, grew up in Mississippi, and had moved to Texas with his father. Roused by the declaration of war, the young Holland volunteered for service and began to keep a diary of his soldiering. His commonplace observations revealed the rigors of the march. Beginning on September 20, American howitzers shelled the Monterrey fortifications. Three days later, Americans penetrated the city with fierce house-to-house fighting. Mexicans inside the main plaza surrendered. General Taylor, who hoped to sway the Mexican government to negotiate, allowed the army at Monterrey to withdraw under an eight-week armistice. President Polk, however, canceled the armistice on October 11. Meanwhile, Holland celebrated the victory and was mustered out of service. After returning to Texas, he launched a successful career in state politics.

Document

24th May—the day of our departure from Harrison county [Texas]—Company commanded by Capt Bird Holland. We left Elysian Field on this day about 11 o'clock—for the Rio Grande—women in tears, God bless them—their tears would make a recreant brave—we all felt gloomy of course for such a separation I look upon as worse if possible than death—for when death comes upon us the grief subsides and now we are parting from our friends perchance never to meet again—which leaves them in miserable suspense as to our future fate but such is the call—let us respond like men—like Texians.

After our gloomy reflections passed away—six cheers was echoed—re-echoed through camp—to the Donor of our Colors—the motto she gave with it will long, long be remembered—the motto will be *Leona memoria in eterna*—Thought of our parting state crept upon us until we crossed the Sabine (4 o'clock) when a general drunken spree ensued at the expense of J. M. Pelham he too sharing a goodly portion—Myself keeping him very good company—Thence to *camp Egg*—2 miles up the River when fun, frolic, drunkenness, and hilarity was the order of the night—The Capt's order to the contrary notwithstanding—other scenes occurring which however are not necessary to mention just here—Jo Pelham, M V Mann, and Spear H[olland] Junior guests at Mess No. 1—all slept pretty well—tho tolerable rough sleeping—but we expected hardship and heres for it with a full determination to see the Elephant and the Monkey [...]

[September] This morning being the 19th we arose and left still without food or forage— Texas went ahead today— now that danger is expected old [General] Taylor has put us in front—Every man in glorious spirits—after running our horses nearly to death, many of them giving out, arrived in sight of the Mexican Batteries about 2 miles and halted when they played upon us with their Balls and many of their balls were directed very well—yet no one was hurt—Genl T. surveyed the situation of Town and retired to camp Walnut Spring—The most beautifull Encampment I ever did see—and that night Taylor formed his plan of *attack*—took several prisoners—learned that they were strongly fortified with about 15000 strong and that they intended to repell us or die—it was cheering to see how The Texians greeted the Mexican Balls—Every fire was met with a hearty response of 3 cheers and such waving of hats and huzzaing Genl T says he never heard—The Texians proved their spunk by the utter carelessness with which the[y] Recd the Enemy's shot— They whizzing by us in all directions—yet no one hurt. I *want sceared a bit* we awaited the arrival of the artillery—which came up in good time and at night was planted in a good position—the main Army came up—and for on[c]e we were all encamped together in 3 miles of Monterrey—prospects most glorious and bright for a fight—

20th. Today being the sabbath, Genl T. did not chose to disturb their worship—all was qui[e]t today yet a cannonading was kept up on those whose curiosity led them to take a peep at the Forts—at night Genl Worth was ordered to take his position above Town—at night he stole a march upon them and passed under their Batteries without harm—

21st. bright and early fire upon them to their great surprise. The Texians were put to order the Monclova and Saltillo passes [General] Worth during the day got possession of one fort on the same day—The Tenn—and Mi. Boy's distinguished themselves in charging upon and storming two of their main Bataries—one of the most vallent deeds—daring and noble charges ever know in the histories of Battles—with a severe loss however—

12 horses of the Flying Artillery were killed on 22nd. Worth stormed several Fort[s] and took good many pieces of artillery—The Mis and Tenn Boy's having taken 4 pieces on day before—on this day our Company was ordered to guard Bragg's Batteries—and to keep

off the Rancheros and Lancers and Worth by the best management in the world got in possession of the old Castle and commanding became the hero of Monterrey—with but little loss—I saw it and it was the prettiest sight I ever saw—he repelled them and drove them into Town and then turned their own pieces upon them from the Castle and created havoc and confusion in their line—he got possession of several of their mills—

Texas on 23rd was ordered to dismount and into the City which was done in quick time under the heaviest firing of grape Cannister and Musketry—we faced it like men—went running in to Town to the astonishment of Genl Taylor—to the great confusion of Enemy—they did not understand such bold movement—when we got in possession of the houses—pick them from housetop to housetop and such fun you never did see—the greatest danger we encountered was in crossing the streets—the hotest place you ever saw—we had penetrated so far into the heart of the City that Genl T. on our progress—taking us to be Mexican retreating— fired upon us—and well nigh ruined us—but it was stoped in time—and on we rushed—bullets whizzing by us on all sides soon got used to it—and about the time we got into it old fashionedly—our own guns commenced fireing upon us—and it put a check upon our progress—in a short time Bragg's Flying Artillery came rolling in and called upon us to protect it—which was done in a very singular man-ner—the Enemy commenced to retreat—and we soon out striped the artillery and give it no show at all—ran nearly half-mile after them—such shooting and huzzaing and hal-lowing seemed by instinct to let the enemy know that Texas had come to Town—just at the time when we had the city almost completely under our command Genl T. not know-ing how far we had penetrated—called us off—for the purpose of bombarding the Town—whereas if he had have let us alone we would soon have had it in such a condition that there would have been no need of it—after the 3rd order we retired—when they, supposing that we were on the retreat, commenced a heavy fireing upon us—at which time we had several killed and wounded—Bradford and Lamar were our heroes—Miss and Texas fought together and bravely too—C G Davenport from our company was wounded, several horses ditto—returned to camp—well pleased with what we had done—a heavy fireing was kept [up] all night—and this morning (24th) a Mexican officer came to Genl T. with a flag of *Truce*. Genl Ampudia had taken blue pills enough he desired to march out of the City with the honors of war—they will abandon the town provided they can take with them their arms—munitions of war and public property—Genl T. answered them by saying no—surrender as prisoners of war—they then asked for an armistice until 12 oclock which was granted—and council of war was held—the result of which was a cessation of hostilities for 8 weeks—he might march out of Town with small arms and 6 pieces of Artillery to keep the Commanches off—it is something astonishing that the victory was taken on the very day on which our time was out—4 mo to a day—

25th. we revelled in the halls—palaces and groceries of Monterrey—the Mex evacuat-ing the town *fast* they have 7 days to leave—I visited the City today and found it the best fortified city in the world except Quebec—the hand of ingenuity as well as nature has been most beautifully displayed—the Stars and Stripes float proudly over the top of the old Hornets next [nest]—it is a beautifull city—many fine Halls well furnished—gardens of unparallel grandeur and bea[u]ty—it is somthing solemn and imposing to see the Mexican[s] marching out—beating the retreat.

Source: James K. Holland, "Diary of a Texan Volunteer in the Mexican War," *Southwestern Historical Quarterly* 30 (1926): 1–33.

Questions for Consideration

1) What did Captain Holland mean in saying that he wanted "to see the Elephant and the Monkey"?
2) How did he describe the defenses in northern Mexico?
3) To what extent did morale seem to impact the tempo of the march?

6.3   Zachary Taylor Describes Buena Vista (1847)

Known among his troops as "Old Rough and Ready," General Zachary Taylor served in uniform for over 40 years. On February 23, 1847, he demonstrated remarkable military leadership during the Battle of Buena Vista. His army of 5,000 soldiers defeated more than 15,000 troops under Mexican General Antonio Lopez de Santa Anna. The victory transformed General Taylor into an American folk hero. The press compared him favorably to Generals Washington and Jackson. Stories circulated about his coolness in the heat of battle, as he sat atop his beloved horse, "Old Whitey," with a tattered straw hat upon his head. According to his own report, his officers unleashed a barrage of heavy artillery fire to turn the tide of battle. The volleys of grape and canister halted the advance of the Mexican infantry, while the Mississippi regiment of Colonel Jefferson Davis valiantly held the line. However, Lieutenant Colonel Henry Clay, Jr., whose father in the Senate disapproved of the war, was among the 264 Americans killed in action. At the end of the day, the Mexican army suffered more than 1,800 casualties. During the night, General Santa Anna ordered his forces to withdraw to San Luis Potosí. General Taylor did not pursue them but instead returned to Monterrey. It was his last battle against Mexico.

Document

This portion of our line having given way, and the enemy appearing in overwhelming force against our left flank, the light troops which had rendered such good service on the mountain were compelled to withdraw, which they did, for the most part, in good order. Many, however, were not rallied until they reached the depot at Buena Vista, to the defence of which they afterwards contributed. Colonel Bissell's regiment (Second Illinois,) which had been joined by a section of Captain Sherman's battery, had become completely outflanked, and was compelled to fall back, being entirely unsupported. The enemy was now pouring masses of infantry and cavalry along the base of the mountain on our left, and was gaining our rear in great force. At this moment I arrived upon the field.

The Mississippi regiment had been directed to the left before reaching the position, and immediately came into action against the Mexican infantry which had turned our flank. The Second Kentucky regiment, and a section of artillery under Captain Bragg, had previously been ordered from the right to reinforce our left, and arrived at a most opportune moment. That regiment, and a portion of the First Illinois, under Colonel Hardin, gallantly drove the enemy, and recovered a portion of the ground we had lost. The batteries of Captains Sherman and Bragg were in position on the plateau, and did much execution, not only in front, but particularly upon the masses which had gained our rear. Discovering that the enemy was heavily pressing upon the Mississippi regiment, the Third Indiana regiment, under Colonel Lane, was dispatched to strengthen that part of our line, which formed a crotchet perpendicular to the first line of battle. At the same time Lieutenant Kilburn, with a piece of Captain Bragg's battery, was directed to support the infantry there engaged. The action was for a long time warmly sustained at that point—the enemy making several efforts both with infantry and cavalry against our line, and being always repulsed with heavy loss. I had placed all the regular cavalry and Captain Pike's squadron of Arkansas horse under the orders of Brevet Lieutenant-Colonel May, with directions to hold in check the enemy's column, still advancing to the rear along the base of the mountain, which was done in conjunction with the Kentucky and Arkansas cavalry, under Colonels Marshall and Yell.

In the meantime our left, which was still strongly threatened by a superior force, was further strengthened by the detachment of Captain Bragg's and a portion of Captain Sherman's batteries to that quarter. The concentration of artillery fire upon the masses of the enemy along the base of the mountain, and the determined resistance offered by the two regiments opposed to them, had created confusion in their ranks, and some of the corps attempted to effect a retreat upon their main line of battle [...]

The position of that portion of the Mexican army which had gained our rear was now very critical, and it seemed doubtful whether it could regain the main body. At this moment I received from General Santa Anna a message by a staff officer, desiring to know what I wanted? I immediately dispatched Brigadier General Wool to the Mexican general in chief, and sent orders to cease firing. Upon reaching the Mexican lines, General Wool could not cause the enemy to cease their fire, and accordingly returned without having an interview. The extreme right of the enemy continued its retreat along the base of the mountain, and finally, in spite of all our efforts, effected a junction with the remainder of the army.

During the day, the cavalry of General Minon had ascended the elevated plain above Saltillo, and occupied the road from the city to the field of battle, where they intercepted several of our men. Approaching the town, they were fired upon by Captain Webster, from the redoubt occupied by his company, and then moved off towards the eastern side of the valley, and obliquely towards Buena Vista. At this time, Captain Shover moved rapidly forward with his piece, supported by a miscellaneous command of mounted volunteers, and fired several shots at the cavalry with great effect. They were driven into the ravines which lead to the lower valley, closely pursued by Captain Shover, who was further supported by a piece of Captain Webster's battery, under Lieutenant Donaldson, which had advanced from the redoubt, supported by Captain Wheeler's company of Illinois volunteers. The enemy made one or two efforts to charge the artillery, but was finally driven back in a confused mass, and did not again appear upon the plain.

In the meantime the firing had partially ceased upon the principal field. The enemy seemed to confine his efforts to the protection of his artillery, and I had left the plateau for a moment, when I was recalled thither by a very heavy musketry fire. On regaining that position, I discovered that our infantry (Illinois and Second Kentucky) had engaged a greatly superior force of the enemy—evidently his reserve—and that they had been overwhelmed by numbers. The moment was most critical. Captain O'Brien, with two pieces, had sustained this heavy charge to the last, and was finally obliged to leave his guns on the field—his infantry support being entirely routed. Captain Bragg, who had just arrived from the left, was ordered at once into battery. Without any infantry to support him, and at the imminent risk of losing his guns, this officer came rapidly into action, the Mexican line being but a few yards from the muzzles of his pieces. The first discharge of canister caused the enemy to hesitate; the second and third drove him back in disorder and saved the day. The Second Kentucky regiment, which had advanced beyond supporting distance in this affair was driven back and closely pressed by the enemy's cavalry. Taking a ravine which led in the direction of Captain Washington's battery, their pursuers became exposed to his fire, which soon checked and drove them back with loss [...]

No further attempt was made by the enemy to force our position, and the approach of night gave an opportunity to pay proper attention to the wounded, and also to refresh the soldiers, who had been exhausted by incessant watchfulness and combat. Though the night was severely cold, the troops were compelled for the most to bivouac without fires, expecting that morning would renew the conflict. During the night the wounded were removed to Saltillo, and every preparation made to receive the enemy, should he again attack our position. Seven fresh companies were drawn from the town, and Brigadier-General Marshall, with a reinforcement of Kentucky cavalry and four heavy guns, under Captain Prentiss, First artillery, was near at hand, when it was discovered that the enemy had abandoned his position during the night. Our scouts soon ascertained that he had fallen back upon Agua Nueva. The great disparity of numbers, and the exhaustion of our troops, rendered it inexpedient and hazardous to attempt pursuit. A staff officer was dispatched to General Santa Anna, to negotiate an exchange of prisoners, which was satisfactorily completed on the following day. Our own dead were collected and buried, and the Mexican wounded, of which a large number had been left upon the field, were removed to Saltillo, and rendered as comfortable as circumstances would permit.

Source: Zachary Taylor, "Official Report," in Henry Montgomery, *The Life of Major General Zachary Taylor* (Buffalo: Derby & Hewson Publishers, 1847), 276–294.

Questions for Consideration

1) What, according to General Taylor, happened to his line before he arrived on the battlefield?
2) Where did he order the artillery to concentrate its fire during the battle?
3) Why did he think it would have been "inexpedient and hazardous" to pursue General Santa Anna after the battle?

6.4 Winfield Scott Lands at Veracruz (1847)

With U.S. forces in control of northern Mexico, Major General Winfield Scott proposed a bold operation at Veracruz, a coastal Mexican city. During the early months of 1847, he amassed nearly 12,000 troops on Lobos Island. He planned an amphibious landing. The U.S. Navy provided specially designed surfboats, which ferried troops and supplies to the shore three miles south of Veracruz. On March 9, 1847, they hit the beaches and began to besiege the city. They faced a Mexican force of over 4,000 troops, who crowded inside the city's fortress of San Juan de Ulúa. Naval guns bombarded the city until March 28, when Mexican officials surrendered. General Scott's army suffered only 80 casualties during the siege. To control his soldiers as well as the civilians, he imposed martial law. He grew concerned about the outbreak of malaria, which caused him to march 8,500 soldiers inland to higher ground. Using Veracruz as a base for operations, they advanced westward along Mexico's national highway. Tragically, thousands perished from disease. Sensitive to criticisms of his command, General Scott's memoir revealed the qualities that earned him the sobriquet, "Grand Old Man of the Army." His overbearing traits prompted another label, "Old Fuss and Feathers."

Document

March 9—the precise day when I had been thirty years a general officer—the sun dawned propitiously on the expedition. There was but little surf on the beach—a necessary condition—as we had to effect a landing from the open sea. Every detail, providing for all contingencies, had been discussed and arranged with my staff, and published in orders. The whole fleet of transports—some eighty vessels, in the presence of many foreign ships of war, stood up the coast, flanked by two naval steamers and five gunboats to cover the movement. Passing through them in the large propeller, the *Massachusetts*, the shouts and cheers from every deck gave me assurance of victory, whatever might be the force prepared to receive us.

We anchored opposite to a point a little beyond the range of the guns of the city and castle, when some fifty-five hundred men instantly filled up the sixty-seven surf boats I had caused to be built for this special occasion—each holding from seventy to eighty men—besides a few cutters belonging to the larger war vessels. Commodore Conner also supplied steerers (officers) and sailors as oarsmen. The whole, again cheering, as they passed my ship wearing the broad pennant, pulled away right for the shore, landed in the exact order prescribed, about half past five P. M., without the loss of a boat or a man, and, to the astonishment of all, without opposition other than a few whizzing shells that did no harm. Another trip or two enabled the row-boats to put ashore the whole force, rather less than twelve thousand men, though I had been promised double the number—my *minimum*; but I never had, at any one time in the campaign, more than thirteen thousand five hundred, until the fighting was over, when I was encumbered with the troops that [General] Taylor found at last he could not use [...]

All sieges are much alike, and as this is not a treatise on engineering, scientific details are here omitted. We took care, in our approaches to keep the city as a shield between us and the terrible fire of the castle; but the forts in the walls of the city were formidable spitfires. They were rarely out of blast. Yet the approaches were so adroitly conducted, that our losses in them were surprisingly small, and no serious sortie was hazarded by the garrison.

The arming of the advanced batteries had been retarded by a very protracted gale *(norther)* which cut off all communication with our vessels in the offing. Ground was, however, broken on the 18th, and by the 22d, heavy ordnance enough for a beginning being in position, the governor of the city, who was also governor of the castle, was duly summoned to surrender. The refusal was no sooner received than a fire on the walls and forts was opened. In the attempt to batter in breach, and to silence the forts, a portion of our shots and shells, in the course of the siege, unavoidably penetrated the city and set fire to many houses.

By the 24th, the landing of additional heavy guns and mortars gave us all the battering power needed, and the next day, as I reported to Washington, the whole was in "awful activity." The same day there came a memorial from the foreign consuls in Vera Cruz, asking for a truce to enable them, and the women and children of the inhabitants, to withdraw in safety. They had in time been duly warned of the impending danger, and allowed to the 22d to retire, which they had sullenly neglected, and the consuls had also declined the written *safe-guards* I had pressed upon them. The season had advanced, and I was aware of several cases of yellow fever in the city and neighborhood. Detachments of the enemy too were accumulating behind us, and rumors spread, by them, that a formidable army would soon approach to raise the siege. Tenderness therefore for the women and children—in the form of delay—might, in its consequences, have led to the loss of the campaign, and, indeed to the loss of the army—two thirds by pestilence, and the remainder by surrender. Hence I promptly replied to the consuls that no truce could be allowed except on the application of the governor (General Morales), and *that* with a view to surrender. Accordingly, the next morning General Landero, who had been put in the supreme command for that purpose, offered to entertain the question of submission. Commissioners were appointed on both sides, and on the 27th terms of surrender, including both the city and castle of Ulloa, agreed upon, signed and exchanged. The garrisons marched out, laying down their arms, and were sent home prisoners of war on parole [...]

Fortunately, the frequency of the gales, called *northers,* had kept off the *vomito,* as an epidemic, though a few cases had occurred in the city; but, unfortunately, the want of road-power—horses and mules—detained the body of the army at Vera Cruz from its capture, March 29, till toward the middle of April.

Source: Winfield Scott, *Memoirs of Lieut.-General Scott, LL.D.,* Volume 2 (New York: Sheldon & Company, 1864), 415–432.

Questions for Consideration

1) What gave General Scott "assurance of victory" during the amphibious landing?
2) How much credit for the success of the operation does he ascribe to others?
3) Why did he express concerns about "the *vomito*" at Veracruz?

6.5   James Walker Views the Storming of Chapultepec (1847)

General Winfield Scott made his military objective "The Halls of Montezuma," that is, Mexico City. At the Battle of Cerro Gordo, he defeated a Mexican army more than 12,000 strong, but General Santa Anna escaped his grasp. General Scott's army then prevailed in a series of battles at Contreras, Churubusco, and Molino del Rey. Afterward, General Santa Anna concentrated his forces on the western approach to Mexico City at Chapultepec, a castle on a rocky bluff looming some 200 feet above the city plain. On the morning of September 13, 1847, Americans stormed the castle. After a few hours of horrific fighting, they captured Chapultepec and raised the American flag. Gazing from the American lines, James Walker witnessed it all. Though born in England, Walker resided in Mexico City at the outbreak of the war. He became an interpreter for the

American troops approaching the city. The next year, Sarony & Major published a lithograph based upon Walker's view of the battle. With Santa Anna fleeing, U.S. forces occupied Mexico City. On February 2, 1848, the Treaty of Guadalupe Hidalgo officially ended the war. U.S. Marines still wear a red stripe on the trousers of their dress uniform to commemorate the storming of Chapultepec.

Document

Source: The Storming of Chapultepec, 1847, Prints and Photographs Division, Library of Congress.

Questions for Consideration

1) What types of armaments appeared in the lithograph?
2) How did the lithograph indicate that U.S. forces were better organized than their Mexican foes?
3) In what ways did the "fog of war" affect the artist's view?

6.6 Matthew C. Perry Steams to Japan (1852)

The American proponents of "Manifest Destiny" viewed expansion as a panacea for national security. After the stunning success of the war against Mexico, the U.S. Navy rode a wave of enthusiasm for new expeditions around the world. They explored the

Amazon River, the Brazilian coast, Rio de la Plata, Rio Paraguay, the Bering Strait, and the China Sea. The most important expedition during the 1850s was undertaken by Commodore Matthew C. Perry, who earlier played a key role in naval operations along the Mexican coast. Called the "Father of the Steam Navy," he took command of an expedition to open Japan to the United States. His dark-hulled sidewheel steamer, the U.S.S. *Mississippi*, served as the flagship for a small squadron. En route to Japan on December 14, 1852, he outlined his strategy for aggressive negotiations in a letter to the Secretary of the Navy, John P. Kennedy. Commodore Perry steamed into Tokyo Bay on July 8, 1853. He threatened to use force if the Tokugawa Shogunate denied him permission to come ashore. Using a combination of persuasion and imposition, his parlays resulted in the signing of the Treaty of Kanagawa on March 31, 1854. Thus, naval professionals delicately balanced economic, scientific, diplomatic, and military objectives as they ventured abroad.

Document

Since leaving the United States I have had leisure to reflect more fully upon the probable result of my visit to Japan, and though there is still some doubt in my mind as to the chances of immediate success in bringing that strange government to any practicable negotiation, yet I feel confident that in the end the great object in view will be effected.

As a preliminary step, and one of easy accomplishment, one or more ports of refuge and supply to our whaling and other ships must at once be secured; and should the Japanese government object to the granting of such ports upon the main land, and if they cannot be occupied without resort to force and bloodshed, then it will be desirable in the beginning, and indeed, necessary, that the squadron should establish places of rendezvous at one or two of the islands south of Japan, having a good harbor, and possessing facilities for obtaining water and supplies, and seek by kindness and gentle treatment to conciliate the inhabitants so as to bring about their friendly intercourse.

The islands called the Lew Chew group are said to be dependencies of Japan, as conquered by that power centuries ago, but their actual sovereignty is disputed by the government of China. These islands come within the jurisdiction of the prince of Satsuma, the most powerful of the princes of the Empire, and the same who caused the unarmed American ship Morrison, on a visit of mercy, to be decoyed into one of his ports and then fired upon from the batteries hastily erected. He exercises his rights more from the influence of the fear of the simple islanders than from any power to coerce their obedience; disarmed, as they long have been, from motives of policy, they have no means, even if they had the inclination, to rebel against the grinding oppression of their rulers.

Now, it strikes me, that the occupation of the principal ports of those islands for the accommodation of our ships of war, and for the safe resort of merchant vessels of whatever nation, would be a measure not only justified by the strictest rules of moral law, but which is also to be considered, by the laws of stern necessity; and the argument may be further strengthened by the certain consequences of the amelioration of the condition of the natives, although the vices attendant upon civilization may be entailed upon them.

In my former commands upon the coast of Africa, and in the Gulf of Mexico, where it fell to my lot to subjugate many towns and communities, I found no difficulty in conciliating the good will and confidence of the conquered people, by administering the unrestricted power I held rather to their comfort and protection than to their annoyance; and when the naval forces left, they carried with them the gratitude and good wishes of their former enemies; and so I believe that the people of the islands spoken of, if treated with strict justice and gentle kindness, will render confidence for confidence, and after a while the Japanese will learn to consider us their friends.

In establishing those ports of refuge it will be desirable to provide the means of supply to the vessels that may resort to them, and hence the necessity of encouraging the natives in the cultivation of fruits, vegetables, &c.; and to carry out, in part, this object, garden seeds have been provided; but to pursue the purpose still further, I have thought that if a few of the more simple agricultural implements of our own country were sent to me for use, and for presents, they would contribute most essentially to the end in view; such, for instance, as the common cultivator, the plough and harrow, spades, hoes of various kinds, the threshing and winnowing machines, and especially those inventions for separating the cotton from its seed, and rice from its husks.

And with reference, also, to the subject of my letter to Mr. Folsom, charge at the Hague, a copy of which has been enclosed to the Department of State, it would be good policy to counteract the discreditable machinations of the Dutch, by circulating printed publications representing the true condition of the various governments of the world, and especially to set forth the extraordinary prosperity of the United States under their genial laws.

To effect this object, I am already provided with works for presentation, descriptive of the civil and political condition of the United States, such as the census tables, post-office and railroad reports, reports of the Indian and Land offices, military and naval registers, also with the magnificent publications of the State of New York, &c. And I have thought that a small printing press, with type and materials, would go far to facilitate our plans, by giving us the means of putting forth information calculated to disabuse the Japanese of the misrepresentations of the Dutch. The government of Japan keeps in employment linguists in all modern languages; and such is their curiosity, that these publications, if admitted at all, will soon be translated.

Having thus, at least in anticipation, established harbors of resort, and organized certain rules of equity to govern our intercourse with the natives in the payment for labor, supplies, &c., and having depots of provisions and coal near at hand, we shall be able to act with more effect in bringing about some friendly understanding with the imperial government. At all events, steamers, or whatever vessels that may be passing to and from California and China, will find safe harbors in their way, and it may reasonably be expected that in the course of time the intercourse thus brought about will lead to a better understanding of our pacific intentions.

It may be said that my anticipations are too sanguine. Perhaps they are, but I feel a strong confidence of success. Indeed, success may be commanded by our government, and it should be, under whatever circumstances, accomplished. The honor of the nation calls for it, and the interest of commerce demands it. When we look at the possessions in the east of our great maritime rival, England, and of the constant and rapid increase of their fortified ports, we should be admonished of the necessity of prompt measures on our part.

Source: Matthew C. Perry to the Secretary of the Navy, 14 December 1852, in Francis L. Hawks, *Narrative of the Expedition of an American Squadron to the China Seas and Japan* (New York: D. Appleton and Company, 1856), 105–108.

Questions for Consideration

1) What did Commodore Perry suggest would be necessary if the U.S. resorted to "force and bloodshed" in Japan?
2) How did he intend to use a small printing press "to facilitate our plans" in Japan?
3) Why do you think he referred to European powers with regard to Asia?

6.7   Elizabeth C. Smith Petitions for Bounty Land (1853)

The American military secured millions of acres in the occupied territories, which once belonged to Mexico. In 1853, the Gadsden Purchase set the final boundary between the United States and Mexico. Upon completing their military service, many ex-soldiers expected to feast upon Mexican land. The Mexican War Bounty Land Act, a wartime measure passed by Congress, promised a federal land warrant of 160 acres for veterans. To claim a bounty, one particular veteran addressed a petition to "the Honorable Senate and House of Representatives of the United States of America in Congress assembled." It was signed by Elizabeth C. Smith. The Committee on Military Affairs reviewed her petition, which documented her enlistment in the Missouri Infantry volunteers. There seemed to be no doubt that she rendered military service as claimed, reported the Committee to Congress. In fact, the ninth section of the Bounty Land Act made no distinction with regard to sex. The Committee concluded that her military service was as useful to the government "as if she had been a man, and regularly enlisted as such." Therefore, she was fully entitled to veteran's benefits. A special bill on her behalf passed both houses of Congress. President Franklin Pierce, also a veteran of the war against Mexico, signed it on March 3, 1854.

Document

On this twenty-third day of July in the year of our Lord One Thousand Eight Hundred and Fifty-three, before me the undersigned Clerk of the Weston Court of Common Pleas in the County and State aforesaid, personally came Mrs. Elizabeth C. Smith, formerly Elizabeth C. Newcome, a resident of the County and State above mentioned, who after being by me duly sworn according to law, upon her oath declares, that she is the identical person who was a Private of Captain Holeshider's (a German whose name she is not confident about) Company "D," in the Regiment commanded by Col. Gilpin of Missouri Infantry Volunteers, that she enlisted under the assumed name of "Bill Newcume" at Fort Leavenworth and was mustered into the service of the United States on or about the 4th day of September in the year of our Lord one thousand eight hundred forty-seven, to serve during the War with Mexico, that she was regularly sworn and mustered into the service aforesaid as other volunteers were, that she marched with the regiment aforesaid to Fort Nan [sic] in New Mexico that she performed all the duties of a soldier regularly under the assumed name of "Bill Newcume," that she wore the uniform dress of a soldier, was to receive the same pay as such, that she served her Government faithfully and honestly, for the space of ten months or about that length of time when she was discharged from the Army of the United States, at Fort Leavenworth, the place of enlistment, to wit: on or about the fifteenth day of June, A.D. 1848, by reason of the discovery before that time made that she was not "Bill or William Newcume" the person represented on the Muster Roll, but that she was Elizabeth Caroline Newcume a female instead of a male and therefore was discharged.

Affiant further declares that she enlisted from the best of motives, that of serving her country, that she did serve as long as she was permitted to for which she has never been remunerated by the Government in any way, and that she makes this application in order to obtain a Bounty-Land Warrant for 160 acres of land. She further declares that she served under the circumstances and in the manner as herein set forth, and that she is now the lawful wife of John Smith and resides in the County of Platte and State of Missouri, further affiant saith not [...]

The petition of Elizabeth C. Smith, a resident of the County of Platte and State of Missouri, respectfully represents that her maiden name was Elizabeth C. Newcom, that under the assumed name of "Bill Newcom," and in male attire she enlisted as a Private in Capt. Holeshider's Company "D" in the Regiment commanded by Colonel Gilpin of Missouri Infantry Volunteers, on the 16th day of September 1847, was mustered into service on the 18th day of the same month to serve in and during the War with Mexico, that she continued in said service, under the assumed name aforesaid and faithfully performed all the duties of a soldier for the space of eight months, at the expiration of which time, to wit: the 14th day of May, 1848, at Santa Fe, New Mexico, her sex was discovered, and she was immediately thereafter sent to Fort Leavenworth, where she was informally discharged from the service by Lieut. Colonel Wharton of the U.S. Army, being about ten months after the date of enlistment.

Your petitioner further represents, that for the services rendered as aforesaid she has received no pay from the Government, except for mileage, for the proof of all which she would respectfully refer to papers on file in the Pension and 2d Auditor's Offices.

Your petitioner therefore prays, that your Honorable Bodies will be pleased to grant to her such quantity of land and allow her such pay for the services aforesaid as to you may seem just and equitable, and your petitioner as in duty bound will ever pray, etc.

(Signed) Elizabeth C. Smith

Source: Elizabeth C. (Newcom) Smith, Mexican War Service Papers, Collection 995, Item 376, The State Historical Society of Missouri Manuscript Collection.

Questions for Consideration

1) What prompted Smith's discharge from military service?
2) To what extent did she perform "all the duties of a soldier"?
3) How do you think she passed her initial physical exam to enlist?

Suggested Readings

Bauer, Jack. *The Mexican War, 1846–1848.* Annapolis: Naval Institute Press, 1974.

Bauer, Jack. *Zachary Taylor: Soldier, Planter, Statesman of the Old Southwest.* Baton Rouge: Louisiana State University Press, 1985.

DeLay, Brian. *War of a Thousand Deserts: Indian Raids and the U.S.–Mexican War*. New Haven: Yale University Press, 2008.

Dugard, Martin. *The Training Ground: Grant, Lee, Sherman, and Davis in the Mexican War, 1846–1848*. New York: Little, Brown, 2008.

Eisenhower, John S. D. *So Far From God: The U.S. War with Mexico, 1846–1848*. New York: Random House, 1989.

Foos, Paul. *"A Short, Offhand, Killing Affair": Soldiers and Social Conflict during the Mexican-American War*. Chapel Hill: University of North Carolina Press, 2002.

Greenberg, Amy S. *Manifest Manhood and the Antebellum American Empire*. Cambridge: Cambridge University Press, 2006.

Heidler, David S., and Jeanne T. Heidler. *The Mexican War*. Westport, CT: Greenwood Press, 2006.

Henderson, Timothy J. *A Glorious Defeat: Mexico and its War with the United States*. New York: Hill and Wang, 2007.

Hietala, Thomas. *Manifest Design: American Exceptionalism and Empire*. Revised Edition. Ithaca: Cornell University Press, 2003.

Johannsen, Robert Walter. *To the Halls of the Montezumas: The Mexican War in the American Imagination*. New York: Oxford University Press, 1985.

Johnson, Timothy D. *Winfield Scott: The Quest for Military Glory*. Lawrence: University Press of Kansas, 1998.

McCaffrey, James M. *Army of Manifest Destiny: The American Soldier in the Mexican War, 1846–1848*. New York: New York University Press, 1992.

Pinheiro, John C. *Manifest Ambition: James K. Polk and Civil–Military Relations During the Mexican War*. Westport, CT: Greenwood Press, 2007.

Wiley, Peter Booth. *Yankees in the Land of the Gods: Commodore Perry and the Opening of Japan*. New York: Viking, 1990.

Winders, Richard Bruce. *Mr. Polk's Army: The American Military Experience in the Mexican War*. College Station: Texas A&M University Press, 1997.

of Congress. Senators and Representatives are therefore summoned to assemble at their respective chambers, at 12 o'clock, noon, on Thursday, the fourth day of July, next, then and there to consider and determine, such measures, as, in their wisdom, the public safety, and interest may seem to demand [...]

Whereas an insurrection against the Government of the United States has broken out in the States of South Carolina, Georgia, Alabama, Florida, Mississippi, Louisiana, and Texas, and the laws of the United States for the collection of the revenue can not be effectually executed therein conformably to that provision of the Constitution which requires duties to be uniform throughout the United States; and

Whereas a combination of persons engaged in such insurrection have threatened to grant pretended letters of marque to authorize the bearers thereof to commit assaults on the lives, vessels, and property of good citizens of the country lawfully engaged in commerce on the high seas and in waters of the United States; and

Whereas an Executive proclamation has been already issued requiring the persons engaged in these disorderly proceedings to desist there from, calling out a militia force for the purpose of repressing the same, and convening Congress in extraordinary session to deliberate and determine thereon:

Now, therefore, I, Abraham Lincoln, President of the United States, with a view to the same purposes before mentioned and to the protection of the public peace and the lives and property of quiet and orderly citizens pursuing their lawful occupations, until Congress shall have assembled and deliberated on the said unlawful proceedings or until the same shall have ceased, have further deemed it advisable to set on foot a blockade of the ports within the States aforesaid, in pursuance of the laws of the United States and of the law of nations in such case provided. For this purpose a competent force will be posted so as to prevent entrance and exit of vessels from the ports aforesaid. If, therefore, with a view to violate such blockade, a vessel shall approach or shall attempt to leave either of the said ports, she will be duly warned by the commander of one of the blockading vessels, who will indorse on her register the fact and date of such warning, and if the same vessel shall again attempt to enter or leave the blockaded port she will be captured and sent to the nearest convenient port for such proceedings against her and her cargo as prize as may be deemed advisable.

And I hereby proclaim and declare that if any person, under the pretended authority of the said States or under any other pretense, shall molest a vessel of the United States or the persons or cargo on board of her, such person will be held amenable to the laws of the United States for the prevention and punishment of piracy.

Source: Abraham Lincoln, "Proclamations," in *Life of Abraham Lincoln*, ed. Frank Crosby (Philadelphia: John E. Potter, 1865), 108–113.

Questions for Consideration

1) What, according to President Lincoln, were the "combinations too powerful" for control by state and local authorities?
2) How many militiamen did he call forth for immediate service to the federal government?
3) Why was he concerned about "pretended letters of marque" in 1861?

7.2 Julia Ward Howe Composes "The Battle Hymn of the Republic" (1862)

During the first year of fighting, military campaigns from Missouri to Virginia produced no decisive victories for either side. As the fighting became more protracted, it demanded the formation of massive armies. Eventually, attritional strategies required advances in battlefield logistics. Congress worked directly with Secretary of War Edwin Stanton to refine the federal "contract" system with businesses manufacturing military goods. Although the rebellion disrupted social life, the Union was not lost. From farms to factories, few songs expressed Northern solidarity more eloquently than "The Battle Hymn of the Republic." In fact, the melody derived from an old African American spiritual adopted by Methodists. Admirers of abolitionist John Brown invented graphic lyrics that claimed his body laid "mouldering in the grave," even as his soul continued "marching on." During October of 1861, Julia Ward Howe of Boston heard Massachusetts regiments singing it during her visit to a military camp in northern Virginia. Afterward, she composed her own version with words that linked the patriotic gore with divine providence. Soon, her martial song became a Union anthem. Blue-clad troops marched to the shouts of "glory" and found meaning in the apocalyptic motif. What began as a fight to preserve the Union soon became a war to end slavery.

Document

Mine eyes have seen the glory of the coming of the Lord:
He is trampling out the vintage where the grapes of wrath are stored;
He hath loosed the fateful lightning of His terrible swift sword:
　　　His truth is marching on.
　　　Glory, glory, hallelujah!
　　　Glory, glory, hallelujah!
　　　Glory, glory, hallelujah!
　　　His day is marching on.

I have seen Him in the watch-fires of a hundred circling camps,
They have builded Him an altar in the evening dews and damps;
I can read His righteous sentence by the dim and flaring lamps:
　　　His day is marching on.
　　　Glory, glory, hallelujah!
　　　Glory, glory, hallelujah!
　　　Glory, glory, hallelujah!
　　　His day is marching on.

I have read a fiery gospel writ in burnished rows of steel:
"As ye deal with my contemners, so with you my grace shall deal;

Let the Hero, born of woman, crush the serpent with his heel,
>Since God is marching on."
>Glory, glory, hallelujah!
>Glory, glory, hallelujah!
>Glory, glory, hallelujah!
>His day is marching on.

He has sounded forth the trumpet that shall never call retreat;
He is sifting out the hearts of men before His judgment-seat:
Oh, be swift, my soul, to answer Him! be jubilant, my feet!
>Our God is marching on.
>Glory, glory, hallelujah!
>Glory, glory, hallelujah!
>Glory, glory, hallelujah!
>His day is marching on.

In the beauty of the lilies Christ was born across the sea,
With a glory in his bosom that transfigures you and me:
As he died to make men holy, let us die to make men free,
>While God is marching on.
>Glory, glory, hallelujah!
>Glory, glory, hallelujah!
>Glory, glory, hallelujah!
>His day is marching on.

Source: Julia Ward Howe, "The Battle Hymn of the Republic," *Atlantic Monthly* 9 (February 1862): 145.

Questions for Consideration

1) What did Julia Ward Howe see in the "watch-fires" of the military camps?
2) Which verses allude to the martyrdom of soldiers?
3) Why do you think the hymn refers to "glory" during the chorus?

7.3 Samuel Dana Greene Operates an Ironclad (1862)

While the Army of the Potomac floundered on the Virginia peninsula, the U.S. Navy attempted to quarantine 3,500 miles of Southern coastline. According to the grand strategy of the "Anaconda Plan," the Union blockade of ports and rivers was likened to the coils of a suffocating snake strangling its victim into submission. The most famous maritime battle of the Civil War took place on March 9, 1862, near Hampton Roads, Virginia. It included ironclad warships, that is, steam-powered vessels protected with armored plating. The Confederate *Virginia*, which had been built from the hull of a burned-out steamship previously dubbed the *Merrimac*, clashed with the U.S.S. *Monitor*, which had been built according to an ingenious design by Swedish inventor John Ericsson. The latter ironclad possessed only two 11-inch cannons stationed on a rotating turret. Though outgunned, it was an incredibly mobile craft. Lieutenant Samuel Dana Greene, its executive officer, wrote a letter to his parents in which he praised the new technology. The first clash of the ironclads ended in a tactical draw, but the blockade of the Chesapeake Bay held. Whatever happened at Hampton Roads, Union ironclads played key roles in virtually all subsequent naval operations against Confederate warships, commerce raiders, and blockade runners.

Document

At four P.M. we passed Cape Henry, and heard heavy firing in the direction of Fortress Monroe. As we approached it increased, and we immediately cleared ship for action. When about half way between Fortress Monroe and Cape Henry, we spoke [with] the pilot-boat. He told us the *Cumberland* was sunk, and the *Congress* was on fire, and had surrendered to the *Merrimac*. We could not credit it at first, but as we approached Hampton Roads, we could see the fine old *Congress* burning brightly, and we then knew it must be true. Sadly, indeed, did we feel to think those two fine old vessels had gone to their last homes with so many of their brave crews. Our hearts were very full, and we vowed vengeance on the *Merrimac*, if it should ever be our lot to fall in with her [...]

At eight A.M. on Sunday, the *Merrimac* got under way, accompanied by several steamers, and started direct for the *Minnesota*. When a mile distant she fired two guns at her. By this time our anchor was up, the men at quarters, the guns loaded, and every thing ready for action. As the *Merrimac* came close, the captain passed the word to commence firing. I triced up the port, run out the gun, and fired the *first* gun, and thus commenced the great battle between the *Monitor* and the *Merrimac*.

Now mark the condition our men and officers were in. Since Friday morning, forty-eight hours, they had had no rest, and very little food, as we could not conveniently cook. They had been hard at work all night, and nothing to eat for breakfast, except hard bread, and were thoroughly worn out. As for myself, I had not slept a wink for fifty-one hours, and had been on my feet almost constantly. But after the first gun was fired we forgot all fatigues, hard work, and every thing else, and fought as hard as men ever fought. We loaded and fired as fast as we could. I pointed and fired the guns myself. Every shot I would ask the captain the effect, and the majority of them were encouraging. The captain was in the pilot-house, directing the movements of the vessel; Acting-master Stodder was stationed at the wheel which turns the tower, but as he could not manage it, was relieved by Steiners. The speaking trumpet from the tower to the pilot-house was broken, so we passed the word from the captain to myself on the berth deck by Paymaster Keeler and Captain's Clerk Toffey. Five times during the engagement we touched each other, and each time I fired a gun at her, and I will vouch the 168 pounds penetrated her sides. Once she tried to run us down with her iron prow, but did no damage whatever. After fighting for two hours we hauled off for half an hour to hoist shot in the tower. At it we went again as hard as we could, the shot, shell, grape, canister, musket and rifle balls flying in every direction, but doing no damage. Our tower was struck several times, and though the noise was pretty loud it did not affect us any.

Stodder and one of the men were carelessly leaning against the tower, when a shot struck it exactly opposite them and disabled them for an hour or two.

At about 11:30 A.M. the captain sent for me. I went forward, and there stood as noble a man as lives, at the foot of the ladder of the pilot-house, his face was perfectly black with powder and iron, and apparently perfectly blind. I asked him what was the matter. He said a shot had struck the pilot-house exactly opposite his eyes and blinded him, and he thought the pilot-house was damaged. He told me to take charge of the ship and use my own discretion. I led him to his room, laid him on the sofa, and then took his position. On examining the pilot-house, I found the iron hatch on top, on the forward side, was completely cracked through. We still continued firing, the tower being under the direction of Steiners. We were between two fires—the *Minnesota* on one side, and the *Merrimac* on the other. The latter was retreating to Sewall's Point, and the *Minnesota* had struck us twice on the tower. I knew if another shot should strike our pilot-house in the same place, our steering apparatus would be disabled, and we should be at the mercy of the batteries on Sewall's Point. We had strict orders to act on the defensive, and protect the *Minnesota*.

We had evidently finished the *Merrimac* as far as the *Minnesota* was concerned. Our pilot-house was damaged, and we had strict orders *not* to follow the *Merrimac* up; therefore, after the *Merrimac* had retreated, I went to the *Minnesota* and remained by her until she was afloat. General [John] Wool and Secretary [Gustavus] Fox both commended me for acting as I did, and said it was the strict military plan to follow. This was the reason we did not sink the *Merrimac*; and every one here, capable of judging, says we acted perfectly right.

The fight was over now, and we were victorious.

Source: Lydia Minturn Post, ed., *Soldiers' Letters from Camp, Battle-field and Prison* (New York: Bunce & Huntington, 1865), 106–115.

Questions for Consideration

1) What, according to Lieutenant Greene, was the condition of the *Monitor*'s crew when the battle commenced?
2) How was the *Monitor*'s captain injured in the battle?
3) Why did the *Monitor* allow the *Merrimac* to retreat from Hampton Roads afterwards?

7.4   Francis Lieber Promulgates Rules for War (1863)

Given the scale and the scope of Union military operations, the Lincoln administration grew concerned about the conduct of the war. A combination of political prudence and moral realism inspired General Orders No. 100, or the Lieber Code. It was named for its drafter, Dr. Francis Lieber, a professor of law at Columbia College in New York and a renowned German-American jurist. On April 24, 1863, the War Department disseminated his "Instructions for the Government of Armies of the United States in the Field." Among other things, it addressed martial law, military jurisdiction, and the treatment of spies and deserters. Specifically, it forbade killing prisoners of war, except in such cases that the survival of the soldiers holding them appeared in jeopardy. The greatest theoretical contribution of the Lieber Code, however, was the identification of "military necessity" as a general legal principle governing violence in wartime. Consequently, the influence of the principle extended well beyond combatants in the Civil War. It offered a precursor to the proceedings of the first Geneva Convention, which promulgated rules for the treatment of the sick and the wounded in 1864. Informing the Brussels Declaration of 1874 and the Hague Regulations of 1899 and 1907, it eventually became the foundation for the international laws regarding land warfare during the twentieth century.

Document

Art. 14. Military necessity, as understood by modern civilized nations, consists in the necessity of those measures which are indispensable for securing the ends of the war, and which are lawful according to the modern law and usages of war.

Art. 15. Military necessity admits of all direct destruction of life or limb of armed enemies, and of other persons whose destruction is incidentally unavoidable in the armed contests of the war; it allows of the capturing of every armed enemy, and every enemy of importance to the hostile government, or of peculiar danger to the captor; it allows of all destruction of property, and obstruction of the ways and channels of traffic, travel, or communication, and of all withholding of sustenance or means of life from the enemy; of the appropriation of whatever an enemy's country affords necessary for the subsistence and safety of the army, and of such deception as does not involve the breaking of good faith either positively pledged, regarding agreements entered into during the war, or supposed by the modern law of war to exist. Men who take up arms against one another in public war do not cease on this account to be moral beings, responsible to one another and to God.

Art. 16. Military necessity does not admit of cruelty—that is, the infliction of suffering for the sake of suffering or for revenge, nor of maiming or wounding except in fight, nor of torture to extort confessions. It does not admit of the use of poison in any way, nor of the wanton devastation of a district. It admits of deception, but disclaims acts of perfidy; and, in general, military necessity does not include any act of hostility which makes the return to peace unnecessarily difficult.

Art. 17. War is not carried on by arms alone. It is lawful to starve the hostile belligerent, armed or unarmed, so that it leads to the speedier subjection of the enemy.

Art. 18. When a commander of a besieged place expels the noncombatants, in order to lessen the number of those who consume his stock of provisions, it is lawful, though an extreme measure, to drive them back, so as to hasten on the surrender.

Art. 19. Commanders, whenever admissible, inform the enemy of their intention to bombard a place, so that the noncombatants, and especially the women and children, may be removed before the bombardment commences. But it is no infraction of the common law of war to omit thus to inform the enemy. Surprise may be a necessity.

Art. 20. Public war is a state of armed hostility between sovereign nations or governments. It is a law and requisite of civilized existence that men live in political, continuous societies, forming organized units, called states or nations, whose constituents bear, enjoy, suffer, advance, and retrograde together, in peace and in war.

Art. 21. The citizen or native of a hostile country is thus an enemy, as one of the constituents of the hostile state or nation, and as such is subjected to the hardships of the war.

Art. 22. Nevertheless, as civilization has advanced during the last centuries, so has likewise steadily advanced, especially in war on land, the distinction between the private individual belonging to a hostile country and the hostile country itself, with its men in arms. The principle has been more and more acknowledged that the unarmed citizen is to be spared in person, property, and honor as much as the exigencies of war will admit.

Art. 23. Private citizens are no longer murdered, enslaved, or carried off to distant parts, and the inoffensive individual is as little disturbed in his private relations as the commander of the hostile troops can afford to grant in the overruling demands of a vigorous war.

Art. 24. The almost universal rule in remote times was, and continues to be with barbarous armies, that the private individual of the hostile country is destined to suffer every privation of liberty and protection, and every disruption of family ties. Protection was, and still is with uncivilized people, the exception.

Art. 25. In modern regular wars of the Europeans, and their descendants in other portions of the globe, protection of the inoffensive citizen of the hostile country is the rule; privation and disturbance of private relations are the exceptions.

Source: "General Orders No. 100, 24 April 1863," *The Miscellaneous Writings of Francis Lieber*, Volume 2 (Philadelphia: J. B. Lippincott, 1881), 245–253.

Questions for Consideration

1) How did the Lieber Code define "military necessity" for armed forces during wartime?
2) When could a commander lawfully expel enemy noncombatants from a besieged place?
3) Do you agree with the assertion in Article 25?

7.5 Joshua Lawrence Chamberlain Defends Little Round Top (1863)

During 1863, Confederate leaders decided upon a risky strategy to entice foreign intervention. The Army of Northern Virginia under the command of General Robert E. Lee moved northward that summer. At the crossroads town of Gettysburg, Pennsylvania, Lee faced the Army of the Potomac under the command of General George Meade. Neither side planned for the greatest land battle in the history of North America, which raged from July 1 to July 3. On the second day of battle, Lee sent a Confederate corps on a coordinated move against the Union left flank. Colonel Strong Vincent, who was mortally wounded, led a Union brigade with four small regiments on high ground known as Little Round Top. In command of the 20th Maine Regiment was a 33-year-old college professor, Colonel Joshua Lawrence Chamberlain, who defended the hill against Alabama and Texas regiments. Both sides opened a brisk fire at close range, as smoke enveloped the steep, rocky slopes. The fighting surged back and forth five times,

Chamberlain reported, but the soldiers from Maine "refused the line." The federal position at Little Round Top was saved by one of the finest small-unit actions of the Civil War. After three days of fighting, the Battle of Gettysburg produced a Union victory.

Document

Somewhere near 4 p.m. a sharp cannonade, at some distance to our left and front, was the signal for a sudden and rapid movement of our whole division in the direction of this firing, which grew warmer as we approached. Passing an open field in the hollow ground in which some of our batteries were going into position, our brigade reached the skirt of a piece of woods, in the farther edge of which there was a heavy musketry fire, and when about to go forward into line we received from Colonel Vincent, commanding the brigade, orders to move to the left at the double-quick, when we took a farm road crossing Plum Run in order to gain a rugged mountain spur called Granite Spur, or Little Round Top.

The enemy's artillery got range of our column as we were climbing the spur, and the crashing of the shells among the rocks and the tree tops made us move lively along the crest. One or two shells burst in our ranks. Passing to the southern slope of Little Round Top, Colonel Vincent indicated to me the ground my regiment was to occupy, informing me that this was the extreme left of our general line, and that a desperate attack was expected in order to turn that position, concluding by telling me I was to "hold that ground at all hazards." This was the last word I heard from him.

In order to commence by making my right firm, I formed my regiment on the right into line, giving such direction to the line as should best secure the advantage of the rough, rocky, and straggling wooded ground.

The line faced generally toward a more conspicuous eminence southwest of ours, which is known as Sugar Loaf, or Round Top. Between this and my position intervened a smooth and thinly wooded hollow. My line formed, I immediately detached Company B, Captain Morrill commanding, to extend from my left flank across this hollow as a line of skirmishers, with directions to act as occasion might dictate, to prevent a surprise on my exposed flank and rear [...]

The enemy seemed to have gathered all their energies for their final assault. We had gotten our thin line into as good a shape as possible, when a strong force emerged from the scrub wood in the valley, as well as I could judge, in two lines in echelon by the right, and, opening a heavy fire, the first line came on as if they meant to sweep everything before them. We opened on them as well as we could with our scanty ammunition snatched from the field.

It did not seem possible to withstand another shock like this now coming on. Our loss had been severe. One-half of my left wing had fallen, and a third of my regiment lay just behind us, dead or badly wounded. At this moment my anxiety was increased by a great roar of musketry in my rear, on the farther or northerly slope of Little Round Top, apparently on the flank of the regular brigade, which was in support of Hazlett's battery on the crest behind us. The bullets from this attack struck into my left rear, and I feared that the enemy might have nearly surrounded the Little Round Top, and only a desperate chance was left for us. My ammunition was soon exhausted. My men were firing their last shot and getting ready to club their muskets.

It was imperative to strike before we were struck by this overwhelming force in a hand-to-hand fight, which we could not probably have withstood or survived. At that crisis, I ordered the bayonet. The word was enough. It ran like fire along the line, from man to man, and rose into a shout, with which they sprang forward upon the enemy, now not 30 yards away. The effect was surprising; many of the enemy's first line threw down their arms and surrendered. An officer fired his pistol at my head with one hand, while he handed me his sword with the other. Holding fast by our right, and swinging forward our left, we made an extended right wheel, before which the enemy's second line broke and fell back, fighting from tree to tree, many being captured, until we had swept the valley and cleared the front of nearly our entire brigade.

Meantime Captain Morrill with his skirmishers sent out from my left flank, with some dozen or fifteen of the U.S. Sharpshooters who had put themselves under his direction, fell upon the enemy as they were breaking, and by his demonstrations, as well as his well-directed fire, added much to the effect of the charge.

Having thus cleared the valley and driven the enemy up the western slope of the Great Round Top, not wishing to press so far out as to hazard the ground I was to hold by leaving it exposed to a sudden rush of the enemy, I succeeded (although with some effort to stop my men, who declared they were "on the road to Richmond") in getting the regiment into good order and resuming our original position.

Four hundred prisoners, including two field and several line officers, were sent to the rear. These were mainly from the Fifteenth and Forty-seventh Alabama Regiments, with some of the Fourth and Fifth Texas. One hundred and fifty of the enemy were found killed and wounded in our front.

Source: Report of Col. Joshua L. Chamberlain, Twentieth Maine Infantry, 6 July 1863, in *War of the Rebellion: A Compilation of the Official Records of the Union and Confederate Armies*, 4 Series, 128 Volumes (Washington, DC: Government Printing Office, 1889), series 1, volume 27, part 1, chapter 39: 622–626.

Questions for Consideration

1) Who, according to Colonel Chamberlain, ordered him to "hold that ground at all hazards" in the battle?
2) What fraction of his regiment did he estimate were dead or wounded?
3) Why did he believe that it was imperative to strike the enemy with bayonets?

7.6   Sam R. Watkins Survives Chickamauga (1863)

As the Civil War widened, the Western theater of operations extended from the Appalachian Mountains to the Mississippi River. Donning the Confederate uniform in early 1861, 21-year-old Sam R. Watkins of Columbia, Tennessee, marched into battle as a private in Company H, First Tennessee Regiment. He survived the Battle of Chickamauga, which began on September 19, 1863. Named for a creek flowing into the Tennessee River, the two-day battle near Chattanooga was the most jarring Union defeat in the Western theater. Once Union reinforcements arrived, however, the Confederates eventually lost control of the battlefield at Missionary Ridge. By smashing the Confederate Army of Tennessee, the Federal Military Division of the Mississippi opened the door for an invasion of the Deep South. Twenty years later, Watkins crafted a remarkable narrative that balanced the tragedy of combat with a sense of humor. His words testified to courage, camaraderie, and compassion in the midst of danger, death, and destruction. Of the 120 enlisted men in so-called "Co. Aytch," he was one of only seven to survive it all. According to his recollections, he held fast to the hope that he would return home to marry his sweetheart, Jennie. They married after the war, and they raised eight children. Watkins died on July 20, 1901.

Document

We camped on the banks of Chickamauga on Friday night, and Saturday morning we commenced to cross over. About twelve o'clock we had crossed. No sooner had we crossed than an order came to double quick. General [Nathan Bedford] Forrest's cavalry had opened the battle. Even then the spent balls were falling amongst us with that peculiar thud so familiar to your old soldier.

Double quick! There seemed to be no rest for us. Forrest is needing reinforcements. Double quick, close up in the rear! *siz, siz,* double quick, *boom,* hurry up, *bang, bang, a rattle de bang, bang, siz, boom, boom, boom,* hurry up, double quick, *boom, bang,* halt, front, right dress, *boom, boom,* and three soldiers are killed and twenty wounded. Billy Webster's arm was torn out by the roots, and he was killed, and a fragment of shell buried itself in Jim McEwin's side, also killing Mr. Fain King, a conscript from Mount Pleasant. Forward, guide center, march, charge bayonets, fire at will, commence firing. We debouched through the woods, firing as we marched, the Yankee line about two hundred yards off. *Bang, bang, siz, siz.* It was a sort of running fire. We kept up a constant fire as we advanced. In ten minutes we were face to face with the foe. It was but a question as to who could load and shoot the fastest. The army was not up. [General Braxton] Bragg was not ready for a general battle.

The big battle was fought the next day, Sunday. We held our position for two hours and ten minutes in the midst of a deadly and galling fire, being enfiladed and almost surrounded, when General Forrest galloped up and said, "Colonel Field, look out, you are almost surrounded; you had better fall back." The order was given to retreat. I ran through a solid line of blue coats. As I fell back, they were upon the right of us, they were upon the left of us, they were in front of us, they were in the rear of us. It was a perfect hornets' nest. The balls whistled around our ears like the escape valves of ten thousand engines. The woods seemed to be blazing; everywhere, at every jump, would rise a lurking foe. But to get up and dust was all we could do. I was running along by the side of Bob Stout. General Preston Smith stopped me and asked if our brigade was falling back. I told him it was. He asked me the second time if it was Maney's brigade that was falling back. I told him it was. I heard him call out, "Attention, forward!" One solid sheet of leaden hail was falling around me. I heard General Preston Smith's brigade open. It seemed to be platoons of artillery. The earth jarred and trembled like an earthquake. Deadly missiles were flying in every direction. It was the very incarnation of death itself. I could almost hear the shriek of the death angel passing over the scene. General Smith was killed in ten minutes after I saw him. Bob Stout and myself stopped. Said I, "Bob, you weren't killed, as you expected." He did not reply, for at that very moment a solid shot from the Federal guns struck him between the waist and the hip, tearing off one leg and scattering his bowels all over the ground. I heard him shriek out, "O, O, God!" His spirit had flown before his body struck the ground. Farewell, friend; we will meet over yonder.

When the cannon ball struck Billy Webster, tearing his arm out of the socket, he did not die immediately, but as we were advancing to the attack, we left him and the others lying where they fell upon the battlefield; but when we fell back to the place where we had left our knapsacks, Billy's arm had been dressed by Dr. Buist, and he seemed to be quite easy. He asked Jim Fogey to please write a letter to his parents at home. He wished to dictate the letter. He asked me to please look in his knapsack and get him a clean shirt, and said that he thought he would feel better if he could get rid of the blood that was upon him. I went to hunt for his knapsack and found it, but when I got back to where he was, poor, good Billy Webster was dead. He had given his life to his country. His spirit is with the good and brave. No better or braver man than Billy Webster ever drew the breath of life. His bones lie yonder today, upon the battlefield of Chickamauga. I loved him; he was my friend. Many and many a dark night have Billy and I stood together upon the silent picket post. Ah, reader, my heart grows sick, and I feel sad while I try to write my recollections of that unholy and uncalled for war. But He that ruleth the heavens doeth all things well.

We remained upon the battlefield of Chickamauga all night. Everything had fallen into our hands. We had captured a great many prisoners and small arms, and many pieces of artillery and wagons and provisions. The Confederate and Federal dead, wounded, and dying were everywhere scattered over the battlefield. Men were lying where they fell, shot in every conceivable part of the body. Some with their entrails torn out and still hanging to them and piled up on the ground beside them, and they still alive. Some with their under jaw torn off, and hanging by a fragment of skin to their cheeks, with their tongues lolling from their mouth, and they trying to talk. Some with both eyes shot out, with one eye hanging down on their cheek. In fact, you might walk over the battlefield and find men shot from the crown of the head to the tip end of the toe. And then to see all those dead, wounded and dying horses, their heads and tails drooping, and they seeming to be so intelligent as if they comprehended everything. I felt like shedding a tear for those innocent dumb brutes.

Reader, a battlefield, after the battle, is a sad and sorrowful sight to look at. The glory of war is but the glory of battle, the shouts, and cheers, and victory.

A soldier's life is not a pleasant one. It is always, at best, one of privations and hardships. The emotions of patriotism and pleasure hardly counterbalance the toil and suffering that he has to undergo in order to enjoy his patriotism and pleasure. Dying on the field of battle and glory is about the easiest duty a soldier has to undergo. It is the living, marching, fighting, shooting soldier that has the hardships of war to carry. When a brave soldier is killed, he is at rest. The living soldier knows not at what moment he, too, may be called on to lay down his life on the altar of his country. The dead are heroes, the living are but men compelled to do the drudgery and suffer the privations incident to the thing called "glorious war."

We rested on our arms where the battle ceased. All around us everywhere were the dead and wounded, lying scattered over the ground, and in many places piled in heaps. Many a sad and heart-rending scene did I witness upon this battlefield of Chickamauga. Our men died the death of heroes. I sometimes think that surely our brave men have not died in vain. It is true, our cause is lost, but a people who loved those brave and noble heroes should ever cherish their memory as men who died for them. I shed a tear over their memory. They gave their all to their country. Abler pens than mine must write their epitaphs and tell of their glories and heroism. I am but a poor writer, at best, and only try to tell of the events that I saw.

Source: Sam R. Watkins, *Co. Aytch, Maury Grays, First Tennessee Regiment; or, A Side Show of the Big Show* (Chattanooga, TN: Times Printing Co., 1900), 77–96.

Questions for Consideration

1) How long did it take Private Watkins to "double quick" through the woods while firing?
2) What did he believe was the "easiest duty a soldier has to undergo" during war?
3) Why do you think he so vividly recalled the death of Billy Webster?

7.7   James Henry Gooding Protests Unequal Pay (1863)

Military commanders contemplated the fate of what General Benjamin Butler called "the contraband of war." The phrase described chattel slaves, who came into the possession of Union armies invading the South. Consequently, they gave the Union the double advantage of taking a labor force away from the Confederacy and, in turn, employing the freed laborers against their former masters. Once the Emancipation Proclamation took effect on January 1, 1863, black enlistments in the armed forces surged. Placed under the command of white officers, black soldiers encountered prejudice at nearly every turn. They served in segregated regiments, inherited degrading assignments, and received lower pay—$10 per month in contrast to the standard $13. When captured in combat, they faced mistreatment and even death at the hands of Confederates. A corporal in the 54th Massachusetts Infantry, James Henry Gooding protested the unequal pay earned by African Americans in the Union army. On September 28, 1863, he wrote a letter to President Lincoln while at Morris Island, South Carolina. Even though his regiment eventually received their due compensation, Gooding did not. Wounded at the Battle of Olustee in Florida, he was seized by Confederate troops. He died inside a prisoner of war camp on July 19, 1864.

Document

Your Excellency, Abraham Lincoln:

Your Excellency will pardon the presumption of a humble individual like myself in addressing you, but the earnest solicitation of my comrades in arms, besides the genuine interest felt by myself in the matter, is my excuse for placing before the executive head of the nation our common grievance.

On the 6th of the last month, the paymaster of the department informed us that if we would decide to receive the sum of $10 (ten dollars) per month, he would come and pay us that sum, but that, on the sitting of Congress, the regiment would, in his opinion, be allowed the other $3 (three). He did not give us any guarantee that this would be as he hoped; certainly *he* had no authority for making such guarantee, and we cannot suppose him acting in any way interested.

Now the main question is, are we *soldiers* or are we *laborers*? We are fully armed and equipped; have done all the various duties pertaining to a soldier's life; have conducted ourselves to the complete satisfaction of general officers who were, if any, prejudiced *against* us, but who now accord us all the encouragement and honor due us; have shared the perils and labor of reducing the first stronghold that flaunted a traitor flag; and more, Mr. President, today the Anglo-Saxon mother, wife, or sister are not alone in tears for departed sons, husbands, and brothers. The patient, trusting descendants of Africa's clime have dyed the ground with blood in defense of the Union and democracy. Men, too, Your Excellency, who know in a measure the cruelties of the iron heel of oppression, which, in years gone by, the very power their blood is now being spilled to maintain, ever ground them to the dust.

But when the war trumpet sounded o'er the land, when men knew not the friend from the traitor, the black man laid his life at the altar of the nation—and he was refused. When the arms of the Union were beaten, in the first year of the war, and the executive called for more food for its ravaging maw, again the black man begged the privilege of aiding his country in her need—to be again refused.

And now he is in the war, and how has he conducted himself? Let their dusky forms rise up out of the mires of James Island and give the answer. Let the rich mold around Wagner's parapets be upturned, and there will be found an eloquent answer. Obedient and patient and solid as a well are they. All we lack is a paler hue and a better acquaintance with the alphabet. Now, your Excellency, we have done a soldier's duty.

Why can't we have a soldier's pay? You caution the Rebel chieftain that the United States knows no distinction in her soldiers. She insists on having all her soldiers of what-ever creed and color to be treated according to the usages of war. Now, if the United States exacts uniformity of treatment of her soldiers from the insurgents, would it not be well and consistent to set the example herself by paying all her *soldiers* alike?

We of this regiment were not enlisted under any "contraband" act. But we do not wish to be understood as rating our service of more value to the government than the service of the ex-slave. Their service *is* undoubtedly worth much to the nation, but Congress made express provision touching their case, as slaves freed by military necessity, and assuming the government to be their temporary guardian. Now so with us. Freemen by birth and consequently having the advantage of *thinking* and acting for ourselves so far as the laws would allow us, we do not consider ourselves fit subjects for the contraband act.

We appeal to you, sir, as the executive of the nation, to have us justly dealt with. The regiment do pray that they be assured their service will be fairly appreciated by paying them as American *soldiers*, not as menial hirelings. Black men, you may well know, are poor; $3 per month, for a year, will supply their needy wives and assure us our whole pay, we are content. Our patriotism, our enthusiasm will have a new impetus to exert our energy more and more to aid our country. Not that our hearts ever flagged in devotion, spite the evident apathy displayed in our behalf, but we feel as though our country spurned us, now we are sworn to serve her. Please give this a moment's attention.

Source: Corporal James Henry Gooding to Abraham Lincoln, 28 September 1863, Letters Received, Series 360, Colored Troops Division, Adjutant General's Office, Record Group 94, National Archives and Records Administration.

Questions for Consideration

1) What was Corporal Gooding's primary argument for receiving equal pay?
2) To what extent did he speak for all African Americans fighting in the Civil War?
3) How do you suppose President Lincoln would have answered his question: "Are we soldiers or are we laborers"?

7.8   Robert E. Lee Requests Additional Troops (1864)

During the first three years of the Civil War, the Army of Northern Virginia conducted successful defensive operations. In two of his finest campaigns, General Lee prevailed at the Battle of Fredericksburg and the Battle of Chancellorsville. However, both of his campaigns to invade the North ended in failure. Though narrowly escaping annihilation at the Battle of Antietam and at the Battle of Gettysburg, he withdrew his army to fight another day. Even if he was a great tactician, General Lee's strategic decision to neglect the Western theater left the Confederacy vulnerable. After the Union army captured Atlanta on September 2, 1864, General William T. Sherman ordered his troops to march overland to Savannah. Remaining in the Eastern theater, General Lee conducted a war of attrition that he could not win. The Union absorbed heavy casualties, to be sure, but the Confederates simply did not have the manpower reserves to replace the losses. They held fast to the notion that the bloodshed would turn voters against the war that fall. In a dispatch to Confederate President Jefferson Davis on September 2, 1864, General Lee even asked to recruit slaves if they would help to defend the Confederacy. With hope waning, he worried about the fate of his vastly outnumbered and poorly supplied troops.

Document

As matters now stand, we have no troops disposable to meet movements of the enemy or strike when opportunity presents, without taking them from the trenches and exposing some important point. The enemy's position enables him to move his troops to the right or left without our knowledge until he has reached the point at which he aims, and we are then compelled to hurry our men to meet him, incurring the risk of being too late to check his progress, and the additional risk of the advantage he may derive from their absence. This was fully illustrated in the late demonstration north of the James River, which called troops from our lines here who, if present, might have prevented the occupation of the Weldon Railroad. These rapid and distant movements also fatigue and exhaust our men, greatly impairing their efficiency in battle. It is not necessary, however, to enumerate all the reasons for recruiting our ranks.

The necessity is as well known to Your Excellency as to myself, and as much the object of your solicitude. The means of obtaining men for field duty, as far as I can see, are only three. A considerable number could be placed in the ranks by relieving all able-bodied white men employed as teamsters, cooks, mechanics, and laborers, and supplying their places with negroes. I think measures should be taken at once to substitute negroes for whites in every place in the army or connected with it where the former can be used. It seems to me that we must choose between employing negroes ourselves and having them employed against us. A thorough and vigorous inspection of the rolls of exempted and detailed men is in my opinion of immediate importance. I think you will agree with me that no man should be excused from service for any reason not deemed sufficient to entitle one already in service to his discharge. I do not think that the decision of such questions can be made so well by any as by those whose experience with troops has made them acquainted with the urgent claims to relief which are constantly brought to the attention of commanding officers, but which they are forced to deny. For this reason I would recommend that the rolls of exempts and details in each State be inspected by officers of character and influence who have had experience in the field and have had nothing to do with the exemptions and details. If all that I have heard be true, I think it will be found that very different rules of action have been pursued toward men in service and those liable to it in the matter of exemptions and details, and I respectfully recommend that Your Excellency cause reports to be made by the enrolling bureau of the number of men enrolled in each State, the number sent to the field, and the number exempted or detailed. I regard this matter as of the utmost moment.

Our ranks are constantly diminishing by battle and disease, and few recruits are received. The consequences are inevitable, and I feel confident that the time has come when no man capable of bearing arms should be excused unless it be for some controlling reason of public necessity. The safety of the country requires this, in my judgment, and hardship to individuals must be disregarded in view of the calamity that would follow to the whole people if our armies meet with disaster. No detail of an arms-bearing man should be continued or granted except for the performance of duty that is indispensable to the army, and that cannot be performed by one not liable to or fit for service. Agricultural details take numbers from the army without any corresponding advantage. I think that the interests of land-owners and cultivators may be relied upon to induce them to provide means for saving their crops if they be sent to the field. If they remain at home, their produce will only benefit the enemy, as our armies will be insufficient to defend them. If the officers and men detailed in the conscript bureau have performed their duties faithfully, they must have already brought out the chief part of those liable to duty, and have nothing to do now except to get such as from time to time reach military age. If this be true, many of these officers and men can be spared to the army. If not, they have been derelict, and should be sent back to the ranks, and their places supplied by others who will be more active. Such a policy will stimulate the energy of this class of men.

The last resource is the reserve force. Men of this class can render great service in connection with regular troops by taking their places in trenches, forts, etc., and leaving them free for active operations. I think no time should be lost in bringing out the entire strength of this class, particularly in Virginia and North Carolina. If I had the reserves of Virginia to hold the trenches here, or even to man those below Richmond on the north side of the river, they would render greater service than they can in any other way. They would give me a force to act with on the offensive or defensive, as might be necessary, without weakening any part of our lines. Their mere presence in the works below Richmond would prevent the enemy from making feints in that quarter to draw troops from here, except in such force as to endanger his own lines around Petersburg. But I feel confident that with vigorous effort, and an understanding on the part of the people of the necessity of the case, we could get more of this class than enough for the purpose last indicated. We could make our regular troops here available in the field. The same remarks are applicable to the reserves of North Carolina, who could render similar services at Wilmington, and allow the regular troops to take the field against any force that might land there. I need not remind Your Excellency that the reserves are of great value in connection with our regular troops to prevent disaster, but would be of little avail to retrieve it. For this reason they should be put in service before the numerical superiority of the enemy enables him to inflict a damaging blow upon the regular forces opposed to him. In my opinion the necessity for them will never be more urgent or their services of greater value than now. And I entertain the same views as to the importance of immediately bringing into the regular service every man liable to military duty. It will be too late to do so after our armies meet with disaster, should such, unfortunately, be the case.

Source: Robert E. Lee to Jefferson Davis, 2 September 1864, in *Memoirs of Robert E. Lee: His Military and Personal History*, ed. Armistead L. Long and Marcus J. Wright (New York: J. M. Stoddart and Company, 1887), 658–660.

Questions for Consideration

1) Which officers, according to General Lee, should inspect each state's rolls of "exempts and details"?
2) What did he consider to be his "last resource" to defend Richmond?
3) Why did he believe that enslaved people would "substitute" for soldiers in the Confederate army?

7.9 Phoebe Yates Pember Nurses at Chimborazo (1864)

The Civil War mobilized a volunteer network of devout civilians to provide essential services to Americans in uniform. Noncombatants volunteered to wash clothes, monitor sanitation, deliver supplies, brew coffee, distribute food, drive ambulances, and treat casualties. Hospitals called "infirmaries" were opened by communities, although many wounded died before reaching them. Thousands of nurses also toiled in field hospitals. They encountered piles of arms and legs left outside tents. They heard the deafening cries of the wounded and smelled the sickening odors of flesh. They challenged the norms of Victorian womanhood by entering the masculine world of military affairs. Mary Edwards Walker worked as a field surgeon for the 52nd Ohio Infantry, becoming the first woman to receive the Medal of Honor. Although outnumbered and less organized than their Northern counterparts, Confederate women rendered services as well. In Richmond, Virginia, Phoebe Yates Pember was a "matron" of the hospital wards of Chimborazo. Her memoirs described widespread demoralization during 1864, when food, medicine, and supplies were exhausted. She alluded to the mistreatment of war prisoners, including those held in the federal camps of the North as well as in the Confederate stockade at Andersonville, Georgia. With their territory mostly overrun and their economy largely ruined, Confederates began to recognize that their "cause" was lost.

Document

Can any pen or pencil do justice to those squalid pictures of famine and desolation? Those gaunt, lank skeletons with the dried yellow flesh clinging to bones enlarged by dampness and exposure? Those pale, bluish lips and feverish eyes, glittering and weird when contrasted with the famine-stricken faces—that flitting, piteous, scared smile which greeted their fellow creatures, all will live forever before the mental vision that then witnessed it.

Living and dead were taken from the flag-of-truce boat, not distinguishable save from the difference of care exercised in moving them. The Federal prisoners we had released were in many instances in a like state, but our ports had been blockaded, our harvests burned, our cattle stolen, our country wasted. Even had we felt the desire to succor, where could the wherewithal have been found? But the foe—the ports of the world were open to him. He could have fed his prisoners upon milk and honey, and not have missed either.

When we review the past, it would seem that Christianity was but a name—that the Atonement had failed, and Christ had lived and died in vain.

But it was no time then for vague reflections. With beating heart, throbbing head and icy hands I went among this army of martyrs and specters whom it was almost impossible to recognize as human beings; powerless to speak to them, choking with unavailing pity, but still striving to aid and comfort. There was but little variety of appearance. From bed to bed the same picture met the eye. Hardly a vestige of human appearance left.

The passion of sympathy could only impede my efforts if yielded to, for my hand shook too tremulously even to allow me to put the small morsels of bread soaked in wine into their mouths. It was all we dared to give at first. Some laid as if dead with limbs extended, but the greater part had drawn up their knees to an acute angle, a position they never changed until they died. Their more fortunate comrades said that the attitude was generally assumed, as it reduced the pangs of hunger and relieved the craving that gnawed them by day and by night. The Federal prisoners may have been starved at the South, we cannot deny the truth of the charge, in many instances; but we starved with them; we had only a little to share with any—but the subject had better be left to die in silence.

One among them lingered in patience the usual three days that appeared to be their allotted space of life on their return. He was a Marylander, heir to a name renowned in the history of his country, the last of seven sons reared in affluence, but presenting the same bluish, bloodless appearance common to them all. Hoping that there would be some chance of his rallying, I gave him judicious nursing and good brandy. Every precaution was taken, but the third day fever supervened and the little life left waned rapidly. He gave me the trinkets cut from *gutta percha* buttons that he had beguiled his captivity in making at Point Lookout, to send to his family, handing me one of them for a souvenir; begged that he might be buried apart from the crowd in some spot where those who knew and cared for him might find him some day, and quietly slept himself to death that night [...]

There is one subject connected with hospitals on which a few words should be said— the distasteful one that a woman must lose a certain amount of delicacy and reticence in filling any office in them. How can this be? There is no unpleasant exposure under proper arrangements, and if even there be, the circumstances which surround a wounded man, far from friends and home, suffering in a holy cause and dependent upon a woman for help, care and sympathy, hallow and clear the atmosphere in which she labors. That woman must indeed be hard and gross, who lets one material thought lessen her efficiency. In the midst of suffering and death, hoping with those almost beyond hope in this world; praying by the bedside of the lonely and heart-stricken; closing the eyes of boys hardly old enough to realize man's sorrows, much less suffer by man's fierce hate, a woman *must* soar beyond the conventional modesty considered correct under different circumstances.

If the ordeal does not chasten and purify her nature, if the contemplation of suffering and endurance does not make her wiser and better, and if the daily fire through which she passes does not draw from her nature the sweet fragrance of benevolence, charity, and love—then, indeed a hospital has been no fit place for her!

Source: Phoebe Yates Pember, *A Southern Woman's Story* (New York: G. W. Carleton & Co., 1879), 120–123, 191–192.

Questions for Consideration

1) How did Pember explain the "state" of the prisoners released by the Confederates?
2) In what ways did she suffer along with her patients at Chimborazo?
3) Why did she say that a woman must "soar beyond the conventional modesty" inside a military hospital?

7.10   Ulysses S. Grant Prevails at Appomattox (1865)

Ulysses S. Grant officially became General in Chief of all Union armies on March 9, 1864. Elevated because of his success in the Western theater, General Grant waged a form of total warfare that destroyed the Confederacy. From May to June in 1864, he concentrated his forces on an overland march into Virginia. His Wilderness campaign produced high casualties, but he relentlessly advanced against Lee's army. At Cold Harbor, thousands of Union soldiers charged the line and died in minutes. However, Grant continued maneuvering his corps toward Lee's flank, turning toward Richmond that summer. The Confederates entrenched near the Appomattox River at Petersburg, which became the central point for combat operations until the next spring. When Grant launched an assault on April 2, 1865, Lee finally abandoned the trenches. Encircled by columns of Union cavalrymen, Lee decided to surrender to Grant at Appomattox Court House. Inside Wilmer McLean's house, they met face-to-face on April 9. Confederate holdouts capitulated over the next few months, when the era of Reconstruction began. After serving two terms as President of the United States, Grant penned his memoirs while virtually destitute. Terminally ill with throat cancer, he finished writing the book just a few days before dying in 1885.

Document

When I had left camp that morning I had not expected so soon the result that was then taking place, and consequently was in rough garb. I was without a sword, as I usually was when on horseback on the field, and wore a soldier's blouse for a coat, with the shoulder straps of my rank to indicate to the army who I was. When I went into the house I found General Lee. We greeted each other, and after shaking hands took our seats. I had my staff with me, a good portion of whom were in the room during the whole of the interview.

What General Lee's feelings were I do not know. As he was a man of much dignity, with an impassible face, it was impossible to say whether he felt inwardly glad that the end had finally come, or felt sad over the result, and was too manly to show it. Whatever his feelings, they were entirely concealed from my observation; but my own feelings, which had been quite jubilant on the receipt of his letter, were sad and depressed. I felt like anything rather than rejoicing at the downfall of a foe who had fought so long and valiantly, and had suffered so much for a cause, though that cause was, I believe, one of the worst for which a people ever fought, and one for which there was the least excuse. I do not question, however, the sincerity of the great mass of those who were opposed to us.

General Lee was dressed in a full uniform which was entirely new, and was wearing a sword of considerable value, very likely the sword which had been presented by the State of Virginia; at all events, it was an entirely different sword from the one that would ordinarily be worn in the field. In my rough traveling suit, the uniform of a private with the straps of a lieutenant-general, I must have contrasted very strangely with a man so handsomely dressed, six feet high and of faultless form. But this was not a matter that I thought of until afterwards.

We soon fell into a conversation about old army times. He remarked that he remembered me very well in the old army; and I told him that as a matter of course I remembered him perfectly, but from the difference in our rank and years (there being about sixteen years' difference in our ages), I had thought it very likely that I had not attracted his attention sufficiently to be remembered by him after such a long interval. Our conversation grew so pleasant that I almost forgot the object of our meeting. After the conversation had run on in this style for some time, General Lee called my attention to the object of our meeting, and said that he had asked for this interview for the purpose of getting from me the terms I proposed to give his army. I said that I meant merely that his army should lay down their arms, not to take them up again during the continuance of the war unless duly and properly exchanged. He said that he had so understood my letter.

Then we gradually fell off again into conversation about matters foreign to the subject which had brought us together. This continued for some little time, when General Lee again interrupted the course of the conversation by suggesting that the terms I proposed to give his army ought to be written out [...]

When I put my pen to the paper I did not know the first word that I should make use of in writing the terms. I only knew what was in my mind, and I wished to express it clearly, so that there could be no mistaking it. As I wrote on, the thought occurred to me that the officers had their own private horses and effects, which were important to them, but of no value to us; also that it would be an unnecessary humiliation to call upon them to deliver their side arms.

No conversation, not one word, passed between General Lee and myself, either about private property, side arms, or kindred subjects. He appeared to have no objections to the terms first proposed; or if he had a point to make against them he wished to wait until they were in writing to make it. When he read over that part of the terms about side arms, horses and private property of the officers, he remarked, with some feeling, I thought, that this would have a happy effect upon his army.

Then, after a little further conversation, General Lee remarked to me again that their army was organized a little differently from the army of the United States (still maintaining by implication that we were two countries); that in their army the cavalrymen and artillerists owned their own horses; and he asked if he was to understand that the men who so owned their horses were to be permitted to retain them. I told him that as the terms were written they would not; that only the officers were permitted to take their private property. He then, after reading over the terms a second time, remarked that that was clear.

I then said to him that I thought this would be about the last battle of the war—I sincerely hoped so; and I said further I took it that most of the men in the ranks were small farmers. The whole country had been so raided by the two armies that it was doubtful whether they would be able to put in a crop to carry themselves and their families through the next winter without the aid of the horses they were then riding. The United States did not want them and I would, therefore, instruct the officers I left behind to receive the paroles of his troops to let every man of the Confederate army who claimed to own a horse or mule take the animal to his home. Lee remarked again that this would have a happy effect [...]

The much talked of surrendering of Lee's sword and my handing it back, this and much more that has been said about it is the purest romance. The word sword or side arms was not mentioned by either of us until I wrote it in the terms. There was no premeditation, and it did not occur to me until the moment I wrote it down. If I had happened to omit it, and General Lee had called my attention to it, I should have put it in the terms precisely as I acceded to the provision about the soldiers retaining their horses.

Source: Ulysses S. Grant, *Personal Memoirs of U.S. Grant*, Volume 2 (New York: Charles L. Webster and Company, 1885), 488–496.

Questions for Consideration

1) What were the terms General Grant offered to General Lee at Appomattox?
2) How did Grant view the "cause" of the war?
3) Why did he refer to the surrender of the sword as the "purest romance"?

Suggested Readings

Davis, William C. *Duel Between the First Ironclads*. Garden City, NY: Doubleday, 1975.

Faust, Drew Gilpin. *This Republic of Suffering: Death and the American Civil War*. New York: Knopf, 2008.

Glatthaar, Joseph T. *Forged in Battle: The Civil War Alliance of Black Soldiers and White Officers*. New York: Free Press, 1990.

Goss, Thomas J. *The War within the Union High Command: Politics and Generalship during the Civil War*. Lawrence: University Press of Kansas, 2003.

Griffith, Paddy. *Battle Tactics of the Civil War*. New Haven: Yale University Press, 1989.

Guelzo, Allen C. *Fateful Lightning: A New History of the Civil War and Reconstruction*. New York: Oxford University Press, 2012.

Hagerman, Edward. *The American Civil War and the Origins of Modern Warfare*. Bloomington: Indiana University Press, 1988.

Hess, Earl. *The Rifle Musket in Civil War Combat: Reality and Myth*. Lawrence: University Press of Kansas, 2008.

Joiner, Gary D. *Mr. Lincoln's Brown Water Navy*. Lanham, MD: Rowman & Littlefield, 2007.

Leonard, Elizabeth. *All the Daring of a Soldier: Women of the Civil War Armies*. New York: W. W. Norton, 1999.

Linderman, Gerald F. *Embattled Courage: The Experience of Combat in the American Civil War*. New York: Free Press, 1987.

Mackey, Robert R. *The Uncivil War: Irregular Warfare in the Upper South, 1861–1865*. Norman: University of Oklahoma Press, 2004.

Manning, Chandra. *What this Cruel War was Over: Soldiers, Slavery, and the Civil War.* New York: Knopf, 2007.

McFeely, William S. *Grant: A Biography.* New York: W. W. Norton, 2002.

McPherson, James. *For Cause and Comrades: Why Men Fought in the Civil War.* New York: Oxford University Press, 1997.

McPherson, James, and James K. Hogue. *Ordeal by Fire: The Civil War and Reconstruction.* Fourth Edition. New York: McGraw-Hill, 2010.

Royster, Charles. *The Destructive War: William Tecumseh Sherman, Stonewall Jackson, and the Americans.* New York: Knopf, 1991.

Stoker, Donald. *The Grand Design: Strategy and the U.S. Civil War.* New York: Oxford University Press, 2010.

Taaffe, Stephen R. *Commanding the Army of the Potomac.* Lawrence: University Press of Kansas, 2006.

Thomas, Emory. *Robert E. Lee: A Biography.* New York: W. W. Norton, 1995.

Weigley, Russell F. *A Great Civil War: A Military and Political History, 1861–1865.* Bloomington: Indiana University Press, 2000.

Wiley, Bell Irvin. *The Life of Johnny Reb: The Common Soldier of the Confederacy.* Indianapolis: Bobbs-Merrill, 1943.

Wiley, Bell Irvin. *The Life of Billy Yank: The Common Soldier of the Union.* Indianapolis: Bobbs-Merrill, 1952.

Witt, John Fabian. *Lincoln's Code: The Laws of War in American History.* New York: Free Press, 2012.

Woodworth, Steven E. *Jefferson Davis and His Generals: The Failure of Confederate Command in the West.* Lawrence: University Press of Kansas, 1990.

8

Twilight of the Indian Wars

Chronology

1864	Sand Creek Massacre
	Navajo Long Walk
1866–1868	Powder River War
1868	Battle of Beecher Island
	Battle of the Washita
1869	Peace Policy announced
1871	Camp Grant Massacre
1872–1873	Modoc War
1874–1875	Red River War
1876	Battle of Rosebud Creek
	Battle of the Little Bighorn
	Battle of Slim Buttes
	Dull Knife Fight
1877	Battle of Wolf Mountains
	Nez Percé War
1878	Paiute-Bannock War
1879	Ute War
1886	Geronimo surrenders
1890	Wounded Knee Massacre

8.1 William T. Sherman Discusses Indian Policy (1868)

With the nation's attention focused on the politics of the Reconstruction era, General William Tecumseh Sherman turned his gaze toward the American West. Beginning in 1865, he assumed command of the Missouri Division, which stretched from the Mississippi River to the Rocky Mountains. He established new military outposts for the Army regulars deployed across the region. He served as a member of the federal peace commission that met with various Indian leaders and negotiated the Medicine Lodge Treaty of 1867 and the Fort Laramie Treaty of 1868. The goal of what came to be known as the "peace policy" was to place Indian people on reservations and to keep them under the surveillance of government agents. Moreover, General Sherman opined that Indian

American Military History: A Documentary Reader, Second Edition. Brad D. Lookingbill.
© 2019 John Wiley & Sons, Inc. Published 2019 by John Wiley & Sons, Inc.

affairs should be directed by the War Department, not the Interior Department. In his official report to Congress on November 1, 1868, he posited that securing peace in the western territories required military power. The next year, he became the Commanding General of the U.S. Army. General Sherman stepped down from his post on November 1, 1883, retiring from military service a few months later. He died in New York City on February 14, 1891, and was buried in St. Louis, Missouri.

Document

A sense of national justice dictates that in taking from these savages the lands whose wild game has hitherto fed, clothed, and sheltered them, we should, in restricting them to the exclusive use of a part, make them a compensation of some sort for the remainder, and, if possible, procure their consent. Influenced by this consideration, the Peace Commissioners, during the Fall and Winter of 1867, and the Spring and Summer of 1868, held councils with all, or nearly all, the tribes and parts of tribes east of the Rocky Mountains, making liberal provisions for all the appointed places of council, according to the terms and ceremonies to which they were long accustomed. Formal written treaties were made with each separate tribe, signed with all the formality, and transmitted to the Senate of the United States for ratification.

The treaties with the Cheyennes, Arapahoes, Kiowas, Comanches, Navajoes, and Crows were duly confirmed, but those with the various bands of Sioux, Snakes, &c., were not confirmed, simply, it is inferred, because they were not complete when the Senate adjourned. But for some reason the Congress did not take any action on the chief proposition of the Peace Commission, which was embraced in their report of last December, viz.: that which related to the setting apart of the two reservations herein before referred to, and providing government therefore, which was designed to precede the confirmation of any of the treaties, and was the only vital principle of them all.

I regret that I felt compelled to refer to this fact, because many persons attribute to it the reason why we failed to secure a lasting peace, and why we are at this moment engaged in a costly war with four of the principal tribes with which we had to deal, viz.: the Cheyennes, Arapahoes, Kiowas, and Comanches.

It has always been most difficult to uncover the exact truth concerning the cause of a rupture with any Indians. They never give notice beforehand of a warlike intention, and the first notice comes after their rifles and lances have done much bloody work. All intercourse then necessarily ceases, and the original cause soon becomes buried in after events […]

It is idle for us longer to attempt to occupy the Plains in common with these Indians, for the country is not susceptible of close settlement with farms like Missouri and Iowa, and is solely adapted to grazing. All of our people are necessarily scattered, and have more or less cattle and horses, which tempt the Indians, hungry, and it may be, starving for the want of his accustomed game; and he will steal rather than starve, and to steal he will not hesitate to kill. Therefore, a joint occupation of that district of the country by these two classes of people with such opposing interests is a simple impossibility, and the Indians must yield.

The Peace Commission has assigned them a reservation, which, if held for fifty years, will make their descendants rich; and in the meantime they are promised food while they are learning to cultivate the earth and to rear tame stock. To labor with their own hands, or even to remain in one place, militates with all the hereditary pride of the Indian, and *force* must be used to accomplish this result. It was for this reason the Peace Commission, at its Chicago session in October, after the events before described had occurred, and were known to them, was forced to the conclusion that the management of Indian affairs should be transferred back to the War Department, where it belonged, prior to 1849. That department of our government is the only one that can use force promptly without the circumlocution now necessary; and no other department of our government can act with promptness and vigor enough to give any hope that the plans and purposes of the Peace Commission will be carried out. Even then, there is doubt that the Indians themselves will make the necessary personal efforts to succeed, and I fear that they will at last fall back upon our hands a mere mass of helpless paupers.

I am fully aware that many of our good people, far removed from contact with these Indians, and dwelling with a painful interest on the past events, such as are described to have occurred in Minnesota in 1863 and at the Chivington massacre of 1864, believe that the whites are always in the wrong, and that the Indians have been forced to resort to war in self-defence, by actual want or by reason of our selfishness.

I am more than convinced that such is not the case in the present instance, and hope I have made it plain. I further believe that the only hope of saving any part of these Indians from utter annihilation is by a fair and prompt execution of the scheme suggested by the Peace Commission, which can alone be done by the Congress, with the concurrence of the Indians themselves. Even then it will require much patience and hard labor on the part of the officers who execute the plan, which I do not wish to assume myself or impose on other Army officers; but it is certain that the only hope to find any end of this eternal Indian war is in the transfer of the entire business to the War Department, and for Congress to enact the laws and provide the necessary money at least a year before it is required to be expended.

Source: "Report of Lieutenant General William T. Sherman, 1 November 1868," in *Message from the President of the United States to the Two Houses of Congress at the Commencement of the Third Session of the Fortieth Congress*, ed. Benjamin Perley Poore (Washington, DC: Government Printing Office, 1869), 333–340.

Questions for Consideration

1) Where, according to General Sherman, would Indian tribes possibly clash with new settlers?
2) How did he propose to bring an end to "this eternal Indian war" in the United States?
3) Why do you think he insisted that it was difficult to uncover "the exact truth" concerning Indian affairs?

8.2   Elizabeth B. Custer Camps with the Cavalry (1873)

Families often traveled with U.S. Army officers during the Indian wars. Given the social obligations of domesticity, wives accepted the directives, customs, and hardships of military service along with their husbands. Nevertheless, many challenged conventional assumptions about gender roles. For instance, Elizabeth Bacon Custer accompanied Lieutenant Colonel George Armstrong Custer, her flamboyant husband and a brevetted general, on a number of his military campaigns. During 1873, she camped with the 7th Cavalry during a deployment to the Northern Plains. Soon, the Great Sioux War erupted as a result of disputes over the Northern Pacific Railroad's right of way through Indian lands and the discovery of gold in the Black Hills. From June 25 to June 26, 1876, 263 soldiers of the 7th Cavalry died at the hands of Lakota Sioux and Northern Cheyenne warriors near the Little Bighorn River. Following the death of her husband, the widowed Custer worked vigorously to memorialize the life of what otherwise might have been another forgotten casualty of the Indian wars. Thus, the American public came to remember him as a gallant hero who sacrificed himself for the progress of his country. Long after "Custer's Last Stand," the glory associated with his career derived to a large extent from her relentless campaigning on behalf of his commemoration.

Document

The length of each day's march varied according to the streams on which we relied for water, or the arrival of the boat. The steamer that carried the forage for the horses and the supplies for the command was tied up to the river-bank every night, as near to us as was possible. The laundresses and ladies of the regiment were on board, except the General's sister, Margaret, who made her first march with her husband, riding all the way on horseback. As usual, I rode beside the General. Our first few days were pleasant, and we began at once to enjoy the plover. The land was so covered with them that the hunters shot them with all sorts of arms. We counted eighty birds in the gunny-sack that three of the soldiers brought in. Fortunately there were several shot-guns in the possession of our family, and the little things, therefore, were not torn to pieces, but could be broiled over the coals of the camp-fire. They were so plump that their legs were like tiny points coming from beneath the rounded outline that swept the grass as they walked. No butter was needed in cooking them, for they were very fat. How good the plover and sandwiches tasted, while we quenched our thirst with cold coffee or tea! Since we were named "The Great Grab Mess," we all dared to reach over and help ourselves, and the one most agile and with the longest arms was the best fed.

No great ceremony is to be expected when one rises before four, and takes a hurried breakfast by the light of a tallow-candle; the soldiers waiting outside to take down the tent, the servants hastily and suggestively rattling the kettles and gridiron as they packed them, made it an irresistible temptation for one hungry to "grab."

We had a very satisfactory little cook-stove. It began its career with legs, but the wind used to lift it up from the ground with such violence it was finally dismembered, and afterward placed flat on the ground. Being of sheet-iron it cooled quickly, was very light, and could be put in the wagon in a few moments after the morning meal was cooked. When we came out from breakfast the wagon stood near, partly packed, and bristling with kitchen utensils; buckets and baskets tied outside the cover, axe and spade lashed to the side, while the little stove looked out from the end. The mess-chest stood open on the ground to receive the dishes we had used. At a given signal the dining-tent went down with all those along the line, and they were stowed away in the wagons in an incredibly short time. The wagon-train then drew out and formed in order at the rear of the column.

At the bugle-call, "Boots and Saddles," each soldier mounted and took his place in line, all riding two abreast. First came the General and his staff, with whom Sister Margaret and I were permitted to ride; the private orderlies and head-quarters detail rode in our rear; and then came the companies according to the places assigned them for the day; finally the wagon-train, with the rear-guard. We made a long cavalcade that stretched over a great distance. When we reached some high bluff we never tired of watching the command advancing, with the long line of supply wagons, with their white covers, winding around bends in the road and climbing over the hills. Every day the breaking of camp went more smoothly and quickly, until, as the days advanced, the General used to call me to his side to notice by his watch how few moments it took after the tents were ordered down to set the whole machinery for the march in motion; and I remember the regiment grew so skillful in preparation that in one campaign the hour for starting never varied five minutes during the whole summer.

The column was always halted once during the day's march to water the horses, then the luncheons were brought forth.

When the stream was narrow, and the hundreds of horses had to be ranged along its banks to be watered, there was time for a nap. I soon acquired the General's habit of sleeping readily. He would throw himself down anywhere and fall asleep instantly, even with the sun beating on his head. It only takes a little training to learn to sleep without a pillow on uneven ground and without shade. I learned, the moment I was helped out of the saddle, to drop upon the grass and lose myself in a twinkling. I think I never got quite over wishing for the shade of a tree; but there was often a little strip of shadow on one side of the travelling wagon, which was always near us on the journey. I was not above selfishly appropriating the space under the wagon, if it had not been taken by somebody else. Even then I had to dislodge a whole collection of dogs, who soon find the best places for their comfort.

We had a citizen-guide with us, who, having been long in the country, knew the streams, and the General and I, following his instructions, often rode in advance as we neared the night's camp. It was always a mild excitement and new pleasure to select camp. The General delighted to unsaddle his favorite horse, Dandy, and turn him loose, for his attachment was so strong he never grazed far from us. He was not even tethered, and after giving himself the luxury of a roll in the grass, he ate his dinner of oats, and browsed about the tent, as tame as a kitten. He whinnied when my husband patted his sleek neck, and looked jealously at the dogs when they all followed us into the tent.

After tramping down the grass, to prevent the fire from spreading, my husband would carry dry sticks and underbrush, and place them against a fallen tree. That made an admirable back-log, and in a little while we had a glorious fire, the General having a peculiar gift of starting a flame on the wildest day. The next thing was to throw himself down on the sod, cover his eyes with his white felt hat, and be sound asleep in no time. The dogs came at once to lie beside him. I have seen them stretched at his back and curled around his head, while the nose and paws of one rested on his breast. And yet he was quite unconscious of their crowding. They growled and scrambled for the best place, but he slept placidly through it all.

When the command arrived, the guidons pointed out the location for each company; the horses were unsaddled and picketed out; the wagons unloaded and the tents pitched. The hewing of wood and the hauling of water came next, and after the cook-fires were lighted, the air was full of savory odors of the soldiers' dinner. After I had changed my riding-habit for my one other gown, I came out to join the General under the tent-fly, where he lay alternately watching the scene and reading one of his well-thumbed books. I always had sewing—either a bit of needle-work that was destined to make our garrison quarters more attractive, or more often, some necessary stitches to take in our hard-worn clothes. As we sat there it would have been difficult for a stranger to believe that it was merely the home of a day.

Source: Elizabeth B. Custer, *Boy General: Story of the Life of Major-General George A. Custer*, ed. Mary E. Burt (New York: Charles Scribner's Sons, 1901), 98–105.

Questions for Consideration

1) What did Elizabeth Custer dub the "the Great Grab Mess"?
2) When did she and her husband find time for sleeping?
3) In what ways did her activities indicate a sexual division of labor in the camps?

8.3 Making Medicine Sketches Warriors and Soldiers (1877)

Whether in deserts, mountains, valleys, or grasslands, the U.S. Army attempted to subdue the indigenous populations of the American West. Army officers believed that cold weather in the winter months severely constrained the range and the mobility of the Plains Indians. Military campaigning posed difficult logistical problems for the bluecoats, but the results often proved decisive. Lacking the manpower, technology, and provisions of industrialized societies, resistant bands resorted to asymmetrical tactics while opposing the "white man's road." Whenever possible, they avoided direct action in pitched battles. Captured near Fort Sill in Indian Territory, a Cheyenne warrior named O-kuh-ha-tuh was exiled along with other Indian war prisoners to Fort Marion in Saint Augustine, Florida. Detained from 1875 until 1878 by the War Department, he participated in an educational experiment initiated by Lieutenant Richard Henry Pratt, the Army officer who supervised the prisoners. After cutting his hair, donning a regimental uniform, and serving as first sergeant, the Cheyenne sketched warriors and soldiers in various ledger books. Showing respect to a tradition of "counting coup," he recorded Cheyenne deeds with paper and pencils. He became known as Making Medicine and later took the name David Pendleton Oakerhater. Ordained an Episcopal deacon, he ministered to his people until passing away in 1931.

Document

Source: Detail from U.S. Cavalry and Native American Indians by Making Medicine (Cheyenne), 17.5 x 33.3 cm, Book of Sketches made at Fort Marion, St. Augustine, Fla., ca. 1875–1878, Manuscript collection, Massachusetts Historical Society.

Questions for Consideration

1) What did Making Medicine's sketch reveal about indigenous warfare?
2) What audience do you think he intended to reach with his sketch?
3) Why do you suppose the Plains Indians in his sketch carried no firearms?

8.4 Emory Upton Evaluates Military Policy (1880)

Combat operations during the Indian wars were plagued by bureaucratic squabbles, poor communication, inadequate planning, and improper training. One particular officer, Emory Upton, began to envision transforming the U.S. Army into a force more powerful than a frontier constabulary. An 1861 graduate of West Point, he mastered all three combat arms—infantry, artillery, and cavalry—on the front lines of the Civil War. He commanded several posts during the Reconstruction era and received the brevet rank of Major General before his 25th birthday. From 1870 to 1875, he served as the commandant of cadets at West Point. To study foreign military organizations, he toured Europe and Asia. On his last assignment, he took command of the 4th Artillery stationed at the Presidio of San Francisco, California. Although his earlier books on infantry tactics and on professional armies attracted attention, his greatest work was an unpublished manuscript called "The Military Policy of the United States." Excessive civilian control over military affairs constituted a fundamental flaw of the armed forces, or so Upton opined. He suffered from severe headaches, possibly caused by a brain tumor, as he revised the pages. On March 15, 1881, he committed suicide by shooting himself in the head. Posthumously, the pages of his manuscript circulated widely among officers before its publication in 1904.

Document

Our military policy, or, as many would affirm, our want of it, has now been tested during more than a century. It has been tried in foreign, domestic, and Indian wars, and while military men, from painful experience, are united as to its defects and dangers, our final success in each conflict has so blinded the popular mind, as to induce the belief that as a nation we are invincible.

With the greater mass of people, who have neither the time nor the inclination to study the requirements of military science, no error is more common than to mistake military resources for military strength, and particularly is this the case with ourselves.

History records our triumph in the Revolution, in the War of 1812, in the Florida War, in the Mexican War, and in the Great Rebellion, and as nearly all of these wars were largely begun by militia and volunteers, the conviction has been produced that with us a regular army is not a necessity.

In relating the events of these wars, the historian has generally limited himself to describing the battles that have been fought, without seeking to investigate the delays and disasters by which they have been prolonged, till, in nearly every instance, the national resources have been exhausted.

The object of this work is to treat historically and statistically our military policy up to the present time, and to show the enormous and unnecessary sacrifice of life and treasure, which has attended all our armed struggles.

Whether we may be willing to admit it or not, in the conduct of war, we have rejected the practice of European nations and with little variation, have thus far pursued the policy of China. All of our wars have been prolonged for want of judicious and economical preparation, and often when the people have impatiently awaited the tidings of victory, those of humiliating defeat have plunged the nation into mourning.

The cause of all this is obvious to the soldier and should be no less obvious to the statesman. It lies partly in the unfounded jealousy of not a large, but even a small standing army; in the persistent use of raw troops; in the want of an expansive organization, adequate for every prospective emergency; in short and voluntary enlistments, carping with them large bounties; and in a variety of other defects which need not here be stated.

In treating this subject, I am aware that I tread on delicate ground and that every volunteer and militiaman who has patriotically responded to the call of his country, in the hour of danger, may possibly regard himself as unjustly attacked. To such I can only reply, that where they have enlisted for the period of three months, and, as at Bladensburg and on many other fields, have been hurled against veteran troops, they should not hold me responsible for the facts of history, which I have sought impartially to present. To such volunteers as enlisted for the period of the Mexican War, and particularly for two and three years during the War of the Rebellion, with whom it is my pride to have served and to whom I owe all of my advancement in the service, I but express the opinion of all military men, in testifying that their excellence was due, not to the fact that they were volunteers, but to the more important fact that their long term of service enabled them to become, in the highest sense, regulars in drill, discipline, and courage [...]

Free from danger and from lust of power, if the noncombatant officers love war more than peace, it is manifest that they, too, should join the ambitious soldier and the demagogue in the cry, "Standing armies are dangerous to liberty." But who are our officers that they should be charged with mere selfishness and ambition? If we take those educated by the Government from their youth, are they not selected by the representatives of the people and from every class of society? Are not their fathers, mothers, and their own sons in civil life, and in common with them, are they not citizens of the same country enjoying the blessings of the same Government? Nurtured by this Government, taught to love and defend its flag, are they alone a large family connection most likely to prove false to the institutions which have placed us first among nations? Is death on the field of battle no evidence of love for one's country? Have the officers of our Army today no sense of duty? In time of universal peace are those who continually expose their lives in Indian wars to open up to civilization the rich lands of the far West, actuated by no other motive than love of promotion? These questions to the reader are all pertinent in enabling him to penetrate the motive of the author. Whether or not he will concede to the Army a patriotism as bright and enduring as that which prevails in civil life, he no doubt will admit that as the man who uses a weapon is the best judge of its fitness, so a professional soldier should be the best judge of what constitutes a good military system.

Source: Emory Upton, *The Military Policy of the United States* (Washington, DC: Government Printing Office, 1904), vii–xv.

Questions for Consideration

1) What, according to General Upton, motivated Army officers to "expose their lives in Indian wars" across the western territories?
2) Why did he fear that he was treading "on delicate ground" in his work?
3) Do you agree with him in that the "want of judicious and economical preparation" prolonged America's wars?

8.5   The *Soldier's Handbook* Gives Healthy Advice (1884)

Military service in the Indian wars demanded true grit. Enlisted men probably yearned for adventure, although the vast majority never encountered an Indian in battle. Some were recent immigrants or unemployed drifters. Others were former slaves. For instance, African Americans served in the 9th and 10th Cavalry and in the 24th and 25th Infantry. According to legend, Indian tribes called them "buffalo" soldiers. In addition to policing Indian reservations, the "Old Army" watched over federal properties such as Yellowstone Park. Typically, the regulars slept in crowded, unsanitary barracks. They carried weapons designed for ruggedness rather than precision. They performed manual labor such as building or repairing fortifications, roads, and bridges. They earned around $13 a month for their toil. Their diets consisted of beef, beans, stew, bacon, and hardtack. Morale was low. Desertion rates were high. Wherever deployed for duty, the rank and file carried a pocket-sized, leather-bound volume titled *Soldier's Handbook*. While dispensing healthy advice on soldiering, it offered basic information about physical fitness, weaponry maintenance, animal care, sentinel duties, and detached service. It included articles of war in addition to sections on discipline and conduct. In the back, it contained pages for recording each year's clothing issue and marksmanship scores. Thus, the War Department gave practical guidance to American soldiers in the Indian wars.

Document

Abundant sleep is essential to bodily efficiency, and to that alertness of mind which is all-important in an engagement. Few things more certainly and more effectually prevent sound sleep than eating heartily after sundown, especially after a heavy march or desperate battle.

Nothing is more certain to secure endurance and capability of long-continued effort than the avoidance of everything as a drink except cold water (and coffee at breakfast). Drink as little as possible of even cold water. Experience teaches old soldiers that the less they drink on a march the better, and that they suffer less in the end by controlling the desire to drink, however urgent.

After any sort of exhausting effort, a cup of coffee or tea, hot or cold, is an admirable sustainer of the strength until nature begins to recover herself.

Never eat heartily just before a great undertaking, because the nervous power is irresistibly drawn to the stomach to manage the food eaten, thus draining off that supply which the brain and muscles so much need [...]

A *cut* is less dangerous than a bullet-wound, and heals more rapidly.

If from any wound the blood spurts out in jets, instead of a steady stream, you will die in a few minutes, unless it be remedied; because an artery has been divided, and that takes the blood direct from the fountain of life. To stop this instantly, tie a handkerchief or other cloth very loosely BETWEEN the wound and the heart, put a stick, bayonet, or ramrod *between* the skin and the handkerchief, and twist it around until the bleeding ceases, and keep it thus until the surgeon arrives.

If the blood flows in a slow, regular stream, a vein has been pierced, and the handkerchief must be on the other side of the wound from the heart, that is, *below* the wound.

Fire low. A bullet through the abdomen (belly or stomach) is more certainly fatal than if aimed at the head or heart; for in the latter cases the ball is often glanced off by the bone, or follows round it under the skin. But when it enters the stomach or bowels, from any direction, death is inevitable, but scarcely ever instantaneous. Generally the person lives a day or two, with perfect clearness of intellect, often *not* suffering greatly. The practical bearing of this statement in reference to the future is clear. *Fire low.*

Whenever possible, take a plunge into any lake or running stream every morning, as soon as you get up; if none at hand, endeavor to wash the body all over, as soon as you leave your bed: for personal cleanliness acts like a charm against all diseases, always either warding them off altogether, or greatly mitigating their severity and shortening their duration.

Keep the hair of the head closely cut, say within an inch and a half of the scalp in every part, repeated on the first of each month, and wash the whole scalp plentifully in cold water every morning.

Wear woolen stockings and moderately loose shoes, keeping the toe and finger nails cut close. Wash the stockings whenever soiled, and the underclothing once a week. Thoroughly dry both.

It is important to wash the feet well every night (not in the morning): because it aids to keep the skin and nails soft, to prevent chafings, blisters, and corns, all of which greatly interfere with a soldier's duty.

If the feet begin to chafe, rub the socks with common soap where they come in contact with the sore places. If you rub the feet well with soap (hard soap) before the march, you will scarcely be troubled with sore feet.

The most universally safe position after all stunnings, hurts, and wounds is that of being placed on the back, the head being elevated three or four inches only—aiding, more than anything else can do, to equalize and restore the proper circulation of the blood.

The more weary you are after a march or other work, the more easily will you take cold, if you remain still, after it is over, unless the moment you cease motion you throw a coat or blanket over your shoulders. This precaution should be taken in the warmest weather, especially if there is even a slight air stirring.

The greatest physical kindness you can show a severely wounded comrade is, first to place him on his back, and then give him some water to drink from a canteen or ambulance-bucket. I have seen a dying man clutch at a single drop of water from the finger's and with the voraciousness of a famished tiger.

If wet to the skin by rain or swimming rivers, keep in motion until the clothes are dried; and no harm will result.

Whenever it is possible, do, by all means, when you have to use water for cooking or drinking from ponds or sluggish streams, boil it well, and, when cool, shake it, or stir it, so that the oxygen of the air shall get to it, which greatly improves it for drinking. This boiling arrests the process of fermentation, which arises from the presence of organic and inorganic impurities, thus tending to prevent cholera and all bowel-diseases. If there is no time for boiling, at least strain it through a cloth, even if you have to use a shirt or trousers-leg.

Water can be made almost ice-cool in the hottest weather, by closely enveloping a filled canteen, or other vessel, with woolen cloth kept plentifully wetted and exposed.

While on a march, lie down the moment you halt for a rest. Every minute spent in that position refreshes more than five minutes standing or loitering about.

A daily evacuation of the bowels is indispensable to bodily health, vigor, and endurance: this is promoted, in many cases, by stirring a table-spoonful of corn (Indian) meal in a glass of water, and drinking it on rising in the morning.

Inattention to nature's calls is a frequent source of disease. The strictest discipline in the performance of these duties is absolutely essential to health, as well as to decency. Men should never be allowed to void their excrement elsewhere than in the regular-established sinks. In the well-regulated camps the sinks are visited daily by a police party, a layer of earth thrown in, and lime and other disinfecting agents employed to prevent them from becoming offensive and unhealthy. It is the duty of the surgeon to call the attention of the commanding officer to any neglect of this important item of camp police, to see that the shambles, where the cattle are slaughtered, are not allowed to become offensive, and that all offal is promptly buried at a sufficient distance from camp, and covered by at least four feet of earth.

Source: Nathaniel Hershler, ed., *Soldier's Handbook: For the Use of the Enlisted Men of the Army* (Washington, DC: Government Printing Office, 1884), 51–56.

Questions for Consideration

1) What, according to the *Handbook*, was "an admirable sustainer" of a soldier's strength following an exhausting effort?
2) Where were soldiers instructed to aim their weapons in combat?
3) Why do you think that the *Handbook* directed soldiers to conduct a "daily evacuation" of the bowels?

8.6   Henry W. Lawton Pursues the Apache (1886)

U.S. Army maps long referred to the American Southwest as Apacheria, which encompassed millions of acres from the Verde River to the Rio Grande River. The major divisions of the Apache included the Western, Chiricahua, Mescalaro, Jicarilla, Lipan, and Kiowa Apache. To blend into the desert landscape, Apache warriors rubbed their bodies with clay and sand. They survived between water holes, living off wild honey, berries, and cactus fruit in the wasteland. Enhanced by the use of horses and firearms, they constituted a resilient guerrilla force. During one of the costliest Indian wars in American history, U.S. forces conducted a series of campaigns that eventually induced the Apache to capitulate. Indian scouts and auxiliaries assisted the regulars. One of the last Apache to surrender was Geronimo, a popular Chiricahua. Though never a chief, he appeared to possess sacred power bestowed upon him by Usen, the Apache god. His band fled the San Carlos Reservation again and again. During the summer of 1886, Captain Henry W. Lawton led a mixed column of the 4th Cavalry and 8th Infantry in hot pursuit. On September 4, Geronimo surrendered for the final time at Skeleton Canyon. Lawton's official report praised the tenacity of the soldiers during the final campaign.

Document

While the trail was being constantly followed and the Indians pushed to the utmost of our power, the base of operations was being changed to a point 150 miles south of the national boundary line.

By the 5th of July the Indians had been driven south and east of Oposura, a supply camp established at this point, and the command equipped and ready to continue operations. Up to this time the hostiles had operated in small parties, making sudden and fatal descents upon settlements at unexpected places. Numbers of other commands were in the field and the hostiles were frequently met and pursued by them. During this portion of the campaign my command marched, including side scouts and reconnaissances, 1390 miles, nearly all of which distance was over rough, high mountains. Most of the country had been burned over, leaving no grass, and water was so scarce that the command frequently suffered greatly. There was accomplished during this period one surprise, and the hostiles were three times placed on foot. They could reap no benefits from their raids, as they were so closely followed that they could not rest for a day, and they were obliged to abandon the animals or fight to protect them; this they carefully avoided. They were obliged to keep a constant and vigilant watch on their back trail and on their camp to prevent surprise. This made it possible for other commands, knowing their course, to fall upon them. Every device known to the Indian was practiced to throw me off their trail, but without avail. My trailers were good, and it was soon proven that there was no spot they could reach where security was assured.

On the 6th of July the command, consisting of infantry and scouts, marched from Oposura. No officer of infantry having been sent with the detachment, and having no officers with the command except Second Lieutenant Brown, Fourth Cavalry, commanding scouts, and Second Lieutenant Walsh, Fourth Cavalry, commanding cavalry, Assistant Surgeon Wood was, at his own request, given command of the infantry. The work during June having been done by the cavalry, they were too much exhausted to be used again without rest, and they were left in camp at Oposura to recuperate [...]

In the meantime scouts were sent in all directions to cut the country for signs. During this time Lieutenant [Charles] Gatewood, Sixth Cavalry, with two Chiricahua Indians, who had been charged with a mission to enter the hostile camp and demand their surrender, joined me.

On the 13th of August I received information that the hostiles were moving towards the Sierras Mountains, through Campus and Nacosuri. I marched immediately to head them off. By making forced marches I arrived near Fronteras on the 20th of August, and learned that the hostiles had communicated to the Mexicans a desire to surrender. Lieutenant Gatewood went forward at once with his Chiricahuas to communicate with them, but found the Mexican authorities trying to negotiate. Lieutenant Gatewood, however, sent his Indians forward and soon learned that the hostiles had moved their camp, going east. This fact he communicated to me and I moved out on their trail at once, Lieutenant Gatewood also following ahead of me. On the evening of the 24th I came up with Lieutenant Gatewood and found him in communication with the hostiles, but on his return from their camp he reported that they declined to make an unconditional surrender and wished him to bear certain messages to General [Nelson] Miles. I persuaded Gatewood to remain with me, believing that the hostiles would yet come to terms, and in this I was not disappointed. The following morning Geronimo came into camp and intimated his desire to make peace, but wished to see and talk with General Miles. I made an agreement with him that he should come down from the mountains, camp near my command, and await a reply to his request to see and talk with General Miles [...]

In the meantime, General Miles had started for my camp at the mouth of Skeleton Canyon, which he reached on the evening of September 3. On the 4th September the hostiles surrendered as agreed, and the leading men placed themselves in General Miles's hands and were taken by him to Fort Bowie. The same day I started for Fort Bowie with the main party of Indians, and by making slow marches reached that post on the morning of September 8. This ended the campaign.

The command taking the field May 5, continued almost constantly on the trail of the hostiles until their surrender, more than four months later, with scarcely a day's rest or intermission. It was purely a command of soldiers, there being attached to it barely one small detachment of trailers. It was the persistent and untiring labor of this command which proved to the hostiles their insecurity in a country which had heretofore afforded them protection and seemingly rendered pursuit impossible. This command, which fairly run down the hostiles and forced them to seek terms, has clearly demonstrated that our soldiers can operate in any country the Indians may choose for refuge, and may not only cope with them upon their own ground but run down and subdue them.

Source: "Report of Captain Lawton, 9 September 1886," in *Annual Report of the Secretary of War for the Year 1886*, Volume 1 (Washington, DC: Government Printing Office, 1886), 176–181.

Questions for Consideration

1) What, according to Captain Lawton, kept him on the trail of the Apache?
2) Who accompanied Lieutenant Gatewood on his mission to enter the "hostile camp"?
3) Why did the report claim that "our soldiers can operate in any country the Indians may choose for refuge"?

8.7   Nelson A. Miles Remembers Wounded Knee (1890)

Written in the twilight of the Indian wars, the memoirs of General Nelson A. Miles revealed the moral ambiguities inherent in the profession of arms. He began his military career as a volunteer infantryman during the Civil War, but he served thereafter in almost every major campaign in the American West. From 1874 to 1875, he served as a field commander in the Red River War. In the aftermath of the Little Bighorn fiasco, he launched a winter campaign against the Lakota Sioux to force them back to the reservation. During the following winter, he conducted a long march to capture the Nez Percé, who outmaneuvered several outfits previously sent to intercept them. During the spring of 1886, he replaced General George Crook in the Department of Arizona to break Apache resistance. As commander of the Division of the Missouri, General Miles responded to the Ghost Dance movement by mobilizing armed forces for action. On December 29, 1890, as many as 300 Sioux were killed or mortally wounded by the 7th Cavalry at Wounded Knee Creek. Officially, 25 soldiers were killed in the clash. Another 39 suffered wounds. Before retiring in 1903, General Miles became the Commanding General of the U.S. Army.

Document

I had hoped that I had heard the last of Indian depredations and war, yet I had scarcely assumed command when I began to hear rumors of disaffection and unrest and a threatened uprising of the different tribes scattered over the western half of our country.

The Indian orators were haranguing large groups wherever they could be assembled in the camps. The exhorters, the so-called prophets, as well as the intriguing leaders, were influencing the Indians in a religious belief and inspiring a hope in the hearts of a doomed race that some divine interposition was about to rescue them from their impending fate. They were being taught certain ceremonies, to chant improvised sacred songs, and the ghost-dance was introduced as a sacred observance. They indulged in this mysterious worship, chanting, crying, or singing weird and solemn music, using various incantations expressing joy or supplication, until they were wrought up, in many cases, to a wild frenzy.

Indian hostilities have originated from a great variety of causes—from gross frauds, injustice, and a total disregard of obligations of treaties on the part of our people; from the aggressive tide of immigration; from acts of violence, and from vague theories of their prophets and dreamers, "medicine men," who under took to fathom the mystery of the future by their limited knowledge of the past [...]

As soon as a sufficient force was assembled and placed the troops were gradually moved toward the Indian position, pressing them back toward their agency. In the meantime the camp under Big Foot, a noted Indian chief, left its agency on the Missouri River with the intention of joining the hostile camp assembled in the Bad Lands. A strong force of cavalry was sent to intercept them, and so far succeeded as to come in close proximity with them, causing them to halt. A parley occurred, but the commanding officer, instead of insisting upon their disarmament and return to their agency, took a promise that they would do so and returned the troops to camp, whereupon the Indians, as soon as night came on, escaped and continued their journey toward the Bad Lands.

Another force was ordered to intercept them, which was done before they reached the main camp of the hostiles, and a demand made for their surrender. This they agreed to do, and camped near the troops that night. The next morning a formal demand was made for their arms, whereupon the Indian warriors came out into the open field and laid their arms on the ground. While they were being searched, and a party that had been sent into camp was searching for arms, a controversy or misunderstanding of some kind occurred, and the Indians getting the impression that they were going to be killed, commenced what was known as a ghost-dance, one of its ceremonies being to take up dust and throw it over the warriors, under the superstitious belief that they could be made invulnerable to the bullets of the troops. This was continued for a brief time when hostilities commenced, the Indians making a rush for their camps, the troops being unfortunately so placed that some of them were in the line of fire. Many of the shots directed at the warriors went straight into the camp of women and children. A general mêlée and massacre occurred, in which a large number of men, women, and children were killed and wounded; so much so that the commanding officer reported that the camp or village had been destroyed.

The Indians fled in all directions, pursued by the troops, and the bodies of the dead and wounded were found on the prairies, some of them at quite long distances from the place where the disturbance occurred. I have never felt that the action was judicious or justifiable, and have always believed that it could have been avoided. It was a fatality, however, that Indian hostilities, uprisings, and wars should finally close in a deplorable tragedy. Regrettable as it was, there is one satisfaction in the fact that for twenty years it has not been repeated, and I hope and trust never will occur again. This tragedy, but a short distance from the great hostile camp, caused additional excitement, and for a time it was feared that nothing could prevent a serious outbreak and devastating war.

Yet the troops continued their slow pressure, moving more and more closely to the main Indian camp, so as to overawe it by force, and at the same time every measure was taken to draw them back to a peaceful condition by sending messages to the principal chiefs. Fortunately I had met many of the leaders on former occasions. Many of them had surrendered to me before—in the campaigns of the Northwest—Broad Trail, Spotted Eagle, and others—and I was enabled to appeal to their sense of reason and better judgment, and to convince them of the impossibility of the theories upon which they were acting. I also assured them, in case they should return to their camp, of strict compliance with the terms of their treaty; that a representation of their condition would be made at Washington, and that I would be their friend if they would surrender and follow my advice.

This, although it required many days and a great effort, finally prevailed, and I succeeded in drawing that large camp back to their agency, where they agreed to abandon their hostile measures and follow my directions. This was one of the most gratifying events of my life, as it saved the country from a devastating war and possibly saved the lives of thousands. It was effected without the Indians breaking into the settlements, and without the loss of a single life outside of those engaged in the military service and the Indians above mentioned [...]

That scene was possibly the closing one that was to bury in oblivion, decay, and death that once powerful, strong, defiant, and resolute race. It was doomed to disappear, leaving behind it no evidence of its former life and power; and as the warm breezes of spring should remove the robe of winter a new life, verdure, and duty would appear. Those prairies would see a new civilization, happy homes, prosperous communities, and great States; and the sound of the merry bells of industrial activity and the music of progress were to take the place of the war-cry and the echoes of alarm and danger. The scene was weird and in some respects desolate, yet it was fascinating to me—possibly on account of the jubilant spirit occasioned by the reflection that one more Indian war had been closed, and closed in the most satisfactory way, without the desolation and devastation in the settlements, as others had closed in former times. I did not even then realize that we had probably reached the close of Indian wars in our country.

Source: Nelson Appleton Miles, *Serving the Republic: Memoirs of the Civil and Military Life of Nelson A. Miles, Lieutenant-General, United States Army* (New York: Harper & Brothers, 1911), 233–247.

Questions for Consideration

1) What did General Miles recollect about his role in the "mêlée and massacre" at Wounded Knee?
2) Which Indian leaders did he recall meeting during previous military campaigns in the American West?
3) How did cultural assumptions seem to color his memories about "the close of Indian wars" in the U.S.?

Suggested Readings

Adams, Kevin. *Class and Race in the Frontier Army: Military Life in the West, 1870–1890.* Norman: University of Oklahoma Press, 2009.

Ambrose, Stephen E. *Upton and the Army.* Baton Rouge: Louisiana State University, 1964.

Coffman, Edward M. *The Old Army: A Portrait of the American Army in Peacetime, 1784–1898.* New York: Oxford University Press, 1988.

Dunlay, Thomas W. *Wolves for the Blue Soldiers: Indian Scouts and Auxiliaries with the United States Army, 1860–1890.* Lincoln: University of Nebraska Press, 1982.

Hutton, Paul Andrew. *The Apache Wars: The Hunt for Geronimo, the Apache Kid, and the Captive Boy Who Started the Longest War in American History.* New York: Crown, 2016.

Leckie, William H. *Buffalo Soldiers: A Narrative of the Negro Cavalry in the West.* Norman: University of Oklahoma Press, 1967.

Lookingbill, Brad D. *War Dance at Fort Marion: Plains Indian War Prisoners*. Norman: University of Oklahoma Press, 2006.

Nacy, Michele J. *Members of the Regiment: Army Officers' Wives on the Western Frontier, 1865–1890*. Westport, CT: Greenwood Press, 2000.

Rickey, Don. *Forty Miles a Day on Beans and Hay: The Enlisted Soldier Fighting the Indian Wars*. Norman: University of Oklahoma Press, 1963.

Smith, Sherry L. *The View from Officers' Row: Army Perceptions of Western Indians*. Tucson: University of Arizona Press, 1990.

Tate, Michael. *The Frontier Army in the Settlement of the West*. Norman: University of Oklahoma Press, 1999.

Utley, Robert M. *Frontier Regulars: The United States Army and the Indian, 1866–1891*. New York: Macmillan, 1973.

Utley, Robert M. *Cavalier in Buckskin: George Armstrong Custer and the Western Military Frontier*. Norman: University of Oklahoma Press, 1988.

Wooster, Robert. *The Military and United States Indian Policy, 1865–1903*. New Haven: Yale University Press, 1988.

Wooster, Robert. *Nelson Miles and the Twilight of the Frontier Army*. Lincoln: University of Nebraska Press, 1993.

9

A Rising Power

Chronology

1885	Naval War College established
1894	Cuban revolt begins
1898	U.S.S. *Maine* explodes
	Spanish–American War
	Battle of Manila Bay
	Battle of El Caney
	Battle of Santiago Bay
	Puerto Rico occupied
	Battle of Manila
	Treaty of Paris
	Hawaii annexed
1899	Naval Personnel Act
1899–1902	Philippine–American War
1900	Boxer Rebellion
1901	Army War College established
1903	Militia Act
	Army General Staff organized
1904	Roosevelt Corollary announced
1907–1909	The Great White Fleet cruises

9.1 Alfred Thayer Mahan Advocates Sea Power (1890)

As the nineteenth century waned, the power of the United States surged. Rear Admiral Stephen B. Luce, the first president of the Naval War College in Newport, Rhode Island, encouraged the development of a new doctrine for modern warfare. He hired Captain Alfred Thayer Mahan, a longtime naval officer who abhorred sea duty, to lecture on maritime tactics. By 1890, Captain Mahan turned his lecture notes into a monumental book about a grand strategy for national defense. Given the fierce competition for world trade, the United States needed a "big" naval fleet of battleships to protect its interests across the globe. Sea power, declared Mahan, required the acquisition of ports, stations, and bases abroad. Accordingly, he recommended annexing the Hawaiian Islands and

American Military History: A Documentary Reader, Second Edition. Brad D. Lookingbill.

developing a Central American canal. Of course, his argument for "command of the sea" echoed the sentiments of other strategists regarding the significance of a decisive battle. Hailed by imperialists in Great Britain, Germany, and Japan, his work profoundly influenced American foreign policy. Eventually, it struck a chord with officials inside the Naval Department. They planned to modernize the U.S. Navy, which gradually replaced small cruisers with massive battleships. After his retirement, Mahan became Rear Admiral by an act of Congress.

Document

As the practical object of this inquiry is to draw from the lessons of history inferences applicable to one's own country and service, it is proper now to ask how far the conditions of the United States involve serious danger, and call for action on the part of the government, in order to build again her sea power. It will not be too much to say that the action of the government since the Civil War, and up to this day, has been effectively directed solely to what has been called the first link in the chain which makes sea power. Internal development, great production, with the accompanying aim and boast of self-sufficingness, such has been the object, such to some extent the result. In this the government has faithfully reflected the bent of the controlling elements of the country, though it is not always easy to feel that such controlling elements are truly representative, even in a free country. However that may be, there is no doubt that, besides having no colonies, the intermediate link of a peaceful shipping, and the interests involved in it, are now likewise lacking. In short, the United States has only one link of the three.

The circumstances of naval war have changed so much within the last hundred years, that it may be doubted whether such disastrous effects on the one hand, or such brilliant prosperity on the other, as were seen in the wars between England and France, could now recur. In her secure and haughty sway of the seas England imposed a yoke on neutrals which will never again be borne; and the principle that the flag covers the goods is forever secured. The commerce of a belligerent can therefore now be safely carried on in neutral ships, except when contraband of war or to blockaded ports; and as regards the latter, it is also certain that there will be no more paper blockades. Putting aside therefore the question of defending her seaports from capture or contribution, as to which there is practical unanimity in theory and entire indifference in practice, what need has the United States of sea power? Her commerce is even now carried on by others; why should her people desire that which, if possessed, must be defended at great cost? So far as this question is economical, it is outside the scope of this work; but conditions which may entail suffering and loss on the country by war are directly pertinent to it. Granting therefore that the foreign trade of the United States, going and coming, is on board ships which an enemy cannot touch except when bound to a blockaded port, what will constitute an efficient blockade? The present definition is, that it is such as to constitute a manifest danger to a vessel seeking to enter or leave the port. This is evidently very elastic […] As for supplies which are contraband of war, is there not reason to fear that the United States is not now able to go alone if an emergency should arise?

The question is eminently one in which the influence of the government should make itself felt, to build up for the nation a navy which, if not capable of reaching distant countries, shall at least be able to keep clear the chief approaches to its own. The eyes of the country have for a quarter of a century been turned from the sea; the results of such a policy and of its opposite will be shown in the instance of France and of England. Without asserting a narrow parallelism between the case of the United States and either of these, it may safely be said that it is essential to the welfare of the whole country that the conditions of trade and commerce should remain, as far as possible, unaffected by an external war. In order to do this, the enemy must be kept not only out of our ports, but far away from our coasts.

Can this navy be had without restoring the merchant shipping? It is doubtful. History has proved that such a purely military sea power can be built up by a despot, as was done by Louis XIV; but though so fair seeming, experience showed that his navy was like a growth which having no root soon withers away. But in a representative government any military expenditure must have a strongly represented interest behind it, convinced of its necessity. Such an interest in sea power does not exist, cannot exist here, without action by the government. How such merchant shipping should be built up, whether by subsidies or by free trade, by constant administration of tonics or by free movement in the open air, is not a military but an economical question. Even had the United States a great national shipping, it may be doubted whether a sufficient navy would follow; the distance which separates her from other great powers, in one way a protection, is also a snare. The motive, if any there be, which will give the United States a navy, is probably now quickening in the Central American Isthmus. Let us hope it will not come to the birth too late.

Source: Alfred Thayer Mahan, *Influence of Sea Power Upon History, 1660–1783* (Boston: Little, Brown, and Company, 1890), 83–88.

Questions for Consideration

1) According to Captain Mahan, what three links in a "chain" were necessary to make any country a sea power?
2) Which conditions of trade and commerce remained essential to the welfare of the United States?
3) Do you agree with him in that "an interest in sea power does not exist, cannot exist here, without action by the government"?

9.2   William McKinley Calls for War (1898)

A combination of internal and external crises compelled the United States to participate to an extent in the worldwide scramble for empire. A prized possession of the Spanish empire, Cuba loomed only 90 miles off the coast of Florida. By 1894, rebels under the banner of "Cuba Libre" had launched an insurrection to end Spanish control of the island. Two years later, William McKinley won the U.S. presidential election on a platform that called for Cuban independence. Having seen death and destruction as a private during the Civil War, President McKinley was reluctant to intervene in Cuba. When riots erupted in Havana, however, he ordered the U.S.S. *Maine* to the harbor. On

February 15, 1898, an explosion on board the battleship left 266 American sailors dead—252 died immediately and another 14 died later from their injuries. Most Americans concluded, as did Assistant Secretary of the Navy Theodore Roosevelt, that Spain was responsible for the explosion. They called for war with the slogan: "Remember the *Maine*! To hell with Spain!" Nevertheless, no evidence was ever found linking Spain to the explosion. On April 11, 1898, President McKinley asked Congress for the authority to force Spain from Cuba. Both houses of Congress supported a declaration of war, although the Teller Amendment stipulated that the U.S. would not annex the island.

Document

Obedient to that precept of the Constitution which commands the President to give from time to time to the Congress information of the state of the Union and to recommend to their consideration such measures as he shall judge necessary and expedient, it becomes my duty now to address your body with regard to the grave crisis that has arisen in the relations of the United States to Spain by reason of the warfare that for more than three years has raged in the neighboring island of Cuba.

I do so because of the intimate connection of the Cuban question with the state of our own Union and the grave relation the course which it is now incumbent upon the nation to adopt must needs bear to the traditional policy of our government if it is to accord with the precepts laid down by the founders of the republic and religiously observed by succeeding administrations to the present day.

The present revolution is but the successor of other similar insurrections which have occurred in Cuba against the dominion of Spain, extending over a period of nearly half a century, each of which, during its progress, has subjected the United States to great effort and expense in enforcing its neutrality laws, caused enormous losses to American trade and commerce, caused irritation, annoyance, and disturbance among our citizens, and, by the exercise of cruel, barbarous, and uncivilized practices of warfare, shocked the sensibilities and offended the humane sympathies of our people [...]

The forcible intervention of the United States as a neutral to stop the war, according to the large dictates of humanity and following many historical precedents where neighboring states have interfered to check the hopeless sacrifices of life by internecine conflicts beyond their borders, is justifiable on rational grounds. It involves, however, hostile constraint upon both the parties to the contest as well to enforce a truce as to guide the eventual settlement.

The grounds for such intervention may be briefly summarized as follows:

First, in the cause of humanity and to put an end to the barbarities, bloodshed, starvation, and horrible miseries now existing there, and which the parties to the conflict are either unable or unwilling to stop or mitigate. It is no answer to say this is all in another country, belonging to another nation, and is therefore none of our business. It is specially our duty, for it is right at our door.

Second, we owe it to our citizens in Cuba to afford them that protection and indemnity for life and property which no government there can or will afford, and to that end to terminate the conditions that deprive them of legal protection.

Third, the right to intervene may be justified by the very serious injury to the commerce, trade, and business of our people, and by the wanton destruction of property and devastation of the island.

Fourth, and which is of the utmost importance, the present condition of affairs in Cuba is a constant menace to our peace, and entails upon this government an enormous expense. With such a conflict waged for years in an island so near us and with which our people have such trade and business relations; when the lives and liberty of our citizens are in constant danger and their property destroyed and themselves ruined; where our trading vessels are liable to seizure and are seized at our very door by warships of a foreign nation, the expeditions of filibustering that we are powerless to prevent altogether, and the irritating questions and entanglements thus arising—all these and others that I need not mention, with the resulting strained relations, are a constant menace to our peace, and compel us to keep on a semi-war footing with a nation with which we are at peace.

These elements of danger and disorder already pointed out have been strikingly illustrated by a tragic event which has deeply and justly moved the American people. I have already transmitted to Congress the report of the Naval Court of Inquiry on the destruction of the battleship *Maine* in the harbor of Havana during the night of the 15th of February. The destruction of that noble vessel has filled the national heart with inexpressible horror. Two hundred and fifty-eight brave sailors and marines and two officers of our Navy, reposing in the fancied security of a friendly harbor, have been hurled to death, grief and want brought to their homes, and sorrow to the nation. The Naval Court of Inquiry, which, it is needless to say, commands the unqualified confidence of the government, was unanimous in its conclusion that the destruction of the *Maine* was caused by an exterior explosion, that of a submarine mine. It did not assume to place the responsibility. That remains to be fixed.

In any event, the destruction of the *Maine*, by whatever exterior cause, is a patent and impressive proof of a state of things in Cuba that is intolerable. That condition is thus shown to be such that the Spanish government cannot assure safety and security to a vessel of the American Navy in the harbor of Havana on a mission of peace, and rightfully there [...] The only hope of relief and repose from a condition which can no longer be endured is the enforced pacification of Cuba. In the name of humanity, in the name of civilization, in behalf of endangered American interests which give us the right and the duty to speak and to act, the war in Cuba must stop.

In view of these facts and of these considerations, I ask the Congress to authorize and empower the President to take measures to secure a full and final termination of hostilities between the government of Spain and the people of Cuba, and to secure in the island the establishment of a stable government, capable of maintaining order and observing its international obligations, insuring peace and tranquility and the security of its citizens as well as our own, and to use the military and naval forces of the United States as may be necessary for these purposes.

And in the interest of humanity and to aid in preserving the lives of the starving people of the island, I recommend that the distribution of food and supplies be continued, and that an appropriation be made out of the public Treasury to supplement the charity of our citizens.

The issue is now with the Congress. It is a solemn responsibility. I have exhausted every effort to relieve the intolerable condition of affairs which is at our doors. Prepared to execute every obligation imposed upon me by the Constitution and the law, I await your action.

Source: William McKinley, "Message to the Congress, 11 April 1898," in *Messages and Papers of the Presidents, 1789–1907*, Volume 10, ed. James D. Richardson (New York: Bureau of National Literature and Art, 1908), 56–67.

Questions for Consideration

1) Who did President McKinley believe was responsible for "the exercise of cruel, barbarous, and uncivilized practices" of warfare?
2) Which event did he say "filled the national heart with inexpressible horror"?
3) Why did he propose using the armed forces to stop the war in Cuba?

9.3   Frank W. Pullen Charges in Cuba (1898)

While celebrating the gallantry of Theodore Roosevelt and the Rough Riders in Cuba, few Americans appreciated the sacrifices of black soldiers at the time. In fact, they constituted approximately 25% of the cavalry and infantry deployed to Cuba. The Spanish forces on the island referred to them as "smoked Yankees." Enlisted in the 25th Infantry, Sergeant Major Frank W. Pullen, Jr., recalled how African Americans impacted the fighting at El Caney and the capture of Santiago. His unit arrived in Cuba on June 22, 1898. They advanced in the Army's V Corps under the command of Major General William R. Shafter. With insufficient equipment and exhausted provisions, however, troops on the ground faced a logistical nightmare. On July 1, they launched an assault on the San Juan Heights around Santiago. Brigadier General Jacob F. Kent's division attacked on the left of the Heights, as Major General Joseph Wheeler sent his dismounted cavalry to the right. The charges succeeded dramatically. Meanwhile, Brigadier General Henry W. Lawton directed a strike against a Spanish garrison nearby at El Caney. In Santiago Bay, Rear Admiral William Sampson bottled up the Spanish vessels that the American naval fleet eventually destroyed. On July 16, 1898, the Spanish forces in Cuba surrendered to the U.S. Army.

Document

On the morning of June 24th the Rough Riders struck camp early and were marching along the trail at a rapid gait, at "route step," in any order suitable to the size of the road. Having marched several miles through a well-wooded country, they came to an opening near where the road forked. They turned into the left fork; at that moment, without the least warning, the Cubans leading the march having passed on unmolested, a volley from the Spanish behind a stone fort on top of the hill on both sides of the road was fired into their ranks. They were at first disconcerted, but rallied at once and began firing in the direction from whence came the volleys. They could not advance and dared not retreat, having been caught in a sunken place in the road, with a barbed-wire fence on one side and a precipitous hill on the other. They held their ground, but could do no more. The Spanish poured volley after volley into their ranks.

   At the moment when it looked as if the whole regiment would be swept down by the steel-jacketed bullets from the Mausers, four troops of the 10th U.S. Cavalry came up on "double time." Little thought the Spaniards that these "smoked Yankees" were so formidable. Perhaps they thought to stop those black boys by their relentless fire, but those boys knew no stop. They halted for a second, and having with them a Hotchkiss gun, soon knocked down the Spanish improvised fort, cut the barb-wire, making an opening for the

---

Rough Riders, started the charge, and, with the Rough Riders, routed the Spaniards, causing them to retreat in disorder, leaving their dead and some wounded behind. The Spaniards made a stubborn resistance. So hot was their fire directed at the men at the Hotchkiss gun that a head could not be raised, and men crawled on their stomachs like snakes loading and firing. It is an admitted fact that the Rough Riders could not have dislodged the Spanish by themselves without great loss, if at all.

The names of Captain A. M. Capron, Jr., and Sergeant Hamilton Fish, Jr., of the Rough Riders, who were killed in this battle, have been immortalized, while that of Corporal Brown, 10th Cavalry, who manned the Hotchkiss gun in this fight, without which the American loss in killed and wounded would no doubt have been counted by hundreds, and who was killed by the side of his gun, is unknown by the public.

At the time the battle of the Rough Riders was fought, the 25th Infantry was within hearing distance of the battle and received orders to reinforce them, which they could have done in less than two hours, but our Brigade Commander in marching to the scene of battle took the wrong trail, seemingly on purpose, and when we arrived at the place of battle twilight was fading into darkness.

The march in the direction of Santiago continued, until the evening of June 30th found us bivouacked in the road less than two miles from El Caney. At the first glimpse of day on the first day of July word was passed along the line for the companies to "fall in." No bugle call was sounded, no coffee was made, no noise allowed. We were nearing the enemy, and every effort was made to surprise him. We had been told that El Caney was well fortified, and so we found it.

The first warning the people had of a foe being near was the roar of our field artillery and the bursting of a shell in their midst. The battle was on. In many cases an invading army serves notice of a bombardment, but in this case it was incompatible with military strategy. Non-combatants, women and children, all suffered, for to have warned them so they might have escaped would also have given warning to the Spanish forces of our approach. The battle opened at dawn and lasted until dark. When our troops reached the point from which they were to make the attack, the Spanish lines of entrenched soldiers could not be seen. The only thing indicating their position was the blockhouse situated on the highest point of a very steep hill. The undergrowth was so dense that one could not see, on a line, more than fifty yards ahead. The Spaniards, from their advantageous position in the blockhouse and trenches on the hill top, had located the American forces in the bushes and opened a fusillade upon them. The Americans replied with great vigor, being ordered to fire at the blockhouse and to the right and left of it, steadily advancing as they fired.

All of the regiments engaged in the battle of El Caney had not reached their positions when the battle was precipitated by the artillery firing on the blockhouse. The 25th Infantry was among that number. In marching to its position some companies of the 2d Massachusetts Volunteers were met retreating; they were completely whipped, and took occasion to warn us, saying: "Boys, there is no use to go up there, you cannot see a thing; they are slaughtering our men!" Such news made us feel "shaky," not having, at the time, been initiated. We marched up, however, in order and were under fire for nine hours. Many barbed-wire obstructions were encountered, but the men never faltered. Finally, late in the afternoon, our brave Lieutenant Kinnison said to another officer: "We cannot take the trenches without charging them."

Just as he was about to give the order for the bugler to sound "the charge," he was wounded and carried to the rear. The men were then fighting like demons. Without a word of command, though led by that gallant and intrepid Second Lieutenant J. A. Moss, 25th Infantry, someone gave a yell and the 25th Infantry was off, alone, to the charge. The 4th U.S. Infantry, fighting on the left, halted when those dusky heroes made the dash with a yell which would have done credit to a Comanche Indian. No one knows who started the charge; one thing is certain, at the time it was made excitement was running high; each man was a captain for himself and fighting accordingly. Brigadier Generals, Colonels, Lieutenant-Colonels, Majors, etc., were not needed at the time the 25th Infantry made the charge on El Caney, and those officers simply watched the battle from convenient points, as Lieutenants and enlisted men made the charge alone.

It has been reported that the 12th U.S. Infantry made the charge, assisted by the 25th Infantry, but it is a recorded fact that the 25th Infantry fought the battle alone, the 12th Infantry coming up after the firing had nearly ceased. Private T. C. Butler, Company H, 25th Infantry, was the first man to enter the blockhouse at El Caney, and took possession of the Spanish flag for his regiment. An officer of the 12th Infantry came up while Butler was in the house and ordered him to give up the flag, which he was compelled to do, but not until he had torn a piece off the flag to substantiate his report to his Colonel of the injustice which had been done to him. Thus, by using the authority given him by his shoulder-straps, this officer took for his regiment that which had been won by the hearts' blood of some of the bravest, though black, soldiers of Shafter's army.

The charge of El Caney has been little spoken of, but it was quite as great a show of bravery as the famous taking of San Juan Hill.

Source: Frank W. Pullen, "The First Battle," in Edward Austin Johnson, ed., *A School History of the Negro Race in America from 1619 to 1890: Combined with the History of the Negro Soldiers in the Spanish-American War*, Rev. Ed. (New York: Isaac Goldmann Company, 1911), 234–242.

Questions for Consideration

1) Which unit, according to Sergeant Major Pullen, provided covering fire for the advance of the Rough Riders?
2) What action did he believe was "incompatible with military strategy" at El Caney?
3) Why do you think the "little spoken of" charge was not as famous as the taking of San Juan Hill?

9.4 Clara Barton Visits a Field Hospital (1898)

During the Spanish–American War, the U.S. Surgeon General's Office established a Nurse Corps Division to coordinate civilian nursing activities. Volunteer nurses toiled on board medical ships as well as at military camps, aid stations, and field hospitals. A few women physicians accompanied the American advance from Cuba to Puerto Rico. Clara Barton, a founder of the American Red Cross, entered Cuba even before the U.S. Army arrived during the summer of 1898. At the age of 77, she tended to the needs of casualties and managed the distribution of supplies. Since many humanitarian workers were skilled medical practitioners, military personnel regarded them highly. Recipients of aid included American soldiers, war prisoners, and Cuban refugees. In her report from Cuba, Barton described civilian volunteers waging war against infections, dysentery, malaria, typhoid, measles, and smallpox. Around 400 Americans died from their wounds in combat; another 2,565 perished from disease. Major combat operations ended after four months of fighting, as the U.S. gained control of Guam, Puerto Rico, and the Philippines. The formal peace treaty was signed in Paris on December 10, 1898, and was ratified by the U.S. Senate on February 6, 1899. After returning home, Barton eventually died at the age of 90 from tuberculosis.

Document

The road was simply terrific—clayey, muddy, wet and cut to the hub. A ride of about four hours brought us to the First Division Hospital of the Fifth Army Corps, General [William] Shafter's headquarters. This was properly the second day after the fight. Two fearful nights had passed.

The sight that greeted us on going into the so-called hospital grounds was something indescribable. The land was perfectly level—no drainage whatever, covered with long, tangled grass, skirted by trees, brush and shrubbery—a few little dog tents, not much larger than would have been made of an ordinary tablecloth thrown over a short rail, and under these lay huddled together the men fresh from the field or from the operating tables, with no covering over them save such as had clung to them through their troubles, and in the majority of cases no blanket under them. Those who had come from the tables, having been compelled to leave all the clothing they had, as having been too wet, muddy and bloody to be retained by them, were entirely nude, lying on the stubble grass, the sun fitfully dealing with them, sometimes clouding over, and again streaming out in a blaze above them. As we passed, we drew our hats over our eyes, turning our faces away as much as possible for the delicacy of the poor fellows who lay there with no shelter either from the elements or the eyes of the passers-by.

Getting past them as quickly as possible, and seeing a smoke ahead of us, and relying upon the old adage that where there is smoke there must be fire, we went to it. A half-dozen bricks had been laid about a yard apart, a couple of pieces of wagon-tire laid across these, so low and so near the ground that no fire of any strength or benefit could be made, the bits of wet wood put under crosswise, with the smoke streaming a foot out on each side, and two kettles of coffee or soup and a small frying-pan with some meat in it, appeared to be the cook-house for these men. They told us there were about eight hundred men under the tents and lying in the grass, and more constantly coming-in [...]

The rain that had been drizzling more or less all day increased. Our supplies were taken from the wagon, a piece of tarpaulin found to protect them, and as the fire began to blaze and the water to heat, Mrs. Gardner and I found the way into the bags and boxes of flour, salt, milk and meal, and got material for the first gallons of gruel. I had not thought to ever make gruel again over a camp-fire; I cannot say how far it carried me back in the lapse of time, or really where or who I felt that I was. It did not seem to be me, and still I seemed to know how to do it, and when the bubbling contents of our kettles thickened and grew white with the condensed milk, and we began to give it out, putting it in the hands of the men detailed as nurses and of our own to take it around to the poor sufferers shivering and naked in the rain, I felt again that perhaps it was not in vain that history had reproduced itself. And when the nurses came back and told us of the surprise with which it was received and the tears that rolled down the sunburned, often bloody, face into the cup as the poor fellow drank his hot gruel and asked where it came from, who sent it, and said it was the first food he had tasted in three, sometimes in four, days (for they had gone into the fight hungry), I felt it was again the same old story, and wondered what gain there had been in the last thirty years. Had anything been worse than this? But still, as we moralized, the fires burned and the gruel steamed and boiled and bucket after bucket went out, until those eight hundred men had each his cup of gruel and knew that he could have another and as many as he wanted. The day waned and the darkness came and still the men were unsheltered, uncovered, naked and wet—scarcely a groan, no word of complaint; no man said he was not well treated.

The operating tables were full of the wounded. Man after man was taken off and brought on his litter and laid beside other men and something given him to keep the little life in his body that seemed fast oozing out. All night it went on. It grew cold—for naked men, bitter cold before morning. We had no blankets, nothing to cover them, only as we tore off from a cut of cotton cloth, which by some means had gotten on with us, strips six or seven feet long, and giving them to our men, asked them to go and give to each uncovered man a piece that should shield his nakedness. This made it possible for him to permit us to pass by him if we needed to go in that direction.

Early in the morning ambulances started, and such as could be loaded in were taken to be carried back over that rough, pitiless road down to Siboney to the hospitals there, that we had done the best we could toward fitting up—where our hundred cots and our hundred and fifty blankets had gone, and our cups and spoons and the delicacies that would help to strengthen these poor fainting men if once they could get there, and where also were the Sisters under Dr. Lesser and Dr. Le Garde to attend them.

They brought out man after man, stretcher after stretcher, to the waiting ambulances, and they took out seventeen who had died in the night—unattended, save by the nurse—uncomplaining, no last word, no dying message, quiet and speechless life had ceased and the soul had fled.

Source: Clara Barton, *The Red Cross: A History of this Remarkable International Movement in the Interest of Humanity* (Washington, DC: American National Red Cross, 1898), 563–573.

Questions for Consideration

1) What, according to Barton, was "indescribable" about the First Division Hospital?
2) How did the men under the tents react to her distribution of gruel?
3) Why did she distribute cuts of cotton cloth in "strips six or seven feet long" to the wounded soldiers upon the litters?

9.5   Frederick N. Funston Operates in the Philippines (1901)

Thanks to the operations of the American Asiatic Squadron under Commodore George Dewey, U.S. forces quickly occupied the Philippine Islands. Filipinos under the leadership of Emilio Aguinaldo formed the Army of Liberation, which began to fight the Americans as they once fought the Spanish. The McKinley administration worried that another European power might seize the archipelago if American regiments left prematurely. After 1899, the U.S. Army began building schools, hospitals, and roads in the Philippines. Despite co-opting many Filipinos, American commanders grew frustrated with the insurgency. They permitted actions such as the "water cure"—an interrogation technique in which water was poured down a captive's throat until information was forthcoming. Taking command in 1900, Major General Arthur MacArthur expanded the operations of the native constabulary and scout units. He authorized Colonel Frederick N. Funston to personally lead a small party that included Filipino auxiliaries known as the Macabebes. They were a tribal population named for their home town in central Luzon. Colonel Funston posed as their prisoner to gain entry to Aguinaldo's headquarters at the village of Palanan. As he recalled for his memoirs, the party captured the Filipino leader on March 23, 1901. Consequently, Aguinaldo wrote a general proclamation to his fellow insurgents asking them to surrender.

Document

About half-way to the town we were disturbed by meeting a Macabebe sergeant and one of the privates coming back along the trail as rapidly as they could. The two men were out of breath, and simply motioned frantically to us to get off the trail and hide in the woods. This we did, and they joined us. The sergeant quickly explained that some real insurgent soldiers were on the way to Dinundungan to take charge of us, in order that all the men of our party might be able to come to Palanan. Soon we heard the men come splashing along laughing and talking. They passed within thirty feet of us, as we lay close to the ground, almost fearing to breathe [...]

We resumed our march, having had a fine scare. It was not desirable to catch up with the main body, as we correctly presumed that some officers might come out from Palanan to meet it, and see that the orders regarding the prisoners were not being carried out, so that we kept some distance behind it until we realized that we were approaching the town, and then hurried on as much as possible.

The main interest now centers in the adventures of the main column, the one by which the actual capture was made. About a mile outside the town it was met by a couple of insurgent officers, who escorted them the remainder of the distance. About three o'clock they approached the Palanan River, here about a hundred yards wide and quite deep, and saw the town on the other side. The only way to cross this stream was by means of a rather good-sized *banca*. Hilario and Segovia crossed with the first load, leaving instructions for the men to follow as rapidly as they could, form on the opposite bank, and then march up to Aguinaldo's house, where they would find him. The boat was to be sent back to await our arrival. Segovia and Hilario now had a most trying half-hour. They called on Aguinaldo at his head-quarters, and found him surrounded by seven insurgent officers, all of them armed with revolvers. Outside, the fifty men of the escort, neatly uniformed and armed with Mausers, were drawn up to do the honors for the reinforcements that had made such a wonderful march to join them. Segovia and Hilario entertained those present with stories of the march from Lacuna's head-quarters, and were warmly congratulated on having made it successfully. Segovia took his position where he could look out of one of the open windows and see when the time had arrived.

Finally, the Macabebes under Dionisio Bató and Gregorio Cadhit marched-up, Segovia stepped to the head of the stairway outside the house, for they were in the second story, and signaled to Gregorio, who called out, "Now is the time, Macabebes. Give it to them." The poor little "Macs" were in such a nervous state from their excitement over the strange drama that they were playing a part in that they were pretty badly rattled. They had loaded their pieces and were standing at "order arms," as were the men of the escort facing them on the other side of the little square. They fired a ragged volley, killing two men of the escort and severely wounding the leader of Aguinaldo's band, who happened to be passing between the lines when fire was opened. Aguinaldo, hearing the firing, and thinking that the men of his escort had broken loose to celebrate the arrival of the rein-forcements, stepped to the window, and called out, "Stop that foolishness. Don't waste your ammunition." Before he could turn around Hilario had grasped him about the waist and thrown him under a table, where he literally sat on him, and Hilario was a fat man. I had given the most positive orders to the effect that under no circumstances should Aguinaldo be killed, and that no lives should be taken unless it was absolutely necessary. But as Segovia dashed back into the room several of the officers started to draw their revolvers, and he opened fire on them, hitting Villa three times, who was tugging to get a Mauser automatic pistol out of its holster, and also wounding Major Alhambra. Villa sur-rendered, as did Santiago Barcelona, treasurer of the so-called republic. Alhambra and the other officers leaped from one of the windows into the river, the house standing on the bank, and escaped by swimming. As Hilario grasped Aguinaldo, he had said, "You are a prisoner of the Americans," so that the fallen "Dictator," as he now called himself, had some sort of a vague idea of what had happened to him.

In the meantime, we Americans with our supposed guard had reached the river, jumped into the *banca* waiting for us, and had paddled across in frantic haste. Running up the bank toward the house, we were met by Segovia, who came running out, his face aglow with exultation and his clothing spattered with the blood of the men he had wounded. He called out in Spanish, "It is all right. We have him." We hastened into the house, and I introduced myself to Aguinaldo, telling him that we were officers of the American army, that the men with us were our troops, and not his, and that he was a prisoner of war […]

It was now the opinion that the war that had wasted the country for so long a time was at its end. In the meantime I had hurried to tell the news of my return to the poor woman who for three long weeks had waited in an agony of suspense. A few days later General MacArthur sent for me, and as I entered his office said, with a very serious look on his face, "Well, Funston, they do not seem to have thought much in Washington of your perfor-mance. I am afraid you have got into trouble." At the same time he handed me a cable-gram announcing my appointment as a brigadier-general in the regular army. The other officers, all of whom had splendidly done their parts, were also given commissions in the regular army, while Segovia, Segismundo, the three Tagalos, and the Macabebes were given appropriate rewards in various sums of money.

Source: Frederick N. Funston, *Memories of Two Wars: Cuban and Philippine Experiences* (New York: Charles Scribner's Sons), 384–426.

Questions for Consideration

1) What prompted Colonel Funston "to get off the trail and hide in the woods" during the operation at Palanan?
2) Did the operation suggest that he was foolhardy, brave, or lucky?
3) Do you believe that he gave proper credit to the Filipino auxiliaries?

9.6 The Committee on Naval Affairs Investigates Submarines (1902)

To make warfare beneath the waters possible, the Navy Department began investing resources in submersible technology. Although underwater boats were used by Americans as early as 1776, the U.S. Navy commissioned its first submarine in 1900. John R. Holland, an engineer living in New Jersey, designed the Type VI craft. He combined the internal-combustion engine for surface cruising with a battery-powered electric motor for submerged operations. Christened the U.S.S. *Holland*, it constituted an effective weapon for close-to-shore coastal defense. However, it lacked the capacity for attacking targets on the high seas. Since the submarine possessed no significant commercial applications, its technological development depended almost entirely on appropriations from Congress. To that end, the House Committee on Naval Affairs held a hearing to investigate the progress of submarines on May 20, 1902. Captain Richard Wainwright, superintendent of the U.S. Naval Academy, testified along with other naval officers. Given the questions of committee members, the hearing involved back-and-forth discussions about construction, design, tactics, and strategy. By 1914, generous federal expenditures enabled the U.S. Navy to acquire 34 underwater vessels. A dozen of them weighed over 500 tons. Eventually, the Holland Torpedo Boat Company evolved into General Dynamics and became the builder of the most technologically advanced submarines in the world.

Document

MR. LESSLER.	Being so new on this subject, I would like to know this, as a mechanical proposition: Is there any certitude as to its present standing as a defensive armament?
CAPTAIN WAINWRIGHT.	I believe it stands on a line with all adopted naval weapons.
MR. LESSLER.	I am asking it as a mechanical proposition.
CAPTAIN WAINWRIGHT.	Yes.
MR. LESSLER.	Has the building of torpedo-boats arrived at such perfectibility that you can say it is mechanically good and sound?
CAPTAIN WAINWRIGHT.	It has.
MR. LESSLER.	And that there is no question mark?

CAPTAIN WAINWRIGHT.	No; there may be improvements, but in its present stage it is what I would call a perfected weapon. You never know that you cannot make a mechanical device a little superior to what it is today; but in its present state it is capable of effective use. It is a good mechanical device […]
THE CHAIRMAN.	How many submarine boats are we building now? Eight of them?
CAPTAIN WAINWRIGHT.	Ten, I think it is.
THE CHAIRMAN.	Ten submarine boats?
MR. FROST.	Seven.
THE CHAIRMAN.	Have you seen these boats?
CAPTAIN WAINWRIGHT.	I have not—I have seen them; yes; but I have not seen them do anything. I have seen the *Shark* launched.
THE CHAIRMAN.	You have been down in the *Holland*?
CAPTAIN WAINWRIGHT.	Yes.
THE CHAIRMAN.	Have you been out on any of these cruises with her?
CAPTAIN WAINWRIGHT.	I was out in Chesapeake Bay with her.
THE CHAIRMAN.	How many times have you been out in her?
CAPTAIN WAINWRIGHT.	I have only been out once in her. I have been out three or four times to see her. You can see more if you are above water than you can if you are down in her, after you have had experience.
THE CHAIRMAN.	What is the temperature inside of the boat? Is there any way of heating it?
CAPTAIN WAINWRIGHT.	They can be heated; yes. I think they get heat in them now by electric heaters.
THE CHAIRMAN.	They are used mostly in warm weather, or have been, I suppose? The tests have been mostly in warm weather.
CAPTAIN WAINWRIGHT.	Mostly in warm weather; yes. There is no difficulty in electrical heating.
THE CHAIRMAN.	Have you electric heaters in connection with them at all, Mr. Frost?
MR. FROST.	No, sir.
THE CHAIRMAN.	I will ask, Lieutenant Caldwell, have you ever made tests of the *Holland* during cold weather?
LIEUTENANT CALDWELL.	Yes, sir.
THE CHAIRMAN.	In what month?
LIEUTENANT CALDWELL.	Practically all the year around, at Annapolis; practically throughout the winter. She made a trip to Norfolk a year ago last January. It was very cold, and we overcame the cold by electric heaters.
THE CHAIRMAN.	What was the temperature, on the average, in the boat?
LIEUTENANT CALDWELL.	I do not remember that. It was above freezing; about forty degrees, I should say, was the average temperature.

Source: Hearings Before the Committee on Naval Affairs, House of Representatives, on Submarine Boats (Washington, DC: Government Printing Office, 1902), 2–10.

Questions for Consideration

1) What, according to Captain Wainwright, indicated that the submarine torpedo-boat was "a perfected weapon" at that time?
2) How many submarines were under construction?
3) Why were the "tests" in cold weather significant?

9.7 Dan Dugal Tours the World (1907–1909)

In 1907, the U.S. Navy abandoned its dispersed squadron deployments to concentrate its 16 battleships in the Atlantic waters. Painted white with gilded scrollwork on their bows, the battleships inspired the nickname, the "Great White Fleet." Under the command of Rear Admiral Robley D. Evans, the U.S.S. *Connecticut* was the flagship for a grand world tour. The battleships departed from Hampton Roads, Virginia, on December 16, 1907. President Theodore Roosevelt, an advocate for developing a large navy, welcomed them home on February 22, 1909. Manned by 14,000 crew members, this particular cruise covered some 43,000 miles and included 20 port calls on six different continents. Dan Dugal, one of the bluejackets, kept a journal of his visit to Magdalena Bay, where the battleships carried out gunnery practice. The schedule for the "sea dogs" was daunting, to say the least. They completed rounds of chores, watches, and drills on deck. The "black gang" in the fire room below deck endured searing heat and coal dust. Of course, most earned liberties to go ashore on occasional diversions. With a global reach that extended well beyond North America, the U.S. Navy enforced the Roosevelt Corollary to the Monroe Doctrine, which asserted that the United States intended to "police" the Western Hemisphere. Thus, the "Great White Fleet" symbolized American military strength in a progressive era.

Document

Last night the *Saturn*, our supply ship, came in from the states, bringing stores, mail, and coal. We were overjoyed to see her being convoyed into the harbor by the torpedo boat destroyer, which brought the mail on in, as the *Saturn* anchored some distance out because of her deep draught. As it has been two weeks or more since we have had any mail, all hands were anxious to hear from friends and home.

The little black destroyer charged down upon us through the dusk, like a phantom ship, her search-light playing from the bridge, and her band playing full blast from the quarter deck, making more noise than some minstrel troupe in front of a Powell street theatre. As she passed between us and the flagship, we gave her a rousing cheer, the flagship did the same, and so she struck up an even livelier air by way of recognition of our applause. We were not applauding her music, however, but her cargo of mail, and the expedient method she had of delivering it. She stopped a few lengths away, and the steam launches of the various ships went alongside and received their mail.

A large bag came to us and was read out as soon as it had been assorted, so we all spent the evening reading letters and papers from almost every quarter of the United States. Among our ship's company are to be found representatives of every state in the union, and some that aren't in the union.

Some of the ships have run short of supplies lately, and eating has been bad all around. Our commissary department ran short of flour, so we have been eating hard tack. I hope the *Saturn* has brought a large supply of flour, for then, if everything else gets so bad it cannot be eaten, we will live upon bread alone.

The hard tack we have been eating was by no means the best in the land, being that twenty-five hole brand which is manufactured in the East, and special care taken lest it be too nice, for in that case the sailors would eat too much of it. There would have been no complaint to make, however, if it had not been full of small bugs. Each piece contained many hundreds of these little animals, and when it was broken on the table preparatory to being eaten, they scrambled hither and thither across the table, running under plates, into the meat pan, or around the coffee cups, anywhere to get out of sight.

In preference to eating our meal, us fellows amused ourselves by having bug races down the center of the table. A dozen or more bugs would be entered into each race. Each member of the mess would own a bug and bet on him. After several try-outs, we could ascertain the distance our bugs were best able to run, and in this way kept the competitive bugs in their respective classes. Some of them could run a speedy two plate length race, while others were longer-winded and could run a dozen plate lengths. If any bug tried to dodge out of the race he was disqualified, and his owner had to drown him in his coffee, and drink him; such was the harsh treatment of an unfair bug [...]

The new week brings no change whatever in our routine drills. We go to morning inspection and quarters at nine-thirty, man the loading machine for about fifteen minutes, then go to "ping pong" and fire a few dozen shots each out of the small gun fast to the big one. After that, we do as we like until one-thirty, when the one-pounders are manned for a half hour or so, which concludes the drills of the day.

The hot day drags on, the bay lies calm and serene; we ride at a slack chain. The incessant boom, boom, of the great guns, being fired out on the range, sweeps in upon us, breaking into the stillness of the afternoon, reminding us drowsy sailors that it will soon be our turn to go out there and break some of those records the other ships have made.

Several of the boys are lying at my feet taking it easy, up here under the fo'castle awning. They are telling each other the gossip of the ship, and stating their varied opinions concerning the food we have been getting lately [...] Every man of them has some sort of grievance to talk about, and when they have nothing better to do, they are fond of criticising their superiors.

Sailors are notorious growlers, and if they cannot find one thing to growl about, they will another; one time it is because they don't get any liberty; the next time it is about their food, whether they are getting the best or not, they can at least find fault with the way it is cooked, and they are usually right about that part and wrong about almost everything else they choose to growl about.

Source: Dan Dugal, "Journal of a Bluejacket Written at Magdalena Bay," *Overland* 52 (August 1908): 137–143.

Questions for Consideration

1) What did the reaction to the supply ship imply about the morale of the battleship crew?
2) When were the "drills of the day" concluded?
3) Why do you think that the sailors found the "bug races" so amusing?

Suggested Readings

Abrahamson, James L. *America Arms for a New Century: The Making of a Great Military Power*. New York: Free Press, 1981.

Boot, Max. *The Savage Wars of Peace: Small Wars and the Rise of American Power*. New York: Basic Books, 2002.

Challener, Richard D. *Admirals, Generals, and American Foreign Policy, 1898–1914*. Princeton: Princeton University Press, 1973.

Cirillo, Vincent J. *Bullets and Bacilli: The Spanish–American War and Military Medicine*. New Brunswick, NJ: Rutgers University Press, 1999.

Gardner, Mark Lee. *Rough Riders: Theodore Roosevelt, His Cowboy Regiment, and the Immortal Charge Up San Juan Hill*. New York: William Morrow, 2016.

Hoganson, Kristin. *Fighting for American Manhood: How Gender Politics Provoked the Spanish-American and Philippine-American Wars*. New Haven: Yale University Press, 1998.

Linn, Brian McAllister. *The Philippine War, 1899–1902*. Lawrence: University Press of Kansas, 1999.

McBride, William M. *Technological Change and the United States Navy, 1865–1945*. Baltimore: Johns Hopkins University, 2000.

McCartney, Paul T. *Power and Progress: American National Identity, the War of 1898, and the Rise of American Imperialism*. Baton Rouge: Louisiana State University Press, 2006.

Musicant, Ivan. *Empire by Default: The Spanish-American War and the Dawn of the American Century*. New York: Henry Holt, 1998.

Reardon, Carol. *Soldiers and Scholars: The U.S. Army and the Uses of Military History, 1865-1920*. Lawrence: University Press of Kansas, 1990.

Shulman, Mark Russell. *Navalism and the Emergence of American Sea Power, 1882-1893*. Annapolis: Naval Institute Press, 1995.

Sibley, David. *War of Frontier and Empire: The Philippine-American War, 1899–1902*. New York: Hill and Wang, 2007.

Spector, Ronald. *Professors of War: The Naval War College and the Development of the Naval Profession*. Newport, RI: Naval War College Press, 1977.

Trask, David F. *The War with Spain in 1898*. Lincoln: University of Nebraska Press, 1996.

10

The War to End all Wars

Chronology

1914 The Great War begins in Europe
1915 Lusitania attacked
1916 Punitive Expedition to Mexico
National Defense Act
1917 Zimmerman Telegram
U.S. declares war on Germany
Selective Service Act
AEF arrives in Europe
Russia withdraws from the Great War
1918 President Wilson's Fourteen Points
Battle of Cantigny
Battle of Château-Thierry
Battle of Belleau Wood
U.S. forces enter Russia
Battle of Meuse-Argonne
Armistice Day
U.S. forces enter Germany
1919 Treaty of Versailles

10.1 Woodrow Wilson Calls for War (1917)

The Great War erupted in Europe during the summer of 1914. The following year, submarine warfare on the high seas fueled American distrust of Germany. One German submarine sank a British passenger liner, the *Lusitania*, which resulted in the death of 124 Americans on board. President Woodrow Wilson spoke of the United States being "too proud to fight," even though he sent a military expedition into Mexico during 1916. Following his reelection that November, he announced plans to bring an end to the war in Europe. However, Germany ignored his plans and launched a major offensive against the British and the French armies along the Western Front. German submarines resumed "unrestricted" warfare to cut off supplies flowing to the Triple Entente. Consequently, they torpedoed three American ships. Furthermore, British officials gave the Wilson

American Military History: A Documentary Reader, Second Edition. Brad D. Lookingbill.
© 2019 John Wiley & Sons, Inc. Published 2019 by John Wiley & Sons, Inc.

administration a secret telegram sent to Mexico from German foreign minister Arthur Zimmerman, who ostensibly proposed an alliance to help them regain "lost provinces" from the U.S. On April 2, 1917, President Wilson asked Congress for a declaration of war on Germany. Before a joint session, he delivered a dramatic speech regarding the mission of the armed forces. Despite fierce opposition from pacifists, Congress declared war four days later. Thus, the U.S. entered the war as an associate power of the Allies.

Document

With a profound sense of the solemn and even tragical character of the step I am taking and of the grave responsibilities which it involves, but in unhesitating obedience to what I deem my constitutional duty, I advise that the Congress declare the recent course of the Imperial German Government to be in fact nothing less than war against the Government and people of the United States; that it formally accept the status of belligerent which has thus been thrust upon it, and that it take immediate steps not only to put the country in a more thorough state of defense but also to exert all its power and employ all its resources to bring the Government of the German Empire to terms and end the war [...]

A steadfast concert for peace can never be maintained except by a partnership of democratic nations. No autocratic government could be trusted to keep faith within it or observe its covenants. It must be a league of honour, a partnership of opinion. Intrigue would eat its vitals away; the plottings of inner circles who could plan what they would and render account to no one would be a corruption seated at its very heart. Only free peoples can hold their purpose and their honour steady to a common end and prefer the interests of mankind to any narrow interest of their own.

Does not every American feel that assurance has been added to our hope for the future peace of the world by the wonderful and heartening things that have been happening within the last few weeks in Russia? Russia was known by those who knew it best to have been always in fact democratic at heart, in all the vital habits of her thought, in all the intimate relationships of her people that spoke their natural instinct, their habitual attitude towards life. The autocracy that crowned the summit of her political structure, long as it had stood and terrible as was the reality of its power, was not in fact Russian in origin, character, or purpose; and now it has been shaken off and the great, generous Russian people have been added in all their naive majesty and might to the forces that are fighting for freedom in the world, for justice, and for peace. Here is a fit partner for a league of honour.

One of the things that has served to convince us that the Prussian autocracy was not and could never be our friend is that from the very outset of the present war it has filled our unsuspecting communities and even our offices of government with spies and set criminal intrigues everywhere afoot against our national unity of counsel, our peace within and without, our industries and our commerce. Indeed, it is now evident that its spies were here even before the war began; and it is unhappily not a matter of conjecture but a fact proved in our courts of justice that the intrigues which have more than once come perilously near to disturbing the peace and dislocating the industries of the country have been carried on at the instigation, with the support, and even under the personal direction of official agents of the Imperial Government accredited to the Government of the United States. Even in checking these things and trying to extirpate them we have sought to put the most generous interpretation possible upon them because we knew that their source lay, not in any hostile feeling or purpose of the German people towards us (who were, no doubt, as ignorant of them as we ourselves were), but only in the selfish designs of a Government that did what it pleased and told its people nothing. But they have played their part in serving to convince us at last that that Government entertains no real friendship for us and means to act against our peace and security at its convenience. That it means to stir up enemies against us at our very doors the intercepted note to the German Minister at Mexico City is eloquent evidence.

We are accepting this challenge of hostile purpose because we know that in such a government, following such methods, we can never have a friend; and that in the presence of its organized power, always lying in wait to accomplish we know not what purpose, there can be no assured security for the democratic governments of the world. We are now about to accept gauge of battle with this natural foe to liberty and shall, if necessary, spend the whole force of the nation to check and nullify its pretensions and its power. We are glad, now that we see the facts with no veil of false pretense about them, to fight thus for the ultimate peace of the world and for the liberation of its peoples, the German peoples included: for the rights of nations great and small and the privilege of men everywhere to choose their way of life and of obedience. The world must be made safe for democracy. Its peace must be planted upon the tested foundations of political liberty. We have no selfish ends to serve. We desire no conquest, no dominion. We seek no indemnities for ourselves, no material compensation for the sacrifices we shall freely make. We are but one of the champions of the rights of mankind. We shall be satisfied when those rights have been made as secure as the faith and the freedom of nations can make them [...]

It is a distressing and oppressive duty, gentlemen of the Congress, which I have performed in thus addressing you. There are, it may be, many months of fiery trial and sacrifice ahead of us. It is a fearful thing to lead this great peaceful people into war, into the most terrible and disastrous of all wars, civilization itself seeming to be in the balance. But the right is more precious than peace, and we shall fight for the things which we have always carried nearest our hearts—for democracy, for the right of those who submit to authority to have a voice in their own governments, for the rights and liberties of small nations, for a universal dominion of right by such a concert of free peoples as shall bring peace and safety to all nations and make the world itself at last free. To such a task we can dedicate our lives and our fortunes, everything that we are and everything that we have, with the pride of those who know that the day has come when America is privileged to spend her blood and her might for the principles that gave her birth and happiness and the peace which she has treasured. God helping her, she can do no other.

Source: Woodrow Wilson, "Address to Congress, 2 April 1917," in *President Wilson's State Papers and Addresses*, intro. by Albert Shaw (New York: George H. Doran Company, 1918), 372–383.

Questions for Consideration

1) Who, according to President Wilson, was waging war against the United States in 1917?
2) Which type of nations did not belong to "a league of honour"?
3) What did he mean in that America "is privileged to spend her blood and her might for the principles that gave her birth and happiness and the peace which she has treasured"?

10.2   George M. Cohan Composes "Over There" (1917)

News of the Great War stirred the emotions of the American people. Communities across the U.S. planned parades and rallies during 1917. While traveling by train in New York, entertainer George M. Cohan composed a song called "Over There." In the verses, he urged a typical young American—Johnnie—to "get your gun." Noted for its catchy melody and clever lyrics, the chorus became a standard of Tin Pan Alley and helped to stimulate enthusiasm for wartime mobilization. Songwriters, performers, and publishers celebrated the call for "100 percent Americanism." A few ridiculed the German monarch, Kaiser Wilhelm II. The patriotic fervor excited audiences in musical theaters, movie houses, churches, and homes. The Committee on Public Information, an independent agency established by an executive order of the Wilson administration, used propaganda techniques to persuade citizens to support the war effort. However, individuals who openly criticized military policy became liable for prosecution under the Espionage and the Sedition Acts. Given the drive for sacrifice and unity, many Americans were convinced not only to accept the war aims but also to join a political crusade. Waging war represented a traditional task of the federal government, to be sure, but selling war pointed the nation in a new direction.

Document

Johnnie get your gun, get your gun, get your gun,
Take it on the run, on the run, on the run,
Hear them calling you and me,
Ev'ry son of liberty.
Hurry right away, no delay, go today,
Make your daddy glad to have had such a lad,
Tell your sweetheart not to pine,
To be proud her boy's in line.
  Over there over there
  Send the word, send the word over there
  That the Yanks are coming, the Yanks are coming,
  The drums rum-tumming ev'rywhere
  So prepare say a pray'r
  Send the word, send the word to beware
  We'll be over, we're coming over,
  And we won't come back till it's over over there!

Johnnie get your gun, get your gun, get your gun,
Johnnie show the Hun you're a son of a gun,
Hoist the flag and let her fly,
Like true heroes do or die.
Pack your little kit, show your grit, do your bit,
Soldiers to the ranks from the towns and the tanks,

Make your mother proud of you
And to liberty be true.
    Over there over there
    Send the word, send the word over there
    That the Yanks are coming, the Yanks are coming,
    The drums rum-tumming ev'rywhere
    So prepare say a pray'r
    Send the word, send the word to beware
    We'll be over, we're coming over,
    And we won't come back till it's over over there!

Source: George M. Cohan, "Over There," 1917, Notated Music, Library of Congress. https://www.loc.gov/item/ihas.100010516 (accessed 6 June 2017).

Questions for Consideration

1) What was Johnnie supposed to show "the Hun"?
2) Which family members of Johnnie were mentioned in the song?
3) Why do you suppose the song insisted that "we won't come back till it's over over there"?

10.3 Congress Passes the Selective Service Act (1917)

The scale and scope of the Great War demanded military service from millions of American citizens. Even though President Wilson previously pledged "preparedness," Army regulars numbered only 133,111 at the time of U.S. entry in the Great War. They were reinforced by no more than 185,000 National Guardsmen. The Army Chief of Staff, Major General Hugh Scott, and his deputy, Major General Tasker Bliss, lacked the manpower to wage war on European battlefields. While recruiting volunteers for enlistment in wartime, the Wilson administration devised a nationwide system of conscription. Secretary of War Newton D. Baker, a pacifist, described it as "selective service." On May 13, 1917, Congress passed the first Selective Service Act. Initially, males between the ages of 21 and 30 were required to register for the draft. Congress amended the law to include ages 18 to 45 the following year. Though coordinated by the War Department, civilian boards examined the registrants. Millions of registrants were called, but not all were drafted. Several were deemed physically unfit, while some received exemptions on the grounds of family dependency, alien status, critical occupations, and religious beliefs. Nevertheless, the selective service system quickly filled the ranks with what American society failed to yield in the past, that is, a truly "National Army."

Document

Be it enacted by the Senate and House of Representatives of the United States of America in Congress assembled, That in view of the existing emergency, which demands the raising of troops in addition to those now available, the President be, and he is hereby, authorized—

First. Immediately to raise, organize, officer, and equip all or such number of increments of the Regular Army provided by the national defense act approved June third, nineteen hundred and sixteen, or such parts thereof as he may deem necessary; to raise all organizations of the Regular Army, including those added by such increments, to the maximum enlisted strength authorized by law [...]

Sec. 4. That the Vice President of the United States, the officers, legislative, executive, and judicial, of the United States and of the several States, Territories, and the District of Columbia, regular or duly ordained ministers of religion, students who are at the time of the approval of this Act are preparing for the ministry in recognized theological or divinity schools, and all persons in the military and naval service of the United States shall be exempt from the selective draft herein prescribed; (and nothing in this act contained shall be construed to require or compel any person to serve in any of the forces herein provided for who is found to be a member of any well-recognized religious sect or organization at present organized and existing and whose existing creed or principles forbid its members to participate in war in any form and whose religious convictions are against war or participation therein in accordance with the creed or principles of said religious organizations, but no person so exempted shall be exempted from service in any capacity that the President shall declare to be noncombatant); and the President is hereby authorized to exclude or discharge from said selective draft and from the draft under the second paragraph of section one hereof, or to draft for partial military service only from those liable to draft as in this act provided, persons of the following classes: County and municipal officials; customhouse clerks; persons employed by the United States in the transmission of the mail; artificers and workmen employed in the armories, arsenals, and navy yards of the United States, and such other persons employed in the service of the United States as the President may designate; pilots; mariners actually employed in the sea service of any citizen or merchant within the United States; persons engaged in industries, including agriculture, found to be necessary to the maintenance of the Military Establishment or the effective operation of the military forces or the maintenance of national interest during the emergency; those in a status with respect to persons dependent upon them for support which renders their exclusion or discharge advisable; and those found to be physically or morally deficient. No exemption or exclusion shall continue when a cause therefore no longer exists: *Provided*, That notwithstanding the exemptions enumerated herein each State, Territory, and the District of Columbia shall be required to supply its quota in the proportion that its population bears to the total population of the United States.

The President is hereby authorized, in his discretion, to create and establish, throughout the several States and subdivisions thereof and in the Territories and the District of Columbia local boards, and where, in his discretion, practicable and desirable, there shall be created and established one such local board in each county or similar subdivision in each State, and one for approximately each thirty thousand of population in each city of thirty thousand population or over, according to the last census taken or estimates furnished by the Bureau of Census of the Department of Commerce. Such boards shall be appointed by the President, and shall consist of three or more members, none of whom shall be connected with the Military Establishment, to be chosen from among the local authorities of such subdivisions or from other citizens residing in the subdivision or area in which the respective boards will have jurisdiction under the rules and regulations prescribed by the President. Such boards shall have power within their respective jurisdictions to hear and determine, subject to review as hereinafter provided, all questions of exemption under this act, and all questions of or claims for including or discharging individuals or classes of individuals from the selective draft, which shall be made under rules and regulations prescribed by the President, except any and every question or claim for including or excluding or discharging persons or classes of persons from the selective draft under the provisions of this act authorizing the President to exclude or discharge from the selective draft "Persons engaged in industries, including agriculture, found to be necessary to the maintenance of the Military Establishment, or the effective operation of the military forces, or the maintenance of national interest during the emergency."

The President is hereby authorized to establish additional boards, one in each Federal judicial district of the United States, consisting of such number of citizens, not connected with the Military Establishment, as the President may determine, who shall be appointed by the President. The President is hereby authorized, in his discretion, to establish more than one such board in any Federal judicial district of the United States, or to establish one such board having jurisdiction of an area extending into more than one Federal judicial district.

Such district boards shall review on appeal and affirm, modify, or reverse any decision of any local board having jurisdiction in the area in which any such district board has jurisdiction under the rules and regulations prescribed by the President. Such district boards shall have exclusive original jurisdiction within their respective areas to hear and determine all questions or claims for including or excluding or discharging persons or classes of persons from the selective draft, under the provisions of this act, not included within the original jurisdiction of such local boards.

The decisions of such district boards shall be final except that, in accordance with such rules and regulations as the President may prescribe, he may affirm, modify, or reverse any such decision.

Any vacancy in any such local board or district board shall be filled by the President, and any member of any such local board or district board may be removed and another appointed in his place by the President, whenever he considers that the interest of the Nation demands it.

The President shall make rules and regulations governing the organization and procedure of such local boards and district boards, and providing for and governing appeals from such local boards to such district boards, and reviews of the decisions of any local board by the district board having jurisdiction, and determining and prescribing the several areas in which the respective local boards and district boards shall have jurisdiction, and all other rules and regulations necessary to carry out the terms and provisions of this section, and shall provide for the issuance of certificates of exemption, or partial or limited exemptions, and for a system to exclude and discharge individuals from selective draft.

Sec. 5. That all male persons between the ages of twenty-one and thirty, both inclusive, shall be subject to registration in accordance with regulations to be prescribed by the

President; and upon proclamation by the President or other public notice given by him or by his direction stating the time and place of such registration it shall be the duty of all persons of the designated ages, except officers and enlisted men of the Regular Army, the Navy, and the National Guard and Naval Militia while in the service of the United States, to present themselves for and submit to registration under the provisions of this act; and every such person shall be deemed to have notice of the requirements of this act upon the publication of said proclamation or other notice as aforesaid given by the President or by his direction; and any person who shall willfully fail or refuse to present himself for registration or to submit thereto as herein provided, shall be guilty of a misdemeanor and shall, upon conviction in the district court of the United States having jurisdiction thereof, be punished by imprisonment for not more than one year, and shall thereupon be duly registered: *Provided*, That in the call of the docket precedence shall be given, in courts trying the same, to the trial of criminal proceedings under this act: *Provided further*, That persons shall be subject to registration as herein provided who shall have attained their twenty-first birthday and who shall not have attained their thirty-first birthday on or before the day set for the registration, and all persons so registered shall be and remain subject to draft into the forces hereby authorized, unless exempted or excused therefrom as in this act provided: *Provided further*, That in the case of temporary absence from actual place of legal residence of any person liable to registration as provided herein such registration may be made by mail under regulations to be prescribed by the President.

Source: Office of the Provost Marshal General, *Selective Service Regulations Prescribed by the President under the Authority Vested in Him by the Terms of the Selective Service Law* (Washington, DC: Government Printing Office, 1917), 222–227.

Questions for Consideration

1) What class of people would not be exempted from "any capacity that the President shall declare to be noncombatant"?
2) Who served on the "local boards" to review exemptions from the draft?
3) Do you think that the punishment for "any person who shall willfully fail or refuse to present himself for registration" was appropriate?

10.4   John J. Pershing Commands the AEF (1917)

President Wilson named General John J. "Black Jack" Pershing the commander of the American Expeditionary Forces—the AEF. Born in Laclede, Missouri, he graduated from West Point in 1886. He commanded American troops on several military forays. Bypassing senior officers while rising through the ranks, he exemplified professionalism in 1917. At the age of 56, General Pershing organized, trained, and supplied what eventually evolved into two armies and included more than two million soldiers. Assessing the Western Front of the Great War, he scorned the trench warfare. Instead, he insisted that the AEF practice large-unit assaults with a tactical emphasis on rifle fire and artillery support. Furthermore, he refused to deploy the AEF to fill the lines of the British and the French. He preferred an independent army, even though his goal could not be met until adequately trained divisions with sufficient supplies reached Europe. Hence, the AEF launched no major offensives until the spring of 1918. Once they engaged in combat, though, General Pershing touted their superiority under fire. On September 1, 1919, he gave his final report to the War Department. Consequently, Congress authorized President Wilson to promote him to General of the Armies, the highest rank possible for an American soldier.

Document

Our mission was offensive, and it was essential to make plans for striking the enemy where a definite military decision could be gained. While the Allied Armies had endeavored to maintain the offensive, the British, in order to guard the Channel ports, were committed to operations in Flanders and the French to the portion of the front protecting Paris. Both lacked troops to operate elsewhere on a large scale.

To the east the great fortified district east of Verdun and around Metz menaced central France, protected the most exposed portion of the German line of communications, that between Metz and Sedan, and covered the Briey iron region, from which the enemy obtained the greater part of the iron required for munitions and material. The coal fields east of Metz were also covered by these same defenses. A deep advance east of Metz, or the capture of the Briey region, by threatening the invasion of rich German territory in the Moselle Valley and the Saar Basin, thus curtailing her supply of coal or iron, would have a decisive effect in forcing a withdrawal of German troops from northern France. The military and economic situation of the enemy, therefore, indicated Lorraine as the field promising the most fruitful results for the employment of our armies.

The complexity of trench life had enormously increased the tonnage of supplies required by troops. Not only was it a question of providing food, but enormous quantities of munitions and material were needed. Upon the railroads of France fell the burden of meeting the heavy demands of the three and one-half million Allied combatants then engaged [...]

The training of our earlier divisions was begun in close association with the French divisions, under conditions set forth in the following paragraph on divisional training: Trench warfare naturally gives prominence to the defensive as opposed to the offensive. To guard against this, the basis of instruction should be essentially the offensive both in spirit and in practice. The defensive is accepted only to prepare for future offensive.

For training our Artillery units, special localities such as Valdahon, Coetquidan, Meucon, and Souge, had to be sought, and the instruction was usually carried on in conjunction with French artillery followed up later, as far as possible, with field practice in cooperation with our own Infantry.

The long period of trench warfare had so impressed itself upon the French and British that they had almost entirely dispensed with training for open warfare [...] Recommendations were cabled to Washington emphasizing the importance of target practice and musketry training, and recommending that instruction in open warfare be made the mission of troops in the United States, while the training in trench warfare so far as necessary be conducted in France. Succeeding divisions, whether serving temporarily with the British or French, were trained as thus indicated. The assistance of the French units was limited to demonstrations, and, in the beginning, French instructors taught the use of French arms and assisted in the preparation of elementary trench warfare problems.

Assuming that divisions would arrive with their basic training completed in the United States, one month was allotted for the instruction of small units from battalions down, a second month of experience in quiet sectors by battalions, and a third month for field practice in open warfare tactics by division, including artillery. Unfortunately many divisions did not receive the requisite amount of systematic training before leaving the States and complete preparation of such units for battle was thus often seriously delayed.

The system of training profoundly influenced the combat efficiency of our troops by its determined insistence upon an offensive doctrine and upon training in warfare of movement. Instruction which had hitherto been haphazard, varying with the ideas and conceptions of inexperienced commanding officers and indifferent instructors, was brought under a system based on correct principles. Approved and systematic methods were maintained and enforced largely by the continual presence of members of the Training Section with the troops both during the training period and in campaign [...]

On December 31, 1917, there were 176,665 American troops in France and but one division had appeared on the front. Disappointment at the delay of the American effort soon began to develop. French and British authorities suggested the more rapid entry of our troops into the line and urged the amalgamation of our troops with their own, even insisting upon the curtailment of training to conform to the strict minimum of trench requirements they considered necessary.

My conclusion was that, although the morale of the German people and of the armies was better than it had been for two years, only an untoward combination of circumstances could give the enemy a decisive victory before American support as recommended could be made effective, provided the Allies secured unity of action. However, a situation might arise which would necessitate the temporary use of all American troops in the units of our Allies for the defensive, but nothing in the situation justified the relinquishment of our firm purpose to form our own Army under our own flag.

While the Germans were practicing for open warfare and concentrating their most aggressive personnel in shock divisions, the training of the Allies was still limited to trench warfare. As our troops were being trained for open warfare, there was every reason why we could not allow them to be scattered among our Allies, even by divisions, much less as replacements, except by pressure of sheer necessity. Any sort of permanent amalgamation would irrevocably commit America's fortunes to the hands of the Allies. Moreover it was obvious that the lack of homogeneity would render these mixed divisions difficult to maneuver and almost certain to break up under stress of defeat, with the consequent mutual recrimination. Again, there was no doubt that the realization by the German people that independent American divisions, corps, or armies were in the field with determined purpose would be a severe blow to German morale and prestige.

Source: John J. Pershing, *Final Report of General John J. Pershing, Commander in Chief, American Expeditionary Forces* (Washington, DC: Government Printing Office, 1920), 9–19.

Questions for Consideration

1) Where, according to General Pershing, was the "field promising the most fruitful results for the employment of our armies"?
2) What reasons did he give for preferring "open warfare"?
3) Why did he resist the "amalgamation" of American with British and French troops?

10.5 Howard Chandler Christy Publicizes the Navy (1917)

Howard Chandler Christy, a renowned illustrator for American magazines, developed a series of military recruitment posters during the Great War. One of his most provocative featured Bernice Smith, a 20-year-old woman, wearing a sailor's outfit. He met her at a naval recruiting office in California. After posing for him, she actually entered naval service. Soon, the Navy Department amassed almost half a million personnel in uniform. The U.S. Navy grew to over 2,000 ships, which ranged in class from submarines to dreadnoughts. Holding the post from 1913 to 1921, Secretary of the Navy Josephus Daniels managed maritime affairs. He chose Franklin D. Roosevelt as his assistant, who helped to establish the Naval Reserve. Anticipating the movement of troops and supplies across the Atlantic Ocean, Admiral William S. Sims traveled to London to persuade the Allies to escort ships in convoys. Thanks to the convoy system, they experienced a sharp decrease in shipping losses. Meanwhile, the U.S. Navy laid a mine barrage across the North Sea to block German access to the North Atlantic. Furthermore, a "splinter fleet" of subchasers probed the waters in search of German submarines lurking near shipping lanes or American shores. Even though sailors seldom received great acclaim, naval operations remained vital to winning the war.

Document

Source: Gee!! I Wish I were a Man, 1917, Prints and Photographs Division, Library of Congress.

Questions for Consideration

1) What was the central message of the poster?
2) Who was the primary target for the recruitment drive?
3) Why do you suppose the woman in uniform appeared to be smiling?

10.6   Ida Clyde Clarke Supports the Troops (1918)

America's home front became a new battleground. The Wilson administration sold "Liberty Bonds" and raised income taxes. Wartime bureaucracies such as the Food Administration and the War Industries Board facilitated mobilization. Meanwhile, manpower shortages created chances for previously excluded populations to enter the industrial labor market. Activists such as Ida Clyde Clarke linked the Great War with opportunities to express "woman power." She, like others who belonged to the Equal Suffrage League, temporarily suspended agitation for the vote and joined with fellow progressives to support the war. During 1918, she explained how the war made it possible for her sex to achieve personal fulfillment and civic goals. In particular, she highlighted the contributions of the Woman's Committee of the National Council of Defense. Women organized fundraising drives, aided the Red Cross, and joined the nurse corps. Perhaps the best-known uniformed women of the war were telephone operators dubbed "hello girls." Indeed, more than a million women participated in "war work" outside the traditional household. One immediate result was President Wilson's decision in 1918 to endorse woman's suffrage. The 19th Amendment was ratified during 1920. Nevertheless, male-dominated unions encouraged many female workers in the labor force to revert to domestic roles once the war ended.

Document

It would be a long story indeed if all of the work women have done in the interest of the health and happiness of our American soldiers were recorded, for in practically all of the splendid plans that have been set on foot for safeguarding the health and morals of the soldiers on land and sea, women have been asked to contribute a large share [...]

In every state where camps of soldiers are in training, the Woman's Committee has been grappling with the grist of problems that they create. First, there is the problem of hospitality. What will be practical and acceptable for them to undertake? One worker divides the work into retail and wholesale hospitality. The former consists of inviting the boys into the homes, taking them on motor drives, and furnishing them healthful amusements and wholesome company. Wholesale hospitality is defined as that undertaken by the big organizations where soldiers and sailors are invited en masse to lectures, entertainments, or dinners.

As soon as the North Carolina Division of the Woman's Committee learned that there was to be a cantonment of some sixty thousand men near Charlotte, the women at once began to lay their plans to cooperate with the city authorities in making the camp what they would desire it to be. The State Chairman, Mrs. Eugene Reilly, said that the Committee on Health and Recreation was most active in arranging with all the women's organizations of the community to provide entertainment for the soldiers. They arranged that every organization in the town should adopt or stand sponsor for one company of men, furnishing them with amusements, magazines, and books, inviting them to church and to dinner, opening their club or society rooms to them, and in every way possible surrounding them with wholesome and friendly influences. The Committee Chairman said that the women were just as attentive to the soldiers who come to them as strangers from New England as they are to their own boys, "and," she adds, "we expect that strangers will do the same for our boys."

Certainly Massachusetts reciprocated this thoughtfulness. A special committee from the women's colleges provided club houses and homes outside the camp. Their purpose is to have as many of these homes as possible where soldiers will find recreation, friendly interest and refined surroundings; the kind of homes from which the majority of them have come. Each home will be provided for by a separate college group, either alumnae, undergraduates, or both, and each will have a college "mother." The college mother will be permanent or as nearly so as possible, but the helpers may vary from week to week. A few will give their services in the home itself and others will provide the things needed to make it attractive—furnishings, games, books, pianos, victrolas. Such an undertaking is particularly practicable in the case of the reserve officer training camps made up largely of college men. With modifications to suit local needs the plan could be worked out to advantage in connection with almost any camp.

A helpful camp service in which many of the State Divisions are preparing to cooperate is that undertaken by the American Library Association. It is organizing committees to collect and distribute reading matter in the training camps and has even prepared to put up libraries in some of the camps. The Missouri Division took hold of this work with particular zest, giving the matter wide publicity and arranging for the collection of books at local libraries throughout the states. It has even furnished boxes of the proper dimensions in which to pack the books collected.

Several of the groups of women involved have reechoed the word laid down by the Library Association, that only worth-while books are wanted. "Do not go up to the garret and pick up material that has been discarded because it is too dull to be kept on the library shelves—give the boys the best. They want good fiction. They are keen for scientific books and periodicals. They want everything you can give them about war, about sports, they want the news of the world. Because a thing has been printed and bound it does not follow that it will be useful to send to a cantonment." No woman, either, need have any doubt about her contributions being well taken care of. The American Library Association is directly responsible to the Government in this work.

Where soldiers are temporarily camped in a town, or where they are traveling, one much appreciated attention is supervising the food that the boys get. This seems to have been managed very well by the women of the Woman's Committee in Grand Rapids, Michigan. They responded immediately not only to the call of furnishing good wholesome amusements for the boys mobilized at their gates, but during the two weeks when the camp of eight hundred boys was at Grand Rapids they furnished their meals. The different days of the week were assigned to various organizations so that while hundreds of women were engaged in the feeding of the soldiers, no one group was in constant service. In the two weeks the women furnished thirteen hundred meals, including breakfasts, dinners, and suppers. They did it so economically that from the allotment of twenty-five cents per head a meal, they had a surplus to go into the mess fund of the Grand Rapids Battalion, and the boys were satisfied, for when the camp broke up the praise came to the women from all sides for the catering they had done.

The greatest of all problems that confront the women in the vicinity of the camps is that of guarding the young girl. Where soldiers are stationed either temporarily or permanently, the problem of preventing girls from being misled by the glamour and romance of war and beguiling uniforms looms large. Maryland has proposed a Patriotic League of Honor which will inspire girls to adopt the highest standards of womanliness and loyalty to their country. From New York comes the suggestion that the teachers of girls may be invaluable in making girls realize the dangers. In clubs formed for war service guidance could be given incidentally with instruction. Girls employed in the big industries are most in danger, but if some happy slogan should be found which would in itself constitute a sort of badge of courage and loyalty, it would be far better than depending on supervision. The number it is possible to chaperone carefully is necessarily limited.

Source: Ida Clyde Gallagher Clarke, *American Women and the World War* (New York: D. Appleton and Company, 1918), 85–91.

Questions for Consideration

1) What, according to Clarke, was the difference between "retail and wholesale hospitality" at training camps?
2) How many meals did the Woman's Committee cater for the soldiers camped in Grand Rapids, Michigan?
3) Why did she say that "guarding the young girl" was a great problem?

10.7 Ben Hur Chastaine Reaches the Front (1918)

There was nothing quiet about the Western Front in 1918. During the Hundred Days Offensive, American divisions battled from St. Mihiel to St. Etienne. Lieutenant Ben Hur Chastaine fought in the 142nd Infantry Regiment of the 36th Division. Organized from activated Oklahoma and Texas National Guard units, his fellow "doughboys" included Hispanics and Native Americans as well as descendants of German, Irish, Italian, and Swedish immigrants. His accurate and colorful dispatches appeared in *The Daily Oklahoman*, which printed them on the front-page of the newspaper's Sunday edition. Stories in early October described soldiers going "over the top." Their salient advanced through heavy shelling, poison gas, barbed wire, machine-gun fire, and aerial strafing. American troops drove through the Meuse–Argonne sector and pushed toward the railroad at Sedan, which supplied the entire German front. As the Hindenburg Line collapsed, General Pershing steered them into Belgium. With defeat imminent, German leaders faced civil unrest and naval mutiny. The Kaiser abdicated. Suddenly, the new German Republic agreed to an armistice with Allied commanders. On November 11, the guns fell silent. Anticipating the historic negotiations of the Versailles Peace Conference, British Prime Minister David Lloyd George mused: "I hope we may say that thus, this fateful morning, came to an end all wars."

Document

With nothing less than awe the men had watched the bursting of the gigantic missiles loosed from the enemy artillery. With widened eyes they watched furtively for the flash and smoke accompanying the bursting of each shell, sometimes as far as a mile away, sometimes near at hand. Each burst shook the ground for a great distance in every direction, and each made a hole in the earth that would have harbored a small delivery wagon or a half-platoon of men. But all of the shells did not burst. Now and then the senses of the soldiers would be drawn taut at the screaming approach of one of the great missiles, but instead of the crash of the explosion with its blinding flash and deafening roar, there would be only the thud of steel against mud. These invariably elicited the expression: "Another friend of the United States in the German munitions factories."

This shelling was directed for the most part on the roads, and as it increased in the early evening, the wandering troops frequently found it necessary to break up into detachments and hug the places of shelter to avoid casualties. This could not but result in confusion. Some of the troops became separated from their commands in this manner and only were located and directed properly after hours of effort. By this time it had been discovered at headquarters that something had gone wrong. Staff officers were sent hurriedly out on all roads regardless of shell craters over which their motorcycles were operated. The confusion gradually was overcome and all units headed in the proper direction.

No one can describe properly the misery of this march. Few thought of making complaint. If a man chose to swear it was done under his breath. All realized that the hardship was a matter of necessity and all demonstrated a training discipline that would have been a credit to any troops. They stuck to the task and "carried on" as long as strength lasted. A few did fall out. In each instance the man would stagger onward until the help of his comrades on either side and the determination to stick it out would avail no longer. But these were few. They had been tired with the march of the morning, and because of the excitement of being under fire, the necessity of securing rations and ammunition and of disposing of their packs, not many had obtained any sleep during the afternoon. There had been no straggling during the day, and there was none in the night. Men and officers who fell by the side of the road were evacuated to the hospitals, but pride kept the others going. Many a man would have given up in the early hours of the night had they been in any other place. But going into battle, each gritted his teeth a little harder and although the straps of even the light combat packs numbed his shoulders, although the rub of a stiff boot heel was like the scorch of a branding iron, although his knees wobbled a bit under his weight, continued to struggle on through the darkness, laughing at the futile blasts of exploding shells, which shook the earth and rumbled their detonations of intended death.

Now and then one of these would make a direct hit on this or that roadway, and one of them took away two men of the 142nd Infantry. These were the only casualties. Although warm enough for comfort while marching, each halt left the ranks shivering from the night air. Midnight came but brought little rest. At stated intervals the columns would be allowed to take a breath. At these times men dropped in their tracks from sheer exhaustion but when the time came for them to move forward again, somehow they managed to get to their feet. As measured by the standards of the American soldier, it always has been a stain on a man's reputation to fall out on a march. Even in times of peace and training periods it had not been approved in the Thirty-sixth, and now that they were going forward in the face of possible death, it was not to be thought of. Rather than fall out it were better to die!

It seemed that dawn would never come. But few kept track of time. The night was divided into periods of marching and stops. Toward morning the men were so exhausted that the officers leading the columns dared not march for periods longer than thirty minutes. But at last the gray of dawn came and with it the blessed announcement that just ahead where the pine trees were dripping with the weight of fine rain the troops dug in by the side of the Second Division men they had come to relieve. In the shallow holes they excavated to secure shelter from the constant fire of the enemy artillery, they made themselves as comfortable as possible. With gravel for a bed and their equipment for a pillow most of them fell into fitful slumber, too weary to know or care how close the shells were falling [...]

As the first gray of dawn began to appear through the pine tops, runners scurried here and there through the brush to all parts of the line summoning company commanders to the battalion command posts. Practically at the same time the batteries in the rear began to thunder their first barrage. It was time for the troops to be under way. Hurried instructions, all too brief, all too indefinite were flung at company commanders, and these hurried back to their commands to state as briefly as possible to their platoon leaders what they had learned at the battalion command post. Before this could be accomplished, it was time for the barrage to move on and for the troops to be pressing forward. Before the company commanders could get back to their commands, the shells from the enemy batteries were beginning to fall thick and fast in the trees, a barrage that was intended to block off the supporting waves from the front, so that they could not assist in the advance.

In the front lines rapidly the word of instruction was passed from captains to lieutenants and from lieutenants to non-commissioned officers and privates. In the din of the barrage bursting well beyond in the open, words of command were drowned, but first one man here and there and then all rose from the places where they had burrowed in the chalky soil and moved steadily forward. Somewhat dazed by the newness of it all, uncertain as just what task they had to perform, handicapped by the lack of complete instruction, yet they never faltered. Sure and confident that they could meet and master any foe, unafraid of any death that might await them, gloriously they went forward in a manner that might do credit to the best trained troops in the world.

For a few moments they were an organized whole, moving as if in practice maneuver. Then they encountered the wire. They had not been able to take full advantage of the barrage where this was properly laid. Some were a little late in starting because the word had not reached them. Picking their way through the strands of wire that had been cut here and there, they were met by a perfect hail of machine gun and rifle bullets. Trained through the months for just this kind of emergency, promptly they sought cover wherever available on the ground and then took up a series of isolated fights for the capture of this or that position from which the enemy had opened fire.

Ensconced behind trees before the 141st and well camouflaged in positions between the 142nd and St. Etienne, in many instances the "boche" machine gunners had not come under the American barrage. This had been laid beyond them. The information that told of the occupation of the village had caused the artillery to lay their fire down beyond this.

Actually between the first line troops and the village was one of the strongest positions held by the Germans. All the "boche" gunners had to do was to lay their sights and wait for the men of the Thirty-sixth to reach the wire.

Source: Ben Hur Chastaine, *Story of the 36th: The Experiences of the 36th Division in the World War* (Oklahoma City: Harlow, 1920), 75–102.

Questions for Consideration

1) What, according to Lieutenant Chastaine, elicited a quip from his comrades about "another friend" in the German munitions factories?
2) Which passages insinuated that the offensive was poorly planned?
3) Why do you think he noted the infantry's training when they encountered "a perfect hail of machine gun and rifle bullets"?

Suggested Readings

Chambers II, John Whiteclay. *To Raise an Army: The Draft Comes to Modern America.* New York: Free Press, 1987.

Coffman, Edward M. *The War to End all Wars: The American Military Experience in World War I.* New York: Oxford University Press, 1968.

Fussell, Paul. *The Great War and Modern Memory.* New York: Oxford University Press, 1975.

Grotelueschen, Mark Ethan. *The AEF Way of War: The American Army and Combat in World War I.* Cambridge: Cambridge University Press, 2007.

Harries, Meirion, and Susie Harries. *The Last Days of Innocence: America at War, 1917–1918.* New York: Random House, 1997.

Hart, Peter. *The Great War: A Combat History of the First World War.* New York: Oxford University Press, 2013.

Jensen, Kimberly. *Mobilizing Minerva: American Women in the First World War.* Urbana: University of Illinois Press, 2008.

Keegan, John. *The First World War.* New York: Knopf, 1999.

Keene, Jennifer. *Doughboys, the Great War, and the Remaking of America.* Baltimore: Johns Hopkins University Press, 2001.

Kennedy, David. *Over Here: The First World War and American Society.* New York: Oxford University Press, 1980.

Kennett, Lee. *The First Air War, 1914–1918.* New York: Free Press, 1991.

Koistinen, Paul A. C. *Mobilizing for Modern War: The Political Economy of American Warfare, 1865–1919.* Lawrence: University Press of Kansas, 1997.

Lengel, Edward G. *To Conquer Hell: The Meuse-Argonne, 1918.* New York: Henry Holt, 2008.

Smythe, Donald. *Pershing: General of the Armies.* Bloomington: Indiana University Press, 1986.

Trask, David F. *Captains & Cabinets: Anglo-American Naval Relations, 1917–1918.* Columbia: University of Missouri Press, 1972.

Trask, David F. *The AEF and Coalition Warmaking, 1917–1918.* Lawrence: University Press of Kansas, 1993.

11

Out of the Trenches

Chronology

1919	League of Nations founded
1920	National Defense Act
1921–1922	Washington Naval Conference
1924	Adjusted Service Certificate Act
	Dawes Plan
1926	Army Air Corps created
1928	Kellogg–Briand Pact
1929	Wall Street Crash
	Young Plan
1930	Veterans Administration organized
1931	Japan invades Manchuria
1932	Bonus March
1933	Civilian Conservation Corps created
1935	First Neutrality Act
1938	Munich Agreement
1939	World War II in Europe begins
1940	Axis Tripartite Pact
1941	Lend-Lease Act
	Atlantic Charter

11.1   The American Legion Rallies Veterans (1919)

The soldiers of the American Expeditionary Forces (AEF) said farewell to arms, but few forgot the lessons of the Great War. While an influenza epidemic spread rapidly around the globe, a cohort of U.S. Army officers caucused in Paris to discuss their military experiences. One of them, Lieutenant Colonel Theodore Roosevelt, Jr., proposed organizing a society to preserve camaraderie among veterans. Meeting again in St. Louis, Missouri, the organizing caucus produced a draft constitution for what was called the American Legion. Chartered by Congress in 1919, they rallied veterans across the U.S. Almost immediately, they emerged as a powerful lobby in state and federal politics. They resolved to protect the rights of veterans as well as

American Military History: A Documentary Reader, Second Edition. Brad D. Lookingbill.
© 2019 John Wiley & Sons, Inc. Published 2019 by John Wiley & Sons, Inc.

to fight radicalism during the Red Scare. Some posts sponsored vigilante measures, but most focused on school curricula and involved citizenship. Furthermore, they became well known across the country for their baseball program. They urged Congress to create the Veterans Office and the Veterans Administration. The federal government also promised to pay veterans an adjusted compensation pension, although the Legion did not endorse the "Bonus March" for early payment during 1932. With their membership exceeding a million by 1941, the Legion constituted the most prominent veterans' organization in American history.

Document

WHEREAS, one of the most important questions of Readjustment and Reconstruction is the question of employment of the returning and returned soldiers and sailors, and,

WHEREAS, no principle is more sound than that growing out of the general patriotic attitude toward the returning soldier vouchsafing to him return to his former employment, or a better job;

BE IT RESOLVED: That the American Legion in national caucus assembled, declares to the people of the United States that no act can be more unpatriotic in these most serious days of Readjustment and Reconstruction than the violation of the principle announced, which pledges immediate reemployment to the returned soldier; and,

BE IT FURTHER RESOLVED: That the American Legion in its National Caucus assembled does hereby declare itself as supporting in every proper way the efforts of the ex-service men to secure reemployment, and recommends that simple patriotism requires that ex-soldiers, sailors, or marines be given preference whenever additional men are to be employed in any private or public enterprise; and,

BE IT FURTHER RESOLVED: That the American Legion recommends to Congress the prompt enactment of a program for internal improvement, having in view the necessity therefore, and as an incident the absorption of the surplus labor of the country, giving preference to discharged ex-service men.

WHEREAS under the provisions of the existing law an obvious injustice is done to the civilian who entered the military service, and as an incident to that service is disabled; therefore,

BE IT RESOLVED: That this Caucus urge upon Congress the enactment of legislation, which will place upon an equal basis as to retirement for disability incurred in active service during the War with the Central Powers of Europe, all officers and enlisted men who served in the Military and Naval forces of the United States during the War, irrespective of whether they happened to serve in the Regular Army or in the National Guard or National Army.

WHEREAS, one of the purposes of this organization is: "To protect, assist, and promote the general welfare of all persons in the Military and Naval service of the United States, and those dependent upon them," and,

WHEREAS, owing to the speedy demobilization of the men in the service, who have not had their rights, privileges, and benefits under the War Risk Insurance Act fully explained to them, and these men, therefore, are losing daily, such rights, privileges, and benefits, which may never again be restored; and,

WHEREAS, it is desirable that every means be pursued to acquaint the men of their full rights, privileges, and benefits under the said Act, and to prevent the loss of the said rights, benefits, and privileges; therefore,

BE IT RESOLVED: That the American Legion pledges its most energetic support to a campaign of sound education and widespread activity to the end that the rights, privileges, and benefits under the War Risk Insurance Act be conserved, and that the men discharged from the service, be made to realize what are their rights under this act; and that the Executive Committee be empowered and directed to confer with the War Risk Insurance Bureau, that it may carry out the purposes herein expressed; and,

BE IT FURTHER RESOLVED: That it is the sense of this Caucus that the War Risk Insurance Act be amended to provide that the insured, under the Act, may be allowed to elect whether his insurance, upon maturity, shall be paid as an annuity, or in one payment; and that he may select his beneficiaries regardless of family relationship.

WHEREAS, there was a law passed by the Congress of these United States in July, 1918, known as an Amendment to Selective Service Act, giving persons within the draft age, who had taken out first papers for American citizenship, the privilege of turning in said first papers to their local exemption board and thereby become exempt from service, and,

WHEREAS, thousands of men within draft age who had been in this country for many years and had signified their intention to become citizens took advantage of this law and thereby became exempted from military service, or were discharged from military service by reason thereof, and have taken lucrative positions in the mills, shipyards, and factories; and,

WHEREAS, in the great world war for democracy the rank and file of the best of our American manhood have suffered and sacrificed itself in order to uphold the principles upon which this country was founded, and for which they were willing to give up their life's blood; and,

WHEREAS, these counterfeit Americans who revoked their citizenship in our opinion would contaminate the 100 percent true American soldier, sailor, or marine who will shortly return to again engage in the gainful pursuits of life; therefore,

BE IT RESOLVED: That we, the American Legion, do demand the Congress of these United States to immediately enact a law to send these aliens, who withdrew their first papers, back to the country from which they came. The country in which we live, and for which we are willing to fight is good enough for us; but this country in which they have lived and prospered, yet for which they were unwilling to fight, is too good for them, and

BE IT FURTHER RESOLVED: That we demand the immediate deportation of every alien enemy who was interned during the war, whether the said alien enemy be now interned or has been paroled.

Source: Resolutions Passed by the St. Louis Caucus, American Legion, 10 May 1919, in George Seay Wheat, *The Story of the American Legion* (New York: G. P. Putnam's Sons, 1919), 199–205.

Questions for Consideration

1) What act did the Legion deem to be "unpatriotic" after the war?
2) How did they address an "obvious injustice" done to disabled veterans?
3) Why do you think they demanded the deportation of "every alien enemy" interned during the war?

11.2 George S. Patton Ponders the Next War (1922)

The interwar period inspired significant innovations in American military affairs. During 1920, the National Defense Act created the "Army of the United States," which involved a regular force of professionals, a civilian-based National Guard, and reserves of both officers and enlisted men. The Reserve Officer Training Corps, or ROTC, became essential to the commissioning of new officers. Additional military schools appeared to provide greater depth in specialized training. Major George S. Patton, who commanded a tank brigade during the Hundred Days Offensive, reflected on the lessons learned from the Great War. During 1922, he wrote an article for *The Cavalry Journal* to underscore the importance of mobility and mechanization going forward. He continued making improvements to armored vehicles, suggesting innovations in radio communications and tank mounts. However, the War Department exhibited little interest in developing tanks at the time. By the late 1930s, Major General Adna Chaffee, Jr., finally organized the first armored divisions within the U.S. Army. By 1940, Colonel Patton commanded a brigade in the 2nd Armored Division. He eventually assumed command of the Third Army, which featured not only fast tanks but also self-propelled howitzers, truck convoys, and scout cars. Unfortunately, he was injured in an automobile accident. He died on December 21, 1945.

Document

While I do not hold with those who consider the World War as the sealed pattern of all future efforts to maintain peace, it is, nevertheless, our most recent source of information, and the tactical tendencies shown will most certainly color to a considerable degree our initial efforts in the next war […]

Now, to safeguard our perspective of the relative importance of these happenings, let us analyze certain features which are bound to crop up in the future with undue emphasis, since they have been grasped by the popular mind and have filled the writings of many thoughtless critics and historians, both civil and military.

The restricted area, long deadlock, and vast resources permitted the employment of masses of guns and ammunition which probably, during our lifetime, cannot be duplicated, certainly not in any other theater of operations. The great results, apparent and real, accomplished by these guns has so impressed the majority of people that they talk of future wars as gun wars. To me, all that is necessary to dispel such dreams, or at least limit their sites to western Europe, is a ten-mile drive along country roads in any State of the Union, except perhaps a favored half dozen along its coasts.

Tactics based on a crushing artillery are, then, impossible except in one place. But, even where roads permit its use in mass, the effect of artillery alone is negative, so far as offensive victory is concerned. Sufficient shells concentrated at the right time and place will, as at Rheims, stop any attack; but all the artillery ever built cannot defeat an enemy unaided; for that the personal touch of the infantry (with the bayonet) is needed.

The guns are the greatest auxiliary, but only that. Infantry without them cannot beat infantry with them. The great range of the present gun has helped both the attack and the defense by making concentrations of great density possible at widely different places from the same gun positions. The same increased range has made it possible to place the artillery in depth, which in turn has made turning movements less deadly and more expensive.

Still, guns in moderation or in excess will not win a war. And the more open the war, the more uncivilized the country where it is fought, the less will they affect the issue; for in war of movement there will be less guns, less time to bring up ammunition, less time to hide batteries. Airplanes will locate them more easily, and they will have to use most of their limited ammunition supply shooting at each other and less of it shooting infantry. Get all the guns you can, and then steal or otherwise procure all the shells possible, but don't deceive yourselves with fancied zero hours and barrages.

Another feature resulting from the war, and which also has left its mark, is the evolution of the specialist. His birth is the result of an unholy union between trench warfare and quick training. Fighting in trenches was more or less stereotyped; hence men apt at bombing, shooting rifle grenades, using automatic rifles, etc., had time and opportunity to ride their hobbies. Further, it was easier and quicker to make a good grenade-thrower than a good soldier. Time pressed, so one-sided men were evolved who knew little and cared less for anything but their one death-dealing stunt. But the evil did not stop here; these one-idea gentry could be more quickly produced by instructors of a like ilk. These instructors and their pupils assembled in schools, with the result that unit commanders did not train their men, did not learn to know them; leadership suffered, and, as one drink leads to another, so the evil grew. The only way to fight such collections of specialists was to devise "set-piece" attacks, where each did his little stunt in his little way. This made necessary voluminous orders defining in detail the littlest operation, and in consequence taking all initiative from the fighting officers. All that was left to them was to set heroic examples; and this they did [...]

Still another development of the war, and one from which we shall surely hear in the future, was the enthusiast of the special arm—the man who would either bomb, gas, or squash the enemy into oblivion, according as he belonged to the Air, Gas, or Tank Service. All these men, and I was one of them, were right within limits; only they were overconfident of the effectiveness of their favorite weapon. In the future there will be many more such, and we must accept all they say and give them a trial, for some may be right; but we must not plan our battles on the strength of what they think they will do until we have more than oral proof.

Source: George S. Patton, "What the World War Did for Cavalry," *The Cavalry Journal* 31 (January 1922): 165–169.

Questions for Consideration

1) According to Major Patton, which features of the Great War "are bound to crop up in the future" with undue emphasis?
2) What did he believe was "taking all initiative from the fighting officers"?
3) Do you agree with him in that "the enthusiast" was overconfident in the effectiveness of the Air, Gas, or Tank Service?

11.3   Billy Mitchell Advocates Air Power (1927)

Advancements in aviation technology elevated the potential of air power. By the 1920s, military leaders had expected airplanes to conduct support operations such as the pursuance of belligerent aircraft, the bombardment of entrenched positions, and the monitoring of troop movements. Brigadier General William "Billy" Mitchell, who commanded Army Air Services during the Great War, foresaw a "winged defense." Influenced by the writings of British General Sir Hugh Trenchard and Italian Air Chief Guilio Douhet, he called for a unified, independent air force. Aeronautics made traditional armed forces on land and at sea obsolete, or so he opined. On July 21, 1921, he staged a spectacular air raid on an ex-German battleship stationed off the Virginia Capes. His squadron of bombers sank the *Ostfriesland*, although the Navy Department scoffed. Eventually, the War Department transferred him to San Antonio, Texas, and demoted him to colonel. During 1925, he was court-martialed for insubordination. He resigned but remained an advocate of air power thereafter. Irrespective of his flamboyance, Congress created the Army Air Corps in 1926. Rear Admiral William A. Moffett rose to acclaim as the Navy's Chief of Aeronautics. Even though General Mitchell's assessments of aircraft carriers missed the mark, his prophecies about long-range bombers largely came to pass.

Document
Each succeeding military epoch has seen an improvement in the mechanics of conducting war. Each improvement in weapons has given the defense more power to arrest the advance of the opposing force. Sixty years ago in our Civil War, one man well entrenched might have been able to hold off five attacking him. Now one man may be able to hold off fifty.

These improvements in weapons have operated to make land armies more and more incapable of obtaining victory over the opposing state. A climax was reached in the European or World War. There the armies, after some preliminary maneuvering, sat down in a series of trenches and indulged, during four years, in an orgy of killing that merely led to the complete exhaustion of all the combatants without substantial gain to any. The armies only advanced or retreated about sixty miles during the whole time. The directing heads of the armies were entirely unable to bring about victory for either side. Had this method of warfare been continued, it might have led to an entire extinction of what we call civilization today. Just as happened in Europe, after the fall of the Roman Empire, when with a destruction of all means for preserving the peace and maintaining a governmental organization, the known world reverted to a state of savagery which we call the dark ages. Armies, therefore, have become holders of ground. They cannot advance over it with rapidity to the vital centers of an opposing nation and bring about a quick and decisive victory. Air forces with the airplane are the means of going straight to the vital centers of the opposing side and paralyzing them […]

Suppose that New York were paralyzed. By this we mean made uninhabitable for its population so they would have to leave it and go to the open fields and forests fifty or a hundred miles away. The population of the area within twenty-five miles of New York is about as great as that of all of Canada, almost twice that of Australia, and more than the populations of some of the countries of Europe. A few shells, gas, explosive, or incendiary, landed in Manhattan would cause a complete evacuation. It is not necessary to destroy the physical structure of a city today to paralyze it. That was a method of ground armies, because they could do nothing else.

Aircraft can stand off a hundred or more miles and launch air torpedoes carrying hundreds of pounds of gas, explosive, or fire-making compounds, and hit a place like New York practically every time. The air torpedo is like an airplane controlled by gyroscopes which will pilot it in the direction and for the distance desired. In case the wind deflects it from its course it may be corrected by radio or wireless control. Either large airplanes or dirigible airships, such as the Zeppelin that last crossed the Atlantic, are able to carry these. Airplanes do not have to fly over a place to attack it. Not only may they use the air torpedo, but they can also put wings on their bombs which will allow them to glide for many miles to their objective. The variety and power of weapons that aircraft can carry are the greatest that the world has ever seen. Poison gas can be sprayed over fields and agricultural areas so as to kill the vegetation, and prevent its being used for long periods. All livestock, as well as people, may be destroyed in a similar manner.

Suppose that New York, Chicago, and the railways south of Sandusky were paralyzed. It would disrupt our whole existence as a nation. Suppose next that Pittsburgh, Detroit, and the Mackinaw Canal were put out of business, and that the air attacks against these places were continued so as to keep them paralyzed. Within a very short time the nation would have to capitulate or starve to death. These places can be attacked directly through the air from Europe now, and either directly or with auxiliary bases from Asia. Such is the carrying capacity and power of navigation of aircraft that can be constructed at this time. Armies and navies are entirely powerless to stop such proceedings, because no weapon or device operated from the ground is able to stop or even remotely hinder air operations [...]

Suppose that this country were menaced by a European nation possessing an immense navy, and that we had no navy but a well-ordered air force. We can exist, fortunately, without outside assistance; in fact we would feel the lack of very little no matter whether we had all the sea communications or not. Should the opposing surface navy venture out into the sea it forms the easiest object of attack and destruction which has ever been presented in warfare. In fact, in a modern war these vessels would probably be destroyed before they ventured forth from their harbors. Aircraft using the air torpedo, the water torpedo, the gliding bomb, the dropped bomb, gas curtains, mines, and gunfire are able to destroy and sink these leviathans with comparatively little effort in lives and expenditure. The submarine alone, or a navy's devices, forms a difficult problem for the airplane to handle. Concealed beneath the surface of the sea it is difficult to find during the day; cruising or lying quietly on the surface of the sea at night it is inconspicuous compared to the great surface vessels. Aircraft, however, provide the best means of defense against submarines, except submarines themselves. As a means of defending our coasts against old-fashioned naval attack, aircraft are an absolute and positive protection. In fact no nation would be foolish enough to send a navy to certain destruction against a nation well provided with an air force [...]

We must relegate armies and navies to a place in the glass case of a dusty museum, which contains examples of the dinosaur, the mammoth, and the cave bear. They still must be kept, because we must always maintain something that is still sure and useful in its particular sphere as the dinosaur was. But we must not entrust our national defense to these honored but obsolete services, because they will surely bring us to the Scylla of the fixed and narrow routine of the armies, and the Charybdis of the "brass hats" and organized buncombe of the navies. The airplane is the future arbiter of the world's destiny.

Source: William Mitchell, "Airplanes in National Defense," *Annals of the American Academy of Political and Social Science* 131 (May 1927), 38–42.

Questions for Consideration

1) What, according to General Mitchell, could arrest the "orgy of killing" among combatants?
2) Which naval vessels posed the greatest problem for air forces defending the coasts?
3) Why did he wish to relegate armies and navies "to a place in the glass case of a dusty museum"?

11.4 Holland M. Smith Studies Marine Landings (1932)

During the interwar period, the U.S. Marine Corps moved to the vanguard of the American military. Marines performed constabulary duties in Nicaragua, Hispaniola, and China, but seizing, holding, and maintaining advanced bases for the U.S. Navy became their paramount mission. Under Commandant Major General John A. Lejeune, Marine schools at Quantico, Virginia, began to analyze amphibious warfare. Contemplating the ship-to-shore movements, Lieutenant Colonel Holland M. Smith contributed significantly to the theoretical and historical study of Marine landings. During 1932, he studied how to overcome potential enemies in the Pacific. In his memoirs, he described a battle to make innovations in strategies and tactics for assaulting supposedly impregnable defenses. He considered the eventual creation of the Fleet Marine Force, or FMF, the most important advance in the history of the Corps, because it established the Marines as a part of the regular organization of the U.S. Fleet. After many years of fine-tuning, the effort culminated in the development of the "Tentative Landing Operations Manual" in 1934. Four years later, the U.S. Navy adopted it as *Landing Operations Doctrine* (FTP 167). "Howlin' Mad" Smith continued to rise through the ranks and conducted significant island campaigns during World War II. Accordingly, General Smith became the "father of amphibious warfare."

Document

Most naval minds refused to contemplate the endless new problems that must be solved to make a landing successful. It scarcely occurred to them that the enemy might resist and fire back, undaunted by the naval demonstration. Even the bitter lessons the British learned at Gallipoli had little effect on the War College.

Let us consider the primary conditions involved. No special troops existed which had been trained for this task. Not a single boat in the naval service was equipped for putting troops ashore and retracting under its own power. The practice was to use 50-foot motor sailers, cram them with Marines or bluejackets, and two additional men in ordinary ships' boats. This method restricted the choice of landing beaches, because the boats could turn only in a wide circle and had difficulty getting back to their mother ships after landing the men.

Determination to put my ideas across resulted in a long and acrimonious struggle with the Navy. When I voiced objections to the accepted naval doctrine I was brushed off with the reminder that the Marines were only a secondary branch of the service anyway. The Marines, it was conceded, could be employed for landings chosen as the progress of operations dictated but only when commanded by a naval officer and reinforced with bluejackets [...]

I foresaw the day when the Marines would land according to a coordinated, carefully prepared plan of action, assisted by naval and air arms, and assault strongly fortified positions with no possibility of failure instead of going ashore in a haphazard, extemporaneous swarm, trusting to hit or miss methods.

Here I ran head on into what happily is today discarded naval doctrine. The use of warships in the way I advocated brought strong objections. All arguments produced the same answer; warships could not stand up to fire from heavier shore batteries and, simultaneously, engage in an effective bombardment of shore positions. The advantage always lay with the shore batteries.

In my efforts to write into these naval operation studies a Marine plan of attack, I stressed the need for heavy and concentrated support from naval gunfire, a subject I cannot refrain from mentioning time and time again because of its vital bearing on the success of amphibious warfare. The original Navy reaction was that such a proposal was impracticable. Warships would be required to carry two types of ammunition: high explosive for land bombardment and armor-piercing for action with an enemy fleet. Such a double load would tax magazine capacity [...]

I got a pretty good illustration of our deficiencies in 1932 when I went to sea again as Battle Force Marine Officer. I was transferred to the USS *California* as FMO on the staff of the Commander Battle Force, U.S. Fleet. Our home station was Long Beach, California. Incidentally, in two years I had the unique experience of serving under four four-star admirals. They were Admirals Frank H. Schofield, Richard H. Leigh, Luke McNamee and William H. Standley.

That year we held combined exercises off the coast of Oahu, the main Hawaiian island on which Honolulu stands. Joint Army and Navy exercises on a smaller scale had been held off Hawaii before and the 1925 operations actually were based upon Gallipoli and its related problems, but in 1932 we were engaged in the first large scale operation held so close to Japanese bases. It was a test of our strength and of our knowledge of amphibious warfare, with Japan actually in mind. A lot of big brass came along to watch the show.

Supported by the Fleet, the Marines went ashore, waded through the surf, secured a beachhead, and carried out all the details of the plan. But what a dismal exhibition! I realized that we had a great deal to learn before we approached anything like efficiency in amphibious warfare.

The Marines landed in standard ships' boats, which were unsuitable for crossing reefs and riding the surf. It was obvious that our elementary need was more efficient landing craft, a retractable type that could get in and out of the surf. Moreover, we didn't have sufficient boats to get enough men ashore at one time to constitute an effective assault force. So small was the number of men we were able to land that the suppositional enemy would have wiped us out in a few minutes.

The Oahu operation revealed our total lack of equipment for such an undertaking, our inadequate training, and the lack of coordination between the assault forces and the simulated naval gunfire and air protection. "If the Japs had been holding that island, we couldn't have captured it," I told myself. "In fact, we couldn't have landed at all." I realized how badly prepared we were and how urgent was our need for further study and improvement of our methods. The doctrine of amphibious warfare was still in the theoretical stage.

Source: Holland M. Smith, *Coral and Brass* (1949; rpt. Washington, DC: United States Marine Corps, 1989), 48–60.

Questions for Consideration

1) What prompted Lieutenant Colonel Smith to undertake "a long and acrimonious struggle" with the Navy?
2) Where did the U.S. Fleet hold combined exercises during 1932?
3) Why do you suppose "naval minds" doubted his doctrine of amphibious warfare?

11.5   Charles E. Humberger Joins the CCC (1933)

Upon taking office in 1933, President Franklin D. Roosevelt compared the Great Depression to "the emergency of a war." Congress immediately passed the Emergency Conservation Work Act, which established a form of national service known as the Civilian Conservation Corps, or CCC. Though jointly administered by four cabinet departments, only the U.S. Army possessed the logistical capabilities to coordinate building roads, constructing dams, reclaiming farmland, restocking waterways, managing wildlife, renovating parks, and planting trees. In the first year, the Army mobilized 310,000 civilians and organized 1,315 camps. Though limited by law to unmarried men from age 18 to 25, an executive order permitted 25,000 veterans to enroll. Among a "vast army of these unemployed," Charles E. Humberger enrolled on June 6, 1933. At Beatrice, Nebraska, he met an Army major, who provided meals and transportation to Fort Crook. CCC activities eventually involved some three million Americans. Participants not only earned a living wage but also received immunization shots, nutritious food, outdoor recreation, and daily calisthenics. The War Department assigned about 3,000 regular officers and many noncommissioned officers to the CCC. By 1935, close to 9,300 reserve officers performed duties at the camps as well. Throughout the Great Depression, young men in uniform experienced the regimentation of Army life.

Document

We mustered at the fort, where hastily pitched tents served as shelter, with straw filled mattress sacks for beds. It was hot, and swarms of flies and mosquitos abounded. It was the first trip away from home for most of the applicants, and many were stricken with fear, apprehension, and homesickness. All were examined by Army doctors and given immunization shots. A very few were rejected and returned to their homes.

The Army did a superb job in managing this emergency operation and soon had the recruits outfitted with clothing that had been surplus from World War I. As far as fit of the clothing was concerned, there was a choice of too large or too small. When immunization and records were completed, companies of about two hundred men each were formed. Company 762 was commanded by Captain C. Williams, a veteran officer, who did an outstanding job of training and organization. Assisting was 1st Sergeant Patrick Eagan, a tolerant but efficient soldier. We were indoctrinated with the basics of sanitation, house-keeping, formations, marching, and discipline. Emphasis was placed upon reading the bulletin board daily to acquaint ourselves with orders, assignments, and duties.

This initial introduction to discipline, rules, and regulations was entirely new to the enrollees, and for most it became the turning point in their lives and careers. They would become aware that self-respect and dignity were important elements in living and further enriched when they bestowed full respect for the rights and privileges of their associates.

When functional, the company was assigned to Chadron State Park, Chadron, Nebraska. Travel to Chadron was by rail, and upon arrival at the park a tent camp was established with a field kitchen and mess, supervised by Army personnel [...]

It was a stroke of genius when President Roosevelt placed the camps under the general administration of the Army with a distinct separation of responsibilities between the Army and work agencies involved. The Army had the experience, supplies, and trained personnel to implement the rapid mobilization and organization that were required. It afforded field experience in administration and organization for the Army Reserve Corps and a ready source of semi-trained manpower upon the outbreak of World War II. I am convinced that the CCC program would have been a failure if this had not been done.

The company leader (first sergeant) was responsible for daily routine operations in the camp. He held morning roll call, sick call, submitted the morning report to the commanding officer, and cooperated with the work administrator to determine their daily manpower requirements. After breakfast there was a work formation, and enrollees were assigned to the leaders and assistant leaders, who then reported for duty with their supervisors.

The supervisors and leaders usually dealt with minor infractions that occurred on the job site. However, if a serious incident took place, it would be referred to the commanding officer for settlement. This procedure seemed to work well with a minimum of friction and misunderstanding. Company 762 was an outstanding unit, since it was comprised mainly of decent young men who came predominantly from rural and small town areas. Collectively, their backgrounds were quite similar. A few had not completed grade school, most had completed the eighth grade, some high school, and a few had attended college. Basically they were honest, industrious, and responsible, with a sprinkling of older malcontents and troublemakers who, with a chip on the shoulder, believed that the world was against them. With friendly counseling and after observing the examples of conduct practiced by their associates, most were motivated to change for the better. A very few, after resisting all normal efforts to help and reform them, either deserted or were shipped out.

As in any society, there were personal, petty disagreements. Animosities between young men were usually aggravated by their buddies, who hoped that they could instigate a fight with boxing gloves. The fracas would be staged with minimum formality with a referee to prevent undue mayhem. The boxing performance of the combatants was not exactly high octane in style and finesse as they tore into each other. It would usually begin with a wild exchange of blows, with glove leather flying in all directions. No doubt it was at this point that one of them wished that he had settled the dispute in a more docile manner. The fray would continue with noisy cheering from the spectators. Usually these bouts ended in a Mexican standoff unless one of them forgot to duck and was felled by a wild haymaker.

A number at first seemed depressed and looked intimidated. They were reluctant to engage in social activities and were shy and withdrawn. As time progressed, subtle changes occurred; they became more responsive and their downcast features took on the appearance of confidence and stability as they adjusted to this new lifestyle. As a unit there were significant changes as they gained weight and their bodies filled with muscle. Improved demeanor and confidence was manifest, and morale was high. They had three nutritious meals a day, clean comfortable quarters, health care, productive work, and knowledge that they were assisting their parents. What with having $5 monthly for spending money, it was like coming from rags to riches! A classic metamorphosis of body and mind.

Source: Charles E. Humberger, "The Civilian Conservation Corps in Nebraska: Memoirs of Company 762," *Nebraska History* 75 (1994): 292–300. Used with permission of the Nebraska State Historical Society.

Questions for Consideration

1) What, according to Humberger, was the "turning point" in the lives and careers of most CCC enrollees?
2) How did Army officers deal with behavioral problems in Company 762?
3) In what ways did CCC enrollees benefit directly from military supervision?

11.6   George C. Marshall Speaks to Historians (1939)

Across the vast oceans, clouds of war formed. Although the democratic nations of the world attempted to outlaw war, Japan, Germany, and Italy posed a gathering threat to international peace. Beginning in 1935, Congress passed a series of neutrality acts inhibiting American participation in conflicts overseas. However, the Roosevelt administration called upon military leaders to prepare to defend the U.S. and the rest of the Western Hemisphere. General George C. Marshall embodied the new breed of American soldier—a thoroughly trained staff officer. Nominated by President Roosevelt to become Army Chief of Staff, General Marshall was sworn in on September 1, 1939. His critical task involved building a force structure ready for battle. At the time, the rank and file lacked appropriate training. Much of their equipment was obsolete. Speaking to the American Historical Association, General Marshall meditated upon the problems of military organization. With the world at war and the possibility of American involvement looming, he began to forge an armed force capable of winning a protracted conflict. Gradual increases in personnel and material gave his staff time to evaluate weapons, equipment, and doctrines. The next year, Congress even approved a peacetime draft. Nevertheless, the American people clung to their traditional notions regarding the efficacy of unilateralism and isolation.

Document

Popular knowledge of history, I believe, is largely based on information derived from school textbooks, and unfortunately these sources often tell only a portion of the truth with regard to our war experiences. Historians have been inclined to record the victories and gloss over the mistakes and wasteful sacrifices. Cause and effect have been, to an important extent, ignored. Few Americans learn that we enrolled nearly 400 000 men in the Revolutionary War to defeat an enemy that numbered less than 45 000, or that we employed half a million in 1812 against an opponent whose strength never exceeded 16 000 at any one place, and fewer still have learned why these overwhelming numbers were so ineffective. The War Between the States pointed numerous lessons for our future protection, yet seldom has a nation entered a war so completely unprepared, and yet so boastfully, as did the United States in 1898. Veterans of the World War often seem to overlook the fact that almost a year and a half elapsed after the declaration of war before we could bring a field army into being and even then its weapons, ammunition, and other materiel were provided by our Allies. And many of them seem unaware of the fact that the partially trained state of our troops proved a costly and tragic business despite the eventual success.

What the casual student does learn is that we have won all our wars and he is, therefore, justified in assuming that since we have defeated the enemies of the past we shall continue to defeat the enemies of the future. This comfortable belief in our invincibility has been reflected legislatively in the inadequate military organization of past years, resulting in stupendous expenditures in each emergency, invariably followed by a parsimonious attitude, if not the complete neglect of ordinary military necessities. In addition to the perils of war there is the issue of huge war debts with their aftermath of bitter years of heavy taxes. I think it apparent that much of this misfortune in the life of our democracy could have been avoided by the influence of a better informed public on the decisions of the Congress.

Personally I am convinced that the colossal wastefulness of our war organization in the past, and the near tragedies to which it has led us, have been due primarily to the character of our school textbooks and the ineffective manner in which history has been taught in the public schools of this country. In other words, I am saying that if we are to have a sound organization for war we must first have better school histories and a better technique for teaching history [...]

I might attempt a philosophical discussion this morning regarding the proper organization of this country for war, or, to put it more tactfully, for the national defense; but however convincing this might be, the effect would be negligible—or at least but momentary. The members of a Congress, wise on heels of a war, will legislate with serious purpose to avoid a repetition of the crises, the plights and frights of their recent experience; but what is done is usually undone, the military arrangements emasculated, the old story of unpreparedness continued on into the next chapter of repetitions because of the pressure of public opinion.

To maintain a sound organization the public must understand the general requirements for the defense of this particular country—the requirements for the maintenance of peace as we soldiers believe, before Congress can be expected, year in and year out, to provide the necessary legislation with due regard both for the economics of the situation and for the essential requirements for an adequate Army and Navy, with the necessary industrial organization behind them. When the high-school student knows exactly what happened, and most important of all, why it happened, then our most serious military problem will be solved. Potentially the strongest nation on earth, we will become the strongest and at a much smaller cost than has been paid for our mistaken course in the past. The historian, the school history, and its teacher are the important factors in the solution of the problem I am discussing so superficially this morning.

History as a science has many specialties. The military historian is a specialist. Normally he is not concerned in the preparation of school textbooks. Furthermore, military history, since it deals with wars, is unpopular, and probably more so today than at any other time. Yet I believe it is very important that the true facts, the causes and consequences that make our military history, should be matters of common knowledge.

War is a deadly disease, which today afflicts hundreds of millions of people. It exists; therefore, there must be a reason for its existence. We should do everything in our power to isolate the disease, protect ourselves against it, and to discover the specific which will destroy it. A complete knowledge of the disease is essential before we can hope to find a cure. Daily we see attacks on war and tabulations regarding its cost, but rarely do we find a careful effort being made to analyze the various factors in order to determine the nature of war; to audit the accounts as it were, and to see to whom or to what each item of the staggering total is really chargeable.

Source: George C. Marshall, "Speech to the American Historical Association," 28 December 1939, in *The Papers of George Catlett Marshall, vol. 2, "We Cannot Delay," July 1, 1939–December 6, 1941,* ed. Larry I. Bland et. al. (Baltimore: The Johns Hopkins University Press, 1986), 123–127. ©1986 The Johns Hopkins University Press. Reprinted with permission of The Johns Hopkins University Press.

Questions for Consideration

1) What, according to General Marshall, was responsible for "the colossal wastefulness of our war organization" in the past?
2) How did public opinion impact national defense during peacetime?
3) Why do you think he said: "War is a deadly disease, which today afflicts hundreds of millions of people"?

11.7 Harold R. Stark Recommends Plan Dog (1940)

By 1940, the Axis powers of Germany, Italy, and Japan pledged mutual assistance if an uncommitted nation went to war against any of them. Hence, the U.S. grappled with a series of critical strategic decisions, which ranged from enforcing the Monroe Doctrine to supplying Great Britain. For years, War Plan Orange supposed that a Pacific war against Japan was in the offing. Other colors denoted contingency plans for military operations against various and sundry belligerents. While seeking to deter Japanese aggression, the Army and Navy Joint Planning Committee compiled what they dubbed the Rainbow Plan to supersede the existing ones. On November 12, 1940, Chief of Naval Operations Harold Rainsford Stark wrote a historic memorandum about military strategy. Contemplating a possible two-front war against Germany and Italy on the one hand and against Japan on the other hand, Admiral Stark described four possible scenarios, lettered A through D. He recommended option D, which took the name "Dog" from the military phonetic alphabet. Plan "Dog" involved a defensive war in the Pacific while giving priority to offensive operations across the Atlantic. Approved by President Roosevelt, it laid the foundation for the armed forces fighting in Europe first. Although the U.S. did not join the fray immediately, military planners anticipated trouble ahead.

Document

The military matters discussed in this memorandum may properly receive consideration in arriving at a decision on the course that we should adopt in the diplomatic field. An early decision in this field will facilitate a naval preparation which will best promote the adopted course.

As I see affairs today, answers to the following broad questions will be most useful to the Navy:

A) Shall our principal military effort be directed toward hemisphere defense, and include chiefly those activities within the Western Hemisphere which contribute directly to security against attack in either or both oceans? An affirmative answer would indicate that the United States, as seems now to be the hope of this country, would remain out of war unless pushed into it. If and when forced into war, the greater portion of our Fleet could remain for the time being in its threatening position in the Pacific, but no major effort would be exerted overseas either to the east or the west; the most that would be done for allies, besides providing material help, would be to send detachments to assist in their defense. It should be noted here that, were minor help to be given in one direction, public opinion might soon push us into giving it major support, as was the case in the World War. Under this plan, our influence upon the outcome of the European War would be small.

B) Shall we prepare for a full offensive against Japan, premised on assistance from the British and Dutch forces in the Far East, and remain on the strict defensive in the Atlantic? If this course is selected, we would be placing full trust in the British to hold their own indefinitely in the Atlantic, or, at least, until after we should have defeated Japan decisively, and thus had fully curbed her offensive power for the time being. Plans for augmenting the scale of our present material assistance to Great Britain would be adversely affected until Japan had been decisively defeated. The length of time required to defeat Japan would be very considerable. If we enter the war against Japan and then if Great Britain loses, we probably would in any case have to reorient towards the Atlantic. There is no dissenting view on this point.

C) Shall we plan for sending the strongest possible military assistance both to the British in Europe, and to the British, Dutch and Chinese in the Far East? The naval and air detachments we would send to the British Isles would possibly ensure their continued resistance, but would not increase British power to conduct a land offensive. The strength we could send to the Far East might be enough to check the southward spread of Japanese rule for the duration of the war. The strength of naval forces remaining in Hawaii for the defense of the Eastern Pacific, and the strength of the forces in the Western Atlantic for the defense of that area, would be reduced to that barely sufficient for executing their tasks. Should Great Britain finally lose, or should Malaysia fall to Japan, our naval strength might then be found to have been seriously reduced, relative to that of the Axis powers. It should be understood that, under this plan, we would be operating under the handicap of fighting major wars on two fronts. Should we adopt Plan (C), we must face the consequences that would ensue were we to start a war with one plan, and then, after becoming heavily engaged, be forced greatly to modify it or discard it altogether, as, for example, in case of a British fold up. On neither of these distant fronts would it be possible to execute a really major offensive. Strategically, the situation might become disastrous should our effort on either front fail.

D) Shall we direct our efforts toward an eventual strong offensive in the Atlantic as an ally of the British, and a defensive in the Pacific? Any strength that we might send to the Far East would, by just so much, reduce the force of our blows against Germany and Italy. About the least that we would do for our ally would be to send strong naval light forces and aircraft to Great Britain and the Mediterranean. Probably we could not stop with a purely naval effort. The plan might ultimately require capture of the Portuguese and Spanish Islands and military and naval bases in Africa and possibly Europe; and thereafter even involve undertaking a full scale land offensive. In consideration of a course that would require landing large numbers of troops abroad, account must be taken of the possible unwillingness of the people of the United States to support land operations of this character, and to incur the risk of heavy loss should Great Britain collapse. Under Plan (D) we would be unable to exert strong pressure against Japan, and would necessarily gradually reorient our policy in the Far East. The full national offensive strength would be exerted in a single direction, rather than be expended in areas far distant from each other. At the conclusion of the war, even if Britain should finally collapse, we might still find ourselves possessed of bases in Africa suitable for assisting in the defense of South America.

Under any of these plans, we must recognize the possibility of the involvement of France as an ally of Germany.

I believe that the continued existence of the British Empire, combined with building up a strong protection in our home areas, will do most to ensure the status quo in the Western Hemisphere and to promote our principal national interests. As I have previously stated, I also believe that Great Britain requires from us very great help in the Atlantic, and possibly even on the continents of Europe or Africa, if she is to be enabled to survive. In my opinion Alternatives (A), (B), and (C) will most probably not provide the necessary degree of assistance, and, therefore, if we undertake war, that Alternative (D) is likely to be the most fruitful for the United States, particularly if we enter the war at an early date. Initially, the offensive measures adopted would, necessarily, be purely naval. Even should we intervene, final victory in Europe is not certain. I believe that the chances for success are in our favor, particularly if we insist upon full equality in the political and military direction of the war.

Source: Harold R. Stark, Memorandum for the Secretary, 12 November 1940, in Franklin D. Roosevelt, Papers as President: The President's Secretary's File (PSF), 1933–1945, Series 1: Safe File, Box 4, Navy Department, "Plan Dog," Franklin D. Roosevelt Presidential Library and Museum.

Questions for Consideration

1) Which plan, according to Admiral Stark, would provide for the most direct defense of the Western Hemisphere?
2) What did he consider to be the "handicap" of operating under plan C?
3) Why did he believe that "the continued existence of the British Empire" served the principle national interests of the U.S.?

Suggested Readings

Biddle, Tami Davis. *Rhetoric and Reality in Air Warfare: The Evolution of British and American Ideas about Strategic Bombing, 1914–1945*. Princeton: Princeton University Press, 2002.

Biddle, Wayne. *Barons of the Sky: From Early Flight to Strategic Warfare*. 1991; rpt. Baltimore: Johns Hopkins University Press, 2002.

Coffman, Edward M. *The Regulars: The American Army, 1898–1941*. Cambridge: Harvard University Press, 2004.

D'Este, Carlo. *Patton: A Genius for War*. New York, Harper Collins, 1995.

Felker, Craig C. *Testing American Sea Power: U.S. Navy Strategic Exercises, 1923–1940*. College Station: Texas A&M University, 2007.

Heinrichs, Waldo H. *Threshold of War: Franklin D. Roosevelt and American Entry into World War II*. New York: Oxford University Press, 1988.

Hone, Thomas C., and Trent Hone. *Battle Line: United States Navy, 1919–1939*. Annapolis: Naval Institute Press, 2006.

Johnson, David E. *Fast Tanks and Heavy Bombers: Innovation in the U.S. Army, 1917–1945*. Ithaca: Cornell University Press, 1998.

Miller, Edward S. *War Plan Orange: The U.S. Strategy to Defeat Japan, 1897–1945*. Annapolis: Naval Institute Press, 1991.

Murray, Williamson, and Allan R. Millett, eds. *Military Innovation in the Interwar Period*. Cambridge: Cambridge University Press, 1996.

Odom, William O. *After the Trenches: The Transformation of U.S. Army Doctrine, 1918–1939*. College Station: Texas A&M University, 1999.

Pencak, William. *For God and Country: The American Legion, 1919–1941*. Boston: Northeastern University Press, 1989.

Pogue, Forrest C. *George C. Marshall: The Education of a General, 1880–1939*. New York: Viking, 1963.

Ross, Steven T., ed. *U.S. War Plans: 1938–1945*. Boulder, CO: Lynne Rienner Publishers, 2002.

Venzon, Anne Cipriano. *From Whaleboats to Amphibious Warfare: Lt. Gen. "Howling Mad" Smith and the U.S. Marine Corps*. Westport, CT: Praeger, 2003.

Weigley, Russell F. *The American Way of War: A History of United States Military Strategy and Policy*. New York: Macmillan, 1973.

12

Fighting World War II

Chronology

1941   Pearl Harbor attacked
1942   Battle of Wake Island
        Bataan Death March
        Doolittle Raid
        Battle of the Coral Sea
        Battle of Midway
        Battle of Guadalcanal
        Operation Torch
1943   Operation Pointblank
        Battle of Kassarine Pass
        Battle of the Atlantic
        Operation Husky
        Allied Offensive in Italy
1944   Battle of Anzio
        Allied Offensives in New Guinea and Saipan
        Operation Overlord
        Operation Cobra
        Battle of the Philippine Sea
        Operation Dragoon
        Battle of Guam
        Operation Market Garden
        Battle of Leyte Gulf
        Battle of the Bulge
1945   Battle of Iwo Jima
        Battle of Okinawa
        Victory in Europe
        Atomic Bombs dropped on Hiroshima and Nagasaki
        Victory in Japan

American Military History: A Documentary Reader, Second Edition. Brad D. Lookingbill.
© 2019 John Wiley & Sons, Inc. Published 2019 by John Wiley & Sons, Inc.

12.1   Franklin D. Roosevelt Calls for War (1941)

World War II began for the United States on December 7, 1941, when Japan launched a surprise attack. Shortly after dawn, Japanese planes roared over the U.S. naval base at Pearl Harbor on the Hawaiian island of Oahu. In less than two hours, their assault devastated the U.S. Pacific Fleet. More than 2,400 Americans died. At least 1,200 were wounded. Furthermore, the U.S. lost 200 aircraft, five battleships, and several other vessels. Meanwhile, Japan authorized simultaneous strikes against military targets all across the Pacific. The only solace for U.S. forces came from the fact that three aircraft carriers and their escorts avoided harm that day. The following day, President Franklin D. Roosevelt addressed both houses of Congress and called for a declaration of war against Japan. For years, he had spoken directly to the American people during "Fireside Chats." Broadcast by radio across the nation, the brief speech that he delivered on December 8, 1941, was one of his most memorable. His words encapsulated the public outrage and general resolve in the aftermath of Pearl Harbor. Within two days, Germany and Italy declared war on the U.S. Their declarations prompted another message on December 11 from the Commander in Chief. Thus, Congress declared war on the Axis powers—Japan, Germany, and Italy.

Document

Yesterday, December 7, 1941—a date which will live in infamy—the United States of America was suddenly and deliberately attacked by naval and air forces of the Empire of Japan.

The United States was at peace with that Nation and, at the solicitation of Japan, was still in conversation with its Government and its Emperor looking toward the maintenance of peace in the Pacific. Indeed, one hour after Japanese air squadrons had commenced bombing in the American Island of Oahu, the Japanese Ambassador to the United States and his colleague delivered to our Secretary of State a formal reply to a recent American message. And while this reply stated that it seemed useless to continue the existing diplomatic negotiations, it contained no threat or hint of war or of armed attack.

It will be recorded that the distance of Hawaii from Japan makes it obvious that the attack was deliberately planned many days or even weeks ago. During the intervening time the Japanese Government has deliberately sought to deceive the United States by false statements and expressions of hope for continued peace.

The attack yesterday on the Hawaiian Islands has caused severe damage to American naval and military forces. I regret to tell you that very many American lives have been lost. In addition American ships have been reported torpedoed on the high seas between San Francisco and Honolulu.

Yesterday the Japanese Government also launched an attack against Malaya.

Last night Japanese forces attacked Hong Kong.

Last night Japanese forces attacked Guam.

Last night Japanese forces attacked the Philippine Islands.

Last night the Japanese attacked Wake Island.

And this morning the Japanese attacked Midway Island.

Japan has, therefore, undertaken a surprise offensive extending throughout the Pacific area. The facts of yesterday and today speak for themselves. The people of the United States have already formed their opinions and well understand the implications to the very life and safety of our Nation.

As Commander in Chief of the Army and Navy, I have directed that all measures be taken for our defense.

But always will our whole Nation remember the character of the onslaught against us.

No matter how long it may take us to overcome this premeditated invasion, the American people in their righteous might will win through to absolute victory. I believe that I interpret the will of the Congress and of the people when I assert that we will not only defend ourselves to the uttermost but will make it very certain that this form of treachery shall never again endanger us.

Hostilities exist. There is no blinking at the fact that our people, our territory, and our interests are in grave danger.

With confidence in our armed forces—with the unbounded determination of our people—we will gain the inevitable triumph—so help us God.

I ask that the Congress declare that since the unprovoked and dastardly attack by Japan on Sunday, December 7, 1941, a state of war has existed between the United States and the Japanese Empire.

Source: United States Government Manual (Washington, DC: Government Printing Office, 1942), iii–v.

Questions for Consideration

1) What, according to President Roosevelt, made December 7, 1941, a "date which will live in infamy"?
2) Where did Japan attack on the morning he delivered the speech?
3) How would the U.S. prevent "this form of treachery" in the future?

12.2 Raymond A. Spruance Defends Midway (1942)

The American military reeled from a series of defeats in the Pacific, including the loss of the Philippines during 1942. Seemingly unstoppable, Japan aimed to establish the Greater East Asia Co-Prosperity Sphere. Unbeknownst to Admiral Isoroku Yamamoto, commander of the Japanese Combined Fleet, U.S. cryptologists were decoding their communications. Meanwhile, the Roosevelt administration dispatched Admiral Chester W. Nimitz to command the U.S. Pacific Fleet. By early May, the involvement of two American carriers in the Battle of the Coral Sea provided their first success against the Japanese thrust. Nevertheless, Admiral Yamamoto planned a major operation in the central Pacific in order to eliminate the American carriers with a decisive battle. From June 4 to June 7, 1942, Admiral Nimitz's forces confronted the Japanese carriers near Midway. Rear Admiral Raymond A. Spruance, commander of Task Force Sixteen, ordered the launch of aircraft from the *Enterprise* and the *Hornet*. The U.S. Fleet defended Midway with great success. Although the U.S. lost the *Yorktown*, four Japanese carriers were wrecked and sunk. Admiral Spruance wisely refrained from pursuing the Japanese vessels in retreat, because he would have collided with Admiral Yamamoto's battleships at nightfall. Although it was not a decisive victory, Midway marked a turning point for World War II in the Pacific.

Document

1) Enclosures are forwarded herewith. Where discrepancies exist between *Enterprise* and *Hornet* reports, the *Enterprise* report should be taken as the more accurate.
2) On 4 June, Task Force SIXTEEN consisted of 2 CVs [carrier], 5 CAs [cruiser], 1 CL [light cruiser], and 9 DD [destroyer].
3) The following is a general outline of the operations of Task Force SIXTEEN during the three days, 4–6 June, during which attacks against Japanese forces took place off Midway. All times given are zone plus ten, which is two hours ahead of Midway time, zone plus twelve.
4) Thursday, 4 June.
   a) We received our first contact report at 0740. Task Force SEVENTEEN was about 10 miles to the N.E. of us with search in the air. Task Force SIXTEEN headed toward the contact at 24 knots. When we got within striking distance, about 0900, we turned south into the wind and launched attack groups. The order of launching was: (1) VF [fighter plane] for fighter patrol, (2) dive bombers armed some with 500, remainder with 1000 lb. bombs, (3) torpedo planes, (4) VF to accompany TBDs [torpedo bomber]. Launching time was about one hour. Carriers then headed for contact at 25 knots.
   b) Our estimate of enemy CV movements was that he would continue into wind to close Midway, so as to recover, re-service, and launch new attack. We felt that we had to hit him before he could launch his second attack, both to prevent further damage to Midway and to ensure our own safety.
   c) Unfortunately, our presence was discovered by an enemy seaplane scout while we were launching. As this plane was to the southward of us, I assume he may have come from a seaplane tender southeast of Midway. Whatever the cause, enemy CV turned back to the northward instead of continuing toward Midway, as we have figured he would. Our dive bombers who were conducting a modified search en route to the target, failed to make contact at first and did not arrive until after the TBDs and their accompanying VF.
   d) By this time enemy CVs, had been recovering their planes and were preparing to launch their second attack, which would undoubtedly have been on our CVs and not on Midway. The presence of the third carrier was not known when we launched our attack; and the presence of a fourth was not realized until much later, as she appears to have been somewhat separated from the first three.
   e) Very unfortunately for themselves but very fortunately for the fate of the action, our TBDs gallantly attacked without waiting for the arrival and support of our dive bombers. The torpedo plane attack, while not in itself very effective, caused the enemy to maneuver radically and prevented him from launching. Our dive bombers arrived in the nick of time, caught one enemy CV (*Akagi*) with most, if not all, of

his planes on deck. The other carriers had some planes on deck. This resulted in the burning and subsequent destruction of the first three carriers. The wiping out of our torpedo plane squadrons was, I believe, done largely by enemy VFs. This seems to have pulled enemy VFs down and left the air clear for our dive bombers. The heavy losses in dive bombers appear to have occurred through forced landings, out of gas. We rescued the crew of one such *Enterprise* plane Friday afternoon. Others have since been sighted and rescued from Midway. *Hornet* dive bombers failed to locate the target and did not participate in this attack. Had they done so, the fourth carrier could have been attacked and later attacks made on *Yorktown* by this carrier prevented.

f) The *Yorktown* air group played an important part in this first attack. Their search gave us that afternoon the information of the location of the fourth carrier. This enabled us to launch the late afternoon attack, which crippled the fourth carrier and gave us incontestable mastery of the air. After the first attack on the *Yorktown* her planes then in the air landed on the *Enterprise* and *Hornet*. They took part in all subsequent attacks and were of the greatest value in making up for planes lost in the first attack.

g) When the first attack was made on the *Yorktown*, she was nearly out of sight of us to the northwestward. From the heavy smoke that appeared, I judged that she had been hit. Our aircraft operations and the relative direction of the light wind prevailing prevented us from ever getting a good look at her until she had been abandoned after the second attack. I sent two CAs and 2 DDs to her assistance after the first attack and continued to furnish VF protection. Our late afternoon attack on the fourth carrier was, except for this, the best action we could take for the protection of all hands.

h) After recovering our air groups following their second attack, Task Force SIXTEEN stood to the eastward and back to the westward during the night. A radar contact while on course north abut 0330 was responsible for some unscheduled movements. I did not feel justified in risking a night encounter with possibly superior enemy forces, but on the other hand, I did not want to be too far away from Midway the next morning. I wished to have a position from which either to follow up retreating enemy forces or to break up a landing attack on Midway. At this time the possibility of the enemy having a fifth CV somewhere in the area, possibly with his Occupation Force or else to the northwestward, still existed.

Source: Raymond A. Spruance to Chester A. Nimitz, Commander Task Force Sixteen, 16 June 1942, TF 16 Action Report, Navy History and Heritage Command, Department of the Navy. http://www.history.navy.mil/research/archives/digitized-collections/action-reports/wwii-battle-of-midway/tf-16-action-report.html (accessed 16 June 2017).

Questions for Consideration

1) What was unknown to Admiral Spruance when he launched his attack?
2) How were the American dive bombers able to cause "the burning and subsequent destruction" of the Japanese carriers?
3) Do you agree with him in that "a night encounter with possibly superior enemy forces" represented an unjustifiable risk?

12.3 Charles C. Winnia Flies in the South Pacific (1943)

Warfare against Japan challenged the U.S. Army, Navy, and Marine Corps in new ways. From Australia, General Douglas MacArthur commanded armed forces in the Southwest Pacific Theater. Outside of his direct command but geographically parallel, the South Pacific Theater fell to Vice Admiral William F. Halsey during 1943. The Solomons—a double string of islands that stretched 600 miles from San Cristobal to Buka—became the most embattled sector. Aircraft squadrons defended Henderson Field at Guadalcanal, which provided an important air base for an ever-widening series of operations in the jungles. A Marine pilot, Lieutenant Charles C. Winnia, kept a secret diary of his wartime experiences. He was considered a "Mustang," that is, an officer who emerged from the enlisted ranks. A pilot in Squadron VMF-213, he flew an F4U Corsair. He became a wingman for the division leader, Lieutenant Alonzo B. Treffer—often called "Tref" in his diary. Lieutenant Winnia conducted missions against Munda, Rendova, and Kahili. Tragically, he was shot down on July 18, 1943. His body was never recovered. Lost but not forgotten, he was an ordinary Marine in no ordinary time. As American fighters and bombers gained air superiority, the U.S. campaigns eventually overwhelmed Japanese forces across the South Pacific.

Document

Sunday 21 February. The big move came today. Bus and truck to West Loch. Ferry to Ford Island. Loaded with baggage we hiked to dock & boarded the carrier U.S.S. *Nassau*. Converted job. I was first aboard, knowing proper procedure, planes & gear were loaded with amazing efficiency. Pulled out about 1630. We were turned around on the tide under own power when band arrived. Played the Marine Hymn. We all stood up. It gives me a funny feeling. Like something in the movies. The marines sailing for the war zone. The effect was ruined when band (could barely hear it) played "Aloha." Everyone laughed. Once clear of land we read GQ. Word passed we are bound for Espiritu Santo, New Hebrides.

Monday 22 February. First day at sea. Slept like a log last night. Eating like the proverbial horse. Our escort DD *Sterett*, credited with 1BB, 1 CA, 3DD, 5 planes. Escort fired at 30″ balloon with 20mm & 40mm. Not bad firing. We heard today that some of us will be catapulted off when we near destination. Reports are coming in re concentration of forces in our zone. Smells like something big doing. The weather is very fine. Becoming warmer all the time [...]

Sunday 7 March. Operations began today. Flew with Tref on tactical flight. A little rusty, but fair enough. Clamped down our shack this afternoon. God have mercy on our souls. The news came in that we lose our Grummans tomorrow and get F4Us. We get 8 tomorrow or the next day. Have a few hops and go to Cactus where we get 10 more, theoretically. We are not particularly happy, being one of the best trained squadrons to reach this area. Resigned to our fate which may not be as bad as expected. Celebration in honor of Lt. Bier's birthday, had several "harmonizing" records.

Monday 8 March. No flying today. The F4Us didn't arrive on schedule. Pilots meeting this afternoon. Tactical problem tomorrow. Will be in my usual place on Treffer's wing. Our division will be interceptor. If we don't reach the bombers, guarded by Maj. Britt's flight we will know our defense is good. If we do we will know the same about our attack tactics. May be our last flights in F4F4s. Discussion on F4Us. The Majors went over one will today. Opinions generally better. With our training and experience we should make a success.

Tuesday 9 March. Tactical problem worked damned well. Tref & I made first pass before any of bogie knew we were near. The rest of the interceptors tangled with the escort. All were in a rolling ball following the Dive Bombers. Tref & I made high speed low side head on attacks & belly strafing. We made four passes without a gun being brought to bear on us. The secret, high speed from high altitude and violent maneuvering in close section. The first F4U-1 arrived. No chance yet for checkout. They look good.

Wednesday 10 March. Cockpit check out in F4U. Not too complicated. Should be OK. Navigation problem this A.M. The sitter sure gets tired after the first two hours. The hydraulic gun charger may cause some trouble. Planes load easily and will fire with negative g's.

Thursday 11 March. Hell of a day. No flying, but chasing around all day on Gunnery business. Will probably start F4U flights tomorrow. Two pilots from Cactus temporarily attached to help with F4U. Pilot conference tonight on F4U. First flight tomorrow. Celebration tonight in honor of Capt. Humberd's 26th birthday. Some dive bombers dropped flares tonight. Made a very brilliant light.

Friday 12 March. Flew the F4U today. Really a wonderful airplane. Goes like hell and handles like a dream. We should really be able to work over the Zeros [...]

Sunday 2 May. Missed mass today due to task force coverage. Rec'd letter from Mother. Nothing doing this PM. Conference tonight on strike tomorrow at Rekata Bay. Should really be good. We have 12 planes strafe.

Monday 3 May. Strike came off this AM perfectly. I got one AA position. Col. Moore stated: "The best coordinated attack we delivered in this area." 12 planes in 3 div, strafe. 12 SBDs with 1000# daisy cutters. 12 TBFs with 2000# daisy cutters. Rekata Bay is about secured after that. Went to local show, cooked some chow & retired dreaming of V.J.

Tuesday. 4 May. Strike today at Vanga Vanga—third strike there. Finally attained demolition of objective. I didn't go this afternoon weather closed down and I didn't fly at all. Rec'd letter from V.J. and replied today. Radio Tokyo as big a laugh & lie as ever. We hear our story and theirs. Anybody would have to be in bad shape to believe anything they say [...]

Tuesday 1 June. Began what will probably be a period of idleness. Wrote Mother. Went to Post Office. Worked on gear, went to show. Opening a bottle of Chablis tonight. Also attempting letter to V.J.

Wednesday 2 June. Slept in until 0715 so missed breakfast. School 1000—1100. Finished letter to V.J. this afternoon. Just layed around rest of afternoon. Sat in cool breeze watching sunset and dreamed a little of Violet Jane. Lord how I want to come home to that girl [...]

Sunday 11 July. Missed mass this AM. Rendova patrol. Feeling badly with bad head. Doc grounded me as I was preparing for an escort this afternoon. Rec'd letter from V.J. written 28 June. Answered tonight though confined to bunk. First I have heard in over two weeks. A small fight this afternoon. Naturally I wasn't in it. Maj. got one, Defab 1, Boag bailed out, hit tail, no news. Thomas had motor failure, water landing, no news.

Monday 12 July. Scrambled for fight this AM. Rendova patrol in morning. Cold getting into ears & sinuses, grounded all afternoon.

Tuesday 13 July. Duty officer most of morning. Flew in afternoon. I'll bull out this cold yet. Hop Rendova patrol with bogie chase but no results. Thomas reported safe at Segi. Two letters from Mother.

Wednesday 14 July. 4.3 hrs this AM. Escorted 5 DC-3 s dropped supplies at New Georgia. Covered Dumbo while evacuating wounded. Afternoon hop cut short—weather closed down. Landed at Russells, returned 1700. Show tonight "Knute Rockne." Writing Mother. Thomas returned today in time for afternoon hop.

Thursday 15 July. Rendova Patrol and fighter sweep over Vella Lavella this morning. This afternoon I was on the deck when 8 of the boys tangled with the Japs. 7 back so far with 16 certain, several probables. Lt. Votaw still missing.

Friday 16 July. Didn't fly at all today. Show tonight interrupted several times by air raid.

Saturday 17 July. Raid to Kahili today. I missed action there, protecting SBDs. Beautiful, six ships sunk. Lt. Garison shot down in flames. MG Hodde made it to Segi, wounded but OK. Lt. Vedder today presented with Purple Heart. Our squadron got 10 Zeros. Total now 57. Today was one of history. Had an egg this morning and a beer this evening. Raid tonight.

Sunday 18 July. [This entry in a different hand. Written by Lt. Treffer] Mission to Kahili well done. Lt. Winnia lost in dog fight over Kahili. Lt. Red Hall shot down Choiseul near Bougainville. Hall made a safe crash landing, 5 zeros strafed him. Only 11 pilots left.

Source: Charles C. Winnia, "The Diary of a Corsair Pilot in the Solomons, 1943," ed. Carl S. Richardson. http://www.monongahelabooks.com/winnia.html (accessed 16 June 2017). Used with permission of Carl S. Richardson and Bradley J. Omanson.

Questions for Consideration

1) What gave Lieutenant Winnia "a funny feeling" as he departed for Espiritu Santo?
2) How did he describe the experience of flying an F4U Corsair?
3) In what ways did his diary reveal a yearning to return home?

12.4   Hiro Higuchi Volunteers for Service (1943)

During World War II, the armed forces of the U.S. provided opportunities for racial and ethnic minorities to serve in uniform. African American units multiplied in the U.S. Army, which included segregated pilots in the Air Forces dubbed the "Tuskegee Airmen." In the Pacific war zones, American Indians in the Marine Corps defied Japanese code-breakers with radio transmissions in their native language. No group, however, encountered more prejudice during wartime than Japanese Americans. The Roosevelt administration authorized the internment of around 110,000 persons with Japanese ancestry—most of them U.S. citizens called *Nisei*. Close to 3,600 left the camps early to join the American military, as did 22,000 others mostly from Hawaii. Hiro Higuchi of Hawaii volunteered to serve as a chaplain with the U.S. Army's 442nd Regimental Combat Team, a Japanese American unit. On November 11, 1943, he typed a letter to his wife Hisako—whom he addressed as "Mom"—from Camp Shelby in Mississippi. He also directed comments to his son Peter and other family members. Upon deploying to Europe, he aided and comforted soldiers, conducted religious and memorial services, transported casualties from the battlefields, and performed various administrative duties. By the war's end, he earned two battlefield commissions and attained the rank of captain.

Document
Dear Mom Armistice Day—but not very peaceful for me. I just got through a dry run on the infiltration course. A dry run in army term[s] means a practice maneuver, and infiltration course is where you creep and crawl through barb wires, shell craters, etc. while they shoot machine gun bullets over your head. You probably have read about these courses in magazines. It's not the least dangerous—provided you don't decide to give up in the middle and walk away. It's a lot of fun. Last night I dropped in to see Horace's brother in his hut. I went there with Kiyoshi Iguchi and Toshio Kikuchi. It was a lot of fun. They have all Hawaiian chaps in that hut except one boy from Utah. The problem at the beginning of the encampment was whether the Hawaiian boys would be taken over by the mainlanders or the mainlanders by the Hawaiians. Well—the boy from Utah was speaking the Hawaiian pigeon like the rest of them—using the slangs so peculiar to Hawaii and the terms we use there. Imagine a boy from Utah saying "Criminy—but she throw for—what he is?" All this talk about the boys being ashamed of their English must have come from the few University grads around here, for the majority are just too anxious to teach the mainlanders Hawaiian English and proud of it. The mainlanders like it too as it is certainly a lazy man's language—a short cut to expression, and as one said to me—the most expressive way of speech. Another thing I found out—the men from the mainlanders don't get along with each other. The men outside of LA dislike the men from California and prefer Hawaiian lads. There must have been quite a misunderstanding at first—between all the different groups until the 100th Infantry came here. Then they came in with their fists and Hawaiianized the whole bunch. The mainlanders to my surprise are not good mixers. They eat (the officers) together at one table and do not mix, while our local fellers mingle with the *haole* officers and are much freer. Perhaps the complex from encampment has quite a bit to do with it. The men from the mainland the *nissei* are quite impressed with the *kanakas*—the way they make friends so easily and mingle with the *haole* population. I found out the meaning of the word "kotonk"—it's the hollow sound when something empty falls or is hit. The 100th Infantry gave these boys the term—guess when they beat up on the mainlanders the resulting sound is quite a "kotonk." The Hawaiian lads call themselves "buraheads." I don't know where they get these nicknames from—but the latter is a breakdown of "boburas." So poor Peter by anthology [analogy] would be half "kotonk" and half "burahead." I don't seem to get enough sleep. I visit these huts every night and usually stay late talking and getting acquainted. It's so much fun to listen to the boys talk and to hear the mainland *nisseis* becoming so Hawaiian in their talk. It's great fun. Had a good lunch—then went out in the field for the final infiltration course. With machine gun bullets flying over your head and occasional bursts of dynamite to kind of give the atmosphere—it isn't exactly what you would call a happy half an hour. However, did do credit to myself.

I have made an allotment to you for 175 dollars, which I hope will come to you regularly. I do not expect to spend the money I am keeping for my own expense so will send you an occasional check to help things along. I don't think I will spend very much except for food and laundry.

During infiltration today—I followed George Kobayashi knowing that his big body will give me ample protection in case [anything happens].

I am kind of glad that we didn't decide to have you come here—of course it would be grand, but the south is definitely no place for my family. The houses are poor and the schools way below average. I passed a little village coming in today where some of the officers' wives are staying—it looked like a replica of Tabaco [Tobacco] Road. I was surprised no end to come into Hattiesburg and find waiting rooms, drinking fountains, lavatories, etc etc–for colored only and another for white only. The AJA [Americans of Japanese Ancestry] are considered more on the white shade but then not too white—however, there is no overt discrimination nor any riots as was rumored in Hawaii. The place for the boys is not really too bad—guess it's lonesomeness and homesickness that makes them dislike this place. The *haole* officers here despise the south—guess there is still a little feeling left from the Civil War [...]

I took some pictures at Alice's and expect to have them developed by next week. You ought to see daddy with his leggings, fatigue, and helmet on—he looks like something out of the comic strip. The fatigues I bought was large for me—so I had the legs cut off a little—nevertheless as the body of the suit was still a little long for me—my legs seem to begin where my knees ought to be. However, it's very comfortable—and comfort is so much more important.

I'll finish off here and right [write] to you again soon.

Source: Wartime Letters of Chaplain Hiro Higuchi, 11 November 1943, Digital Resources, University Archives and Manuscripts Department, University of Hawaii at Manoa Library. https://library.manoa. hawaii.edu/departments/archives/mss/aja/higuchi/hiro.ph (accessed 26 July 2017). Used with permission of the University Archives and Manuscripts Department.

Questions for Consideration

1) How was Chaplain Higuchi able to "do credit" to himself?
2) What surprised him about the towns and villages near Camp Shelby?
3) Why do you suppose that slang, nicknames, and pejoratives became commonplace among the soldiers?

12.5 Dwight D. Eisenhower Invades Normandy (1944)

The Soviet Union battled Germany along the Eastern Front, as the U.S. and Great Britain planned a "second front" in France. Initially, British war planners preferred to conduct peripheral operations against the "soft underbelly" of the Axis in the Mediterranean. General Dwight D. Eisenhower, an aid to Army Chief of Staff, General George C. Marshall, served as the American Commanding General, European Theater. In late 1943, he became the Supreme Commander of Allied Expeditionary Forces in Europe. Known affectionately to associates as Ike, he commanded Operation Torch in

North Africa as well as Operation Husky in Sicily. From June 14, 1943, to April 19, 1944, Operation Pointblank included round-the-clock bombing of German defenses in Europe. Most significantly, Operation Overlord involved the Allied invasion of Normandy. The amphibious landings on June 6, 1944—D-day—succeeded, although the American assault on Omaha Beach proved costly. Within weeks of establishing the beachhead, the Allies landed more than a million men on the shore. General Eisenhower's official after-action report of the "crusade in Europe" revealed the attention to detail that made the invasion possible. As the year ended, he was promoted to the rank of General of the Army. After serving two terms as President of the United States, he passed away in 1969.

Document

Despite the massive air and naval bombardments with which we prefaced our attack, the coastal defenses in general were not destroyed prior to the time when our men came ashore. Naval gunfire proved effective in neutralizing the heavier batteries, but failed to put them permanently out of action, thanks to the enormous thickness of the concrete casemates. Air bombing proved equally unable to penetrate the concrete, and after the action no instances were found of damage done by bombs perforating the covering shields. Such of the guns as were silenced had been so reduced by shellfire through the ports. The pre-D-day bombing had, nevertheless, delayed the completion of the defense works, and the unfinished state of some of the gun emplacements rendered them considerably less formidable than anticipated.

The defenses on the beaches themselves were also not destroyed prior to H-hour as completely as had been hoped. The beach-drenching air attacks, just before the landing, attained their greatest success on UTAH beach, where the Ninth Air Force bombed visually below cloud level. But elsewhere patches of cloud forced the aircraft to take extra safety precautions to avoid hitting our own troops, with the result that their bombs sometimes fell too far inland, especially at OMAHA beach.

Nevertheless, the air and naval bombardments combined did afford invaluable assistance in assuring the success of our landings, as the enemy himself bore witness. Although the strongly protected fixed coastal batteries were able to withstand the rain of high explosives, the field works behind the beaches were largely destroyed, wire entanglements were broken down, and some of the mine fields were set off. Smoke shells also blinded the defenders and rendered useless many guns which had escaped damage. The enemy's communications network and his radar system were thrown into complete confusion, and during the critical period of the landings the higher command remained in a state of utter ignorance as to the true extent, scope, and objectives of the assault. The German gun crews were driven into their bomb-proof shelters until our forces were close inshore, and the sight which then confronted them was well calculated to cause panic. The terrible drumfire of the heavy naval guns especially impressed the defenders, and the moral effect of this bombardment following a night of hell from the air was perhaps of greater value than its material results. Such return fire as was made from the heavy batteries was directed mainly against the bombarding ships, not the assault forces, and it was generally inaccurate. The close-support fire from destroyers, armed landing craft, rocket craft, and craft carrying self-propelled artillery, which blasted the beaches as the infantry came close to shore, was particularly effective [...]

It was in the St-Laurent-sur-Mer sector, on OMAHA beach, where the American V Corps assault was launched, that the greatest difficulties were experienced. Not only were the surf conditions worse than elsewhere, causing heavy losses to amphibious tanks and landing craft among the mined obstacles, but the leading formations—the 116th Infantry of the 29th Division at Vierville-sur-Mer and the 16th Infantry of the 1st Division at Colleville-sur-Mer—had the misfortune to encounter at the beach the additional strength of a German division, the 352d Infantry, which had recently reinforced the coastal garrison. Against the defense offered in this sector, where the air bombing had been largely ineffective, the naval guns were hampered by the configuration of the ground which made observation difficult and were able to make little impression. Exhausted and disorganized at the edge of the pounding breakers, the Americans were at first pinned to the beaches but, despite a murderous fire from the German field guns along the cliffs, with extreme gallantry, they worked their way through the enemy positions. The cost was heavy; before the beaches were cleared some 800 men of the 116th had fallen and a third of the 16th were lost, but by their unflinching courage they turned what might have been a catastrophe into a glorious victory.

The American 4th Division (VII Corps) assault on the UTAH beaches just west of the Vire Estuary met with the least opposition of any of our landings. Moreover, an error in navigation turned out to be an asset, since the obstacles were fewer where the troops actually went ashore than in the sector where they had been intended to beach. The enemy had apparently relied upon the flooding of the rear areas here to check any forces which might attempt a landing, and the beaches themselves were only lightly held. Complete surprise was achieved and a foothold was obtained with minimum casualties, although it was here that we had expected our greatest losses. The airborne troops having seized the causeway through the inundated hinterland and prevented the enemy from bringing up reinforcements, the 4th Division struck northwest toward Montebourg, on the road to Cherbourg [...]

On 7 June I toured the assault area by destroyer, in company with Admiral Ramsay, and talked with Field Marshal Montgomery, General Bradley, and the Naval Force Commanders. All were disappointed in the unfavorable landing conditions and longed for an improvement in the weather that would enable our troops to exploit to the full their initial successes. After noon on this day the weather did show some signs of moderating, and a chance was offered for us to catch up in part with our delayed unloading schedule. On OMAHA beach, which continued to cause us most anxiety, General Bradley reported some improvement, but in view of the check received here I decided to alter the immediate tactical plan to the extent of having both V and VII Corps concentrate upon effecting a link-up through Carentan, after which the original plan of operations would be pursued. Of the morale of the men whom I saw on every sector during the day I cannot speak too highly. Their enthusiasm, energy, and fitness for battle were an inspiration to behold. During the next five days our forces worked to join up the beachheads into one uninterrupted lodgment area and to introduce into this area the supplies of men and materials necessary to consolidate and expand our foothold.

Source: Dwight D. Eisenhower, *Report by the Supreme Commander to the Combined Chiefs of Staff on the Operations in Europe of the Allied Expeditionary Force, 6 June 1944 to 8 May 1945* (Washington, DC: Government Printing Office, 1946), 21–25.

Questions for Consideration

1) How, according to General Eisenhower, did air and naval bombardments support the landings at Normandy?
2) Where were the "greatest difficulties" experienced on the beaches?
3) Why do you think he decided "to alter the immediate tactical plan" regarding the link-up through Carentan?

12.6   Congress Passes the GI Bill (1944)

More than 16 million Americans served in uniform during World War II. In all likelihood, the initials GI derived from military slang for their "government issue" of clothing, equipment, supplies, and rations. A 1942 comic strip titled "GI Joe" widely popularized the term. According to the U.S. Army, the average GI was nearly 26 years old. Most had not completed high school before marching to war. Prodded by the American Legion, Congress passed legislation to help them transition back into civilian life after the war. Officially named the Servicemen's Readjustment Act, the GI Bill was signed into law by President Roosevelt on June 22, 1944. Accordingly, it turned the Veterans Administration into "an essential war agency," subordinate only to the War and Navy Departments in regard to military affairs. The first title of the law expanded federal support for hospital facilities and medical care. Other provisions promised low interest loans for veterans buying homes and starting businesses or farms. One clause enabled veterans to receive $20 a week for 52 weeks while seeking employment. With the second title, it offered higher education benefits. Over the course of the next decade, more than seven million veterans benefited from the educational opportunities afforded to them.

Document
Title II
1) Any person who served in the active military or naval service on or after September 16, 1940, and prior to the termination of the present war, and who shall have been discharged or released there-from under conditions other than dishonorable, and whose education or training was impeded, delayed, interrupted, or interfered with by reason of his entrance into the service, or who desires a refresher or retraining course, and who either shall have served ninety days or more, exclusive of any period he was assigned for a course of education or training under the Army specialized training program or the Navy college training program, which course was a continuation of his civilian course and was pursued to completion, or as a cadet or midshipman at one of the service academies, or shall have been discharged or released from active service by reason of an actual service-incurred injury or disability, shall be eligible for and entitled to receive education or training under this part: *Provided,* That such course shall be initiated not later than two years after either the date of his discharge or the termination of the present war, whichever is the later: *Provided further,* That no such education or training shall be afforded beyond seven years after the termination of

the present war: *And provided further*, That any such person who was not over 25 years of age at the time he entered the service shall be deemed to have had his education or training impeded, delayed, interrupted, or interfered with.

2) Any such eligible person shall be entitled to education or training, or a refresher or retraining course, at an approved educational or training institution, for a period of one year (or the equivalent thereof in continuous part-time study), or for such lesser time as may be required for the course of instruction chosen by him. Upon satisfactory completion of such course of education or training, according to the regularly prescribed standards and practices of the institutions, except a refresher or retraining course, such person shall be entitled to an additional period or periods of education or training, not to exceed the time such person was in the active service on or after September 16, 1940, and before the termination of the war, exclusive of any period he was assigned for a course of education or training under the Army specialized training program or the Navy college training program, which course was a continuation of his civilian course and was pursued to completion, or as a cadet or midshipman at one of the service academies, but in no event shall the total period of education or training exceed four years: *Provided*, That his work continues to be satisfactory throughout the period, according to the regularly prescribed standards and practices of the institution: *Provided, however*, That wherever the additional period of instruction ends during a quarter or semester and after a major part of such quarter or semester has expired, such period of instruction shall be extended to the termination of such unexpired quarter or semester.

3) Such person shall be eligible for and entitled to such course of education or training as he may elect, and at any approved educational or training institution at which he chooses to enroll, whether or not located in the State in which he resides, which will accept or retain him as a student or trainee in any field or branch of knowledge which such institution finds him qualified to undertake or pursue: *Provided*, That, for reasons satisfactory to the Administrator, he may change a course of instruction: *And provided further*, That any such course of education or training may be discontinued at any time, if it is found by the Administrator that, according to the regularly prescribed standards and practices of the institution, the conduct or progress of such person is unsatisfactory.

4) From time to time the Administrator shall secure from the appropriate agency of each state a list of the educational and training institutions (including industrial establishments), within such jurisdiction, which are qualified and equipped to furnish education or training (including apprenticeship and refresher or retraining training), which institutions, together with such additional ones as may be recognized and approved by the Administrator, shall be deemed qualified and approved to furnish education or training to such persons as shall enroll under this part: *Provided*, That wherever there are established state apprenticeship agencies expressly charged by state laws to administer apprentice training, whenever possible, the Administrator shall utilize such existing facilities and services in training on the job when such training is of one year's duration or more.

5) The Administrator shall pay to the educational or training institution, for each person enrolled in full time or part time course of education or training, the customary cost of tuition, and such laboratory, library, health, infirmary, and other similar fees as are customarily charged, and may pay for books, supplies, equipment, and other

necessary expenses, exclusive of board, lodging, other living expenses, and travel, as are generally required for the successful pursuit and completion of the course by other students in the institution [...]

6) As used in this part, the term "educational or training institutions" shall include all public or private elementary, secondary, and other schools furnishing education for adults, business schools and colleges, scientific and technical institutions, colleges, vocational schools, junior colleges, teachers colleges, normal schools, professional schools, universities, and other educational institutions, and shall also include business or other establishments providing apprentice or other training on the job, including those under the supervision of an approved college or university or any State department of education, or any State apprenticeship agency or State board of vocational education, or any State apprenticeship council or the Federal Apprentice Training Service established in accordance with Public, Numbered 308, Seventy-fifth Congress, or any agency in the executive branch of the Federal Government authorized under other laws to supervise such training.

Source: *United States Statutes at Large*, 1944, Volume 58, Part 1 (Washington, DC: Government Printing Office, 1945), 287–290.

Questions for Consideration

1) How many days of active service were required for eligibility to receive education or training after the war?
2) Who received payment for the cost of tuition and related fees?
3) Why do you think the law provided GIs with multiple options for educational or training institutions?

12.7 Bill Mauldin Draws Willie and Joe (1944)

Pursuant to a grand strategic vision, Allied armies advanced toward victory in Europe. After D-day, General Eisenhower asked General Omar Bradley to command Operation Cobra. His forces broke out from Normandy and liberated Paris on August 25, 1944. However, autumn mud and winter cold slowed the momentum of American divisions late in the year. German forces counterattacked on December 16 in the Ardennes Forest, although they were defeated during the Battle of the Bulge. Despite the ferocity of American infantrymen up front, a minority actually fired their weapons in combat. Few recalled the scenes of war more distinctly than Sergeant Bill Mauldin, who served in the 180th Infantry Regiment of the 45th Division. His cartoon characters, Willie and Joe, appeared on the pages of *Stars and Stripes*. One even graced the cover of *Time* in 1944. Unshaven, dirty, and fatigued, they faced the destructive warfare with a sense of humor. They endured as archetypes of American "dogfaces." For example, Sergeant Mauldin depicted combat engineers sweeping for mines with a caption: "Don't hurry for me, son. I like to see young men take an interest in their work." Obsessed with spit-and-polish, General George S. Patton complained that the depictions were "lousy." Nevertheless, Sergeant Mauldin eventually received the Pulitzer Prize for editorial cartooning.

Document

Questions for Consideration

1) What did the cartoon illustrate about technology in World War II?
2) How did it suggest that rank bestowed privileges?
3) Do you agree that the demeanor of Willie and Joe seemed "lousy"?

12.8   Melvin E. Bush Crosses the Siegfried Line (1945)

Allied victory during 1945 brought an end to World War II in Europe. Early in the year, General Eisenhower ordered a riposte that destroyed the last reserves of the German thrust in the Ardennes Forest. As the Soviets rolled into eastern Germany, the Americans penetrated the vaunted Siegfried Line in the west. They soon encountered the death camps of the Holocaust in which the Nazi regime exterminated six million Jews. Allied commanders announced the unconditional surrender of Germany on May 8. Wherever deployed in the European theater, military personnel tried to remain in contact with loved ones waiting nervously at home. Mail call and letter writing were vital activities to ease anxieties and to pass time. On May 17, Sergeant Melvin E. Bush wrote a letter from Pilsen, Czechoslovakia, to his "folks" in Clackamas, Oregon. Serving as a platoon leader in the 38th Infantry Regiment of the 2nd Division, he testified that "things happen hard and fast" in combat. With great humility, he recalled his wounding in battle and his promotions in rank. He recounted the fighting from D-day to V-E Day, although he never boasted about his unit citations or Purple Heart. His correspondence illustrated the kind of communication that friends and family often received from those fighting World War II.

Document

Dear Folks

This is a wonderful summer evening, and this is just as pretty and nice a city as when we came here ten days ago, only more so.

We are seeing some of the greatest changes here since their war began. Street lights and windows are bright at night again. Busses are beginning to run, and the trains are moving some freight and passengers. Boy, they are swamped!

You have asked so many questions I haven't been able to answer since D-day last June. Maybe now I can answer a few of them as censorship has been lifted somewhat […]

After three days in holes dug good and deep we launched the attack on Krinkelt. The snow was from eighteen inches to two feet deep and the wind blowing quite strong. I was working with tanks as I had on several light attacks in Normandy. It isn't quite so hard physically as to be a rifleman, but those big tanks sure draw lots of big stuff in the line of fire. I got shook up a couple of times and had lots of fun calling fire on German positions I had spotted.

After this deal we had three days rest then went into Hellenthal. What a deal! We took the town in one night, and the next night moved out and took two hills just outside of town. These hills were so situated that they even sniped at us with 88 artillery fire. The second morning we lost a few men in hand to hand fighting. Out of eighty some odd Germans we took eleven prisoners. The snow had nearly all gone when we took Hellenthal. This is the town where Vernon, my buddy, joined us.

We were relieved here by another division and moved back about ten miles where we built log cabins and lived in them for eight days—a pretty nice little rest. It was from here we launched the final attack to break through the Siegfried line.

The following two weeks there was so much rough fighting that I shudder even yet when I think about it. It was on this attack that I took over as a platoon leader.

Our company was the first of the Allies through the Siegfried. It was attack, attack, attack the same as in Normandy, only more so. If we had six hours all together, to rest, out of the twenty-four, we were lucky. Finally we stopped in the town of Regensdorf, and it was from this place we began the wild tank and motorized attack which spearheaded across Germany to within forty miles of Berlin.

My outfit bypassed Leipsig and were about twelve miles east of the city while other elements of our division took the city. I am very thankful we missed that fight. A few miles out of Leipsig we encountered the Hitler youth, and they were plumb rough.

Some of the towns we captured were Lemburg, Eilenburg, Grimme, Borne, and almost hundreds of small towns. It was just one solid attack halfway across Germany. Every outfit was trying to meet the Russians first. We were within about fifteen miles of them when we finally had to stop for lack of supplies. We had been on the go for over twenty days nearly day and night. Boy! Were we glad to stop for a while and pull back to Grimma, a town we had captured some three or four days earlier.

After about eight days in this beautiful little town where we had rest and quietness, and were happy as we believed the conflict to be the same as ended for us, we received orders to spearhead a motorized convoy into Czechoslovakia, what a let down! But we had no "fire" fighting on this trip. When we entered a town we could tell if it was German or Czech. Very few people were to be seen in the German towns, but when we came to the Czech towns all the people from nine days to ninety years were out to greet us.

May 7th and 8th were two days I shall remember as long as I live.

Every place the German soldiers were surrendering by the thousands. The most trouble we had was just trying to catch up with the Jerries and disarm them. All the fight seemed to have been taken out of them, but they especially the Gestapo and the S.S. troops are a surley arrogant lot.

The Czech civilians had homemade American and Czech flags and flowers in bouquets and garlands. All the people were waving and throwing flowers and kisses as we passed. Honestly I saw more than a few waving with both hands, tears in their eyes and running unheeded down their cheeks. After the years of slavery and occupation by the Germans, all are financially poor but a healthy lot [...]

It is really hard to believe that it is all over now. Every one of us feels the same way—like we were dreaming or something. One thing though we are not building up any false hopes. There is to be an army of occupation, and a war is still going on in the Pacific.

This morning they had a church service for us in a fine large church with a swell pipe organ. This was the first service to be held in this church for more than five years. The civilians held a service first and then several joined with us. It was a wonderful service and we enjoyed it immensely. Our old chaplain who was with us on the Siegfried line was back.

All our fights here are now in the past and I sure thank the good Lord he carried me through it all.

Source: World War II Letters, 1940–1946, Collection 0068, Box 4, Folder 390, The State Historical Society of Missouri Manuscript Collection.

Questions for Consideration

1) How did Sergeant Bush describe the "rough fighting" across the Siegfried line?
2) Did he seem to respect the Germans that he encountered?
3) Why was he reluctant to express "any false hopes" about the end of the war?

12.9 Jacqueline Cochran Praises the WASPs (1945)

Throughout World War II, the American military included uniformed branches for women's auxiliary service. The advent of "total warfare," which rarely distinguished civilians from combatants, rendered traditional notions about the "home front" untenable. Nevertheless, senior military officers maintained a division of labor based upon gendered assumptions. In other words, female service skills supported male combat missions. Remarkably, the Women's Airforce Service Pilots, or the WASPs, elevated female aviators known as "flygirls." In 1942, General Henry "Hap" Arnold, the commander of the U.S. Army Air Forces, asked Jacqueline Cochran, a world-famous aviatrix, to help women earn their wings. Another renowned pilot, Nancy Harkness Love, also suggested the formation of a small squadron of trained ferry pilots. The next year, the training programs were merged under Cochran's leadership. As the head of the WASPs, Cochran supervised training in Sweetwater, Texas. Although General Arnold eventually ordered the WASPs to disband, Cochran tried unsuccessfully to convince the brass otherwise. In 1945, she praised the capabilities of female aviators in her final report. For her wartime service, she received the Distinguished Service Medal and the Distinguished Flying Cross. After the war, she flew jet-engine aircraft and became the first woman pilot to "go supersonic." When she died in 1980, Cochran held more distance and speed records than any other pilot—male or female.

Document

Facts

More than 25,000 women applied for women pilot training. Eighteen hundred and thirty (1,830) were inducted. 30.7% of inductees were eliminated during training for flying deficiency and another 2.2% for other reasons, with consequent lower elimination rate than among male cadet pilots. 8% of inductees resigned and 1,074 graduated, or 58.7% of the ones inducted. Of the 1,074 who graduated, 900 remained at time of inactivation, or 83.6% of the graduates, to which should be added 16 of the original WAFS [Women's Auxiliary Ferrying Squadron] employed who were still with the program at time of inactivation.

The women pilots, subsequent to graduation from the training program, flew approximately 60 million miles for the Army Air Forces; the fatalities were 38, or one to about 16,000 hours of flying. Both the accident rate and the fatality rate compared favorably with the rates for male pilots in similar work.

The WASP, according to the overwhelming opinion of station commanders where they were on duty, were as efficient and effective as the male pilots in most classes of duties; and were better than the men in some duties, as for example, towing of targets for gunnery practice. Almost uniformly the WASP were reported eager to learn, willing to work, and well behaved. The WASPs did ferrying, target towing, tracking and searchlight missions, simulated strafing, smoke laying and other chemical missions, radio control flying, basic and instrument instruction, engineering test flying, administrative and utility flying. The WASPs flew during operational duties nearly every type of airplane used by the AAF, from the small primary trainer to the Superfortress (B-29), including the Mustang, Thunderbolt, B-17, B-26, and C-54.

The WASPs, according to the medical surveys, had as much endurance and were no more subject to fatigue and flew as regularly and for as long hours as the male pilots in similar work. Aptitude and psychological tests, including the Stanine test, were found to be equally determinative and selective in the case of WASPs as in the case of males. The conclusion of the medical studies is, "It is no longer a matter of speculation that graduate WASPs were adapted physically, mentally, and psychologically to the type of flying assigned."

Conclusions

1) Women can meet the standard WD-AGO Form 64 physical examination for flying; and those meeting the proper height and weight requirements can be trained, approximately as quickly and as economically as men in the same age group, to fly all types of planes safely, efficiently, and regularly.
2) The best women pilot material is in the lower age brackets, down to 18 years.
3) It follows from conclusion 1 above that women can effectively release male pilots for other duties; and they have done so with the WASP program.
4) Physiology peculiar to women is not a handicap to flying or dependable performance of duty in a properly selected group.
5) The psychological, aptitude, and other tests used in the case of male pilots have approximately the same usefulness in the case of women pilots.
6) The flying safety record of women pilots approximates that of male pilots in the same type of work, whether training or operational. The elimination rate for women in training as pilots is approximately the same as for the flying cadets in the same age groups.
7) Women pilots have as much stamina and endurance and are not more subject to operational or flying fatigue than male pilots doing similar work. Women pilots can safely fly as many hours per month as male pilots.
8) Even limiting the selection of women pilots to the age and height groups named below, and also discounting for all factors incident to the fact that the WASP program was comparatively small and therefore somewhat more selective than even the aviation cadet program, an effective women's air force of many scores of thousands of good dependable pilots could be built up in the case of need from the nearly 13 million young women of our country between the ages of 18 and 28, about 6 million of whom are single.

Recommendations

1) Any future women pilot program should be militarized from the beginning.
2) For general economy and efficiency, the upper age limit should be 27 or 28 years for women to be trained as pilots for subsequent operational flying duties.
3) The minimum height for women accepted for service as pilots with the Army Air Forces, with the present types of planes in use, should be 64 inches, with a minimum weight of 110 pounds. Above these limits the weight allowance in relationship to height should be the same as for men, less about 7 pounds.
4) The next of kin of WASPs who died in the service should receive compensation comparable to what would have been received if the WASP had been on military status with insurance privileges and benefits. This requires Congressional action. Second to this, the WASP who finished the program in good standing should receive veterans' rights when veterans' rights are granted to any non-military group, and this also would require legislation.

Source: Jacqueline Cochran, WASP Final Report, 1 June 1945, Jacqueline Cochran Papers, WASP Series, Box 12, NAID #12004155, Eisenhower Presidential Library. https://www.eisenhower.archives.gov/research/online_documents/jacqueline_cochran/BinderN.pdf (accessed 18 May 2017).

Questions for Consideration

1) How, according to Cochran, did the accident and the fatality rates for female pilots compare with the rates for male pilots during training?
2) What evidence did she offer to support her conclusion that "physiology peculiar to women is not a handicap" for flying?
3) Which of her recommendations seemed most likely to spark controversy?

12.10   B-29s Drop Atomic Bombs on Japan (1945)

The armed might of the U.S. brought World War II in the Pacific to an end. Once Americans secured the Marianas, new B-29 bombers were placed within striking distance of the Japanese homeland. With Japanese carriers devastated by the Battle of Leyte Gulf, "kamikazes" began to launch suicide attacks in desperation. During 1945, bloody fights for Iwo Jima and Okinawa took a terrible toll. Nevertheless, American command of the skies permitted aircraft to "firebomb" many of Japan's largest cities. The U.S. Strategic Bombing Survey, which included statesmen such as John Kenneth Galbraith, George W. Ball, and Paul H. Nitze, began evaluating the military effectiveness of the air raids. For the next step in strategic bombing, the U.S. Army Air Forces trained the 509th Bombardment Group, commanded by Colonel Paul W. Tibbets. On August 6, a B-29 named *Enola Gay* dropped an atomic bomb dubbed "Little Boy." The explosion produced massive destruction in Hiroshima. On August 9, a B-29 named *Bockscar* dropped an atomic bomb called "Fat Man" on Nagasaki. Within a week, Japanese leaders relented. On September 2, General MacArthur and other Allied representatives received their formal surrender on board the battleship U.S.S. *Missouri* in Tokyo Bay. Ultimately, the U.S. emerged from the war as the strongest military power in history.

Document

On 6 August and 9 August 1945, the first two atomic bombs to be used for military purposes were dropped on Hiroshima and Nagasaki respectively. One hundred thousand people were killed, 6 square miles or over 50 percent of the built-up areas of the two cities were destroyed. The first and crucial question about the atomic bomb thus was answered practically and conclusively; atomic energy had been mastered for military purposes and the overwhelming scale of its possibilities had been demonstrated. A detailed examination of the physical, economic, and morale effects of the atomic bombs occupied the attention of a major portion of the Survey's staff in Japan in order to arrive at a more precise definition of the present capabilities and limitations of this radically new weapon of destruction.

Eyewitness accounts of the explosion all describe similar pictures. The bombs exploded with a tremendous flash of blue-white light, like a giant magnesium flare. The flash was of short duration and accompanied by intense glare and heat. It was followed by a tremendous pressure wave and the rumbling sound of the explosion. This sound is not clearly recollected by those who survived near the center of the explosion, although it was clearly heard by others as much as fifteen miles away. A huge snow-white cloud shot rapidly into the sky and the scene on the ground was obscured first by a bluish haze and then by a purple-brown cloud of dust and smoke.

Such eyewitness accounts reveal the sequence of events. At the time of the explosion, energy was given off in the forms of light, heat, radiation, and pressure. The complete band of radiations, from X- and gamma-rays, through ultraviolet and light rays to the radiant heat of infra-red rays, travelled with the speed of light. The shock wave created by the enormous pressures built up almost instantaneously at the point of explosion but moved out more slowly, that is at about the speed of sound. The superheated gases constituting the original fire ball expanded outward and upward at a slower rate.

The light and radiant heat rays accompanying the flash travelled in a straight line and any opaque object, even a single leaf of a vine, shielded objects lying behind it. The duration of the flash was only a fraction of a second, but it was sufficiently intense to cause third degree burns to exposed human skin up to a distance of a mile. Clothing ignited, though it could be quickly beaten out, telephone poles charred, thatch-roofed houses caught fire. Black or other dark-colored surfaces of combustible material absorbed the heat and immediately charred or burst into flames; white or light-colored surfaces reflected a substantial portion of the rays and were not consumed. Heavy black clay tiles which are an almost universal feature of the roofs of Japanese houses bubbled at distances up to a mile. Test of samples of this tile by the National Bureau of Standards in Washington indicates that temperatures in excess of 1,800° C must have been generated in the surface of the tile to produce such an effect. The surfaces of granite blocks exposed to the flash scarred and spalled at distances up to almost a mile. In the immediate area of ground zero (the point on the ground immediately below the explosion), the heat charred corpses beyond recognition.

Penetrating rays such as gamma-rays exposed X-ray films stored in the basement of a concrete hospital almost a mile from ground zero. Symptoms of their effect on human beings close to the center of the explosion, who survived other effects thereof, were generally delayed for two or three days. The bone marrow and as a result the process of blood formation were affected. The white corpuscle count went down and the human processes of resisting infection were destroyed. Death generally followed shortly thereafter. The majority of radiation cases who were at greater distances did not show severe symptoms until 1 to 4 weeks after the explosion. The first symptoms were loss of appetite, lassitude, and general discomfort. Within 12 to 48 hours, fever became evident in many cases, going as high as 104° to 105° F, which in fatal cases continued until death. If the fever subsided, the patient usually showed a rapid disappearance of other symptoms and soon regained his feeling of good health. Other symptoms were loss of white blood corpuscles, loss of hair, and decrease in sperm count [...]

The blast wave which followed the flash was of sufficient force to press in the roofs of reinforced concrete structures and to flatten completely all less sturdy structures. Due to the height of the explosion, the peak pressure of the wave at ground zero was no higher than that produced by a near miss of a high-explosive bomb, and decreased at greater distances from ground zero. Reflection and shielding by intervening hills and structures produced some unevenness in the pattern. The blast wave, however, was of far greater extent and duration than that of a high-explosive bomb and most reinforced-concrete structures suffered structural damage or collapse up to 700 feet at Hiroshima and 2,000 feet at Nagasaki. Brick buildings were flattened up to 7,300 feet at Hiroshima and 8,500 feet at Nagasaki. Typical Japanese houses of wood construction suffered total collapse up to approximately 7,300 feet at Hiroshima and 8,200 feet at Nagasaki. Beyond these distances structures received less serious damage to roofs, wall partitions, and the like. Glass windows were blown out at distances up to 5 miles. The blast wave, being of longer duration than that caused by high-explosive detonations, was accompanied by more flying debris. Window frames, doors, and partitions which would have been shaken down by a near-miss of a high-explosive bomb were hurled at high velocity through those buildings which did not collapse. Machine tools and most other production equipment in industrial plants were not directly damaged by the blast wave, but were damaged by collapsing buildings or ensuing general fires [...]

The Survey has estimated that the damage and casualties caused at Hiroshima by the one atomic bomb dropped from a single plane would have required 220 B-29s carrying 1,200 tons of incendiary bombs, 400 tons of high-explosive bombs, and 500 tons of antipersonnel fragmentation bombs, if conventional weapons, rather than an atomic bomb, had been used. One hundred and twenty-five B-29s carrying 1,200 tons of bombs would have been required to approximate the damage and casualties at Nagasaki. This estimate pre-supposed bombing under conditions similar to those existing when the atomic bombs were dropped and bombing accuracy equal to the average attained by the Twentieth Air Force during the last 3 months of the war.

Source: United States Strategic Bombing Survey, *Summary Report*, Pacific War (Washington, DC: Government Printing Office, 1946), 22–25.

Questions for Consideration

1) What question was answered "practically and conclusively" by the survey?
2) How high were the temperatures around "ground zero"?
3) Why did the survey estimate tonnage "if conventional weapons, rather than an atomic bomb, had been used" by the military?

Suggested Readings

Adams, Michael C. C. *The Best War Ever: Americans and World War II*. Baltimore: Johns Hopkins University Press, 1994.

Altschuler, Glenn C., and Stuart M. Blumin. *The G.I. Bill: A New Deal for Veterans*. New York: Oxford University Press, 2009.

Ambrose, Stephen E. *Citizen Soldiers: The U.S. Army from the Normandy Beaches to the Bulge to the Surrender of Germany, June 7, 1944–May 7, 1945*. New York: Simon & Schuster, 1997.

Blum, John Morton. *V Was for Victory: Politics and American Culture during World War II*. New York: Harcourt Brace, 1986.

Crane, Conrad C. *Bombs, Cities, and Civilians: American Airpower Strategy in World War II*. Lawrence: University Press of Kansas, 1993.

Dower, John. *War Without Mercy: Race and Power in the Pacific War*. New York: Pantheon, 1986.

Gambone, Michael D. *The Greatest Generation Comes Home: The Veteran in American Society*. College State: Texas A&M University Press, 2005.

Giangreco, D. M. *Hell to Pay: Operation Downfall and the Invasion of Japan, 1945–1947*. Annapolis: Naval Institute Press, 2009.

Gordin, Michael D. *Five Days in August: How World War II Became a Nuclear War*. Princeton: Princeton University Press, 2007.

Kennedy, David M. *Freedom from Fear: The American People in Depression and War, 1929–1945*. New York: Oxford University Press, 2005.

Kennett, Lee. *G.I.: The American Soldier in World War II*. 1987; rpt. Norman: University of Oklahoma Press, 1997.

Koistinen, Paul A. C. *Arsenal of World War II: The Political Economy of American Warfare, 1940–1945*. Lawrence: University Press of Kansas, 2004.

Korda, Michael. *Ike: An American Hero*. New York: Harper Collins, 2007.

Linderman, Gerald F. *The World Within War: America's Combat Experience in World War II*. New York: Free Press, 1997.

McManus, John C. *The Deadly Brotherhood: The American Combat Soldier in World War II*. Novato: Presidio Press, 1998.

Merryman, Molly. *Clipped Wings: The Rise and Fall of the Women Airforce Service Pilots (WASPs) of World War II*. New York: New York University Press, 1997.

Murray, Williamson, and Allan R. Millett. *A War to Be Won: Fighting the Second World War*. Cambridge: Harvard University Press, 2000.

Overy, Richard. *Why the Allies Won*. New York: W. W. Norton, 1995.

Perret, Geoffrey. *Winged Victory: The Army Air Forces in World War II*. New York: Random House, 1993.

Rhodes, Richard. *The Making of the Atomic Bomb*. New York: Simon & Schuster, 1986.

Scrijvers, Peter. *The G.I. War against Japan: American Soldiers in the Pacific and Asia during World War II*. New York: New York University Press, 2005.

Sherry, Michael S. *The Rise of American Air Power*. New Haven: Yale University Press, 1987.

Spector, Ronald H. *Eagle Against the Sun: The American War with Japan*. New York: Free Press, 1984.

Weinberg, Gerhard L. *A World at Arms: A Global History of World War II*. Second Edition. New York: Cambridge University Press, 2005.

Zeiler, Thomas. *Annihilation: A Global Military History of World War II*. New York: Oxford University Press, 2010.

13

A Cold War Begins

Chronology

1945   The United Nations chartered
1947   The Truman Doctrine
       The Marshall Plan
       The National Security Act
       USAF established
1948   Executive Order 9981
       Berlin Airlift
1949   NATO formed
1950   Korean War erupts
       UN Security Council Resolution
       Operation Chromite
       Chinese troops intervene
1951   General MacArthur relieved
1953   Operation Little Switch
       Korean Armistice
       Operation Big Switch
1957   Sputnik launched
1958   National Defense Education Act
       NASA formed
1960   U2 incident
1961   Bay of Pigs
       Berlin Wall constructed
1962   Cuban Missile Crisis
1963   President Kennedy assassinated

13.1   James V. Forrestal Manages the Pentagon (1948)

After 1945, the United States readied its defenses for a long and bitter conflict known as the Cold War. The Truman Doctrine of containment committed the U.S. to supporting "free peoples" in their ongoing struggles against totalitarian regimes. Following months of Congressional hearings, the National Security Act in 1947 created the National

American Military History: A Documentary Reader, Second Edition. Brad D. Lookingbill.
© 2019 John Wiley & Sons, Inc. Published 2019 by John Wiley & Sons, Inc.

Security Council as well as the Central Intelligence Agency. The Department of Defense (DoD) replaced the War Department. All military affairs were handled at the Pentagon— the headquarters for the DoD. James V. Forrestal, the last cabinet-level Secretary of the Navy, became the first Secretary of Defense. During 1948, Secretary Forrestal issued his first report on the Pentagon. His tenure involved a series of unexpected challenges: Communist governments came to power in Czechoslovakia and China; the Soviets blockaded West Berlin; and war erupted between Israel and the Arab states. Abruptly, President Truman asked him to resign after only 18 months on the job. On May 22, 1949, he committed suicide. Amendments to the National Security Act eventually expanded the authority of the Secretary of Defense. Meanwhile, the U.S. pledged to contribute armed forces to the North Atlantic Treaty Organization, or NATO. Henceforth, an attack on one member would constitute an attack on all.

Document

Our position, as a democratic nation dedicated to the preservation of our liberty and desirous of maintaining peace, is less vulnerable today than it was in September 1947. That position is improving, but the time has not come when we can afford to relax our efforts to make our country sufficiently strong that it will never invite attack.

We must continue to support our armed services—our Army, Navy, and Air Force— weld them into a unified combat team, supply them with the weapons and equipment they need, and determine how they can be employed most advantageously in the event of a national emergency.

We must conserve and develop our natural resources, replenish depleted stock piles of strategic and critical raw materials, foster scientific research and development, and plan now the emergency utilization of manpower and industrial machinery and facilities, so that both civilian and military production needs will be filled with the least disturbance to the national economy.

We must see that expenditures for national security yield full value; that they are made for essential projects only, and that they are kept within the country's capacity to pay for them. This nation must hold a position of military readiness, created within reasonable limits. One of the great problems from which the Military Establishment cannot divorce itself is the complex one of securing proper balance between military necessities and national solvency. The capacity for making war is not separable from economics any more than it is from diplomacy.

These are the vital tasks on which the Military Establishment has been at work since it was created. The accomplishment of these tasks is designed to prevent rather than to provoke war; for until the nations of the world take effective action to abolish armed warfare as an instrument of national policy, our greatest guarantee of peace and security is our own strength and the strength of the free peoples throughout the world who look to us for friendship, help, and inspiration. The greater our ability to defend ourselves, the less likelihood that we or they will be attacked [...]

It would be the height of folly for us to assume that a war could be won by any single weapon. If we should ever have to fight another war, I cannot visualize a situation in which any one of the services would operate independently. We must have a strong

Army, a strong Navy, and a strong Air Force, and we must have them all working together in the closest cooperation under all circumstances.

This defines the real problem of unification on which I should like to enlarge on the basis of experience gained to date. The mere passage of the National Security Act did not mean the accomplishment of its objectives overnight. The most difficult part of the task of unification is to bring conflicting ideas into harmony. It is not strange that professional military men should think in terms of the service to which they have devoted their entire adult lives; it is to be expected. Differences of opinion can be reconciled by free and frank discussion, conducted without rancor and with an open mind. That is the democratic process on which the Government of this country is founded. With all its limitations, it is a sound and sane process.

In the task of unifying and integrating the Army, Navy, and Air Force, I have been working with men in the three services, both military and civilian, whose patriotism is beyond question and who are animated fundamentally by the same motive: the creation of a system of national defense which will provide us, at the least expense, with a strong and effective war-making machine, both actual and potential, if we should have to fight another war. We have had many arguments and disagreements, because while all agree on the end result, there have been profound differences as to the methods of attaining that result.

These differences are being resolved. How fast we complete the process of resolution will depend on the speed with which we achieve the harmony of thought which is inherent in true unification. I am confident that we shall reach that accord. I believe that the decisions on the questions of our national security will come far better from a group reflecting varying experience than from any single arbitrary source.

I have stated to the Congress my position on the expression of personal views by the Secretaries and Chiefs of the Departments in the National Military Establishment. I have told those officials that I want them to feel perfectly free to express their personal views when called upon to do so by the Congress. The public and the Congress are entitled to know the personal views of the Secretaries and the Chiefs, but the public and the Congress are also entitled to know whenever there is a material distinction between such personal views and the official conclusion which the Military Establishment has arrived at after mature consideration [...]

In conclusion I should like to reemphasize two thoughts implicit in this report. The first is that this nation has endeavored constantly to maintain peace. The United States came out of the war with the atomic bomb, the most deadly and devastating weapon that man ever devised. As proof of our good faith and peaceful intentions, we have offered voluntarily to deny ourselves the use of this lethal instrument. We have proposed that it be placed under international control and have offered to surrender our proprietary rights, including the right of visitation and inspection of atomic energy plants, to an international commission. This proposal, still pending before the United Nations, has been continuously blocked by the exercise of the veto power in that organization.

Our ownership of the atomic bomb undoubtedly engendered to a wide extent the mistaken sense of security and complacency which pervaded the public mind immediately after the war and which was in some measure responsible for demobilization. The atomic bomb does not give us automatic immunity from attack, as some people would like to believe, nor does its mere possession guarantee victory if war should come. With or without the atomic bomb, there can be no absolute security for the United States or for any other nation in the world until all nations agree to the regulation of armed forces and the substitution therefore of peaceful methods in the settlement of international disputes.

The second thought I should like to reemphasize is that true unification of the armed might of the United States cannot spring from legislation alone. The spark generated by the Unification Act must be fanned into a flame by the thoughts and actions of generals and admirals, ensigns, and lieutenants, soldiers, sailors, and airmen, and civilians. We must all learn that we are working together for a common cause—the security of our country—and that the good of all transcends that of the few.

Source: James Forrestal, *First Report of the Secretary of Defense* (Washington, DC: Government Printing Office, 1948), 1–19.

Questions for Consideration

1) What, according to Secretary Forrestal, was one of the "great problems from which the Military Establishment cannot divorce itself" in 1948?
2) How did he intend to reconcile "differences of opinion" among the services?
3) Do you agree with him in that "true unification of the armed might of the United States cannot spring from legislation alone"?

13.2   Omar Bradley Discusses Desegregation (1949)

Given the service of African Americans in uniform, civil rights leaders urged the Truman administration to desegregate the military. Rather than pursuing Congressional legislation, President Truman decided to use his executive powers. On July 26, 1948, he issued Executive Order 9981. It made ending segregation the official policy of the Commander in Chief. It declared that "there shall be equality of treatment and opportunity for all persons in the armed services without regard to race, color, religion, or national origin." To implement the order as rapidly as possible, President Truman established the Committee on Equality of Treatment and Opportunity in the Armed Services. Chaired by jurist Charles Fahy, the seven member advisory body examined the rules, procedures, and practices of the Army, Navy, and Air Force. During hearings, the Fahy Committee compelled the military brass to discuss desegregation. The Army Chief of Staff, General Omar Bradley, appeared before them on March 28, 1949, and indicated a desire to avoid radical changes. That summer, the Secretary of Defense approved the desegregation plans of both the Air Force and the Navy. However, the Army continued to drag its boots. After delivering a final report during 1950, the Fahy Committee was disbanded by President Truman.

Document

Any system of handling manpower and any principles of organization must be based upon what will obtain best results in carrying out our mission, i.e., winning battles in case of war. We must not do anything that will jeopardize National Security.

Any system of use of manpower must be applicable in peace and in war. It must be applicable to both the Regular Army and the National Guard, because in war our replacement systems must be as simple as possible. It is complicated enough at best. You cannot have different rules apply to units of the same type. You certainly could not have some units with complete integration of Negroes and Whites while others practiced segregation. It naturally follows that the same principles must be applied to National Guard units of every state in the Union.

Complete integration of units would greatly simplify our administrative problems, and I believe that steps towards such integration should be taken as fast as our social customs will permit. I think that we have made great strides towards further integration in the last few years. However, we still have a great divergence in customs in different parts of the country. In certain instances, such as schools or other temporary assignments, we can follow the customs of the locality. However, in our permanent units, the problem is more difficult.

Neither is integration in a military unit as simple as integration in public gatherings or places of work during the day. The big problems arise after work or training hours, in living quarters and social gatherings. At the same time we must have equality of opportunity, of facilities, and of treatment. This is being provided under present policies [...] It is especially necessary that we give every gradient of our population which is transposed from civilian to Army life an opportunity to accept responsibility, learn the basic tenants [*sic*] of leadership, and reap the democratic benefits and results.

Furthermore, in our training and administrative practices we have tried to reduce the number and amount of changes from civil life to military life to a minimum. Of course, some changes are necessary. A man must become a member of a team with more consideration for the rights of his fellows. He becomes more dependent on them, and they on him. This is highly important, especially in battle. But we do try to have the Army reflect the best points of our civilian social and political structure. For one thing this makes our job easier, because the transition from civilian life to military life is abrupt enough without our throwing any unnecessary stumbling blocks in the way. Secondly, any organization should take full advantage of the best features of any background that its personnel may have. We all realize that the donning of a uniform does not change a man's personality, his aptitude, or his prejudices.

To a large extent the success of the American Army has been the result of taking advantage of the adaptation of the native American ingenuity to military problems, not upon the re-stamping of men into the military stereotype attempted by some nations in the past. Our success in winning battles and in winning wars would attest to the soundness of the adaptation [...]

In conclusion may I point out that primarily our peacetime Army is a volunteer organization depending upon the free acceptance of the conditions within the Army by men who volunteer for such service, both at home and abroad. I hope that we can keep it a volunteer Army without resorting to the Selective Service Act, or at least keep conscription to a minimum. On the other hand, our wartime service is not a volunteer proposition, but in service by conscription in which men have less opportunity to select their branch of services, their type of service, or where they serve. The ultimate winning or losing of battles with this conscript Army is our military problem. I am sure that you realize that any radical changes in this Army, which might seriously affect its ability to accomplish this mission, would be a very serious one.

Source: Statement by General Omar Bradley, 28 March 1949, Record Group 220, Box 10, Records of the President's Committee on Equality of Treatment and Opportunity in the Armed Services, National Archives and Records Administration.

Questions for Consideration

1) According to General Bradley, what would "greatly simplify our administrative problems" in different parts of the country?
2) When did "big problems" for integrating a military unit usually arise?
3) What do you think he meant by referencing "native American ingenuity" in the Army?

13.3   Harry S. Truman Intervenes in Korea (1950)

Beginning in 1950, the Truman administration conducted a critical reassessment of American military commitments around the world. The National Security Council prepared NSC-68, which offered a "blueprint" for strategic defense initiatives. Accordingly, the U.S. needed to build more nuclear weapons as well as to expand its conventional forces. Meanwhile, Secretary of State Dean Acheson omitted South Korea from a speech about the American "defense perimeter" in Asia. Eager to forcibly reunite the peninsula, North Korea prepared to cross the 38th parallel. After exploding its own atomic weapon and allying with Communist China, the Soviet Union secretly supported aggressive actions. On June 25, the North invaded the South. The United Nations Security Council passed Resolution 83 asking members to provide military assistance to South Koreans. Conducting a press conference a few days later, President Truman declared: "We are not at war." One reporter suggested calling it "a police action under the United Nations," to which the Commander in Chief retorted: "Yes. That is exactly what it amounts to." On July 19, President Truman delivered a radio and television address on the situation in Korea, which corresponded with a message that he sent to Congress that day. Thus, he articulated his reasons for intervening in Korea that summer.

Document

At noon today I sent a message to the Congress about the situation in Korea. I want to talk to you tonight about that situation, and about what it means to the security of the United States and to our hopes for peace in the world.

Korea is a small country, thousands of miles away, but what is happening there is important to every American. On Sunday, June 25th, Communist forces attacked the Republic of Korea. This attack has made it clear, beyond all doubt, that the international Communist movement is willing to use armed invasion to conquer independent nations. An act of aggression such as this creates a very real danger to the security of all free nations.

The attack upon Korea was an outright breach of the peace and a violation of the Charter of the United Nations. By their actions in Korea, Communist leaders have demonstrated their contempt for the basic moral principles on which the United Nations is founded. This is a direct challenge to the efforts of the free nations to build the kind of world in which men can live in freedom and peace. This challenge has been presented squarely. We must meet it squarely [...]

One of the main reasons the Security Council was set up was to act in such cases as this—to stop outbreaks of aggression in a hurry before they develop into general conflicts. In this case the Council passed a resolution which called for the invaders of Korea to stop fighting and to withdraw. The Council called on all members of the United Nations to help carry out this resolution. The Communist invaders ignored the action of the Security Council and kept right on with their attack. The Security Council then met again. It recommended that members of the United Nations help the Republic of Korea repel the attack and help restore peace and security in that area. Fifty-two of the 59 countries which are members of the United Nations have given their support to the action taken by the Security Council to restore peace in Korea.

These actions by the United Nations and its members are of great importance. The free nations have now made it clear that lawless aggression will be met with force. The free nations have learned the fateful lesson of the 1930s. That lesson is that aggression must be met firmly. Appeasement leads only to further aggression and ultimately to war.

The principal effort to help the Koreans preserve their independence and to help the United Nations restore peace has been made by the United States. We have sent land, sea, and air forces to assist in these operations. We have done this because we know that what is at stake here is nothing less than our own national security and the peace of the world [...]

Furthermore, the fact that Communist forces have invaded Korea is a warning that there may be similar acts of aggression in other parts of the world. The free nations must be on their guard, more than ever before, against this kind of sneak attack. It is obvious that we must increase our military strength and preparedness immediately. There are three things we need to do.

First, we need to send more men, equipment, and supplies to General MacArthur.

Second, in view of the world situation, we need to build up our own Army, Navy, and Air Force over and above what is needed in Korea.

Third, we need to speed up our work with other countries in strengthening our common defenses.

To help meet these needs, I have already authorized increases in the size of our Armed Forces. These increases will come in part from volunteers, in part from Selective Service, and in part from the National Guard and the Reserves. I have also ordered that military supplies and equipment be obtained at a faster rate. The necessary increases in the size of our Armed Forces and the additional equipment they must have will cost about $10 billion, and I am asking the Congress to appropriate the amount required. These funds will be used to train men and equip them with tanks, planes, guns, and ships in order to build the strength we need to help assure peace in the world [...]

We have the resources to meet our needs. Far more important, the American people are unified in their belief in democratic freedom. We are united in detesting Communist slavery.

We know that the cost of freedom is high. But we are determined to preserve our freedom—no matter what the cost. I know that our people are willing to do their part to support our soldiers and sailors and airmen who are fighting in Korea. I know that our fighting men can count on each and every one of you.

Our country stands before the world as an example of how free men, under God, can build a community of neighbors, working together for the good of all. That is the goal we seek not only for ourselves, but for all people. We believe that freedom and peace are essential if men are to live as our Creator intended us to live. It is this faith that has guided us in the past, and it is this faith that will fortify us in the stern days ahead.

Source: Harry S. Truman, "Radio and Television Address to the American People on the Situation in Korea," 19 July 1950, Online by Gerhard Peters and John T. Woolley, The American Presidency Project. http://www.presidency.ucsb.edu/ws/?pid=13561 (accessed 23 May 2017).

Questions for Consideration

1) What type of language did President Truman use to describe the Communist forces in Korea?
2) How did he plan to achieve the size increases in U.S. forces?
3) To what extent did "the fateful lesson of the 1930s" inform his support for the Republic of Korea in 1950?

13.4 Douglas MacArthur Addresses Congress (1951)

General Douglas MacArthur, the commander of United Nations forces in Korea, intended to turn the conflict into a showdown with international Communism. One of the most controversial military figures in American history, his titles included Far East Commander and General of the Army. Given sufficient air and naval support to operate in the Korean peninsula, he acted boldly to reverse the Communist tide. On September 15, 1950, he launched an amphibious landing at Inchon called Operation Chromite. Within two weeks, American troops liberated Seoul, the South Korean capital. Meanwhile, General Walton H. Walker's Eighth Army broke out from the Pusan Perimeter and joined forces with other corps in a coordinated advance northward. On October 19, South Korean troops captured the North Korean capital, Pyongyang. North Korean troops retreated to the Yalu River, where they reconstituted into new divisions for a winter offensive. Between November 27 and December 13, the Chinese Volunteer Army struck UN forces at the Chosin Reservoir and drove them back. General MacArthur, who disagreed with the civilian decision to avoid striking China, grew insubordinate. On April 11, 1951, President Truman relieved him from command. Eight days later, General MacArthur made his last public appearance before a joint session of Congress.

Document

While I was not consulted prior to the President's decision to intervene in support of the Republic of Korea, that decision, from a military standpoint, proved a sound one as we hurled back the invader and decimated his forces. Our victory was complete, and our objectives within reach, when Red China intervened with numerically superior ground forces. This created a new war and an entirely new situation—a situation not contemplated when our forces were committed against the North Korean invaders—a situation which called for new decisions in the diplomatic sphere to permit the realistic adjustment of military strategy. Such decisions have not been forthcoming. While no man in his right mind would advocate sending our ground forces into continental China, and such was never given a thought, the new situation did urgently demand a drastic revision of strategic planning if our political aim was to defeat this new enemy as we had defeated the old.

Apart from the military need, as I saw it, to neutralize the sanctuary protection given the enemy north of the Yalu, I felt that military necessity in the conduct of the war made necessary:

1) The intensification of our economic blockade against China.
2) The imposition of a naval blockade against the China coast.
3) Removal of restrictions on air reconnaissance of China's coastal area and of Manchuria.
4) Removal of restrictions on the forces of the republic of China on Formosa with logistical support to contribute to their effective operations against the common enemy.

For entertaining these views, all professionally designed to support our forces committed to Korea and to bring hostilities to an end with the least possible delay and at a saving of countless American and Allied lives, I have been severely criticized in lay circles, principally abroad, despite my understanding that from a military standpoint the above views have been fully shared in the past by practically every military leader concerned with the Korean campaign, including our own Joint Chiefs of Staff.

I called for reinforcements, but was informed that reinforcements were not available. I made clear that if not permitted to destroy the enemy build-up bases north of the Yalu, if not permitted to utilize the friendly Chinese force of some six hundred thousand men on Formosa, if not permitted to blockade the China coast to prevent the Chinese Reds from getting succor from without, and if there were to be no hope of major reinforcements, the position of the command from the military standpoint forbade victory.

We could hold in Korea by constant maneuver and at an approximate area where our supply-line advantages were in balance with the supply-line disadvantages of the enemy, but we could hope at best for only an indecisive campaign with its terrible and constant attrition upon our forces if the enemy utilized his full military potential. I have constantly called for the new political decisions essential to a solution.

Efforts have been made to distort my position. It has been said in effect that I was a warmonger. Nothing could be further from the truth. I know war as few other men now living know it, and nothing to me is more revolting. I have long advocated its complete abolition, as its very destructiveness on both friend and foe has rendered it useless as a means of settling international disputes […]

But once war is forced upon us, there is no other alternative than to apply every available means to bring it to a swift end. War's very object is victory, not prolonged indecision. In war there is no substitute for victory.

There are some who for varying reasons would appease Red China. They are blind to history's clear lesson, for history teaches with unmistakable emphasis that appeasement but begets new and bloodier war. It points to no single instance where this end has justified that means, where appeasement had led to more than a sham peace. Like blackmail, it lays the basis for new and successively greater demands until, as in blackmail, violence becomes the only alternative. Why, my soldiers asked of me, surrender military advantages to an enemy in the field? I could not answer. Some may say to avoid spread of the conflict into an all-out war with China. Others, to avoid Soviet intervention. Neither explanation seems valid, for China is already engaging with the maximum power it can commit, and the Soviet will not necessarily mesh its actions with our moves. Like a cobra, any new enemy will more likely strike whenever it feels that the relativity in military or other potential is in its favor on a worldwide basis.

The tragedy of Korea is further heightened by the fact that as military action is confined to its territorial limits, it condemns that nation, which it is our purpose to save, to suffer the devastating impact of full naval and air bombardment, while the enemy's sanctuaries are fully protected from such attack and devastation. Of the nations of the world, Korea alone, up to now, is the sole one which has risked its all against communism. The magnificence of the courage and fortitude of the Korean people defies description. They have chosen to risk death rather than slavery. Their last words to me were: "Don't scuttle the Pacific."

I have just left your fighting sons in Korea. They have met all tests there, and I can report to you without reservation that they are splendid in every way. It was my constant effort to preserve them and end this savage conflict honorably and with the least loss of time and a minimum sacrifice of life. Its growing bloodshed has caused me the deepest anguish and anxiety. Those gallant men will remain often in my thoughts and in my prayers always.

I am closing my fifty-two years of military service. When I joined the Army, even before the turn of the century, it was the fulfillment of all my boyish hopes and dreams. The world has turned over many times since I took the oath on the plain at West Point, and the hopes and dreams have long since vanished. But I still remember the refrain of one of the most popular barracks ballads of that day which proclaimed most proudly that old soldiers never die—they just fade away.

And like the old soldier of that ballad, I now close my military career and just fade away—an old soldier who tried to do his duty as God gave him the light to see that duty.

Good-bye.

Source: General Douglas MacArthur's "Old Soldiers Never Die" Address to Congress, 19 April 1951, American Memory, Library of Congress. http://memory.loc.gov/cgi-bin/query/r?ammem/mcc:@field(DOCID+@lit(mcc/034)) (accessed 23 May 2017).

Questions for Consideration

1) What, according to General MacArthur, created "a new war and an entirely new situation" in Korea?
2) How did he respond to the charge that he was a "warmonger"?
3) Why do you think he closed by saying that "old soldiers never die—they just fade away"?

13.5   Spike Selmyhr Maneuvers in Korea (1951)

During 1951, President Truman authorized General Matthew Ridgway, who succeeded General MacArthur, to arrange armistice talks with the North Koreans. A stalemate ensued near the 38th parallel. Under the banner of the United Nations, U.S. forces maneuvered to gain ground. Whenever Communists attacked, American troops conducted delaying actions. Once they paused, a counterattack began. The counterattacks rarely involved tanks, because the mountainous landscape made them ineffective. Instead, infantrymen maintained constant contact with enemy lines and directed massive firepower against forward positions. They battled with bayonets, knives, grenades, and rifles—even their bare hands. They engaged in combat night and day. They fought through frigid winters and sweltering summers. Casualties mounted along the front. Despite occasional breaches, neither side made significant advances in the rough terrain. A platoon leader in the 1st Marine Regiment, Lieutenant Garlen "Spike" Selmyhr arrived in Korea on May 23. That summer, he maneuvered up high ground in the face of deadly mortar and artillery fire. His most vivid memories involved fierce fighting on September 13, when he was wounded twice. Following treatment in a Mobile Army Surgical Hospital, or MASH, he eventually departed Korea in March of 1952. Awarded the Purple Heart, he retired from the Marine Corps two decades later.

Document
Armed with a .45 caliber automatic pistol, the Marine Corps K-bar knife, and several hand grenades, I was assigned to George Company, 3rd Battalion, 1st Marine Regiment. When I got to my unit, I knew no one. I was briefed on the tactical situation by the Company Commander Captain Frisbie, who told me that I was assigned to the 3rd Platoon. Their Platoon Leader had been killed several days earlier, and the platoon was being temporarily led by a Staff Sergeant. Staff Sergeant "Blackjack Jones" came down to the Company CP [command post] and took me to the platoon sector. There I was briefed on the platoon area of responsibility, toured the platoon position on line, was introduced to the three squad leaders and platoon guide, selected a CP for myself, and checked on supplies of rations and ammo for the platoon. I made a map study of our position and area, and checked with the Korean unit on my left flank. Walking along the ridge line, I attracted a round of incoming fire from what they told me was a 76 mm field piece that whistled overhead. Welcome to Korea! Actually, I doubt that they had fired at me specifically, as it would be a waste of ammunition to fire such a weapon at an individual [...] After we moved out of reserves, we went up north of the 38th parallel in the Imjin area near Soyang Gang River. There we launched the last battle I was in and the one for which I have the most vivid memory of all. It was there that I was shot on September 13, 1951. Our objectives were to take the high ground on Hill 1052 and an even larger one, Hill 1161 [Kanmu-Bong]. There were about 2,200 troops on our side and an unknown number on the enemy's side. The enemy that I saw were young, generally tenacious and determined fighters. They fought differently than us in that they seemed to have less concern for any casualties they might suffer in a headlong charge. Not too much finesse. About 0900, Lieutenant Connolly, the Company Commander, and Lieutenants Marsh, Morton, and I made a reconnaissance of the area where we would attack. We spotted a

group of enemy moving along the ridge line above us. Suddenly two enemy soldiers came out of the bush with their hands in the air, waving surrender leaflets. Because of the enemy on the ridge line, Lieutenant Morton and I motioned with our .45 pistols for them to move back against a bank so we would not be observed by their friends on the ridge line. They sort of went hysterical in the probable belief that they were about to be shot. They got down on their knees and drew diagrams of the positions where their comrades were. They said there were "many, many machine guns." Were they ever correct! There were heavy concentrations of small arms and automatic weapons fire, skillfully used to cover avenues of approach to their positions. They made good use of camouflage and were tenacious in holding their positions, although there was little initiative on the part of subordinates.

During the attack to take Hill 1052, my platoon was driving along a very narrow ridge line covered with trees and brush. We began to receive small arms and automatic weapons fire on Hill 751, and I moved forward to encourage the men and to direct their fire and maneuver. A major difficulty in battle is the total confusion of noise, shouting, the crack of bullets, and making sure the troops know where their officers are and that they are there sharing their danger. If the officers are all down behind rocks, trees, etc., and say "Go get 'em" or "charge," no one is going to go. However, if as the leader one stands up and says, "Let's go," they will all go. The tough part is that when the first person stands up, he feels as if a large bull's eye has been painted on his body.

When the firing intensified, I threw myself down into a prone position and received a bullet in my left shoulder. There was not a lot of pain, and when I tried to move my arm I found that it worked fine, so I again moved forward behind the leading squad. The firing was pretty brisk, and the troops were doing well in returning the fire and in moving to covered and concealed positions. Maybe ten or fifteen minutes later, I saw a North Korean come out from behind some rocks and start to point his rifle at me. He was about 30 yards away from me when I shot him. I had reacted to the small arms and automatic weapons fire from the enemy by directing the fire of my troops and encouraging them, and by dropping the enemy I faced.

After that, I was in a prone position looking for a target. I picked what I thought was an arm or shoulder of an enemy and as I moved my head to the right to look through the sights, I took a bullet that entered my left cheek and in grazing fashion exited behind my left ear, taking out part of the mastoid bone. The shock was as if someone had hit me with a baseball bat. No pain, but lots of blood. I do not know whether it was a stray round, a machine gun round, or a rifle round. God knows why, but I tried to stand up and discovered that the damage to my inner ear was such that I had no sense of balance. I immediately fell down.

At that time, Sergeant English from the machine gun platoon came out and said, "Lieutenant, put your arm around my neck and I'll walk you back behind the ridge line to first aid." I told him to get the hell out of there as bullets were flying all around us. He ignored that remark, and with my arm around his neck we walked back maybe 25–30 yards with bullets kicking up dust around our feet and clipping leaves from the trees overhead. Neither of us was touched again. "War Hero" is a term tossed about too freely, in my opinion. A war hero to me is someone who does something beyond the normal. He does something dangerous that he might not normally choose to do to execute a mission or to save another Marine, but it must be above the normal responsibilities. Sergeant English fits that perception. He came out to assist me under a hail of small arms fire when I was hit.

H. M. Paglia of New Jersey was the Navy corpsman assigned to my unit. He was a fine young man. H. N. William Mackelfres of California was a good man, too. We got to a corpsman who took off my helmet, looked at my head wound, and then covered his face with his hands and said, "Oh My God!" I took that as a discouraging word. I had no idea how badly I was hit. I just knew that I was bleeding a lot. He bandaged me up and they put me on a stretcher to evacuate me. I refused to go until some of my men who had been wounded were taken away first. Evacuation of the dead was not a priority at that time. Then one of my BAR [Browning Automatic Rifle] men, Jake Jakovec, went down the hill with me and the four Korean stretcher bearers. I was damn lucky, even though I had been wounded. The instant I was hit in the head, I had just moved my head to the right about two or three inches to look through the sights of my weapon. Had I not done so, that shot would have been right between the head lamps. When I was evacuated, I really hated leaving my buddies behind.

Source: Garlen L. "Spike" Selmyhr Interview, Veteran's Memoirs, Korean War Educator. http://www.koreanwar-educator.org/memoirs/selmyhr_spike/index.htm (accessed 23 May 2017). Used with permission of Garlen L. "Spike" Selmyhr and Lynnita Brown of the Korean War Educator.

Questions for Consideration

1) What kinds of weaponry did Lieutenant Selmyhr encounter while moving up the hills on September 13?
2) Did the platoon leader face greater danger in battle than other Marines?
3) Why did he consider himself "damn lucky" despite his wounds?

13.6 Maxwell D. Taylor Suggests a Flexible Response (1955)

The Eisenhower administration worried that rising defense costs threatened the affluence of American society. Inside the Pentagon, military planners wanted "no more Koreas" but "more bang for the buck." As explained by Secretary of State John Foster Dulles, the New Look for national defense involved massive retaliatory strikes in response to Soviet-sponsored wars around the globe. Atomic weaponry promised to provide a deterrent to Communist aggression, he predicted, as well as a means to reduce spending on military personnel. However, General Maxwell D. Taylor in 1955 called for "a flexible response" to the challenges of the Cold War. As Army Chief of Staff, he expressed frustration with the New Look. He foresaw a durable role for conventional forces as a credible deterrent to international threats. In addition, basic combat units gave the U.S. an option, if warranted, for intervention in the Third World. Congressional appropriations strengthened both conventional and unconventional forces, funded strategic and tactical defense initiatives, and maintained American troops at forward bases close to areas of national interest. Thanks to the steady supply of manpower through the retention of conscription, the force structure grew larger and more complex. In fact, the doctrine of "a flexible response" became popular among defense experts during the 1960s.

Document

In our present inability to predict future developments, our country must be prepared to cope with aggression of varying forms. It is most dangerous to commit ourselves rigidly to one strategy built around one weapon to be used in only one way. The strategy and forces of the United States must be sufficiently flexible to meet any and all threats—atomic, non-atomic; local, or general war. We must be prepared to fight a war with atomic weapons, and at the same time we must be prepared to fight a war in which atomic weapons will be restricted to the smaller types for employment on the battlefield and against targets of military significance. These smaller atomic weapons may eventually become the "conventional" weapons of the future with the larger atomic weapons reserved for a retaliatory threat. Since it is impossible to foretell what will happen, it is evident that the United States must have a versatile military structure capable of successfully dealing with all principle eventualities […]

Ground combat will always consist of fire and maneuver, but frozen concepts of battle and rigid adherence to formalized battle organizations will not meet the needs of the new era. Optimum flexibility must be the keynote in all ground combat. Tactics and techniques for offensive and defensive operations must be constantly modified to keep pace with weapons and developments. The orthodox principles underlying our tactics and techniques are valid for either atomic or non-atomic war. The possible introduction of atomic weapons on the battlefield, however, requires continuous reexamination of the manner in which these principles can be applied.

Future combat will be characterized by greatly increased tactical and strategic mobility. Consequently, new and improved methods of command, controls, and communications are essential and are being introduced. Timely and accurate intelligence to reduce to a minimum all uncertainty regarding the enemy, weather, and terrain is vital and is being emphasized, as is effective counter-intelligence to assist in concealing our own intentions and activities. The need to disperse to avoid catastrophic losses, to bring adequate force to bear swiftly at decisive points, and to exploit atomic weapons will set the pattern for both the defense and the offense.

Defensive formations in depth over a wide area are more necessary than ever before. Elasticity is the basis of defense. Because of the destructiveness of atomic weapons, defense on an atomic battlefield must consist of staggered tactical formations dispersed in great depth. Such a defense places heavy emphasis on reconnaissance and surveillance to cover unoccupied areas. Units must be so composed and dispersed that they can absorb atomic strikes without shattering. They must be conditioned to accept as normal combat in any direction. At the same time, units must be capable of swift movement to prevent enemy exploitation of his strikes, and to maneuver the enemy into forming lucrative atomic targets.

In the offensive, men and equipment must move from dispersed positions with great speed to the focal point of the attack. Supporting fires will include those of guided missiles and rockets directed from divergent and far distant points to achieve the fire superiority necessary to support the attack. Atomic warheads will give to a single round the effect of many TOTs [Time on Target] of conventional artillery. Attacking forces must be able to seize an objective without inviting disaster from enemy atomic attacks. Once an objective is seized, attacking forces must be capable of rapid dispersion to avoid a counter blow.

To give us this essential superior mobility and to meet the threats of atomic weapons, our basic combat units will probably take the form of small, integrated battle groups of all arms—infantry, artillery, armor, and engineer, with the required service support. These units must be semi-independent, self-contained, and capable of operating over extended distances on a fluid battlefield for prolonged periods with minimum control and support by higher headquarters. These units may be grouped into combat commands comparable to the present armored division, but the numbers and types of units under combat command control may vary. The weapons systems available to the units will include guided missiles (both ground-to-ground and ground-to-air), rockets, artillery, and demolitions employing both atomic and conventional explosives. By employing the latest electronic and other scientific and technological developments, the weapons systems must be capable of reliable, accurate, timely delivery in spite of adverse weather, poor visibility, or enemy countermeasures [...]

Although solutions to the problems raised by new weapons and techniques are essential to success in the battles of tomorrow, nothing can ensure success except men who are properly trained and led. Man remains what he has been throughout history—the only truly indispensable element in waging war. The awesome arsenals of modern weapons have as their sole purpose the extension and strengthening of his arm for the purpose of imposing his will on the enemy. They will be no more effective than the man who directs and applies them. As these weapons gain in complexity, the demands on the men who serve them increase in proportion. The training and leadership provided them must be of the highest professional quality if they are to wield modern weapons with effect on the atomic battlefield herein envisaged.

It is evident that the Army is in an era of evolutionary change in weapons, organization, and concepts of employment. It must be prepared to fight under varying circumstances. Its soldiers must have the best possible training, the most competent leadership, and the most effective weapons and equipment which American technology and inventive genius can provide. In short, while retaining its strength in being, the Army is seeking to develop the best combinations to fight tomorrow's war with tomorrow's weapons and techniques. Only in this way can the Army be prepared to accomplish the vital task of defeating an enemy's land forces and destroying at a minimum cost the vital resources of his power rooted in the land.

Source: Maxwell D. Taylor, *Officer's Call: The Army in the Atomic Age,* Department of the Army Pamphlet, No. 355-21 (Washington, DC: Government Printing Office, 1955), 3–9.

Questions for Consideration

1) What, according to General Taylor, must be "the keynote" in all ground combat?
2) Which weapons systems will be available to basic combat units?
3) Do you agree that "nothing can ensure success except men who are properly trained and led" on the atomic battlefield?

13.7 Presidential Candidates Debate the Cold War (1960)

The challenges of the Cold War tested the mettle of the Commander in Chief. The 1957 launch of the Sputnik satellite confirmed the fears of the Pentagon regarding Soviet missile capabilities. That same year, the Eisenhower administration began working on a Single Integrated Operational Plan, or SIOP. It included provisions for a preemptive nuclear attack if an early warning system detected an imminent Soviet strike. Despite its intermediate range for missile delivery, the Navy's Polaris submarine program gave the U.S. a mobile nuclear strike force. On behalf of the Air Force, the Strategic Air Command, or SAC, maintained around-the-clock delivery capabilities. Meanwhile, the CIA conducted high-altitude spy missions with U-2 planes. During the presidential election of 1960, American voters were alarmed by the perceived disparities in the respective arsenals of the U.S. and the Soviet Union. The Democrats nominated Massachusetts Senator John F. Kennedy, who called for a concerted national effort to close a "missile gap" with Communist rivals. Standing before television cameras, Vice President Richard M. Nixon debated him as the Republican candidate for the nation's highest office. Broadcast on October 13, the third debate revealed the views of the two candidates regarding potential "hot spots" in the Cold War.

Document	
MR. McGEE:	Senator Kennedy, yesterday you used the words "trigger happy" in referring to Vice President Richard Nixon's stand on defending the islands of Quemoy and Matsu. Last week on a program like this one you said the next President would come face to face with a serious crisis in Berlin. So the question is: Would you take military action to defend Berlin?
MR. KENNEDY:	Mr. McGee, we have a contractual right to be in Berlin coming out of the conversations at Potsdam and of World War II. That has been reinforced by direct commitments of the President of the United States. It's been reinforced by a number of other nations under NATO. I've stated on many occasions that the United States must meet its commitment on Berlin. It is a commitment that we have to meet if we're going to protect the security of Western Europe. And, therefore, on this question I don't think that there is any doubt in the mind of any American; I hope there is not any doubt in the mind of any member of the community of West Berlin. I am sure there isn't any doubt in the mind of the Russians. We will meet our commitments to maintain the freedom and independence of West Berlin.
MR. SHADEL:	Mr. Vice President, do you wish to comment?
MR. NIXON:	Yes. As a matter of fact, the statement that Senator Kennedy made was that—was to the effect that there were trigger happy Republicans, that my stand on Quemoy and Matsu was an indication of trigger happy Republicans. I resent that comment. I resent it because that's an implication that Republicans have been trigger happy and, therefore, would lead this Nation into war. I would remind Senator Kennedy of the past 50 years. I would ask him to name one Republican President who led this

Nation into war. There were three Democratic Presidents who led us into war. I do not mean by that that one party is a war party and the other party is a peace party. But I do say that any statement to the effect that the Republican party is trigger happy is belied by the record. We had a war when we came into power in 1953. We got rid of that; we've kept out of other wars; and certainly that doesn't indicate that we're trigger happy.

We've been strong, but we haven't been trigger happy. As far as Berlin is concerned, there isn't any question about the necessity of defending Berlin; the rights of people there to be free, and there isn't any question about what the united American people, Republicans and Democrats alike, would do in the event there were an attempt by the Communists to take over Berlin.

Source: "Face-to-Face, Nixon-Kennedy," Vice President Richard M. Nixon and Senator John F. Kennedy Third Joint Television-Radio Broadcast, 13 October 1960, John F. Kennedy Presidential Library and Museum. http://www.jfklibrary.org/Research/Research-Aids/JFK-Speeches/3rd-Nixon-Kennedy-Debate_19601013.aspx (accessed 23 May 2017).

Questions for Consideration

1) What did Senator Kennedy propose to do in defense of West Berlin?
2) How did Vice President Nixon respond to the claim that Republicans were "trigger happy"?
3) Which candidate answered the reporter's question most effectively?

Suggested Readings

Aliano, Richard A. *American Defense Policy from Eisenhower to Kennedy*. Athens: Ohio University Press, 1975.

Bacevich, Andrew J. *The Pentomic Era: The U.S. Army between Korea and Vietnam*. Washington, DC: National Defense University Press, 1986.

Brands, H. W. *The General vs. the President: MacArthur and Truman at the Brink of Nuclear War*. New York: Doubleday, 2016.

Crane, Conrad C. *American Airpower Strategy in Korea, 1950–1953*. Lawrence: University Press of Kansas, 2000.

Gaddis, John Lewis. *We Now Know: Rethinking Cold War History*. New York: Oxford University Press, 1997.

Halberstam, David. *The Coldest Winter: America and the Korean War*. New York: Hyperion, 2007.

Hastings, Max. *The Korean War*. New York: Simon & Schuster, 1987.

Hoopes, Townsend, and Douglas Brinkley. *Driven Patriot: The Life and Times of James Forrestal*. Annapolis: Naval Institute Press, 1992.

House, Jonathan M. *A Military History of the Cold War, 1944–1962*. Norman: University of Oklahoma Press, 2012.

Kaplan, Fred. *The Wizards of Armageddon*. New York: Simon & Schuster, 1983.

Mershon, Sherie, and Steven Schlossman. *Foxholes and Color Lines: Desegregating the U.S. Armed Forces*. Baltimore: Johns Hopkins University Press, 1998.

Miller, David. *The Cold War: A Military History*. New York: St. Martin's Press, 1998.

Newhouse, John. *War and Peace in the Nuclear Age*. New York: Knopf, 1989.

Pash, Melinda L. *In the Shadow of the Greatest Generation: The Americans Who Fought the Korean War*. New York: New York University Press, 2012.

Sherry, Michael S. *In the Shadow of War: The United States Since the 1930s*. New Haven: Yale University Press, 1995.

Strueck, William. *The Korean War: An International History*. Princeton: Princeton University Press, 1995.

14

The Tragedy of Vietnam

Chronology

1964   Gulf of Tonkin Resolution
1965   Operation Rolling Thunder
       Operation Market Time
       Operation Game Warden
       Battle of Ia Drang
1966   Operation Sea Dragon
1967   Operation Cedar Falls
       Operation Junction City
1968   Battle of Khe Sanh
       Operation Niagara
       Tet Offensive
       U.S.S. *Pueblo* Incident
       My Lai Massacre
       Operation Sealords
1969   Vietnamization begins
1970   Kent State Shootings
1971   Winter Soldier Hearings
       Operation Lam Son 719
1972   Easter Offensive
       Operation Linebacker I and II
1973   Paris Peace Accords
       War Powers Resolution
1974   President Nixon resigns
1975   Operation Frequent Wind
       Saigon falls

14.1   Herbert L. Ogier Patrols in the Tonkin Gulf (1964)

As French armed forces withdrew from Indochina, the Geneva Accords of 1954 mandated a temporary partition between North and South Vietnam. Backed by the Democratic Republic of Vietnam in Hanoi, Communist insurgents known as the Viet Cong operated in the southern provinces. Meanwhile, the United States

American Military History: A Documentary Reader, Second Edition. Brad D. Lookingbill.
© 2019 John Wiley & Sons, Inc. Published 2019 by John Wiley & Sons, Inc.

provided military and economic assistance to the Republic of Vietnam in Saigon. Within the Tonkin Gulf, American destroyers patrolled international waters. On August 2, 1964, three North Vietnamese P-4 torpedo boats attacked the U.S.S. *Maddox* operating near the coast. According to the report of Captain Herbert L. Ogier, the skipper of the *Maddox*, the destroyer evaded torpedoes and returned fire. Aircraft launched from the carrier U.S.S. *Ticonderoga* strafed the retiring P-4s. Two days later, the *Maddox* and the *C. Turner Joy* received radar, sonar, and radio signals indicating another incident. Although later investigations raised doubts about the reports, no one at the time seriously questioned what happened. At the request of President Lyndon Johnson, Congress overwhelmingly passed the Gulf of Tonkin Resolution. It authorized all actions necessary to protect U.S. forces and to provide for the defense of allies in Southeast Asia. Thanks to the Congressional authorization, the Johnson administration proceeded to expand American military operations inside Vietnam.

Document

1) On 2 August, the *Maddox* was conducting a routine DESOTO Patrol in international waters in the Gulf of Tonkin, in accordance with instructions found in reference (a). The primary purpose of the patrol was to determine the coastal patrol activity furnished by the Democratic Republic of Vietnam (DRV) along the North Vietnam coast. Other intelligence requirements included collecting ELINT and hydrographic information, monitoring of junk density and junk traffic patterns, conducting radarscope photography, and photographing landmarks (At no time that day did *Maddox* approach the mainland nearer than 8 nautical miles or an island nearer than 4 miles).

2) Our own forces in the area included CTG 72.1 (COMDESDIV 192) embarked in the *Maddox*; CTF 77 (COMCARDIV 5) embarked in the *Ticonderoga* (CVA 14), operating in the vicinity of 16′N, 110′E; the *C. Turner Joy* (DD 951) on station at 17 [degrees] 30′N 108 [degrees] 00′E; and the *Samuel N. Moore* (DD 747) on station at 17 [degrees] 30′N, 109 [degrees] 40′E.

3) During the morning of 2 August, the *Maddox* proceeded northward towards Point DELTA (19 [degrees] 47′N, 106 [degrees] 08′E) arriving in the vicinity at 1145I and then turned south on the first leg of an 8 hour orbit. The *Maddox* continued in a southerly direction during the early afternoon headed for a point 4 miles seaward of HON ME. About 1330I three patrol craft believed to be motor torpedo boats were sighted to the northwest, also on a southerly course apparently headed towards HON ME. The *Maddox* reversed course and headed back towards Point DELTA on a northeast heading. At 1350I two more patrol craft, believed to be Swatow patrol boats, were sighted to the northwest, and they were also apparently headed towards HON ME. The three PT boats and the two Swatow PGM's were tracked by radar into a cove on the north side of HON ME. At 1445I the *Maddox* altered course 35 degrees to starboard to avoid a large junk fleet fishing in the vicinity of Point DELTA. By 1600 the *Maddox* was 12 miles due east of Point DELTA still headed on a northeast course when a radar contact

bearing 230 range 30 miles was detected just north of HON ME. The contact was tracked on a course of 050, speed 30 knots, and it was evaluated as a probable patrol craft due to its high speed [...]

During the next 45 minutes the *Maddox* increased speed from 10 knots to 25 knots and headed east momentarily and then southeast in order to open the contacts, which also were increasing speed and closing. By 1700l the *Maddox* was 25 miles from the DRV coast, headed southeast at 27 knots. The contacts could be seen visually bearing 269, range of 8 miles, and they were being tracked by the Fire Control radar on a closing course of 120 with a speed of 50 knots. It was apparent that the contacts were motor torpedo boats and that they were intercepting the *Maddox*. By 1705 the boats were identified as three P-4's in column formation. They had closed to 9800 yards off the starboard quarter at which time the *Maddox* fired three 5"/38 caliber warning shots, which were unheeded.

4) The torpedo boats continued to close and were taken under fire with 151 5" rounds and 132 3" rounds of continuous fire. Although receiving numerous hits and near misses, two boats (second and third in a column) closed to 2700 yards and, because of the volume of fire, only the second boat was able to launch torpedoes. The lead boat received a direct hit at 3000 yards as it launched a third torpedo; the torpedo was not observed to run. The first two torpedoes passed near the starboard side after the *Maddox* turned to evade. During the attack, 12.7 mm machine gun fire was also directed at the *Maddox* but resulted in only one hit and no casualties. After having turned away, the first and third boats slowed apparently to assist the second boat, which had been hit and had retired earlier. The *Maddox* turned and pursued the boats for 4 minutes after it was known that the torpedoes had cleared. By this time the high relative opening range rate had opened the boats to 5 miles. At 1729l the pursuit was broken off because of the possibility of spent torpedoes in the area and that carrier aircraft had started their strafing runs. The *Maddox* remained in the area in order to render possible assistance to damaged or downed aircraft and then retired to the southeast.

Source: USS *Maddox* "Report of Action, Gulf of Tonkin, 2 August 1964," Formerly Classified Documents Subsequent to 4 August 1964, Tonkin Gulf Crisis, Navy History and Heritage Command, Department of the Navy. https://www.history.navy.mil/research/library/online-reading-room/title-list-alphabetically/t/tonkin-gulf-crisis/tonkin-gulf-incidents-of-2-4-aug-1964/uss-maddox-reports-2-4-aug-1964.html#maddox003 (accessed 23 May 2017).

Questions for Consideration

1) What, according to Captain Ogier, was the purpose of the naval patrols in the Tonkin Gulf?

2) How did the torpedo boats indicate that they were "intercepting the *Maddox*" on August 2?

3) Why do you think that only the second boat was able to launch torpedoes before retiring?

14.2   Lyndon Johnson Escalates the War (1965)

The Johnson administration assumed responsibility for the war in Vietnam. During Operation Rolling Thunder, a monsoon of ordnance rained down on targets from the Ho Chi Minh Trail to Hanoi. Secretary of Defense Robert McNamara, a proponent of gradual escalation, demanded the quantification of the results. He surrounded himself with a staff of "Whiz Kids," that is, technocrats schooled in systems analysis. In support of "Mr. McNamara's War," the Joint Chiefs of Staff insisted that the American military must not allow the Saigon "domino" to fall. Regarding the Vietnamese conflict as a crucial test of American willingness to counter wars of national liberation throughout the Third World, President Johnson intended to disrupt the flow of insurgents from the North into the South. On April 7, 1965, he explained the strategy to an audience at Johns Hopkins University. The demonstration of military strength, he reasoned, would be sufficient for a limited war. Moreover, he voiced the idealism that many Americans in uniform initially brought with them to the jungles of South Vietnam. Unfortunately, they underestimated the human and psychological dimensions of the Vietnamese Communist strategy of *dau tranh*—a mosaic of nonmilitary and military actions over long periods of time designed to achieve victory in a violent struggle.

Document

Why are we in South Viet-Nam?

We are there because we have a promise to keep. Since 1954 every American President has offered support to the people of South Viet-Nam. We have helped to build, and we have helped to defend. Thus, over many years, we have made a national pledge to help South Viet-Nam defend its independence.

And I intend to keep that promise. To dishonor that pledge, to abandon this small and brave nation to its enemies and to the terror that must follow, would be an unforgivable wrong.

We are also there to strengthen world order. Around the globe, from Berlin to Thailand, are people whose well-being rests, in part, on the belief that they can count on us if they are attacked. To leave Viet-Nam to its fate would shake the confidence of all these people in the value of an American commitment and in the value of America's word. The result would be increased unrest and instability, and even wider war.

We are also there because there are great stakes in the balance. Let no one think for a moment that retreat from Viet-Nam would bring an end to conflict. The battle would be renewed in one country and then another. The central lesson of our time is that the appetite of aggression is never satisfied. To withdraw from one battlefield means only to prepare for the next. We must say in Southeast Asia—as we did in Europe—in the words of the Bible: "Hitherto shalt thou come, but no further."

There are those who say that all our effort there will be futile—that China's power is such that it is bound to dominate all Southeast Asia. But there is no end to that argument until all of the nations of Asia are swallowed up.

There are those who wonder why we have a responsibility there. Well, we have it there for the same reason that we have a responsibility for the defense of Europe. World War II was fought in both Europe and Asia, and when it ended we found ourselves with continued responsibility for the defense of freedom.

Our objective is the independence of South Viet-Nam and its freedom from attack. We want nothing for ourselves—only that the people of South Viet-Nam be allowed to guide their own country in their own way.

We will do everything necessary to reach that objective. And we will do only what is absolutely necessary.

In recent months attacks on South Viet-Nam were stepped up. Thus, it became necessary for us to increase our response and to make attacks by air. This is not a change of purpose. It is a change in what we believe that purpose requires.

We do this in order to slow down aggression.

We do this to increase the confidence of the brave people of South Viet-Nam, who have bravely borne this brutal battle for so many years with so many casualties.

And we do this to convince the leaders of North Viet-Nam—and all who seek to share their conquest—of a very simple fact: We will not be defeated. We will not grow tired. We will not withdraw, either openly or under the cloak of a meaningless agreement.

We know that air attacks alone will not accomplish all of these purposes. But it is our best and prayerful judgment that they are a necessary part of the surest road to peace.

We hope that peace will come swiftly. But that is in the hands of others besides ourselves. And we must be prepared for a long continued conflict. It will require patience as well as bravery, the will to endure as well as the will to resist.

I wish it were possible to convince others with words of what we now find it necessary to say with guns and planes: Armed hostility is futile. Our resources are equal to any challenge. Because we fight for values and we fight for principles, rather than territory or colonies, our patience and our determination are unending.

Once this is clear, then it should also be clear that the only path for reasonable men is the path of peaceful settlement [...]

This will be a disorderly planet for a long time. In Asia, as elsewhere, the forces of the modern world are shaking old ways and uprooting ancient civilizations. There will be turbulence and struggle and even violence. Great social change—as we see in our own country now—does not always come without conflict.

We must also expect that nations will on occasion be in dispute with us. It may be because we are rich or powerful; or because we have made some mistakes; or because they honestly fear our intentions. However, no nation need ever fear that we desire their land, or to impose our will, or to dictate their institutions.

But we will always oppose the effort of one nation to conquer another nation. We will do this because our own security is at stake. But there is more to it than that. For our generation has a dream. It is a very old dream. But we have the power and now we have the opportunity to make that dream come true.

For centuries nations have struggled among each other. But we dream of a world where disputes are settled by law and reason. And we will try to make it so.

For most of history men have hated and killed one another in battle. But we dream of an end to war. And we will try to make it so.

For all existence most men have lived in poverty, threatened by hunger. But we dream of a world where all are fed and charged with hope. And we will help to make it so [...]

We may well be living in the time foretold many years ago when it was said: "I call heaven and earth to record this day against you, that I have set before you life and death, blessing and cursing: therefore choose life, that both thou and thy seed may live."

This generation of the world must choose: destroy or build, kill or aid, hate or understand. We can do all these things on a scale never dreamed of before.

Well, we will choose life. In so doing we will prevail over the enemies within man and over the natural enemies of all mankind.

Source: Lyndon B. Johnson, "Address at Johns Hopkins University: Peace without Conquest," 7 April 1965, Online by Gerhard Peters and John T. Woolley, The American Presidency Project. http://www.presidency. ucsb.edu/ws/?pid=26877 (accessed 23 May 2017).

Questions for Consideration

1) What specific goals did President Johnson expect to achieve in South Vietnam?
2) How did he intend to convince others that armed hostility was "futile"?
3) Do you agree with him in that the U.S. "will always oppose the effort of one nation to conquer another nation"?

14.3   Sarah L. Blum Encounters Casualties (1967)

The armed forces of the U.S. battled the Vietnamese Communists in thousands of places. Aerial sorties dropped more than a million tons of explosives from 1965 to 1967, while herbicides such as Agent Orange destroyed approximately half of the timberlands. In the absence of front lines, combat units swept into the dense jungles, inundated marshes, and rice paddies. Aided by U.S. Navy river-support squadrons and river-assault squadrons, the "search and destroy" missions multiplied. Howitzers and mortars provided artillery support for infantry patrols. Helicopters offered airmobility for cavalry assaults. Given the scale and the scope of the military operations, the "tooth-to-tail" ratio reached 1 to 10. It indicated the low number of troops engaged in combat duties versus the high number deployed for noncombat roles. After joining the Army Nurse Corps and receiving her commission, Lieutenant Sarah L. Blum volunteered for a tour of duty in Vietnam. She encountered a steady flow of casualties while serving as an operating room nurse at the 12th Evacuation Hospital in Cu Chi. Arriving in January of 1967, she worked grueling shifts and saved countless lives. Once the war ended, she served on the National Board of Directors of the Vietnam Veterans of America and remained active in veteran's affairs.

Document

The first thing that hit me when I arrived in Vietnam was the incredible heat and the new smells. I was one of a couple hundred nurses arriving at Bien Hoa airbase searching among the 200 identical looking olive drab duffle bags for mine, as the sweat penetrated my uniform, rolled down my face, and into my eyes. After that ordeal I was taken on an Army bus with heavy cross-cross metal grills over the windows, to the 90th replacement battalion. I learned that the window covering was to prevent grenades from coming through. For three days we learned how to receive and send mail, what the Vietnamese money was and how to get it and get paid. We also learned a bit about the culture and areas where we had hospitals. Finally we were all assigned to hospitals and sent on our way. I went to the 12th Evacuation Hospital at Cu Chi [...]

My footlocker and duffle bag were taken by truck, and I was put on a Huey helicopter to go to the 12th Evacuation Hospital. My first helicopter ride was scary, because they do not have doors. I felt very vulnerable sitting in a canvas seat in the wide open space while flying in a war zone, and if you think that was frightening the landing was worse. When they arrived at the hospital, the helicopter crew would not land the helicopter. They told me I had to jump out onto the helipad. The helicopter is very loud, and it is hard to be heard over the sounds of the rotor blades. I kept pointing down with my arm and finger, "put this thing down," and they kept shaking their heads and saying, "jump." They hovered the helicopter about six feet over the helipad but would not land it, and I had to jump. I guess that was my initiation. Or was it?

Next I was saluting our very STRAC [standing tall around the clock] executive officer to find out where to report. He looked starched and professional and did not like my answer to his question, "What is that?" pointing to my ukulele case. I brought a baritone ukulele with me so that I had some instrument to play while there. My answer was a joke to lighten up the situation, "It is a machine gun; I thought I might need it over here." That was the wrong thing to say to him, and for the next twenty minutes he yelled at me for being disrespectful to an officer and finally told me where to report [...]

We had two Quonset huts for our operating rooms. The main one was called Arizona and in it we had five different partitioned areas that counted as a room. Each area had an operating room (OR) table, equipment for giving anesthesia, a large stainless steel table I would use for instruments and sterile supplies for each case, an over the table stand that we used during the operation to hold instruments, and supplies like suture material and extra instruments. We had one shift only and that was from 9 AM until we were done with scheduled cases for the day and then all the cases generated by the war. We often worked around the clock, but the average was about 16 hours a day. I was on call four nights a week.

We had soldiers with wounds all over the bodies or only parts of their body. Often they lost arms, legs, eyes, or they had shrapnel that tore through major organs in their bodies, which we had to repair. I definitely saw the worst of war and what war does to the land and human beings on it. Yes, we were targets and were mortared often. Fortunately I was never hit, and the worst hit to our hospital occurred the month after I left.

After I had been there about six months I had a major emotional experience. A young red-headed soldier was hit by American artillery and had the lower half of his body blasted severely. From his hipbones down he was black, charred, and bleeding. We had four surgeons look at him to decide what they could save and what they could do for him.

I was standing in his blood for hours as we worked on him, and what was left at the end were some large skin flaps to cover the remainder of his pelvis. He was literally half a man. I was OK during the surgery because I learned to be numb to it all—but then on his day three, the day he came into the OR for the closure of his skin flaps, I snapped. He was at one end of the Quonset hut on a stretcher, and I came in from the opposite end. As I walked toward him I saw the flat sheet covering the stretcher and half the length of it was flat, because there was nothing there. Finally my eyes saw the bump that was his bandaged hips and then his torso covered with the sheet and finally his face and eyes. My eyes followed all that up to his face, and when I saw his red hair and blue eyes something inside me snapped, and I ran out the doors at his end. There were some assault helicopters flying overhead at that moment, and I shouted as loudly as I could through my rage and tears at the choppers, "Kill, Kill, Kill—that is all you know how to do! I hate this war!" I have no memory of what I did or how long I was going around the hospital yelling at the sky, but I ended up in front of my chief nurse telling her, "You have got to get me out of the OR; I can't take it anymore. Put me on the malaria ward or something." She shook her head and said, "I cannot do that; you just need a rest. Take a few days and go down to the beach at Vung Tau and get yourself together."

Source: Sarah L. Blum, "Sarah, Army Nurse in Vietnam," Women Under Fire. http://womenunderfire.net/ sarah-army-nurse-in-vietnam (accessed 22 July 2017).

Questions for Consideration

1) What did Lieutenant Blum say was the "first thing" to hit her in Vietnam?
2) How did she feel about her helicopter ride to Cu Chi?
3) Why do you think she "learned to be numb to it all" at the hospital?

14.4   William C. Westmoreland Reacts to Tet (1968)

The Vietnam War reached a breaking point. Since 1964, General William C. Westmoreland served as the senior U.S. officer for the Military Assistance Command in Vietnam (MACV). During 1967, he posited that the war was entering a new phase "when the end begins to come into view." American intelligence discovered that almost 40,000 North Vietnamese regulars were massed near a Marine base in Khe Sanh. Predictably, Westmoreland authorized Operation Niagara to pulverize them with air strikes. He also shifted numerous combat units into forward positions near the Demilitarized Zone, or DMZ. On January 31, 1968, however, the Viet Cong defied the holy truce of Tet and launched surprise attacks throughout South Vietnam. The Tet offensive enabled them to overrun five major cities, including the ancient capital of Hue. In a telegram from Saigon on February 9, 1968, General Westmoreland requested reinforcements for a major counteroffensive. President Johnson denied his request but instead prepared to negotiate with Hanoi. The new Secretary of Defense Clark Clifford saw no prospect for military victory. Although the Viet Cong suffered enormous casualties after Tet, public opinion in the U.S. turned dramatically against the war. Horrific acts such as the My Lai massacre raised unsettling questions about the conduct of American soldiers.

Document

To put the situation in context, it might be desirable to give you my views of the enemy's strategy and the plans that he developed in Hanoi during early fall. It would seem that the enemy concluded that a protracted war was not in his long-range interest in view of the success of our ground and air actions against his forces, supplies, and facilities. He therefore decided to adopt an alternate strategy to bring the war to an early conclusion.

Stemming from this strategy, there evolved a plan that I reconstruct in three phases. Phase I, which started at the end of October and was scheduled to go until the first of the year, had as its objective the seizure of selected areas in remote provinces along the ` borders and consolidation of these areas pending further operations to expand his area of control. Also during this phase, he proceeded to concentrate on district towns to disrupt the political and military control structure outside the cities. During this phase, we saw the major attack on Dak To; attacks by fire on Kontum, Pleiku, and Ban Me Thuot; and major ground attacks against Loc Ninh, Bu Dop, and Song Be; and attacks against innumerable district towns and outposts. As you know, this phase achieved very limited success, resulted in large casualties to the enemy, and a failure to physically control more territory in South Vietnam. An enclave strategy would have played into his hands. The second phase, which we saw start at Tet, involved infiltration of cities to destroy the political and military control apparatus and to bring about a public uprising. In the border areas, this phase was designed to support his plan to seize control of Pleiku and Darlac Provinces, which would give him de facto control of the eastern portion of the country from the Ashau Valley in western Thua Thien all the way down through War Zone C in northern Tay Ninh. The third phase, which is yet to begin, would involve consolidation of his position and strong attacks across the DMZ and against Khe Sanh with the objective of establishing military control over the two northern provinces, thereby bringing about a de facto partition of the country from wherein he would control Quang Tri and Thua Thien, western Quang Nam, western Quang Tin, and the Provinces of Kontum, Pleiku, Darlac, Quang Duc, and at least the northern portions of Phuoc Long, Bien Long, and Tay Ninh. Under the circumstances, he would have created a situation similar to that which now prevails in Laos and would therefore be in a strong negotiating position, particularly if he were successful in his design to assume control of the cities and bring about a public uprising [...]

Needless to say, I would welcome reinforcements at any time they can be made available:

A) To put me in a stronger posture to contain the enemy's major campaign in the DMZ-Quang Tri-Thua Thien area and to go on the offensive as soon as his attack is spent.
B) To permit me to carry out my campaign plans despite the enemy's reinforcements from North Vietnam which have influenced my deployments and plans.
C) To off-set the weakened Vietnamese forces resulting from casualties and Tet desertions. Realistically, we must assume that it will take them at least six months to regain the military posture of several weeks ago. I should point out in this connection that when one considers the casualties inflicted on the enemy, this is not an expected [unexpected?] price to pay.
D) To take advantage of the enemy's weakened position by going on the offensive against him [...]

In summary, I would much prefer a bird in the hand than two in the bush, but would like the birds to be deployed to the I Corps area and not in the II Corps or III Corps. Elements that I have had to deploy from III Corps could perhaps be returned and therefore expand our operations in that area. It is conceivable that a six-month loan of these units would turn the tide to the point where the enemy might see the light or be so weakened that we could return them, particularly if the ARVN can rebuild itself following its recent battles and improves its fighting quality by virtue of the modern weapons it is scheduled to receive.

Source: William Westmoreland, Telegram From the Commander, Military Assistance Command, Vietnam, to the Chairman of the Joint Chiefs of Staff and the Commander in Chief, Pacific, 9 February 1968, in *Foreign Relations, 1964–1968*, Volume VI, Vietnam, January-August 1968, Document 63, U.S. Department of State. http://history.state.gov/historicaldocuments/frus1964-68v06/d63 (accessed 23 May 2017).

Questions for Consideration

1) How credible were General Westmoreland's views on "the enemy's strategy" after Tet?
2) Where did he believe the enemy's major campaign could be contained with reinforcements?
3) What did he mean in that he would "much prefer a bird in the hand than two in the bush"?

14.5   George T. Olsen Hunts the Enemy (1969)

Richard M. Nixon won the U.S. presidential election of 1968 while promising "peace with honor" in Vietnam. He kept his plan a secret until assuming office the next year. The new policy commonly known as Vietnamization called for the training and equipping of a strong, self-reliant South Vietnamese military, which would enable the American military to turn over primary responsibility for the war to the Army of the Republic of Vietnam (ARVN). Meanwhile, the Pentagon continued to opine that North Vietnam would stop the insurgency if convinced that Communist forces could not successfully infiltrate the countryside. General Creighton W. Abrams replaced General Westmoreland, who became the Army Chief of Staff. After taking charge of MACV, General Abrams launched a concerted effort to improve population security throughout South Vietnam. The U.S. infantry, nicknamed the "grunts," slogged through the jungles and swamps in pursuit of an elusive enemy. They patrolled for weeks while avoiding booby traps and ambushes. Specialist George T. Olsen, an Army Ranger with Company G of the 75th Infantry, arrived in South Vietnam during 1969. His letter on August 31 to Rosemary Dresch, a college friend from New York, described combat missions near Chu Lai. He was killed in action on March 3, 1970.

Document

Dear Red,

I am living in a green world with a green canvas roof over me, green sandbags all around me, dressed in green camouflage fatigues and sitting on a green cot that once was white, now is mildewed while all around me an act of God is blowing this little radio station apart. We're getting the tail end of a tropical storm that has moved in down by Da Nang and is moving up north towards us. The monsoons are almost upon us […]

Actually I'm writing this because I have to write or go out of my mind, and you're "it," so to speak. Things happen over here that you just can't keep to yourself—if you do, you brood on them, slowly go "flak happy," get careless, and eventually get zapped when your mind has strayed from the job at hand. Sometimes, especially when inactivity has you going crazy and staring at the walls, you've got to talk things out, and it helps a lot if the other person is either a buddy over here who's been through the fire too and can understand, or a member of the opposite sex who can't and you hope is never able to. Even if I don't mail this, at least I'll have written it out, which will make me feel better.

Last Monday I went on my first hunter-killer operation and saw Mars close up for the first time. We had two teams—12 men—inserted at dawn about two miles inland and slightly north of Chu Lai about an hour off the choppers. We set up around a trail, and a lone NVA [North Vietnamese Army] officer walked into the middle of us. We tried for a POW, but he panicked and took off in a blizzard of shells. I had him in my sights, threw three slugs at him and he just disappeared. No Hollywood theatrics—one minute he's a living, running human being, the next second he's down, just a red lump of clay. At first, I thought it was I that got him, but it was a shotgun blast that brought him down. After that everyone in hearing distance knew we were in the area, but on hunter-killer operations we stay to fight rather than extract upon breaking contact. We found some huts the NVA had been working on, then moved out across a dried-up paddy when all hell broke loose. We were strung out on open ground with the point man less than 10 feet from the NVA when we were ambushed with grenades and automatic weapons. If they'd had a heavy MG [machine gun] or a mortar, we'd all be dead, but as it was, we were unbelievably lucky and not a man was killed. Two men took shrapnel in the face, and I took some in the shoulder, and then our NCO and point assaulted the ambushing force, the wounded man rushed the NVA after them and Victor [enemy combatant] broke contact and ran. We ran into the wood line, beat the NVA back twice without taking any more casualties, then after being pinned down for about two hours were extracted under air support. Only one of us was really wounded—my wound and one other man's being insignificant—but we really lucked out that time.

The frightening thing about it all is that it is so very easy to kill in war. There's no remorse, no theatrical "washing of hands" to get rid of nonexistent blood, not even any regrets. When it happens, you are more afraid [than] you've ever been in your life—my hands shook so much I had trouble reloading and it took a visible effort to perform each motion and control what would normally be called panic but which, somehow, isn't. You're scared, really scared, and there's no thinking about it. You kill because that little SOB is doing his best to kill you and you desperately want to live, to go home, to get drunk or walk down the street on a date again. And suddenly the grenades aren't going off any more, the weapons stop and, unbelievably fast it seems, it's all over and you're alive because someone else is either dead or so anxious to stay alive that he's run away and you are the victor—if there is such a thing in war. You don't think about it.

I have truly come to envy the honest pacifist who honestly believes that no killing is permissible and can, with a clear conscience, stay home and not take part in these conflicts. I wish I could do the same, but I can't see letting another take my place and my risks over here, and the pacifist ideal cannot drive one burning objection to it from my mind: the fact that the only reason pacifists such as the Amish can even live in an orderly society is because someone—be they police or soldiers—is taking risks to keep the wolves away. To be a sheep in a world of sheep is one thing; to be a sheep in a world of predators is something else [...] I guess that's why I'm over here, why I fought so hard to come here, and why, even though I'm scared most of the time, I'm content to be here. At least I'm doing my part according to what I believe. The only thing keeping the wolves from the flock are the hounds. But I tell you that, allegorically speaking, it is a hard and scary task to be a wolfhound.

Source: "Letter by George T. Olsen" by George T. Olsen, from *Dear America: Letters Home from Vietnam*, ed. Bernard Edelman. © 1985 The Vietnam Veterans Memorial Commission. Used by permission of W. W. Norton & Company, Inc.

Questions for Consideration

1) What, according to Specialist Olsen, was the objective of a hunter-killer operation?
2) How did writing enable him to think about the war?
3) Why do you think he mentioned "wolves," "sheep," and "hounds" in the letter?

14.6 The Gates Commission Proposes an All-Volunteer Force (1970)

While continuing to provide military and economic aid to Saigon, the Nixon administration implemented a phased disengagement of American troops. From a peak of 543,000 troops in early 1969, U.S. force levels in Vietnam fell to 24,000 by the end of 1972. Unfortunately, the lack of a clear military objective contributed to a deterioration of morale and a lapse in discipline among the rank and file. Meanwhile, President Nixon announced plans to replace the military draft with a lottery system. Army officials internally conducted a classified study called Project Volunteer in Defense of the Nation, or PROVIDE, which highlighted issues of recruitment and retention. Thomas S. Gates, a former Secretary of Defense, chaired the President's Commission on an All-Volunteer Armed Force. Commission members included civilians such as Milton Friedman, W. Allen Wallis, and Alan Greenspan—all free-market economists. Through voluntary enlistments, competitive pay, and enhanced benefits, a smaller but more highly trained military appeared feasible. Moreover, the National Guard and Reserves contained replacement troops to complete the total force structure. President Nixon received their report in late 1969; it was released to the public on February 20, 1970. Although the Pentagon preferred retaining a system of selective service, President Nixon pushed ahead to eliminate conscription.

Document

We unanimously believe that the nation's interests will be better served by an all-volunteer force, supported by an effective stand-by draft, than by a mixed force of volunteers and conscripts; that steps should be taken promptly to move in this direction; and that the first indispensable step is to remove the present inequity in the pay of men serving their first term in the armed forces.

The United States has relied throughout its history on a voluntary armed force except during major wars and since 1948. A return to an all-volunteer force will strengthen our freedoms, remove an inequity now imposed on the expression of the patriotism that has never been lacking among our youth, promote the efficiency of the armed forces, and enhance their dignity. It is the system for maintaining standing forces that minimizes government interference with the freedom of the individual to determine his own life in accord with his values.

The Commission bases its judgments on long-range considerations of what method of recruiting manpower will strengthen our society's foundations. The Commission's members have reached agreement on their recommendations only as the result of prolonged study and searching debate and in spite of initial division. We are, of course, fully aware of the current and frequently emotional public debate on national priorities, foreign policy, and the military, but are agreed that such issues stand apart from the question of when and how to end conscription.

To judge the feasibility of an all-volunteer force, it is important to grasp the dimensions of the recruitment problem in the next decade. If conscription is continued, a stable mid-range force of 2.5 million men (slightly smaller than pre-Vietnam) will require 440,000 new enlisted men per year. To maintain a fully voluntary stable force of the same effective strength, taking into account lower personnel turnover, we estimate that not more than 325,000 men will have to be enlisted annually. In recent years about 500,000 men a year have volunteered for military service. Although some of these volunteered only because of the threat of the draft, the best estimates are that at least half—250,000 men—are "true volunteers." Such men would have volunteered even if there had been no draft, and they did volunteer in spite of an entry pay that is roughly 60 percent of the amount that men of their age, education, and training could earn in civilian life.

The often ignored fact, therefore, is that our present armed forces are made up predominantly of volunteers. All those men who have more than four years of service—38 percent of the total—are true volunteers; and so are at least a third of those with fewer than four years of service.

The return to voluntary means of raising and maintaining our armed forces should be seen in this perspective. With true volunteers now providing some 250,000 enlisted men annually, a fully volunteer force of 2.5 million men can be achieved by improving pay and conditions of service sufficiently to induce approximately 75,000 additional young men to enlist each year from the 1.5 million men who will annually turn 19 and who will also meet the physical, moral, and mental requirements. A voluntary force of 3.0 million men would require 400,000 enlistments each year, or 150,000 additional volunteers from the 1.5 million eligible 19-year olds. Smaller forces would require fewer than 75,000 additional volunteers annually. Reasonable improvements in pay and benefits in the early years of service should increase the number of volunteers by these amounts.

In any event, such improvements are called for on the ground of equity alone. Because conscription has been used to provide raw recruits, the pay of men entering the services has been kept at a very low level. It has not risen nearly as rapidly as the pay of experienced military personnel, and it is now about 60 percent of comparable civilian pay. Similarly, the pay of first-term officers has not been kept in line with the pay of more experienced officers, or with comparable civilians [...]

Although the budgetary expense of a volunteer armed force will be higher than for the present mixed force of volunteers and conscripts, the actual cost will be lower. This seemingly paradoxical statement is true because many of the costs of manning our armed forces today are hidden and are not reflected in the budget. Men who are forced to serve in the military at artificially low pay are actually paying a form of tax, which subsidizes those in the society who do not serve. Furthermore, the output of the civilian economy is reduced because more men serve in the military than would be required for an all-volunteer force of the same strength. This cost does not show up in the budget. Neither does the loss in output resulting from the disruption in the lives of young men who do not serve. Neither do the costs borne by those men who do not serve, but who rearrange their lives in response to the possibility of being drafted. Taking these hidden and neglected costs into account, the actual cost to the nation of an all-volunteer force will be lower than the cost of the present force.

The Commission has attempted to allow for the uncertainties of the future. In the event of a national emergency requiring a rapid increase in the number of men under arms, the first recourse should be to ready reserves, including the National Guard. Like the active duty forces, these reserves can and should be recruited on a voluntary basis. Whatever advantages may be claimed for it, conscription cannot provide emergency forces: it takes many months of training for civilians to become soldiers. However, to provide for the possibility of an emergency requiring a major increase in forces over an extended period, we recommend that machinery be created for a standby draft, to take effect by act of Congress upon the recommendation of the President.

The draft has been an accepted feature of American life for a generation, and its elimination will represent still another major change in a society much buffeted by change and alarmed by violent attacks on the established order. Yet the status quo can be changed constructively, and the society improved peacefully by responsible and responsive government. It is in this spirit that the Commission has deliberated and arrived at its recommendations. However necessary conscription may have been in World War II, it has revealed many disadvantages in the past generation. It has been a costly, inequitable, and divisive procedure for recruiting men for the armed forces. It has imposed heavy burdens on a small minority of young men while easing slightly the tax burden on the rest of us. It has introduced needless uncertainty into the lives of all our young men. It has burdened draft boards with painful decisions about who shall be compelled to serve and who shall be deferred. It has weakened the political fabric of our society and impaired the delicate web of shared values that alone enables a free society to exist. These costs of conscription would have to be borne if they were a necessary price for defending our peace and security. They are intolerable when there is an alternative consistent with our basic national values.

Source: Report of the President's Commission on an All-Volunteer Armed Force (Washington, DC: Government Printing Office, 1970), 5–10.

Questions for Consideration

1) Which issues did the report suggest "stand apart from the question of when and how to end conscription" in the U.S.?
2) How many additional recruits did the report claim would be induced by "reasonable improvements" in pay and benefits?
3) Do you agree with the report that an all-volunteer force offered "an alternative consistent with our basic national values"?

14.7 George J. Eade Assesses the Christmas Bombings (1972)

The balance of power in Vietnam shifted rapidly to Hanoi. To strengthen the position of Saigon, the Nixon administration ordered secret bombings of Viet Cong sanctuaries as well as military incursions into Cambodia and Laos. During 1972, President Nixon responded vigorously to North Vietnam's Easter Offensive. From May to October, Operation Linebacker involved strategic nonnuclear bombardments across North Vietnam. The peace talks in Paris stalled during November. Operation Linebacker II, which was dubbed the "Christmas Bombings," included another 700 sorties by high-flying B-52s. The next month, the U.S. signed the Paris Peace Accords. With a thawing in the Cold War, the Nixon Doctrine encouraged allies to accept a larger share of their own defense burdens. Clearly, American troops in South Vietnam, once withdrawn, seemed unlikely to return. Given the changing defense posture, the precise application of air power made the cease-fire appear viable. Military planners within the U.S. Air Force, particularly General George J. Eade, pointed with confidence to the efficacy of bombing campaigns. Following a long career in the Strategic Air Command, he served as the Deputy Chief of Staff, Plans and Operations. He became Deputy Commander in Chief, United States European Command, before retiring. Tragically, Saigon fell into the hands of North Vietnamese forces during 1975.

Document

Throughout this long and unpopular war, the North Vietnamese had shown little willingness to negotiate a settlement, primarily because they were able to sustain their logistic networks and maintain constant pressure on the armies of South Vietnam, Laos, and, in the latter stages, Cambodia. Their intransigence signaled long-held intentions of eroding the will of their enemies to resist and ultimately the taking over of all of Indochina. However, after the decision of the President in 1972 to resume the bombing of NVN (this time with determined intent and less restrained application of air power), coupled with intensified diplomatic overtures, the North Vietnamese backed away from their intransigence and entered into serious negotiations to conclude a peace settlement.

In actuality the 1972 campaign can be analyzed in two distinct phases. Phase I began with the resumption of full-scale bombing of North Vietnam following the Easter offensive in the South and lasted until mid-October when it appeared that peace was at hand. Phase II, in December 1972, lasted only eleven days, but those eleven days may well prove to be the most decisive period of the entire war; a period that, when the final accounting is taken, should provide unprecedented evidence of the capability of air power to achieve national objectives [...]

A post-operation summary of the eleven-day bombing campaign provides irrefutable evidence on the nature of the targets struck and the crippling effect that air power had on North Vietnam's war-making potential. Bombing the rail system alone resulted in an almost total suspension of rail traffic in the Hanoi-Haiphong area. In the past when North Vietnamese rail installations had been struck, repair crews were at work immediately building bypasses to the damaged areas. During the eleven-day campaign, the rail system was struck with such intensity and regularity that, as post-mission photography reveals, repair crews made no attempt to restore even token rail traffic. Concurrent with raids on the rail system, B-52s and fighter-bombers struck major supply depots where the North Vietnamese stored war materiel prior to shipment to the South. Resultant damage, confirmed by photography, was the virtual destruction of several hundred warehouses and storage buildings. Raids on North Vietnam's three major power plants reduced the country's electrical power output from 92,000 kilowatts to between 17,000 and 24,000 kilowatts, causing a complete blackout of all but the critical functions of government and defense that required electrical power. Militarily, the December bombing campaign achieved the intended objective of seriously degrading the enemy's capability to wage war in the South. Far more significant, however, is the fact that our nation's political objectives were supported by the rapid, concentrated application of air power in an effort to bring about a cease-fire and the ultimate end of the war for the United States in Southeast Asia.

There are several conclusions that can be drawn from this examination of the role of air power throughout the Indochina War. First, there is the realization that air power along with other U.S. and allied forces had been engaged since 1965 in one of the longest wars in U.S. history. Militarily, a long war is disadvantageous. If we possess a capability to apply force rapidly and massively (massively in relation to the opposition, not in absolute terms), presumably we can end a war quickly. With such an alternative available, if we allow the war to continue over an extended period it is because of a decision to impose restrictions on the forces we employ—a decision prompted by a desire to limit the scope of the conflict.

Nevertheless, from the purely military point of view, such restrictions produce numerous disadvantages. The enemy is given time to study, adjust to, and counteract our strategy, tactics, and weapons. He is given time to deploy new weapon systems or to perfect and expand existing ones (witness the formidable North Vietnamese air defenses built up during the earlier bombing campaign); to create different routes of supply (the jungle highways through Laos and sea-fed routes through Cambodia); to train large numbers of people to be effective troops; to redistribute, his population; to disperse his vital industries; to duplicate and build bypasses to critical communications links; to develop and employ successful propaganda themes. In short, we may surrender or seriously compromise the initiative and so make the war much more expensive and difficult to win.

Second, when the political climate requires the imposition of constraints on military forces, serious consideration must be given to existing limitations in force capabilities.

This is not to say that military forces can achieve an objective only when unconstrained and given a free rein; but, rather, a balance must be reached in the decision-making process between political constraints and force limitations so that the ability to achieve a desired objective is optimized. It is in this area that the "can-do" spirit of the military sometimes works at cross-purposes to the accomplishment of an assigned task. The overriding tradition in the military is to salute smartly and move out even when faced with limited capabilities. Just as military leaders must face the reality of political constraints, so is it important that a nation's policy-makers understand that extensive political constraints in concert with force limitations may produce an outcome that falls short of anticipated objectives.

Finally, as the limitations in force capabilities are reduced by advancing technology and the changing face of the war brings about a lessening of political constraints, the appropriate application of military power can indeed contribute significantly to the achievement of desired objectives. I believe that the experience of the eleven-day campaign in December 1972 should provide convincing lessons in the future employment of air power as an effective instrument to be used in support of national policy. Perhaps these valuable lessons will allow us to update the findings of the World War II *Strategic Bombing Survey* to show that "no nation can long endure the swift, accurate, concentrated application of air power and still hope to achieve any measure of victory."

The ultimate objective in Southeast Asia has been identified as a just and honorable peace. Air power alone cannot take full credit for bringing the war to an end; but the establishment of serious peace negotiations and the long-awaited cease-fire agreement that followed were in large part due to the application of air power.

Source: George J. Eade, "Reflections on Air Power in the Vietnam War," *Air University Review* 24 (November–December 1973), 2–9.

Questions for Consideration

1) What, according to General Eade, forced North Vietnam to enter into serious negotiations to conclude a peace settlement?
2) How did the bombing campaign seriously degrade "the enemy's capability to wage war" in South Vietnam?
3) Why did he say that the "can-do" spirit of the military sometimes works at cross-purposes to the accomplishment of an assigned task?

Suggested Readings

Appy, Christian G. *Working-Class War: American Combat Soldiers and Vietnam*. Chapel Hill: University of North Carolina Press, 1993.

Clodfelter, Mark. *The Limits of American Air Power: The American Bombing of North Vietnam*. New York: Free Press, 1989.

Daddis, Gregory A. *Westmoreland's War: Reassessing American Strategy in Vietnam*. New York: Oxford University Press, 2014.

Heardon, Patrick J. *The Tragedy of Vietnam*. Third Edition. New York: Pearson Longman, 2008.

Herring, George C. *America's Longest War: The United States and Vietnam, 1950–1975.* Fourth Edition. New York: McGraw-Hill, 2002.

Karnow, Stanley. *Vietnam: A History.* New York: Viking, 1983.

Kindsvatter, Peter S. *American Soldiers: Ground Combat in the World Wars, Korea, and Vietnam.* Lawrence: University Press of Kansas, 2003.

McMaster, H. R. *Dereliction of Duty: Lyndon Johnson, Robert McNamara, The Joint Chiefs of Staff, and the Lies that Led to Vietnam.* New York: Harper Collins, 1997.

Moise, Edwin E. *Tonkin Gulf and the Escalation of the Vietnam War.* Chapel Hill: University of North Carolina Press, 1996.

Olson, James S., and Randy Roberts. *Where the Domino Fell: America and Vietnam, 1945–2010.* Sixth Edition. Malden, MA: Wiley Blackwell, 2014.

Prados, John. *Vietnam: The History of an Unwinnable War, 1945–1975.* Lawrence: University Press of Kansas, 2009.

Schulzinger, Robert D. *A Time for War: The United States and Vietnam, 1941–1975.* New York: Oxford University Press, 1997.

Sorley, Lewis. *A Better War: The Unexamined Victories and Final Tragedy of America's Last Years in Vietnam.* New York: Harcourt, 1999.

Spector, Ronald H. *After Tet: The Bloodiest Year in Vietnam.* New York: Free Press, 1993.

Stanton, Shelby. *The Rise and Fall of an American Army: U.S. Ground Forces in Vietnam, 1965–1973.* Novato: Presidio Press, 1985.

Vuic, Kara D. *Officer, Nurse, Woman: The U.S. Army Nurse Corps in the Vietnam War.* Baltimore: Johns Hopkins University Press, 2009.

15

A New Military

Chronology

1979   Iranian Hostage Crisis
1983   Beirut barracks bombed
       Operation Urgent Fury
1986   Operation El Dorado Canyon
       Goldwater–Nichols Act
       Tower Commission
1988   INF Treaty ratified
       Al-Qaeda founded
1989   Berlin Wall falls
       Operation Just Cause
1990   Iraq invades Kuwait
       Operation Desert Shield
1991   Operation Desert Storm
       Cease-Fire in Iraq
1993   World Trade Center bombed
       Battle of Mogadishu
1994   Operation Uphold Democracy
1995   Operation Joint Endeavor
1996   Khobar Towers bombed
1998   Operation Infinite Reach
       Operation Desert Fox
1999   Operation Allied Force
2000   U.S.S. *Cole* bombed

15.1   N. W. Ayer Rebrands the Army (1981)

The United States suffered from the cultural fallout of the Vietnam War, which eroded the compulsion for national service. The Pentagon attempted to publicize the benefits of "buddy" systems, international travel, vacation leave, free housing, job training, educational funds, and increased pay. The Air Force urged a new generation to "aim high," while the Navy promised that they would "see the world." With great pride, the Marine Corps boasted about wanting only a "few good men." No one did more to upgrade the marketing of the

American Military History: A Documentary Reader, Second Edition. Brad D. Lookingbill.
© 2019 John Wiley & Sons, Inc. Published 2019 by John Wiley & Sons, Inc.

Document

GO FROM HIGH SCHOOL TO FLIGHT SCHOOL.

With over 8,500 aircraft, the Army needs twice as many pilots as the nation's largest airline.

That's why, if you have what it takes, you could qualify for the Army's Warrant Officer Flight Training Program. It's a rigorous 40-week long course of study where you earn both your pilot's wings and an appointment as an Army Warrant Officer. What's more, you can enter the program with a high school diploma.

If you want an opportunity where not even the sky's the limit, call toll free 800-421-4422. In California, call 800-252-0011. Alaska and Hawaii, 800-423-2244. Better yet, visit your nearest Army Recruiter, listed in the Yellow Pages.

ARMY. BE ALL YOU CAN BE.

Job #US-NPS-P10149
Pg A/c Bleed
8-1/4 x 11-1/8
(7-1/4 x 10) LM
Newsweek—Dec. 7-81
National Future Farmer—Dec./Jan. '81

NW Ayer Incorporated

Source: N. W. Ayer & Son Advertising Records, Archives Center, National Museum of American History, Smithsonian Institution.

Army than General Maxwell R. Thurman, who earned the nickname "Mad Max" after taking over Recruiting Command in 1979. After several intense meetings with the advertising firm N. W. Ayer, he pushed their creative team to craft a clear and coherent message for an All-Volunteer Force, or AVF. Earl Carter, an employee of the firm, suggested "Be All You Can Be" for a catchy slogan. Rebranding the Army became the focus of newspaper, magazine, radio, and television advertisements in 1981. Recruiters utilized the techniques of consumer product marketing while targeting quality young men and women for enlistment. Throughout the decade, the advertising campaigns resonated with positive imagery about a revival of military professionalism and the opportunities for upward mobility.

Questions for Consideration

1) How did the Army advertisement illustrate the benefits of military training?
2) What kind of audience do you think the message may have reached?
3) Why do you suppose that the slogan "Be All You Can Be" appeared in bold text?

15.2 Ronald Reagan Envisions SDI (1983)

First elected in 1980, President Ronald Reagan hoped to secure world peace through American military strength. While calling the Soviet Union an "evil empire," he attempted to reduce the influence of Communist forces around the globe. He dispatched American troops to Grenada and to Lebanon. He authorized an air strike on Libya. Moreover, the Reagan administration orchestrated a buildup of national defense. Thanks to annual increases in the military budget, nearly $2 trillion flowed to the Pentagon. Larger budgets meant investments in the research and the development of new weaponry. On March 23, 1983, President Reagan announced plans to pursue a state-of-the-art system through the Strategic Defense Initiative, or SDI. While critics dubbed it "Star Wars," he foresaw the construction of orbiting battle stations able to vaporize intercontinental ballistic missiles. Promising a celestial defense shield, SDI potentially made nuclear warheads obsolete. Even though SDI was never fully funded, it redefined the arms race into terms giving the U.S. an upper hand with the Soviet Union. Confronted with the possibilities of space-based interceptors and high-energy lasers, the new Soviet leader Mikhail Gorbachev bargained with President Reagan from a position of weakness. During 1987, the two "superpowers" negotiated a historic treaty eliminating their intermediate-range nuclear forces.

Document
The subject I want to discuss with you, peace and national security, is both timely and important. Timely, because I've reached a decision which offers a new hope for our children in the 21st century, a decision I'll tell you about in a few minutes. And important, because there's a very big decision that you must make for yourselves. This subject involves the most basic duty that any President and any people share, the duty to protect and strengthen the peace [...]

When I took office in January 1981, I was appalled by what I found: American planes that couldn't fly and American ships that couldn't sail for lack of spare parts and trained personnel and insufficient fuel and ammunition for essential training. The inevitable result of all this was poor morale in our armed forces, difficulty in recruiting the brightest young Americans to wear the uniform, and difficulty in convincing our most experienced military personnel to stay on.

There was a real question then about how well we could meet a crisis. And it was obvious that we had to begin a major modernization program to ensure we could deter aggression and preserve the peace in the years ahead.

We had to move immediately to improve the basic readiness and staying power of our conventional forces, so they could meet—and therefore help deter—a crisis. We had to make up for lost years of investment by moving forward with a long-term plan to prepare our forces to counter the military capabilities our adversaries were developing for the future.

I know that all of you want peace, and so do I. I know too that many of you seriously believe that a nuclear freeze would further the cause of peace. But a freeze now would make us less, not more, secure and would raise, not reduce, the risks of war. It would be largely unverifiable and would seriously undercut our negotiations on arms reduction. It would reward the Soviets for their massive military buildup while preventing us from modernizing our aging and increasingly vulnerable forces. With their present margin of superiority, why should they agree to arms reductions knowing that we were prohibited from catching up?

Believe me, it wasn't pleasant for someone who had come to Washington determined to reduce government spending, but we had to move forward with the task of repairing our defenses, or we would lose our ability to deter conflict now and in the future. We had to demonstrate to any adversary that aggression could not succeed, and that the only real solution was substantial, equitable, and effectively verifiable arms reduction—the kind we're working for right now in Geneva.

Thanks to your strong support and bipartisan support from the Congress, we began to turn things around. Already, we're seeing some very encouraging results. Quality recruitment and retention are up dramatically—more high school graduates are choosing military careers, and more experienced career personnel are choosing to stay. Our men and women in uniform at last are getting the tools and training they need to do their jobs.

Ask around today, especially among our young people, and I think you will find a whole new attitude toward serving their country. This reflects more than just better pay, equipment, and leadership. You the American people have sent a signal to these young people that it is once again an honor to wear the uniform. That's not something you measure in a budget, but it's a very real part of our nation's strength [...]

Let me share with you a vision of the future which offers hope. It is that we embark on a program to counter the awesome Soviet missile threat with measures that are defensive. Let us turn to the very strengths in technology that spawned our great industrial base and that have given us the quality of life we enjoy today.

What if free people could live secure in the knowledge that their security did not rest upon the threat of instant U.S. retaliation to deter a Soviet attack, that we could intercept and destroy strategic ballistic missiles before they reached our own soil or that of our allies?

I know this is a formidable, technical task, one that may not be accomplished before the end of this century. Yet, current technology has attained a level of sophistication where it's reasonable for us to begin this effort. It will take years, probably decades of effort on many fronts. There will be failures and setbacks, just as there will be successes and breakthroughs. And as we proceed, we must remain constant in preserving the nuclear deterrent and maintaining a solid capability for flexible response. But isn't it worth every investment necessary to free the world from the threat of nuclear war? We know it is.

In the meantime, we will continue to pursue real reductions in nuclear arms, negotiating from a position of strength that can be ensured only by modernizing our strategic forces. At the same time, we must take steps to reduce the risk of a conventional military conflict escalating to nuclear war by improving our nonnuclear capabilities.

America does possess—now—the technologies to attain very significant improvements in the effectiveness of our conventional, nonnuclear forces. Proceeding boldly with these new technologies, we can significantly reduce any incentive that the Soviet Union may have to threaten attack against the United States or its allies.

As we pursue our goal of defensive technologies, we recognize that our allies rely upon our strategic offensive power to deter attacks against them. Their vital interests and ours are inextricably linked. Their safety and ours are one. And no change in technology can or will alter that reality. We must and shall continue to honor our commitments.

I clearly recognize that defensive systems have limitations and raise certain problems and ambiguities. If paired with offensive systems, they can be viewed as fostering an aggressive policy, and no one wants that. But with these considerations firmly in mind, I call upon the scientific community in our country, those who gave us nuclear weapons, to turn their great talents now to the cause of mankind and world peace, to give us the means of rendering these nuclear weapons impotent and obsolete.

Tonight, consistent with our obligations of the ABM [anti-ballistic missile] treaty and recognizing the need for closer consultation with our allies, I'm taking an important first step. I am directing a comprehensive and intensive effort to define a long-term research and development program to begin to achieve our ultimate goal of eliminating the threat posed by strategic nuclear missiles. This could pave the way for arms control measures to eliminate the weapons themselves. We seek neither military superiority nor political advantage. Our only purpose—one all people share—is to search for ways to reduce the danger of nuclear war.

My fellow Americans, tonight we're launching an effort which holds the promise of changing the course of human history. There will be risks, and results take time. But I believe we can do it. As we cross this threshold, I ask for your prayers and your support.

Source: Ronald Reagan, "Address to the Nation on Defense and National Security," 23 March 1983, Online by Gerhard Peters and John T. Woolley, The American Presidency Project. http://www.presidency.ucsb.edu/ws/?pid=41093 (accessed 9 June 2017).

Questions for Consideration

1) What, according to President Reagan, would raise the risks of war?
2) How did strategic offensive power deter attacks?
3) Was he correct that SDI gave "a new hope" to Americans?

15.3 Colin L. Powell Evaluates National Security (1989)

To maintain a high state of combat readiness, American military leaders worked to solve structural and strategic problems. During 1986, Congress passed the Goldwater–Nichols Defense Reorganization Act. It elevated the Chairman of the Joint Chiefs of Staff as the principle military advisor to the Commander in Chief. Consequently, the Reagan administration crafted a "joint" operational doctrine influenced to a large extent by General Colin L. Powell. A professional soldier for over three decades, he was the highest ranking African American in the military. Before becoming a four-star general, his positions ranged from senior assistant for Secretary of Defense Caspar Weinberger to National Security Advisor for President Reagan. During 1989, he headed U.S. Forces Command, or FORSCOM. He offered an optimistic yet sober evaluation of national security, which appeared in an article for the *ARMY* magazine. Meanwhile, President George H. W. Bush tapped him for the Chairman of the Joint Chiefs of Staff. Over the next four years, he advocated an approach to armed conflict that maximized force and minimized casualties. On his watch, the Cold War thawed fast. The Communist bloc came apart. Free men and women danced atop the Berlin Wall. Americans in uniform faced the prospects of a new world order.

Document

If we consult the experts, we find a wide variety of opinions. I think one of the key reasons we find such a wide variety is no one knows—or at least very few are confident of their answers—and those experts who are confident aren't very convincing.

As an example, our best experts can't even tell us with any degree of accuracy where our chief adversaries, the Soviets, are going. There are those who see President Mikhail S. Gorbachev as some sort of a Machiavellian schemer, able to orchestrate the mammoth Soviet bureaucracy toward a clever plan to dismember the NATO alliance. Some say that he is risking chaos in the Balkans, the Baltics, Eastern Europe, Georgia, and elsewhere just to get us out of NATO; that he retired one-third of the Central Committee just to impress the European public; and that he is cutting forces just to de-nuke Europe. Oh, he wants all these things but, I submit, the real imperative for his programs is Soviet domestic and foreign impotence and failure. Other experts say we are on the threshold of a new historical era—the Cold War is over—swords into plowshares or microchips [...]

Underlying everything, the Soviet military machine is still as big, bad, and ugly as it ever was. That fact hasn't changed—yet. But I hope it will. We all should hope it will. The Soviets still have enough nuclear warheads to destroy us and we them. That fact hasn't changed—yet. The Soviets have an empty ideology. That fact hasn't changed either. The difference now seems to be that they are recognizing the results of that empty ideology, if not the barrenness of the ideology itself. As the Soviets undergo these fundamental, long-range changes, the perception will grow that the threat is receding more and more. Whether the reality of a lessened threat will follow remains to be seen.

These historic changes in the Soviet Union are back-dropped against a quieter world. Nations seem to be moving their own way—Islamic fundamentalists, for example—or in the direction of freedom and democracy, our way—not the Soviet way. The dangers in this world seem to spring more from its enormous debt problems and the poverty and joblessness that those problems generate than from irreconcilable East–West tensions. The free world, responding to its own love for peace and prosperity, welcomes the respite from East–West tension to work on its own domestic problems. Much of the West wants rapid movement in accommodating Mr. Gorbachev's initiatives.

On balance, there is in the free world a lessened appreciation of the threat and therefore a lessened desire to pay for armed forces to meet it. So what is the consensus now and how do we keep up with it?

First, the American people want us to continue to act the part of world superpower and leader. I believe they continue to want a strong defense. They don't want a hollow military establishment, but they do want our strength maintained with fiscal constraints dictated by our having to solve other problems in the world and in our domestic situation—and increasingly by Moscow's apparently softer approach and by the generally improved world atmosphere. To the American public, and more so to European audiences, there appear to be very few points of conflict in the world with the potential to lead to superpower confrontation. So we have not lost the consensus for a strong defense, but that consensus has changed. The bottom line is that we can't act in the 1990s as if we had the same public consensus of the early 1980s or as if the geopolitical situation is the same.

You can't count on real growth in the defense budget, in terms of the kind of growth we had in the early 1980s. The last five negative growth years each started out as a real growth proposal. Will the Soviets, who can't meet the demands of the next century except to stagger into it like a punch-drunk behemoth, any time soon generate the threat necessary to convince Americans to return to the defense spending levels of the early eighties? I don't believe so—in fact, I believe the American public wants us to take advantage, cautiously, of these new opportunities.

In this world where television cameras are on the scene before the ambulances and fire trucks, perceptions are reality. In fact, perceptions are frequently more than reality, because a perception that's wrong but taken for real is ten times more volatile and dangerous than an adverse reality perceived correctly. The perception in some circles seems to be that, given the historical ups and downs of the defense budget, all we need to do is hang on for a couple of years and the Bear will be back and real growth will be restored, that having too much program for the dollars available will somehow work itself out. I don't believe it will. I believe we're going to have to make some hard choices [...]

While we still want and will support a strong defense, we want it to be at a reasonable cost. I believe Americans still want a strategic, trained, ready, war-fighting Army, too. They expect a good-looking Army they can have confidence in and be proud of. I believe they recognize such a force as the cornerstone of a strong defense. They support us, but not at any cost. They don't see that as reasonable under the changed circumstances in the world. So our challenge in the Army is to keep what we've gained over the past eight years. To do that, to keep the best Army we've ever fielded in peacetime, we've got to spend wisely and well.

Source: Colin L. Powell, "National Security Challenges in the 1990s: The Future Just Ain't What it Used to Be," *ARMY* 39 (July 1989): 12–14. Reprinted with permission from *ARMY* magazine.

Questions for Consideration

1) What, according to General Powell, was "the real imperative" for changes inside the Soviet Union?
2) In which directions did the nations of "a quieter world" seem to be moving?
3) Why did he trumpet "a strong defense" in peacetime?

15.4   H. Norman Schwarzkopf Defends the Persian Gulf (1990)

The armed forces of the U.S. marched into the turbulence of the Middle East. On August 2, 1990, Saddam Hussein, the brutal ruler of Iraq, invaded Kuwait, a tiny, oil-rich neighbor. Within hours, the UN Security Council passed a resolution demanding the withdrawal of Iraqi forces. Because Saddam posed a direct threat to Saudi Arabia and its oil fields, the Bush administration took action. The primary mission of Operation Desert Shield was to prevent Iraq from invading another neighbor. Along with carriers, battleships, and aircraft, massive quantities of armaments flowed into the region. American troops joined with a coalition that included British, French, Egyptian, and Saudi troops. General H. Norman Schwarzkopf, who headed U.S. Central Command, or CENTCOM, prepared to defend the Persian Gulf. Hoping to make Saddam think twice before crossing "a line in the sand," he measured his words carefully in interviews and in briefings. When sanctions failed to bring an end to Iraq's occupation of Kuwait that November, the UN delivered an ultimatum for them to withdraw by January 15, 1991. Both houses of Congress voted to authorize the use of force, albeit reluctantly. Combat units waited in the desert for what Saddam would call "The Mother of All Battles."

Document
A rotation policy has probably been the top priority that we've worked recently. We asked each commander—Army, Navy, Air Force, Marine Corps—what they thought the policy should be, based on operational requirements and personnel policies. I don't think it's right to have one group, for example, rotating at six months and another group rotating at nine months or a year just because they're wearing different uniforms. I think the fair thing is to start with one policy for the entire theater. There will be some difference, I know. For example, if a reserve unit runs out of mobilization days, it's going home. By and large, we're looking for a universal policy. But the most important thing, of course, is to ensure we maintain our fighting ability. It's a complicated thing: maintaining equity, maintaining combat readiness, and meeting our goals and objectives.
First, we'll establish a rotation policy, and then we'll work on the R&R policy. Presently we're not in combat. But that's not to say I don't want to get the troops out of this harsh environment. We're looking at three different levels of R&R. First would be a short-term R&R in-country. We've already opened one of these in the Dhahran area, and we're rotating people through. It's a place where they can, for one day, have a great time lying around a swimming pool or watching movies. The second is something close to what would normally be an R&R center: someplace for a weekend getaway, two or three days

or something like that in countries close by. In the long term, we're thinking of the routine R&R for people here six months who will be here an entire year. Give them a chance to go someplace for a week or 10 days and then come back. European locations immediately come to mind. But we're a long way from that six-month point when we really would be thinking about R&R.

There aren't many people in the United States who understand this part of the world. One of the greatest benefits from Desert Shield will be the goodwill from having more than 170,000 really fine, high-quality Americans here—each an ambassador of the United States. The Saudi Arabians will learn that Americans are, for the most part, fine, upstanding young men and women with high moral and ethical standards—and that's a big plus. On the other hand, the Americans will learn the same thing about the Arabs. If by the actions of a few, we demonstrate that all the terrible things that extremists say about Americans are true, then we could very easily win the war and lose the peace. In fact, I get good comments every day about American troops and about the lack of incidents.

I don't think we've come up with any problem areas between nations at all. We're working very well together. I think we're all here for a common cause. Every nation that's involved knows why we're here, and that's probably helped to alleviate some problems that ordinarily would come up. Since we have a common understanding, that helps to break through a lot of red tape that you would ordinarily have to face.

I'm proud of the way all services are working together. The attitude is that we're here to do a job, let's do it right, and let's get on with it. One of my jobs as a theater commander is to make decisions, if needed, on doctrinal disputes. However, I haven't had to make a single judgment, because people have worked things out together. The interoperability thing was a concern after Grenada. But since then, we've made our equipment and ammunition compatible. So I don't think there's a major interoperability problem.

I visited an Air National Guard unit from Tennessee, and they're doing a magnificent job. They're happy to be here, and, as a matter of fact, the only problem was that more of their buddies in the United States wanted to join them. But everywhere the National Guard and the Reserve are doing a great job. You can't tell the difference between one unit and another.

One of my first initiatives was to get a radio station and start broadcasting to the troops. The men and women of the armed forces are bright, intelligent, informed young men and women, and they want information. I visited in the field, and they asked, for example, "What are the diplomatic efforts occurring in the world to try and put this crisis to bed?" It was obvious they wanted information. That's when I said to get a radio station here, now. I wanted radios in the hands of as many soldiers and Marines as possible, including those on the front line. We wanted to provide news, sports, and music. We succeeded. Every time there's a rumor, you should jump on it right away and put out the correct story. If "rumors" actually prove to be true, say so, and explain them in the proper context. We want to provide as much information as possible.

The armed forces are obviously going toward contingency-based forces instead of forward-deployed forces. I think in the future you'll see forces in the United States organized contingency-wise to go anywhere there's a crisis. Desert Shield will be a great learning experience as to the type of force design for the future. I would tell you in a heartbeat that this operation is going superbly well. From the flow standpoint, even though you hear about sealift breakdowns and some supplies haven't come fast enough—there has never been a show-stopper. There was no time when I said, "Hey, the troops are in danger." We learn little things all the time about how to flow the forces during every exercise. But I don't think there's anybody who wouldn't say the Desert Shield deployment was an overwhelming success.

As President Bush said: We're going to be here until the job's done. I couldn't even begin to speculate how long that'll be. I hope it won't be very long. I want to get home to my family just like everybody else. How long will it take to redeploy to the United States? I think we can do it pretty quickly. We would probably bring the equipment to the rear, park and marshal it, and then leave a rear party behind to get the equipment home. We'd load troops on wide-body airplanes and fly them home as fast as possible. People first, equipment later.

Beyond a shadow of a doubt, it is worth it. Detractors say our troops are fighting for oil. Others say, well, they are protecting a monarchy. Anybody who says that is dumb. That's the only description you can give. We would not be here for one minute if it were not in the best interest of the United States. The president would never have sent us if it weren't in our best interest to ensure stability in this part of the world. We're here to protect the interests of the United States and the entire free world in the Middle East. It would not be in our best interest to have Saddam Hussein controlling oil resources. But we're not fighting for oil *per se*. We're not fighting for gasoline *per se*. We're fighting for world order. If we turn our backs, then we're saying to every other pipsqueak dictator who gets a little bit of power to go ahead and take your neighbor. I don't think the world is going to let that happen anymore, as it did in World War II.

Source: "Desert Shield Boss Talks Issues," *Airman* 34 (November 1990), 24–25.

Questions for Consideration

1) What did General Schwarzkopf say was "one of the greatest benefits" of Desert Shield?
2) How did he intend to squelch "rumors" among the troops?
3) Did his tone suggest that he was hawkish, dovish, or owlish?

15.5   Daniel L. Davis Sees Action in Desert Storm (1991)

Operation Desert Storm involved the most impressive collection of weaponry ever utilized in battle. Beginning on January 16, 1991, the aerial phase of the war included surgical strikes that devastated Iraq's infrastructure. During the Great Scud Hunt, mobile missile launchers were targeted by Air Force and Navy jets. People around the world watched on television, which broadcast footage of "smart bombs" as well as scenes of "collateral damage." At General Schwarzkopf's direction, the overland campaign started on February 23. With lightning speed, the main spearhead on the ground liberated Kuwait within four days. First Lieutenant Daniel L. Davis, the Fire Support Officer for Eagle Troop in the 2d Armored Cavalry Regiment, monitored the fighting. As tank units from the squadron breached the Iraqi lines, he transmitted fire missions over the communications network to the supporting artillery. Thanks to the "net," he experienced combat in a unique way. Afterward, he pondered Eagle Troop's smashing success at the longitudinal reading of 73 Easting. President Bush halted combat operations before continuing an advance on to Baghdad, which left Saddam's regime in power. On February 27, a cease-fire ended the Gulf War. For the rest of the decade, the American military patrolled no-fly zones and sparred with Iraqi forces.

Document

On the early afternoon of 26 February 1991, the 2d ACR was leading VII (US) Corps' eastward drive toward the heart of the Iraqi Army—the Republican Guards. Just before contact, the regiment changed its formation to three squadrons abreast: 1st Squadron in the south, 3d Squadron in the middle, and 2d Squadron in the north.

The 2d Squadron was in a box formation moving east. G Troop (Ghost) was to the north with F Troop (Fox) behind it, and E Troop (Eagle) was in the south with H Company (Hawk tank company) behind Eagle. The 2d Howitzer Battery was under the operational control of (OPCON) the 2d Squadron's direct support (DS) 6th Battalion, 41st Field Artillery (6-41 FA) and moved just behind the squadron's trail maneuver units [...]

As had been the case since mid-morning, a driving dust storm limited our visibility to no more than 1,000 meters. The wind and dust had also grounded the regiment's OH-58Ds [scout helicopters], depriving it of the usual 5 to 10 kilometers of advanced warning that had become the norm.

At 1600, Eagle 1st Platoon (Bradley-mounted scouts), using 13X thermal sights, located what appeared to be about 10 revetted positions some 3,500 meters away. Almost simultaneously, Eagle 3d Platoon (scouts) began taking fire from a bunker building complex on the troop's right front at about 67 Easting.

With the immediate threat, Eagle Troop commander, Captain H. R. McMaster, directed 2d and 4th Platoons (tanks) to come on-line beside his tank and prepare to place a troop one-round high-explosive anti-tank (HEAT) volley into the complex. To provide cover as the tanks were moving on line, 3d Platoon's Bradleys pumped 25-mm high-explosive incendiary tracer (HE-IT) rounds and tube-launched optically tracked, wire-guided (TOW) missile fire into the complex. This kept the attention of the Iraqi BMP-1s (Soviet-made tracked infantry combat vehicles) and machinegun nests that were returning fire.

Meanwhile, on the troop's left front with 1st Platoon, the Eagle FIST [Fire Support Team] chief realized he didn't have time during the movement-to-contact to stop, align the targeting system, and erect the head of his M981 fire support vehicle (FIST-V). So he jumped into the turret of the nearest Bradley, located the enemy using the Bradley's thermals, obtained a direction with his M2 compass, and used the Bradley's sight to determine a range. He returned to the FIST-V and, using data from the global positioning system (GPS), input the direction, distance, and observer's known location into the FIST digital message device (DMD), and obtained an enemy grid for a fire mission [...]

At exactly 1619 hours, Eagle 6's tank crested a nearly imperceptible rise in the terrain at 70 Easting and stared down the gun tubes of eight enemy T-72 tanks, the closest one 450 meters away. In only seven seconds, Eagle 6's tank destroyed the first three enemy tanks. Simultaneously, 2d and 4th Platoons engaged enemy tanks, using fire distribution techniques to near textbook perfection, and within 10 seconds, all eight enemy tanks were burning. Eagle continued to press the attack into the supporting positions, driving through and sometimes over minefields. Within a span of only seven minutes, the first of two Iraqi armored battalions was laid to waste.

Eagle FIST quickly reported the action to Cougar 13. As all squadron FISTs eavesdrop on the fire support (FS) net, Ghost, Fox, and Hawk FISTs along with the 2d Howitzer Battery knew of the contact with the enemy and where. Each troop FSO then quickly alerted his commander, and the necessary actions began taking place all over the squadron. News traveled faster over the FS net than the squadron command net [...]

Lieutenant General Frederick M. Franks, Jr., VII Corps Commander, had given the 2d ACR the mission of finding and fixing the enemy while not becoming decisively engaged. The squadron was to be prepared to help the 1st Infantry Division (Mechanized)—the "Big Red One"—in a forward passage-of-lines. Therefore, once Eagle and Ghost had made contact with the leading elements of what was the Iraqi Tawakalna Division, it was the regimental commander Colonel L. D. Holder's intent to fix the enemy force and prepare to pass the 1st Infantry Division through.

But in the confusion of combat, staying within the parameters of the commander's intent isn't as easy as drawing a line on a map. When the troop Executive Officer Lieutenant John Gifford called McMaster on the radio to remind him the limit of advance was 70 Easting, McMaster responded, "We're already past 70 and in contact. Tell them I'm sorry!"

After McMaster had consolidated his unit near 73 Easting, he formed a 360-degree defensive perimeter oriented east. He stopped with his nine M1A1 tanks on line facing forward with his 12 Bradleys providing left and right flank security, connecting in the troop's rear to form a full circle. Eagle 13 positioned himself forward, some 50 meters behind the tanks [...]

As the night wore on and the battle began to wane, Eagle 13 noticed an area on the back side of a slight rise, just out of reach of the direct-fire weapons. He had seen several enemy vehicles come from that direction during the previous three hours of combat. They had quickly been destroyed by TOW missiles or tank HEAT rounds—depending on who could get the round off first. However, as no one could see that far and the squadron wasn't allowed to carry the attack any farther, only indirect fire could reach beyond the rise.

At 2204 hours after a lull in firing, Eagle sent a mission in with the deep grid. The first fire-for-effect resulted in numerous secondary explosions. As repeat was called for—more secondary explosions. A third call with augmenting fires resulted in still more secondary explosions. It was clear that something was over the rise, and whatever it was, it was big.

The time for passage of the 1st Infantry Division was at hand, so the final repeat had to be coordinated through corps. In the meantime, as the direct-fire fight was now over, tankers and scouts ventured outside their vehicles for the first time since the previous afternoon. As permission for the final mission was granted, cavalrymen all along the squadron front sat atop their vehicles and watched the show.

At exactly 2240, 6-41 FA Howitzer Battery and C/4-27 FA (multiple launch rocket system, or MLRS) fired on an area more than three kilometers wide and one kilometer deep. They fired a total of 228 DPICM rounds, 92 HE/PD rounds, and 12 MLRS rockets. It was a spectacular sight—the booms and flashes of the guns to the rear, the rush and streaks of light from the rockets, and, finally, the peppering impact on ground of the ICM bomblets finding their marks. The nearly non-stop thunder created by the explosions could be felt as clearly as they were heard. One would have thought it was the grand finale to a 4th of July fireworks show; the cavalrymen's "ooohs" and "ahhhs" were followed closely by rousing applause.

As ground reconnaissance later revealed, the battalion mass destroyed 27 ammunition bunkers, three tanks, four BMP-1s, two SA-9s (Soviet-made antiaircraft missiles), 35 trucks (of various sizes) and five fuelers. Additionally, the 6-41 FA Battle Group destroyed 11 tanks, damaged four more and destroyed three BTRs (Soviet-made amphibious armored personnel carriers) and caused numerous enemy personnel casualties during the Battle of 73 Easting. By firing hundreds of other rounds all over the battlefield, the artillery clearly aided the direct-fire assets in destroying many other targets.

Source: Daniel L. Davis, "Artillerymen in Action—The 2d ACR at the Battle of 73 Easting," *Field Artillery*, April 1992, 48–53.

Questions for Consideration

1) What, according to Lieutenant Davis, was difficult about the parameters of battle near 73 Easting?
2) Who was the commanding officer for Eagle Troop?
3) Do you think that the artillerymen actually heard "ooohs" and "ahhhs" along the squadron front?

15.6 Congress Approves "Don't Ask, Don't Tell" (1993)

In the wake of the Gulf War, the American military faced recruiting and retention issues. The service branches grew culturally diverse, as women and minorities enlisted more frequently. Responding to the fiscal crisis created by exploding federal deficits, the Pentagon gradually downsized the force structure. Promising to guarantee equal opportunity regardless of sexual orientation, President Bill Clinton wanted to lift the military's ban on the service of gays and lesbians. Whereas the Joint Chiefs of Staff defended the preexisting restrictions, the Clinton administration encountered stern opposition. Eventually, Senator Sam Nunn of Georgia helped to broker a compromise in Congress. On November 30, 1993, Congress approved the National Defense Authorization Act with revised provisions regarding the ban. Subtitle G of the public law formulated what was popularly called "Don't Ask, Don't Tell." Accordingly, military personnel faced a discharge from service for engaging in homosexual conduct but not for suspicion of sexual orientation. If a person openly acknowledged his or her homosexuality, then he or she seemed likely to engage in homosexual conduct. However, investigation became warranted only if "credible information" arose regarding homosexual acts. Otherwise, superiors were not to ask men and women in uniform questions about it. The policy of "Don't Ask, Don't Tell" officially ended in 2011.

Document

a) FINDINGS-Congress makes the following findings:

1) Section 8 of article I of the Constitution of the United States commits exclusively to the Congress the powers to raise and support armies, provide and maintain a Navy, and make rules for the government and regulation of the land and naval forces.

2) There is no constitutional right to serve in the armed forces.

3) Pursuant to the powers conferred by section 8 of article I of the Constitution of the United States, it lies within the discretion of the Congress to establish qualifications for and conditions of service in the armed forces.

4) The primary purpose of the armed forces is to prepare for and to prevail in combat should the need arise.

5) The conduct of military operations requires members of the armed forces to make extraordinary sacrifices, including the ultimate sacrifice, in order to provide for the common defense.

6) Success in combat requires military units that are characterized by high morale, good order and discipline, and unit cohesion.

7) One of the most critical elements in combat capability is unit cohesion, that is, the bonds of trust among individual service members that make the combat effectiveness of a military unit greater than the sum of the combat effectiveness of the individual unit members.

8) Military life is fundamentally different from civilian life in that—(A) the extraordinary responsibilities of the armed forces, the unique conditions of military service, and the critical role of unit cohesion, require that the military community, while subject to civilian control, exist as a specialized society; and (B) the military society is characterized by its own laws, rules, customs, and traditions, including numerous restrictions on personal behavior, that would not be acceptable in civilian society.

9) The standards of conduct for members of the armed forces regulate a member's life for 24 hours each day beginning at the moment the member enters military status and not ending until that person is discharged or otherwise separated from the armed forces.

10) Those standards of conduct, including the Uniform Code of Military Justice, apply to a member of the armed forces at all times that the member has a military status, whether the member is on base or off base, and whether the member is on duty or off duty.

11) The pervasive application of the standards of conduct is necessary because members of the armed forces must be ready at all times for worldwide deployment to a combat environment.

12) The worldwide deployment of United States military forces, the international responsibilities of the United States, and the potential for involvement of the armed forces in actual combat routinely make it necessary for members of the armed forces involuntarily to accept living conditions and working conditions that are often Spartan, primitive, and characterized by forced intimacy with little or no privacy.

13) The prohibition against homosexual conduct is a longstanding element of military law that continues to be necessary in the unique circumstances of military service.

14) The armed forces must maintain personnel policies that exclude persons whose presence in the armed forces would create an unacceptable risk to the armed forces' high standards of morale, good order and discipline, and unit cohesion that are the essence of military capability.

15) The presence in the armed forces of persons who demonstrate a propensity or intent to engage in homosexual acts would create an unacceptable risk to the high standards of morale, good order and discipline, and unit cohesion that are the essence of military capability [...]

d) SENSE OF CONGRESS–It is the sense of Congress that—

1) the suspension of questioning concerning homosexuality as part of the processing of individuals for accession into the Armed Forces under the interim policy of January 29, 1993, should be continued, but the Secretary of Defense may reinstate that questioning with such questions or such revised questions as he considers appropriate if the Secretary determines that it is necessary to do so in order to effectuate the policy set forth in section 654 of title 10, United States Code, as added by subsection (a); and

2) the Secretary of Defense should consider issuing guidance governing the circumstances under which members of the Armed Forces questioned about homosexuality for administrative purposes should be afforded warnings similar to the warnings under section 831(b) of title 10, United States Code (article 31(b) of the Uniform Code of Military Justice).

Source: United States Statutes at Large, 1993, Volume 107, Part 2 (Washington, DC: Government Printing Office, 1994), 1670–1673.

Questions for Consideration

1) How, according to the statute, was military life "fundamentally different" from civilian life?

2) Who should consider "issuing guidance" on the questioning of service members about homosexuality?

3) Why do you suppose the findings emphasized the importance of "unit cohesion" within the armed forces?

15.7   Richard I. Thornton Readies the Marines (1999)

As the millennium ended, U.S. forces continued to conduct disparate missions in troubled areas of the world. They became entangled with a policy for "engagement," which meant that the American military attempted to shape the international environment to bring about a more peaceful and stable globe. American troops delivered relief supplies in Somalia, although 18 died in the Battle of Mogadishu. A civil war in Haiti prompted another humanitarian effort called Operation Uphold Democracy. In the failed state of Yugoslavia, the U.S. participated in tactical air strikes and strategic bombing missions to disrupt the Serbian campaign of "ethnic cleansing." President Clinton dispatched "peacekeepers" to the Balkans region as well. Moreover, the Pentagon rotated military personnel into the Middle East to monitor the regime of Saddam Hussein. The U.S. launched Operation Desert Fox, a series of aerial assaults against Iraq to degrade Saddam's weapons of mass destruction program. Retaliating against terrorists, U.S. warships lobbed cruise missiles into Afghanistan and Sudan during Operation Infinite Reach. Consequently, service members did more with less. Facing budget constraints, Sergeant Major Richard I. Thornton readied the 8th Marine Regiment of the 2nd division. On March 22, 1999, he testified to the Military Readiness Subcommittee of the House Committee on Armed Services.

Document

As a regimental sergeant major I have three battalions and the headquarters company. At the risk of not going over everything that has already been said, I just want to speak shortly and briefly about a couple of things.

Number one is the deployment tempo. Right now—I will go back to last fiscal year, one of the battalions was deployed 250 days. Of those 250 days—as I say to them, to you—are deploy days. They are not training days that we also have them out in the field. Within a battalion, one of my companies was deployed for a total of 300 days last year. So that is 300 days that those Marines were, in fact, away from their families, and again that does not take into account any of the training days.

So we are definitely keeping our Marines deployed. We are keeping them ready, but as you can see or hear, that readiness comes on the backs of our young Marines. That readiness falls on the quality of life of their family. So we pay a high price for what we do. Marines expect to deploy. The families want them to deploy because that is what we come into the Marine Corps to do, but at the same time they also expect to have some good quality downtime with their families. Because of the equipment that we have today, they are unable to do that. Marines come from deployment, and they are into a maintenance cycle. I will give you a case in point. As I mentioned, in my last CAC [Combined Arms Company] deployment we brought those Marines back and we gave them four days off. Of those four days, there were Marines working every single day, not because we ordered them to, but because they wanted to be there. They knew that they needed to be there so that when they came back to work, if a contingency came up, they had gear that was fit to go. Had they not been there and not come into work, they would have worked around the clock to get it down. It is what we do.

So deployments are nothing new. The problem is the maintenance. The problem is the gear. If you take a look at a vehicle, and I like to just kind of draw an analogy here—if I give your teenage son a vehicle today and you let him drive it for 14 years, I doubt very seriously you would take that vehicle across country and not expect to spend a lot out of your pocket on maintenance. That is what we are doing today.

We are paying for not putting a lot—for not investing—in new gear years before. We have taken from our modernization account, and we are spending on maintenance today. I just—recently Colonel [Robert B.] Neller and I were up talking to the commanding general and took a look at a graph. Today, right now with the 2nd Marine Division, we spend more money on maintenance than we do on training. It is what we do. It is what we have come down to [...]

Sir, I would like to say I think the biggest threat within the 8th Marine Regiment is the equipment that we have: the age of the equipment, the rust, the cancer that eats away at that equipment on a daily basis.

I related in my statement a story of metal fatigue while we were doing a combined arms exercise. I don't know how many of you gentlemen have been behind a machine gun, but it is a horrible thing when a machine—when a machine gun or a weapon explodes because of metal fatigue. We actually had a weapon that exploded while we were out doing live fire from metal fatigue.

It is the equipment that we have. It is old. It is really old. And we can fix the parts, and we have good mechanics that fix the parts; and we have good armors that fix the parts, and we have outstanding Marines who know how to take those weapons apart and put them back together and take care of them and shoot them straight; but the problem is they are old. The equipment is old, and it is worn out; and it is tired; and if there is any one threat that we live, it is the threat that we won't be able to get where we need to go because the equipment won't allow us to get there. Not that the Marines don't want to go, not that we're not willing, not that we don't want to be there. We are ready. Your Marines are ready, but the equipment may not allow us to get where we need to go [...]

Being a regiment, those battalions are always going to be young. We are—the Marine Corps, in fact, is a young force. We are young just by nature. So that 75 percent of a regiment is first termers is really not unusual.

Insofar as retention, Marines stay in the Marine Corps because they want to be Marines. It is because of who we are. It is because of what we do. It is because we enjoy defending this nation. It is not about money. It is not about material things. It is about knowing that this Marine on my right, if anything ever happened to me, I would come back home; that this Marine on my right, if he knew that I was having problems, he would come directly to my aid. There would be no second thought about it. That is who we are; that is what we do, and we make sure that our young Marines understand that. So it is not always about anything material. Marines stay because Marines want to stay. And I don't think I could put it any plainer than that.

Source: House Committee on Armed Services, H.R. 1401, Fiscal Year 2000 National Defense Authorization Act—Military Readiness Issues, Military Readiness Subcommittee Hearing, 106th Congress, 22 March 1999, Serial No. 106–5. http://commdocs.house.gov/committees/security/has081030.000/has081030_0. HTM#0 (accessed 16 June 2017).

Questions for Consideration

1) What, according to Sergeant Major Thornton, was the "biggest threat" to the regiment?
2) How many "deploy days" did a battalion experience that fiscal year?
3) Do you agree that "Marines stay in the Marine Corps because they want to be Marines"?

Suggested Readings

Atkinson, Rick. *Crusade: The Untold Story of the Persian Gulf War*. Boston: Houghton Mifflin, 1993.

Bailey, Beth. *America's Army: The Making of the All-Volunteer Force*. Cambridge: Harvard University Press, 2009.

Baucom, Donald R. *The Origins of SDI, 1944–1983*. Lawrence: University Press of Kansas, 1992.

Bowden, Mark. *Black Hawk Down: A Story of Modern War*. New York: Atlantic Monthly, 1999.

FitzGerald, Frances. *Way Out There in the Blue: Reagan, Star Wars, and the End of the Cold War*. New York: Simon & Schuster, 2000.

Gordon, Michael R., and Bernard E. Trainor. *The General's War: The Inside Story of the Conflict in the Gulf*. Boston: Little, Brown, 1995.

Halberstam, David. *War in a Time of Peace: Bush, Clinton, and the Generals*. New York: Scribner, 2001.

Hallion, Richard P. *Storm Over Iraq: Air Power and the Gulf War*. Washington, DC: Smithsonian Institution Press, 1992.

Hutchthausen, Peter. *America's Splendid Little Wars: A Short History of U.S. Military Engagements, 1975–2000*. New York: Viking, 2003.

Iskra, Darlene M. *Women in the United States Armed Forces: A Guide to the Issues*. Santa Barbara, CA: Praeger, 2010.

Kagan, Frederick W., and Chris Kubik, eds. *Leaders in War: West Point Remembers the 1991 Gulf War*. New York: Frank Cass, 2005.

Lambeth, Benjamin S. *The Transformation of American Air Power*. Ithaca: Cornell University Press, 2000.

Locher, James R. *Victory on the Potomac: The Goldwater-Nichols Act Unifies the Pentagon*. College Station: Texas A&M University Press, 2002.

Oberdorfer, Don. *From the Cold War to a New Era: The United States and the Soviet Union, 1983–1991*. Baltimore: Johns Hopkins University Press, 1998.

Powell, Colin A., with Joseph E. Persico. *My American Journey*. New York: Ballantine Books, 1995.

Scales, Robert H. *Certain Victory: The U.S. Army in the Gulf War*. Washington, DC: Brassey's, 1994.

Wirls, Daniel. *Buildup: The Politics of Defense in the Reagan Era*. Ithaca: Cornell University Press, 1992.

16

Global War on Terror

Chronology

2001 9/11 Attacks
      Operation Enduring Freedom
2002 Operation Anaconda
      Iraq Disarmament Crisis
      Department of Homeland Security established
2003 Operation Iraqi Freedom
      Saddam Hussein captured
2004 NATO expands
      Abu Ghraib abuses revealed
2005 Hurricane Katrina
      Detainee Treatment Act
2006 Iraq Study Group Report
      Islamic State of Iraq formed
2007 The Surge in Iraq begins
2008 Global Financial Crisis
2009 Cyber Command established
      The Surge in Afghanistan begins
2010 Operation New Dawn
2011 Arab Spring
      Operation Odyssey Dawn
      Operation Neptune Spear
2014 Operation Inherent Resolve

16.1   George W. Bush Calls for War (2001)

On September 11, 2001, terrorists attacked the United States. They steered hijacked planes into the World Trade Center in New York City and the Pentagon in Washington, DC. Another hijacked plane crashed into the Pennsylvania countryside. Osama bin Laden, a Saudi-born dissident, was behind the attacks that day. Hiding in the mountains of Afghanistan, he headed a terrorist network of stateless operatives called Al-Qaeda. President George W. Bush, who entered office following a disputed election, announced the Global War on Terror after the attack. He delivered an address to a joint session of

American Military History: A Documentary Reader, Second Edition. Brad D. Lookingbill.
© 2019 John Wiley & Sons, Inc. Published 2019 by John Wiley & Sons, Inc.

Congress nine days later, which identified the perpetrators. Because the Taliban regime of Afghanistan refused to surrender bin Laden, Operation Enduring Freedom began with an aerial bombardment. In three months, the tribes of the Northern Alliance captured Kabul, the capital, with assistance from U.S. forces. After a series of bloody but decisive battles, the enemy was routed. The Taliban regime collapsed, while bin Laden eluded capture in the mountains of Tora Bora. In early 2002, the American military launched Operation Anaconda to clear the Shah-i-kot Valley of Taliban forces. Consequently, the Bush Doctrine posited that the U.S. reserved the right to defend itself by conducting offensive operations against nation-states that harbored or aided terrorists.

Document

On September the 11th, enemies of freedom committed an act of war against our country. Americans have known wars—but for the past 136 years, they have been wars on foreign soil, except for one Sunday in 1941. Americans have known the casualties of war—but not at the center of a great city on a peaceful morning. Americans have known surprise attacks—but never before on thousands of civilians. All of this was brought upon us in a single day—and night fell on a different world, a world where freedom itself is under attack.

Americans have many questions tonight. Americans are asking: Who attacked our country? The evidence we have gathered all points to a collection of loosely affiliated terrorist organizations known as Al-Qaeda. They are the same murderers indicted for bombing American embassies in Tanzania and Kenya and responsible for bombing the USS *Cole*. Al-Qaeda is to terror what the mafia is to crime. But its goal is not making money; its goal is remaking the world—and imposing its radical beliefs on people everywhere.

The terrorists practice a fringe form of Islamic extremism that has been rejected by Muslim scholars and the vast majority of Muslim clerics—a fringe movement that perverts the peaceful teachings of Islam. The terrorists' directive commands them to kill Christians and Jews, to kill all Americans, and make no distinction among military and civilians, including women and children.

This group and its leader—a person named Osama bin Laden—are linked to many other organizations in different countries, including the Egyptian Islamic Jihad and the Islamic Movement of Uzbekistan. There are thousands of these terrorists in more than 60 countries. They are recruited from their own nations and neighborhoods and brought to camps in places like Afghanistan, where they are trained in the tactics of terror. They are sent back to their homes or sent to hide in countries around the world to plot evil and destruction.

The leadership of Al-Qaeda has great influence in Afghanistan and supports the Taliban regime in controlling most of that country. In Afghanistan, we see Al-Qaeda's vision for the world. Afghanistan's people have been brutalized—many are starving and many have fled. Women are not allowed to attend school. You can be jailed for owning a television. Religion can be practiced only as their leaders dictate. A man can be jailed in Afghanistan if his beard is not long enough.

The United States respects the people of Afghanistan—after all, we are currently its largest source of humanitarian aid—but we condemn the Taliban regime. It is not only repressing its own people, it is threatening people everywhere by sponsoring and sheltering and supplying terrorists. By aiding and abetting murder, the Taliban regime is committing murder.

And tonight, the United States of America makes the following demands on the Taliban: Deliver to United States authorities all the leaders of Al-Qaeda who hide in your land. Release all foreign nationals, including American citizens, you have unjustly imprisoned. Protect foreign journalists, diplomats, and aid workers in your country. Close immediately and permanently every terrorist training camp in Afghanistan, and hand over every terrorist and every person in their support structure to appropriate authorities. Give the United States full access to terrorist training camps, so we can make sure they are no longer operating.

These demands are not open to negotiation or discussion. The Taliban must act, and act immediately. They will hand over the terrorists, or they will share in their fate.

I also want to speak tonight directly to Muslims throughout the world. We respect your faith. It's practiced freely by many millions of Americans and by millions more in countries that America counts as friends. Its teachings are good and peaceful, and those who commit evil in the name of Allah blaspheme the name of Allah. The terrorists are traitors to their own faith, trying, in effect, to hijack Islam itself. The enemy of America is not our many Muslim friends; it is not our many Arab friends. Our enemy is a radical network of terrorists and every government that supports them.

Our war on terror begins with Al-Qaeda, but it does not end there. It will not end until every terrorist group of global reach has been found, stopped, and defeated.

Americans are asking, why do they hate us? They hate what we see right here in this chamber—a democratically elected government. Their leaders are self-appointed. They hate our freedoms—our freedom of religion, our freedom of speech, our freedom to vote and assemble and disagree with each other.

They want to overthrow existing governments in many Muslim countries, such as Egypt, Saudi Arabia, and Jordan. They want to drive Israel out of the Middle East. They want to drive Christians and Jews out of vast regions of Asia and Africa [...]

We are not deceived by their pretenses to piety. We have seen their kind before. They are the heirs of all the murderous ideologies of the 20th century. By sacrificing human life to serve their radical visions—by abandoning every value except the will to power—they follow in the path of fascism, and Nazism, and totalitarianism. And they will follow that path all the way to where it ends: in history's unmarked grave of discarded lies.

Americans are asking: How will we fight and win this war? We will direct every resource at our command—every means of diplomacy, every tool of intelligence, every instrument of law enforcement, every financial influence, and every necessary weapon of war—to the disruption and to the defeat of the global terror network.

This war will not be like the war against Iraq a decade ago, with a decisive liberation of territory and a swift conclusion. It will not look like the air war above Kosovo two years ago, where no ground troops were used and not a single American was lost in combat.

Our response involves far more than instant retaliation and isolated strikes. Americans should not expect one battle but a lengthy campaign, unlike any other we have ever seen. It may include dramatic strikes, visible on TV, and covert operations, secret even in success. We will starve terrorists of funding, turn them one against another, drive them from place to place, until there is no refuge or no rest. And we will pursue nations that provide aid or safe haven to terrorism. Every nation, in every region, now has a decision to make. Either you are with us, or you are with the terrorists. From this day forward, any nation that continues to harbor or support terrorism will be regarded by the United States as a hostile regime.

Source: George W. Bush, "Address Before a Joint Session of the Congress on the United States Response to the Terrorist Attacks of September 11," September 20, 2001. Online by Gerhard Peters and John T. Woolley, The American Presidency Project. http://www.presidency.ucsb.edu/ws/?pid=64731 (accessed 9 June, 2017).

Questions for Consideration

1) According to President Bush, what happened on September the 11th?
2) Who did he say was the "enemy of America"?
3) Why should Americans expect a war "unlike any other we have ever seen" against terrorism?

16.2 Jessica Lynch Soldiers in Iraq (2003)

Americans focused their attention on Saddam Hussein and demanded an end to Iraq's programs for weapons of mass destruction, or WMD. Beginning on March 19, 2003, Operation Iraqi Freedom involved a spectacular display of power and speed. Dubbed "shock and awe," the initial air and missile strikes seriously degraded the capabilities of Saddam's military. CENTCOM commander General Tommy Franks ordered American divisions to roll northward from Kuwait. On March 23, a convoy that included the U.S. Army's 507th Maintenance Company made a wrong turn in the desert. A Humvee driven by Private Lori Piestewa was ambushed near Nasiriyah, a major crossing point over the Euphrates River. Eleven American soldiers died during the ambush, but Private Jessica Lynch, a supply clerk riding in the Humvee, survived. Weeks later, U.S. forces launched a nighttime raid and rescued her from an Iraqi hospital. Thanks to sensational media coverage, she represented a new symbol of American heroism. She eventually told her story before a Congressional oversight committee. After receiving medical treatment and an honorable discharge, she returned home to Palestine, West Virginia. The American military overwhelmed the Iraqi defenses around Baghdad. On May 1, President Bush announced the end of major combat operations in Iraq. Saddam was captured, tried, and executed months later.

Document
I loved my time in the Army, and I am grateful for the opportunity to have served this nation during a time of crisis.
In 2003, I received word that my unit had been deployed. I was part of a 100-mile long convoy going to Baghdad to support the Marines. I drove the 5-ton water buffalo truck. Our unit drove the heaviest vehicles. The sand was thick—our vehicles just sank. It would take us hours to travel the shortest distance. We decided to divide our convoy so the lighter vehicles could reach our target. But then came the city of An Nasiryah and a day I will never forget.
The truck I was driving broke down. I was picked up by my roommate and best friend, Lori Piestewa, who was driving our First Sergeant Robert Dowdy. We also picked up two other soldiers from a different unit to get them out of harm's way.
As we drove through An Nasiryah, trying to get turned around to try to leave the city, the signs of hostility were increasing with people with weapons on roof tops and the street watching our entire group. The vehicle I was riding in was hit by a rocket propelled grenade and slammed into the back of another truck in the convoy. Three people in the vehicle were killed upon impact. Lori and I were taken to a hospital where she later died,

and I was held for nine days. In all eleven soldiers died that day; six others from the unit, plus two others, were taken prisoner.

Following the ambush, my injuries were extensive. When I awoke in the Iraqi hospital, I was not able to move or feel anything below my waist. I suffered a six inch gash in my head. My fourth and fifth lumbars were overlapping causing pressure on my spine. My right humerus bone was broken. My right foot was crushed. My left femur was shattered. The Iraqis in the hospital tried to help me by removing the bone and replacing it with a metal rod. The rod they used was a model from the 1940s for a man and was too long. Following my rescue, the doctors in Landstuhl, Germany, found in a physical exam that I had been sexually assaulted. Today, I continue to deal with bladder, bowel, and kidney problems as a result of my injuries. My left leg still has no feeling from the knee down, and I am required to wear a brace so that I can stand and walk.

When I awoke, I did not know where I was. I could not move, or fight or call for help. The nurses at the hospital tried to soothe me and tried unsuccessfully at one point to return me to American troops.

Then on April 1, while various units created diversions around Nasiryah, a group came to the hospital to rescue me. I could hear them speaking in English, but I was still very afraid. Then a soldier came into my room. He tore the American flag from his uniform and pressed it into my hand and he told me, "We're American soldiers, and we're here to take you home." As I held his hand, I told him, "Yes, I am an American soldier too."

When I remember those difficult days, I remember the fear. I remember the strength. I remember the hand of a fellow American soldier reassuring me that I was ok now.

At the same time, tales of great heroism were being told. My parent's home in Wirt County was under siege of the media all repeating the story of the little girl Rambo from the hills who went down fighting. It was not true.

I have repeatedly said, when asked, that if the stories about me helped inspire our troops and rally a nation, then perhaps there was some good. However, I am still confused as to why they chose to lie and tried to make me a legend when the real heroics of my fellow soldiers that day were, in fact, legendary. People like Lori Piestewa and First Sergeant Dowdy who picked up fellow soldiers in harm's way. Or people like Patrick Miller and Sergeant Donald Walters who actually fought until the very end. The bottom line is the American people are capable of determining their own ideals for heroes, and they don't need to be told elaborate tales.

My hero is my brother Greg who continues to serve this country today. My hero is my friend Lori who died in Iraq but set an example for a generation of Hopi and Native American women and little girls everywhere about the important contributions just one soldier can make in the fight for freedom. My hero is every American who says my country needs me and answers the call to fight. I had the good fortune and opportunity to come home, and I told the truth. Many other soldiers, like Pat Tillman, do not have the opportunity.

The truth of war is not always easy to hear, but it is always more heroic than the hype.

Source: House Committee on Oversight and Government Reform, Testimony of Jessica Lynch, Hearing on Misleading Information from the Battlefield, 110th Congress, 24 April 2007, Serial No. 110-54 (Washington, DC: Government Printing Office, 2008), 21–26.

Questions for Consideration

1) What, according to Private Lynch, were "the signs of hostility" in Nasiryah?
2) How were her injuries treated in the Iraqi hospital?
3) Why do you think she became known as "the little girl Rambo" during Operation Iraqi Freedom?

16.3 Craig M. Mullaney Deploys to Afghanistan (2003)

The calculation of the Bush administration that the Global War on Terror would be won with speed and precision left many military problems unresolved. Inside Afghanistan, NATO assumed responsibility for the International Security Assistance Force, or ISAF. Hamid Karzai won that nation's first direct election for the presidency. Thanks to opium trafficking, however, Al-Qaeda and Taliban fighters retained influence outside of Kabul. They also established sanctuaries in Pakistan, where they reconstituted their strength for cross-border strikes. They hid in caves and bunkers in the mountain ranges while terrorizing the countryside. They fired rockets at U.S. bases and ambushed ISAF patrols. Likewise, they raided the convoys of the Afghan National Army troops, Afghan militia forces, and nongovernmental organizations. During 2003, U.S. Army Captain Craig M. Mullaney of the 10th Mountain Division deployed to Afghanistan and led a rifle platoon in the eastern border region. He participated in a spectrum of operations, ranging from humanitarian assistance to combat missions. After returning home safely, he published an autobiographical account that traced his experiences from West Point to the battlefield. He eventually left the military to serve in the federal government, becoming the Principal Director of Afghanistan, Pakistan, and Central Asia Policy at the Department of Defense.

Document
Deploying to Afghanistan was a slow immersion, like Dante's descent into the Inferno. The journey began at Fort Drum's rapid deployment facility—an airport terminal with X-ray scanners, uncomfortable seats, and television sets tuned to Major League Baseball games. Apart from the boots and body armor, we could have been at the Syracuse airport. The wait was interminable. Soldiers did what soldiers do when any delay passes the fifteen-minute mark: They fell asleep. Six-foot-tall Mitchell Markham curled into the fetal position with an unloaded pistol firmly in his grip. Markham's Connecticut upbringing clashed with the gangster persona he tried to project to the rest of the platoon. A digital photo of this pose set his cause back several months. After perhaps four hours, Markham awoke to the sound of a dozen soldiers carrying large insulated vats of food. Thoroughly embarrassed, he joked with a hint of gallows humor that this was our "Last Supper." Servers gave us each a rubbery T-bone, spicy Mexican rice, and three brownies. After dinner an Air Force sergeant ushered us into a holding area behind a big blue curtain decorated with the 10th Mountain Division crest and its motto, "Climb to Glory." The platoon folded into seats before the projector screen. The much-awaited intelligence briefing began with a list of the dangers awaiting us in Afghanistan: camel spiders

running faster than thirty miles an hour, cobras, ticks. I gave a half-comical, half-serious look at Markham and another soldier snickering in the back row about giving each other tick checks. Our next briefing curiously interposed the threat of dehydration with the perils of flash flooding.

We knew more about Afghanistan's flora and fauna than the tribes inhabiting the districts we patrolled. We could identify the Hindu Kush Mountains and the Helmand River on a map of Afghanistan, but knew little about the dry riverbeds surrounding our bases. We knew politics at a national level, but not at the local level where it mattered. We had Arabic phrase books that were useless in Pashto-speaking provinces. Success in Afghanistan wouldn't hinge on our ability to thwart camel spiders.

We walked out of the terminal and stretched in a long line across the shimmering hot tarmac toward an enormous cargo plane. Its cavernous fuselage slowly swallowed our small profiles. The departure for Afghanistan lacked the Hollywood drama I had expected. There was no flourish of trumpets and drums to send us off, no cheering crowds. Whatever nervousness I had had about deployment dissipated during the countless delays, briefings, and speeches we were subjected to for weeks. Even the youngest privates approached the journey overseas as a novelty rather than a life-changing embarkation. If they were nervous, they hid it well, perhaps eager not to show their butterflies before the nonchalance of the veteran sergeants.

Two long columns of webbed seats stretched toward the cargo pallets loaded high against the rear ramp of the plan. Fort Drum's summer humidity baked us as we waited to taxi. I fought the impulse to undress, remembering from the previous flights how cold an unheated cargo plane gets as it reaches altitude. Before long we were airborne to Frankfurt, Germany. Soldiers splayed out in the aisles and on the web seats, wearing earphones and earplugs to dull the roar of the jet engines. As the temperature dropped, soldiers unpacked poncho liners and wrapped themselves in the soft quilted camouflage. I drifted off to sleep, thinking of the last thing Meena had told me before we said goodbye: "Keep me in your heart and know that however great the distance, I am with you always."

Two flights and seven thousand miles later, we walked off the back ramp of the cargo plan and into Afghanistan. The heat nearly knocked us over, sucking the oxygen out of the air and leaving us breathless. It was like walking into a furnace. My boots felt as if they were melting into the black tarmac. The sky was a red canvas of dust obscuring the setting sun. As we deplaned, soldiers standing guard at posts scattered around the airfield scanned the horizon. Beyond them, barely visible through the choking haze, a ring of barren mountains stuck up out of the flat plain like shards of glass embedded in concrete [...]

Two hours after landing in Gardez and less than twenty-four hours after arriving in Afghanistan, I went on my first combat patrol. I sat in the backseat of the Humvee as we sped out past the guard post and gunned the engine to forty miles an hour. My brain was like cotton candy from the combination of sleeplessness, obscure Afghan names, and altitude.

That first patrol introduced me to dust. Layers of dust, settling in thick layers on every surface, horizontal and vertical. Inhaling dust, making it even harder to breathe whatever oxygen existed in the thin atmosphere. Dust stinging my eyes, as it swirled around our Humvee. Over the course of the deployment, I swallowed my own body weight in Afghan dust.

The sheer scale of the area we were attempting to secure was daunting. We drove for four hours and covered only half of our area of operations, a neat circle on the map twenty miles across. No census had been done in nearly thirty years, but Gardez's population was estimated at more than one hundred thousand. If the estimate was correct, then I had roughly one soldier for every three thousand Afghans [...]

The next generation of Afghans was the one we needed most for Afghanistan's long-term stability, but it was the hardest demographic of all. Walking through town on patrol, I often felt like the Pied Piper of Gardez, trailing children behind me in anticipation of more food, water, or candy. *How are you? Gimme water. How are you? Gimme food, mister.* We must have looked like alien invaders with our laser sights, reflective sunglasses, and dangling antennas. They called us the "Helmeted Ones." I thought about gesturing with three fingers and addressing them in jest: "Greetings. We are from Planet America. We are here to help you." As I walked, the kids laughed and smiled and ran laps around the squad in hand-me-down pajamas and bare feet. Red [Specialist Lucas White] gave one of the kids some sweets secreted away in his cargo pocket. The flock swarmed around him like a celebrity. Ten steps away stood their elders; their faces spelled indifference. I asked a few questions through my interpreter. Have you seen any bad men in the village lately? Have the police been through recently? The answer was always no, but I asked anyway, for the report I needed to fill out when I returned. What happened between ages eight and eighteen? It occurred to me that it would be the same if strange men with guns and sunglasses walked through my hometown: The strangers would be a curiosity for the young and an intrusion for the old.

Years of training had shaped the way I interpreted my environment. Every door and crooked tree was a potential ambush. I peered at shadows in expectation of trouble and searched for cover that my men and I could use to protect us. Military officers plan for the worst and hope for the best. *Stay alert and stay alive.*

The attitude was well suited for a battlefield or training exercise. Gardez was neither. I wasn't prepared to walk through a village that was neither "friendly" nor "enemy." I wanted to take kids' pictures, not imagine them in suicide vests. This was the frustration of Gardez in a microcosm: how to stay focused on protecting my men while simultaneously engaging the local population. One pundit called this "armed social work," evoking the image of Peace Corps volunteers with pistols. The real difficulty, however, was psychological: seeing every local as indeterminate, neither friend nor foe, but potentially both, at different times, in different circumstances. Lieutenant Colonel La Camera's warning echoed in my head: Be polite. Be professional. Be prepared to kill everyone you meet.

Questions for Consideration

1) What did Captain Mullaney say was "interminable" about deploying?
2) How did he express empathy for the population of Gardez?
3) Do you agree with the pundit in that the rifle platoon engaged in a form of "armed social work"?

16.4   David H. Petraeus Counters an Insurgency (2007)

Before 2007, the American military struggled to find a way forward in Iraq. Ethno-sectarian rivalries and violence fueled discord. Al-Qaeda in Iraq evolved into an entity that called itself the Islamic State, which eventually came to be known as Daesh, ISIL, or ISIS. With a propensity for asymmetrical tactics, insurgents conducted bombings, abductions, and assassinations. U.S. commanders needed more soldiers and resources to conduct counterinsurgency operations, which were identified by the acronym COIN. Despite unease in Congress, President Bush ordered a "surge" of additional troops to clear, hold, and build neighborhoods. He appointed a new commander for the Multi-National Force in Iraq, General David H. Petraeus, who previously led the 101st Airborne Division during Operation Iraqi Freedom. Holding a doctorate from Princeton University, he helped to rewrite the Army field manual, FM 3-24, on COIN. While expending more blood and treasure, he increased the focus on stability and reconstruction efforts. On September 11, 2007, he appeared before the Senate Committee on Foreign Relations to give a progress report on Iraq. Bolstered by "awakenings" among former enemies, his actions in Baghdad and beyond countered the insurgency. As conditions on the ground improved, he recommended drawing down U.S. forces and transitioning responsibilities to Iraqi forces.

Document
In January 2007, in response to the horrific ethno-sectarian violence that spiraled out of control in 2006 and to an assessment in December 2006 that we were failing to achieve our objectives, a surge of forces began flowing into Iraq, focusing on protecting the population and reducing sectarian violence, especially in Baghdad.

In so doing, these forces have employed counterinsurgency practices, such as living among the people they are securing. In mid-June, with all the surge brigades in place, we launched a series of offensive operations in partnership with Iraqi security forces. These operations focused on expanding the gains achieved in the preceding months in Anbar province, pursuing Al-Qaeda in the Diyala River Valley and several other areas, and clearing Baqubah, several key Baghdad neighborhoods, the remaining sanctuaries in Anbar province and important areas around Baghdad. And, with coalition and Iraqi forces located among the populations they are securing, we have sought to keep areas clear and to help Iraqis in rebuilding them. All the while, we have engaged in dialog with insurgent groups and tribes, leading to additional elements standing up to oppose Al-Qaeda and other extremists [...]

To summarize, the security situation in Iraq is improving, and Iraqi elements are slowly taking on more of the responsibility for protecting their citizens. Innumerable challenges lie ahead; however, coalition and Iraqi security forces have made progress toward achieving sustainable security. As a result, the United States will be in a position to reduce its forces in Iraq in the months ahead.

Two weeks ago, I provided recommendations for the way ahead in Iraq to the members of my chain of command and the Joint Chiefs of Staff. The essence of the approach I recommended is captured in its title, "Security While Transitioning: From Leading to |

Partnering to Overwatch." This approach seeks to build on the security improvements our troopers and our Iraqi counterparts have achieved in recent months. It reflects recognition of the importance of securing the population and the imperative of transitioning responsibilities to Iraqi institutions and Iraqi forces as quickly as possible, but without rushing to failure. It includes substantial support for the continuing development of Iraqi security forces. It also stresses the need to continue the counterinsurgency strategy that we have been employing, but with Iraqis gradually shouldering more of the load. And it highlights the importance of regional and global diplomatic approaches. Finally, in recognition of the fact that this war is not only being fought on the ground in Iraq, but also in cyberspace, it also notes the need to contest the enemy's growing use of that important medium to spread extremism.

The recommendations I've provided were informed by operational and strategic considerations. The operational considerations include recognition that military aspects of the surge have achieved progress and generated momentum. Iraqi security forces have slowly been shouldering more of the security burden. A mission focused on either population security or transition alone will not be adequate to achieve our objectives. Success against Al-Qaeda–Iraq and Iranian-supported militia extremists requires conventional forces as well as special-operations forces. And the security and local political situations will enable us to draw down the surge forces.

My recommendations also took into account a number of strategic considerations. Political progress will only take place if sufficient security exists. Long-term U.S. ground-force viability will benefit from force reductions as the surge runs its course. Regional, global, and cyberspace initiatives are critical to success. And Iraqi leaders, understandably, want to assume greater sovereignty in their country, although, as they recently announced, they do desire a continued presence of coalition forces in Iraq in 2008 under a new U.N. Security Council resolution, and, following that, they want to negotiate a long-term security agreement with the United States and other nations.

Based on these considerations and having worked the battlefield geometry with LTG General Ray Odierno, Commander of the Multinational Corps–Iraq, to ensure that we retain and build on the gains for which our troopers have fought, I have recommended a drawdown of the surge forces from Iraq. In fact, later this month the Marine Expeditionary Unit deployed as part of the surge will depart Iraq. Beyond that, if my recommendations are approved, this will be followed by the withdrawal of a Brigade Combat Team, without replacement, in mid-December, and the further redeployment, without replacement, of four additional Brigade Combat Teams and two Marine battalions in the first 7 months of 2008, until we reach the pre-surge level of 15 Brigade Combat Teams by mid-July 2008.

Force reductions will continue beyond the pre-surge levels of Brigade Combat Teams that we will reach by mid-July 2008. In my professional judgment, however, it would be premature to make recommendations on the pace of such reductions at this time. In fact, our experience in Iraq has repeatedly shown that projecting too far into the future is not just difficult, it can be misleading and even hazardous. In view of this, I do not believe it is reasonable to have an adequate appreciation for the pace of further reductions and mission adjustments beyond the summer of 2008 until about mid-March of next year. We will, no later than that time, consider factors similar to those on which I base the current recommendations, having, by then, of course, a better feel for the security situation, the improvements in the capabilities of our Iraqi counterparts, and the enemy situation [...]

Our assessments underscore, in fact, the importance of recognizing that a premature drawdown of our forces would likely have devastating consequences. That assessment is supported by the findings of a 16 August Defense Intelligence Agency report on the implications of a rapid withdrawal of U.S. forces from Iraq. Summarizing it in an unclassified fashion, it concludes that a rapid withdrawal would result in the further release of the strong centrifugal forces in Iraq, and produce a number of dangerous results, including a high risk of disintegration of the Iraqi security forces, rapid deterioration of local security initiatives, Al-Qaeda-Iraq regaining lost ground and freedom of maneuver, a marked increase in violence, and further ethno-sectarian displacement and refugee flows, alliances of convenience by Iraqi groups with internal and external forces to gain advantages over their rivals, and exacerbation of already challenging regional dynamics, especially with respect to Iran. Lieutenant General Odierno and I share this assessment and believe that the best way to secure our national interests and avoid an unfavorable outcome in Iraq is to continue to focus our operations on securing the Iraqi people while targeting terrorist groups and militia extremists, and, as quickly as conditions are met, transitioning security tasks to Iraqi elements.

Source: General David H. Petraeus, Statement to Congress, 11 September 2007, *Iraq: The Crocker-Petraeus Report*, Hearing before the Committee on Foreign Relations, United States Senate, 110th Congress, First Session (Washington, DC: Government Printing Office, 2008), 16–41.

Questions for Consideration

1) How did General Petraeus view the "security situation" in Iraq?
2) What kind of "counterinsurgency practices" seemed most effective?
3) Why did he say that it was "premature to make recommendations" on the pace of U.S. force reductions?

16.5   Sean Householder Shares "The Warrior Song" (2009)

Whatever the technological advantages of the American military, overseas contingency operations continued to depend upon the human element. Following troop "surges" in Iraq and Afghanistan, the Global War on Terror eventually became the longest war in American history. The Pentagon sent soldiers, sailors, marines, and airmen on multiple deployments, which stretched the force structure to its limits. With less than 1 percent of the U.S. population in uniform, the number was the smallest at any time since World War II. Nevertheless, service members learned to "embrace the suck." Thanks to the instantaneous communication afforded by cell phones, electronic mail, and streaming video, many sustained connections to family and friends elsewhere. Sean Householder, a musician and artist from California, shared "The Warrior Song" as a morale-booster for military personnel. He dedicated it to all members of the armed forces—past, present, and future. It went viral on YouTube in November of 2009. While selling millions of copies, it generated thousands of dollars for the Armed Forces Relief Trust. Copies circulated free of charge to veterans and others. Moreover, the lyrics became a running cadence in basic training facilities across the U.S. By 2017, "The Warrior Song" YouTube channel had received over 30 million hits.

Document

I've got the reach and the teeth of a killing machine,
    with the need to bleed you when the light goes green,
best believe, I'm in a zone to be,
    from my yin to my yang to my Yang Tze.
Put a grin on my chin,
    come to me, 'cuz I'll win,
I'm a one-of-a-kind and I'll bring death to the place you're about to be:
    another river of blood runnin' under my feet.
Forged in a fire lit long ago,
    stand next to me, you'll never stand alone.
I'm last to leave, but the first to go,
    Lord, make me dead before you make me old.
I feed on the fear of the devil inside of the enemy faces in my sights:
    aim with the hand, shoot with the mind, kill with a heart like arctic ice

I am a soldier and I'm marching on, I am a warrior and this is my song.

I bask in the glow of the rising war,
    lay waste to the ground of the enemy shore,
wade through the blood spilled on the floor,
    and if another one stands I'll kill some more.
Bullet in the breech and a fire in me,
    like a cigarette thrown to gasoline,
if death don't bring you fear I swear,
    you'll fear these marching feet.
Come to the nightmare, come to me,
    deep down in the dark where the devil be,
in the maw with the jaws and the razor teeth,
    where the brimstone burns and the angel weeps.
Call to the gods if I cross your path and my silhouette hangs like a body bag;
    hope is a moment now long past, the shadow of death is the one I cast.

I am a soldier and I'm marching on, I am a warrior and this is my song.
My eyes are steel and my gaze is long, I am a warrior and this is my song.

Now I live lean and I mean to inflict the grief,
    and the least of me's still out of your reach.
The killing machine's gonna do the deed,
    until the river runs dry and my last breath leaves.
Chin in the air with a head held high,
    I'll stand in the path of the enemy line.
Feel no fear, know my pride:
    for God and Country I'll end your life.

> I am a soldier and I'm marching on, I am a warrior and this is my song.
> My eyes are steel and my gaze is long, I am a warrior and this is my song.
>
> *Source:* Sean Householder, "The Warrior Song," Echo Sonic Music. http://www.thewarriorsong.com (accessed 30 June 2016). Used with permission of Sean Householder.

Questions for Consideration

1) How did "The Warrior Song" convey a sense of patriotism?
2) What phrases indicate that the primary goal of a warrior is to kill the enemy?
3) Why do you suppose the lyrics use a first person voice?

16.6   William H. McRaven Commands SEALs (2011)

For most Americans, the long hunt for Osama bin Laden remained the most important objective of the Global War on Terror. The CIA gathered clues about the Al-Qaeda leader and his possible whereabouts. The trail led to a fortress-like compound in Abbottabad, Pakistan. In early 2011, the Obama administration shared details with Admiral William H. McRaven, the head of Joint Special Operations Command, or JSOC. They agreed on a plan for a commando raid to kill or to capture bin Laden at the compound. Code-named Operation Neptune Spear, it involved two MH-60 Black Hawks modified with stealth technology. It depended upon the martial skills of the U.S. Navy's SEAL Team-6, an elite unit capable of infiltrating hostile territory. Admiral McRaven commanded the special operation, monitoring it through a video feed at a U.S. base in Afghanistan. He later recounted his observations during an interview for CNN. Before the dawning of May 2, 2011, the SEALs reached the compound. Despite a helicopter mishap, they surprised the Al-Qaeda leader and killed him. Following exfiltration, the corpse of bin Laden was buried in the North Arabian Sea. The appeal of terrorist organizations persisted, but the American military brought a mass murderer of innocent men, women, and children to justice.

Document

The living quarters were barricaded. They had some steel gates that the guys had to breach, had to blow down in order to get through. The guys on the outside swung through initially what appeared to be a door. Turned out to be a false door. So the compound had actually been built with the express purpose of protecting bin Laden in ways that we were not able to detect ahead of time. We assumed there would be some booby traps, we assumed that the whole place actually could have been loaded with explosives. We had seen this a number of times in Iraq, where an entire compound was set to detonate if Allied forces came in.

So they had to come through another entrance. They all kind of collectively got together and then moved accordingly up the, the three flights of stairs to get where bin

Laden was on the third deck. They moved up. They obviously engaged one of the facilitators on the bottom floor. Bin Laden's son came, moving very quickly, down. He was killed, I think, on the second deck. And then, as they moved up to the third level, the first operator coming up saw bin Laden peeking out through the door.

And as he and I talked later, he said, I knew immediately it was bin Laden. Again, you have to understand it was dark inside the house. The operators are wearing night vision goggles, so your view is not perfect. It's not like daylight. It's very good, but it's not perfect. Your adrenaline is pumping. You've just come up three flights of stairs. You've, you've had to engage a couple of combatants and, now all of a sudden, you get to the top of the stairs, and there bin Laden is. And, and the operators did what they, again, what they had planned to do, which was they flowed into the room as a normal practice [...]

I got the code word Geronimo back, but it took me a minute to wonder whether or not Geronimo meant we had captured bin Laden or we had killed bin Laden. So when the word came across from the, the ground force commander and he said, for God and country, Geronimo, Geronimo, Geronimo, I had to go back and ask the question, was Geronimo EKIA, enemy killed in action? And the word came back that, yes, Geronimo EKIA [...]

We began to receive word that the operators had gone down to the second floor, and now all of a sudden found this kind of treasure trove of hard drives and documents. And, and so they were trying to pull all this information. So as 30 minutes turned into, you know, 35 and 40, and I think we were finally on target. By the time we actually got off target, about 48 minutes. After about 40 minutes, I was getting a little bit anxious probably because I just didn't want to be too long on target. And at some point in time, I, I relayed to the ground force commander, get everything you can, but it's time to wrap this up and, and get out of Abbottabad [...]

As the helicopters were landing, at some point in time the President asked me, he said, Bill, can you confirm that it's bin Laden? And I said, Mr. President, I can't until I go visually ID the body. And the landing field was about five minutes or so from where I was positioned. So I left the video teleconference with the President and Director Panetta. We, we traveled over to the, to the airfield.

About the time I got into the hangar, the guys had, had landed. They'd offloaded the body, brought it into the hangar. I unzipped the body bag, took a look at bin Laden. Obviously, he had—he didn't look terrific, he had two, two rounds in his head, and his beard was a little shorter. But we had several photos and, as soon as you pulled the photo close to the face, it was immediately obvious that it was bin Laden.

One of the interesting stories that comes out of this was I knew bin Laden was about six foot four. So as, as I removed his remains from the body bag, I looked at it, and there was a young SEAL standing nearby, and I asked the SEAL, I said, son, how tall are you? He said, well, sir, I'm about six foot two. I said good. Come here, I want you to lie down next to the remains here. He kind of gave me that look and said, I'm sorry, sir. You want me to do what? I said, I want you to lie down next to the remains. OK, sir. So, he did. And of course the remains were a couple inches taller.

I didn't think much of it at the time, so but I, I came back to the, to my headquarters. And I told the President, I said, Mr. President, I can't be certain without DNA that it's bin Laden, but frankly—it's probably about a 99 percent chance that it is bin Laden. And then

I told the President, I said, in fact I had a young SEAL lie down next to him, and I know he was about six foot four, and the remains were a little taller. And there was a pause on the other end of the, of the video conference.

And of course by this time, we had bin Laden, the troops were back safely, the mission was for all intents and purposes over, and the President comes up on the video and he says, Bill, let me get this straight. We had $60 million for a helicopter, and you didn't have $10 for a tape measure? And it was one of those light moments in the middle of, you know, a very anxious time in our nation's history. And it was, again, kind of perfectly timed. It, it lightened a very tough moment, and, and was the right thing to say. A couple of days later the President presented me with a, a tape measure, so that next time we did a mission like this, I'd be prepared.

Source: "We Got Him: Obama, Bin Laden, and The War On Terror," CNN Special, Aired 2 May 2016. http://edition.cnn.com/TRANSCRIPTS/1605/02/se.01.html (accessed 5 July 2016). Courtesy CNN.

Questions for Consideration

1) According to Admiral McRaven, what had not been detected in the compound ahead of Operation Neptune Spear?
2) How were the SEALs able to see in the dark?
3) Do you agree that there was "about a 99 percent" confirmation of the EKIA without a DNA test?

16.7 The Pentagon Secures Cyberspace (2015)

The American military entered a new kind of battlefield. The Defense Advanced Research Projects Agency invented the precursor to the Internet as early as 1969. Nearly a half-century later, the U.S. became reliant on uninterrupted access to cyberspace. High-technology proliferated, which created opportunities for state and nonstate actors to disrupt civil society. Hacking, phishing, trolling, malware, worms, and viruses began to threaten national security almost every day in the digital age. Because the Department of Defense assumed responsibility for protecting critical infrastructure, service members conducted cyber missions with increasing frequency. Working at terminals, they monitored the firewalls of computers and networks. They blocked and hunted down electronic intruders. Furthermore, they penetrated and infected the information systems of adversaries. An array of cyber weapons targeted enemy air and sea defenses as well as command-and-control centers. As the director of the National Security Agency, General Keith B. Alexander became the first head of U.S. Cyber Command, or USCYBERCOM. Full operational capability was achieved in 2010. Wholly unclassified and distributed worldwide, *The DoD Cyber Strategy* of 2015 established clear and specific objectives for the Pentagon to achieve in this operational domain within five years. Thus, Americans in uniform moved forward together with an extraordinary history of resilience and resourcefulness behind them.

Document

We live in a wired world. Companies and countries rely on cyberspace for everything from financial transactions to the movement of military forces. Computer code blurs the line between the cyber and physical world and connects millions of objects to the Internet or private networks. Electric firms rely on industrial control systems to provide power to the grid. Shipping managers use satellites and the Internet to track freighters as they pass through global sea lanes, and the U.S. military relies on secure networks and data to carry out its missions.

The United States is committed to an open, secure, interoperable, and reliable Internet that enables prosperity, public safety, and the free flow of commerce and ideas. These qualities of the Internet reflect core American values—of freedom of expression and privacy, creativity, opportunity, and innovation. And these qualities have allowed the Internet to provide social and economic value to billions of people. Within the U.S. economy alone, anywhere from three to 13 percent of business sector value-added is derived from Internet-related businesses. Over the last ten years Internet access increased by over two billion people across the globe. Yet these same qualities of openness and dynamism that led to the Internet's rapid expansion now provide dangerous state and non-state actors with a means to undermine U.S. interests.

We are vulnerable in this wired world. Today our reliance on the confidentiality, availability, and integrity of data stands in stark contrast to the inadequacy of our cybersecurity. The Internet was not originally designed with security in mind, but as an open system to allow scientists and researchers to send data to one another quickly. Without strong investments in cybersecurity and cyber defenses, data systems remain open and susceptible to rudimentary and dangerous forms of exploitation and attack. Malicious actors use cyberspace to steal data and intellectual property for their own economic or political goals. And an actor in one region of the globe can use cyber capabilities to strike directly at a network thousands of miles away, destroying data, disrupting businesses, or shutting off critical systems […]

Among DoD's cyber personnel and forces, the Cyber Mission Force (CMF) has a unique role within the Department. In 2012, DoD began to build a CMF to carry out DoD's cyber missions. Once fully operational, the CMF will include nearly 6,200 military, civilian, and contractor support personnel from across the military departments and defense components. The Cyber Mission Force represents a major investment by the Department of Defense and the United States as whole, and a central aim of this strategy is to set specific goals and objectives to guide the development of the Cyber Mission Force and DoD's wider cyber workforce to protect and defend U.S. national interests.

The Cyber Mission Force will be comprised of cyber operators organized into 133 teams, primarily aligned as follows: Cyber Protection Forces will augment traditional defensive measures and defend priority DoD networks and systems against priority threats; National Mission Forces and their associated support teams will defend the United States and its interests against cyber attacks of significant consequence; and Combat Mission Forces and their associated support teams will support combatant commands by generating integrated cyberspace effects in support of operational plans and contingency operations. Combatant commands integrate Combat Mission Forces and Cyber Protection Teams into plans and operations and employ them in cyberspace, while the National Mission Force operates under the Commander of USCYBERCOM. Outside of this construct, teams can also be used to support other missions as required by the Department.

In 2013 the Department began to integrate the CMF into the larger multi-mission U.S. military force to achieve synergy across domains, assure the CMF's readiness within the force, and restructure the military and civilian workforce and infrastructure to execute DoD's missions. During the course of implementing this strategy, DoD will continue to build the CMF, and will continue to mature the necessary command, control, and enabling organizations required for effective operations. DoD will focus on ensuring that its forces are trained and ready to operate using the capabilities and architectures they need to conduct cyber operations, continue to build policy and legal frameworks to govern CMF employment, and integrate the CMF into DoD's overall planning and force development.

This strategy recognizes that effective cybersecurity will require close collaboration within DoD and across the federal government, with industry, with international allies and partners, and with state and local governments. The pursuit of security in cyberspace requires a whole-of-government and international approach due to the number and variety of stakeholders in the domain, the flow of information across international borders, and the distribution of responsibilities, authorities, and capabilities across governments and the private sector. For each of DoD's missions, DoD must continue to develop routine relationships and processes for coordinating its cyber operations.

Source: Department of Defense, *The DoD Cyber Strategy*, April 2015. http://www.defense.gov/Portals/1/features/2015/0415_cyber-strategy/Final_2015_DoD_CYBER_STRATEGY_for_web.pdf (accessed 25 May 2017).

Questions for Consideration

1) According to the DoD, what made "cybersecurity" inadequate?
2) When did the military begin to build a CMF to carry out key missions?
3) Why did the strategy require "a whole-of-government and international approach" to military affairs?

Suggested Readings

Anderson, Terry H. *Bush's Wars*. New York: Oxford University Press, 2011.

Atkinson, Rick. *In the Company of Soldiers: A Chronicle of Combat*. New York: Henry Holt, 2004.

Bacevich, Andrew J. *America's War for the Greater Middle East: A Military History*. New York: Random House, 2016.

Bailey, Beth, and Richard H. Immerman, eds. *Understanding the U.S. Wars in Iraq and Afghanistan*. New York: New York University Press, 2015.

Bergen, Peter L. *The Longest War: The Enduring Conflict between America and Al Qaeda*. New York: Free Press, 2011.

Bowden, Mark. *The Finish: The Killing of Osama Bin Laden*. New York: Atlantic Monthly Press, 2012.

Cloud, David, and Greg Jaffe. *The Fourth Star: Four Generals and the Epic Struggle for the Future of the United States Army*. New York: Crown, 2009.

Hahn, Peter L. *Missions Accomplished? The United States and Iraq since World War I*. New York: Oxford University Press, 2012.

Jones, Seth G. *In the Graveyard of Empires: America's War in Afghanistan*. New York: W. W. Norton, 2009.

Kaplan, Fred. *The Insurgents: David Petraeus and the Plot to Change the American Way of War*. New York: Simon & Schuster, 2013.

Kaplan, Fred. *Dark Territory: The Secret History of Cyber War*. New York: Simon & Schuster, 2016.

Lewis, Adrian R. *The American Culture of War: The History of U.S. Military Force from World War II to Operation Iraqi Freedom*. Second Edition. New York: Routledge, 2012.

May, Ernest R., ed. *The 9/11 Commission Report with Related Documents*. New York: St. Martin's Press, 2007.

Moyar, Mark. *A Question of Command: Counterinsurgency from the Civil War to Iraq*. New Haven: Yale University Press, 2009.

Naylor, Sean. *Relentless Strike: The Secret History of Joint Special Operations Command*. New York: St. Martin's Press, 2015.

Ricks, Thomas E. *The Gamble: General David Petraeus and the American Military Adventure in Iraq, 2006-2008*. New York: Penguin, 2009.

Scales, Robert H., Jr., and Williamson Murray. *The Iraq War: A Military History*. Cambridge: Harvard University Press, 2003.

Singer, P. W. *Wired for War: The Robotics Revolution and Conflict in the 21st Century*. New York: Penguin, 2009.

Wright, Evan. *Generation Kill: Devil Dogs, Iceman, Captain America, and the New Face of American War*. New York: Penguin, 2008.

Full Chronology

1492	Europeans invade the Americas
1565	The Spanish establish Saint Augustine
1607	The English establish Jamestown
1608	The French found Quebec
1609–1613	First Anglo-Powhatan War in Virginia
1614	The Dutch erect Fort Nassau
1620	The Pilgrims settle Plymouth
1636–1637	The Pequot War in New England
1644–1646	Second Anglo-Powhatan War in Virginia
1675–1676	King Philip's War in New England
	Bacon's Rebellion in Virginia
1698	King William's War
1702–1712	Queen Anne's War
1715–1716	Yamasee War in South Carolina
1739–1748	King George's War (War of Jenkins' Ear)
1754–1763	Great War for Empire (French and Indian War)
1770	Boston Massacre
1775	Battles of Lexington and Concord
	Battle of Bunker Hill (Breed's Hill)
	The Continental Army and Navy formed
1776	Declaration of Independence
	Battle of New York
	Battle of Trenton
1777	Battle of Princeton
	Battle of Brandywine
	Battle of Germantown
	Battle of Saratoga
1778	Battle of Monmouth
	France allies with the United States
1779	John Paul Jones captures the *Serapis*
	Battle of Stony Point
1780	Battle of Waxhaws
	Battle of Camden
	Battle of King's Mountain
1781	Battle of Cowpens
	Battle of Guilford Courthouse
	Battle of Yorktown
1783	Treaty of Paris signed
	General George Washington retires
1786	Shays' Rebellion
1787	Constitutional Convention

American Military History: A Documentary Reader, Second Edition. Brad D. Lookingbill.
© 2019 John Wiley & Sons, Inc. Published 2019 by John Wiley & Sons, Inc.

1788	The Constitution ratified
1791	The Bill of Rights ratified
1792	Congress Passes the Uniform Militia Act
	The Legion of the United States formed
1794	Whiskey Rebellion
	Battle of Fallen Timbers
	Jay's Treaty
1795	Pinckney's Treaty
1798	The Quasi-War against France begins
	Navy Department created
	Marine Corps created
1799	George Washington dies
1800	Convention of Mortefontaine
1802	Congress Passes the Military Peace Establishment Act
1803	Tripolitan War begins
	The Louisiana Purchase
1804–1806	The Lewis and Clark Expedition
1805	Battle of Derne
1807	Aaron Burr Trial
	The Chesapeake–Leopard Affair
1811	Battle of Tippecanoe
1812	Declaration of War
	Surrender of Forts Mackinac, Detroit, and Dearborn
	U.S.S. *Constitution* sails
	Battle of Queenston Heights
1813	River Raisin Massacre
	Battle of York
	Battle of Sacket's Harbor
	Battle of Lake Erie
	Battle of the Thames
	Battle of Chrysler's Farm
	Battle of Chateauguay
1814	The Second Niagara Campaign
	Battle of Bladensburg
	Battle of Plattsburgh Bay
	Battle of Baltimore
	Treaty of Ghent
1815	Battle of New Orleans
	Battle of the Sinkhole
	Army Reduction Act
1816	Naval Expansion Act
	The Fortifications Board formed
1819	The Long Expedition
1824	General Survey Act
	The National Guard designated in New York
	Artillery School established at Fort Monroe
1826	Infantry School established at Jefferson Barracks
1829	U.S.S. *Vincennes* sailed from New York
1830	Indian Removal Act
1832	Black Hawk War
	U.S.S. *Potomac* intervenes in Sumatra
1835–1842	The Second Seminole War
1836	The Creek War
	The Cherokee Trail of Tears
	The Texas Revolution
1838	Army Topographical Corps established

1838–1842	The United States Exploring Expedition
1842	U.S.S. *Mississippi* and U.S.S. *Missouri* launched
	U.S.S. *Somers* mutiny
	Navy Observatory established
1842–1846	The Frémont Expeditions
1843	U.S.S. *Princeton* launched
1845	U.S. Naval Academy established
1846	U.S. troops ambushed in Texas
	Battle of Palo Alto
	Battle of Resaca de la Palma
	Congress passes the War Bill
	New Mexico and California occupied
	Battle of San Pascual
1847	Battle of San Gabriel
	Battle of Sacramento
	Battle of Buena Vista
	Veracruz captured
	Battle of Cerro Gordo
	Battle of Contreras
	Battle of Churubusco
	Battle of Molino del Rey
	Battle of Chapultepec
	The Occupation of Mexico City
1848	Treaty of Guadalupe Hidalgo
	U.S. troops depart Mexico
1849	California Gold Rush
1853–1854	The Perry Expedition
1860	Abraham Lincoln elected President
	South Carolina secedes
1861	Confederate States of America formed
	Attack on Fort Sumter
	Battle of First Bull Run
1862	Peninsula Campaign
	First Battle of Ironclads
	Battle of Shiloh
	Battle of Second Bull Run
	Battle of Antietam
	The Emancipation Proclamation
	Battle of Fredericksburg
	Confederate Draft begins
1863	Battle of Murfreesboro
	Federal Conscription begins
	Battle of Chancellorsville
	Battle of Gettysburg
	Vicksburg captured
	Battle of Chickamauga
	Battle of Chattanooga
1864	Battle of the Wilderness
	Battle of Cold Harbor
	Battle of the Crater
	Red River Campaign
	Battle of Atlanta
	March to the Sea
	President Lincoln reelected
	Sand Creek Massacre
	Navajo Long Walk

1865	Surrender at Appomattox Court House
	President Lincoln assassinated
1866–1868	Powder River War
1868	Battle of Beecher Island
	Battle of the Washita
1869	Peace Policy announced
1871	Camp Grant Massacre
1872–1873	Modoc War
1874–1875	Red River War
1876	Battle of Rosebud Creek
	Battle of the Little Bighorn
	Battle of Slim Buttes
	Dull Knife Fight
1877	Battle of Wolf Mountains
	Nez Percé War
1878	Paiute-Bannock War
1879	Ute War
1886	Geronimo surrenders
1885	Naval War College established
1890	Wounded Knee Massacre
1894	Cuban revolt begins
1898	U.S.S. *Maine* explodes
	Spanish–American War
	Battle of Manila Bay
	Battle of El Caney
	Battle of Santiago Bay
	Puerto Rico occupied
	Battle of Manila
	Treaty of Paris
	Hawaii annexed
1899	Naval Personnel Act
1899–1902	Philippine–American War
1900	Boxer Rebellion
1901	Army War College established
1903	Militia Act
	Army General Staff organized
1904	Roosevelt Corollary announced
1907–1909	The Great White Fleet cruises
1914	The Great War begins in Europe
1915	Lusitania attacked
1916	Punitive Expedition to Mexico
	National Defense Act
1917	Zimmerman Telegram
	U.S. declares war on Germany
	Selective Service Act
	AEF arrives in Europe
	Russia withdraws from the Great War
1918	President Wilson's Fourteen Points
	Battle of Cantigny
	Battle of Château-Thierry
	Battle of Belleau Wood
	U.S. forces enter Russia
	Battle of Meuse-Argonne
	Armistice Day
	U.S. forces enter Germany
1919	Treaty of Versailles

1919	League of Nations founded
1920	National Defense Act
1921–1922	Washington Naval Conference
1924	Adjusted Service Certificate Act
	Dawes Plan
1926	Army Air Corps created
1928	Kellogg–Briand Pact
1929	Wall Street Crash
	Young Plan
1930	Veterans Administration organized
1931	Japan invades Manchuria
1932	Bonus March
1933	Civilian Conservation Corps created
1935	First Neutrality Act
1938	Munich Agreement
1939	World War II in Europe begins
1940	Axis Tripartite Pact
1941	Lend-Lease Act
	Atlantic Charter
	Pearl Harbor attacked
1942	Battle of Wake Island
	Bataan Death March
	Doolittle Raid
	Battle of the Coral Sea
	Battle of Midway
	Battle of Guadalcanal
	Operation Torch
1943	Operation Pointblank
	Battle of Kassarine Pass
	Battle of the Atlantic
	Operation Husky
	Allied Offensive in Italy
1944	Battle of Anzio
	Allied Offensives in New Guinea and Saipan
	Operation Overlord
	Operation Cobra
	Battle of the Philippine Sea
	Operation Dragoon
	Battle of Guam
	Operation Market Garden
	Battle of Leyte Gulf
	Battle of the Bulge
1945	Battle of Iwo Jima
	Battle of Okinawa
	Victory in Europe
	Atomic Bombs dropped on Hiroshima and Nagasaki
	Victory in Japan
	The United Nations chartered
1947	The Truman Doctrine
	The Marshall Plan
	The National Security Act
	USAF established
1948	Executive Order 9981
	Berlin Airlift
1949	NATO formed
1950	Korean War erupts

	UN Security Council Resolution
	Operation Chromite
	Chinese troops intervene
1951	General MacArthur relieved
1953	Operation Little Switch
	Korean Armistice
	Operation Big Switch
1957	Sputnik launched
1958	National Defense Education Act
	NASA formed
1960	U2 incident
1961	Bay of Pigs
	Berlin Wall
1962	Cuban Missile Crisis
1963	President Kennedy assassinated
1964	Gulf of Tonkin Resolution
1965	Operation Rolling Thunder
	Operation Market Time
	Operation Game Warden
	Battle of Ia Drang
1966	Operation Sea Dragon
1967	Operation Cedar Falls
	Operation Junction City
1968	Battle of Khe Sanh
	Operation Niagara
	Tet Offensive
	U.S.S. *Pueblo* Incident
	My Lai Massacre
	Operation Sealords
1969	Vietnamization begins
1970	Kent State Shootings
1971	Winter Soldier Hearings
	Operation Lam Son 719
1972	Easter Offensive
	Operation Linebacker I and II
1973	Paris Peace Accords
	War Powers Resolution
1974	President Nixon resigns
1975	Operation Frequent Wind
	Saigon falls
1979	Iranian Hostage Crisis
1983	Beirut barracks bombed
	Operation Urgent Fury
1986	Operation El Dorado Canyon
	Goldwater–Nichols Act
	Tower Commission
1988	INF Treaty ratified
	Al-Qaeda founded
1989	Berlin Wall falls
	Operation Just Cause
1990	Iraq invades Kuwait
	Operation Desert Shield
1991	Operation Desert Storm
	Cease-Fire in Iraq
1993	World Trade Center bombed
	Battle of Mogadishu

1994	Operation Uphold Democracy
1995	Operation Joint Endeavor
1996	Khobar Towers bombed
1998	Operation Infinite Reach
	Operation Desert Fox
1999	Operation Allied Force
2000	U.S.S. *Cole* bombed
2001	9/11 Attacks
	Operation Enduring Freedom
2002	Operation Anaconda
	Iraq Disarmament Crisis
	Department of Homeland Security established
2003	Operation Iraqi Freedom
	Saddam Hussein captured
2004	NATO expands
	Abu Ghraib abuses revealed
2005	Hurricane Katrina
	Detainee Treatment Act
2006	Iraq Study Group Report
	Islamic State of Iraq formed
2007	The Surge in Iraq begins
2008	Global Financial Crisis
2009	Cyber Command established
	The Surge in Afghanistan begins
2010	Operation New Dawn
2011	Arab Spring
	Operation Odyssey Dawn
	Operation Neptune Spear
2014	Operation Inherent Resolve

Sources and Credits

1.1 Powhatan Describes War among the Natives (1607)
John Smith, *The Generall Historie of Virginia, New England, and the Summer Isles*, Volume 1 (London, 1624; rpt. New York: Macmillan, 1907), 157–161, 225–226.

1.2 John Mason Campaigns against the Pequot (1637)
John Mason, *A Brief History of the Pequot War* (Boston: Printed by S. Kneeland and T. Green, 1736), 1–9.

1.3 Elizabeth Bacon Observes Skirmishes in Virginia (1676)
"Bacon's Rebellion," *William and Mary Quarterly* 9 (July 1900), 1–10.

1.4 Benjamin Church Plans for Action in New England (1704)
Benjamin Church, *The Entertaining History of King Philip's War. As Also of Expeditions More Lately Made Against the Common Enemy, and Indian Rebels, in the Eastern Parts of New-England* (Boston, 1716; rpt. Newport, RI: Solomon Southwick in Queen Street, 1772), 245–249.

1.5 James Oglethorpe Strikes Spanish Outposts (1739–1741)
"A Ranger's Report of Travels with General Oglethorpe in Georgia and Florida, 1739–1742," in *Travels in the American Colonies*, ed. Newton D. Mereness (New York: Macmillan, 1916), 215–236.

1.6 Robert Rogers Provides Rules for the Rangers (1757)
Robert Rogers, *Journals of Major Robert Rogers* (London: J. Millan, 1765), 43–51.

1.7 An Unknown Soldier Sings "Yankee Doodle" (1775)
"Father and I Went Down to Camp," in *Report on "The Star-Spangled Banner," "Hail Columbia," "America," "Yankee Doodle,"* comp. Oscar Sonneck (Washington, DC: Library of Congress, 1909), 134–137, 195.

2.1 James Monroe Goes to War (1776)
James Monroe, *Autobiography of James Monroe*, ed. S. G. Brown (Syracuse: Syracuse University Press, 1959), 22–26. Used with permission of Syracuse University Press.

2.2 Albigence Waldo Treats Soldiers at Valley Forge (1777)
"The Diary of Surgeon Albigence Waldo of the Connecticut Line," in *Pennsylvania Magazine of History and Biography*, Volume 21 (Philadelphia: Historical Society of Pennsylvania, 1897), 309–313.

American Military History: A Documentary Reader, Second Edition. Brad D. Lookingbill.
© 2019 John Wiley & Sons, Inc. Published 2019 by John Wiley & Sons, Inc.

2.3   Jeffrey Brace Fights for Liberty (1778)
Jeffrey Brace, *The Blind African Slave* © 2005 The Board of Regents of the University of Wisconsin System. Reprinted by permission of The University of Wisconsin Press.

2.4   John Paul Jones Captures a British Frigate (1779)
John Paul Jones, "Official Account," in *Life and Correspondence*, comp. Janette Taylor (New York: D. Fanshaw, 1830), 180–187.

2.5   A French Officer Draws the Continental Line (1781)
Jean Baptiste Antoine de Verger, "American Foot Soldiers during the Yorktown Campaign, 1781," Anne S. K. Brown Military Collection, Brown University Library.

2.6   Deborah Sampson Wears a Uniform (1782)
Deborah Sampson Gannet, *An Address, Delivered with Applause, at the Federal Street Theatre, Boston, Four Successive Nights of the Different Plays, Beginning March 22, 1802* (Dedham, MA: Printed and sold by H. Mann, 1802), 11–16.

2.7   George Washington Bids Farewell to the Army (1783)
"Washington's Farewell Address to the Army, 2 November 1783," *Founders Online*, National Archives. http://founders.archives.gov/documents/Washington/99-01-02-12012 (accessed May 4, 2017).

3.1   Alexander Hamilton Considers National Forces (1787)
"The Federalist No. XXIV," in *The Federalist: A Commentary on the Constitution of the United States* (New York: M. W. Dunne, 1901), 158–163.

3.2   Henry Knox Arranges the Militia (1790)
Henry Knox, "Plan submitted to Congress, January 1790," in U.S. Congress, *American State Papers: Military Affairs*, Volume 1 (Washington, DC: Gales and Seaton, 1832), 6–14.

3.3   Anthony Wayne Prevails at Fallen Timbers (1794)
"Letter to the Secretary of War, 28 August 1794," in Horatio Newton Moore, ed., *The Life and Services of General Anthony Wayne* (Philadelphia: John B. Perry, 1845), 190–197.

3.4   Thomas Truxtun Recruits Seamen for the Quasi-War (1798)
Naval Documents Related to the Quasi-War Between the United States and France: Naval Operations From February 1797 to October 1798 (Washington, DC: Government Printing Office, 1935), 49–50.

3.5   Congress Passes the Military Peace Establishment Act (1802)
"An Act Fixing the Military Peace Establishment of the United States," in *Military Laws of the United States*, comp. John F. Callan (Philadelphia: Henry B. Ashmead, 1863), 141–149.

3.6   William Eaton Arrives on the Shores of Tripoli (1805)
Naval Documents Related to the United States Wars with the Barbary Powers, Volume 5 (Washington, DC: Government Printing Office, 1939), 553–555.

3.7   James Wilkinson Faces a Court Martial (1811)
"Copy of the Charges, 7 July 1811," in James Wilkinson, *Memoirs of My Own Times*, Volume 2 (Philadelphia: Abraham Small, 1816), 35–41.

4.1   James Madison Calls for War (1812)
James Madison, "Special Message to Congress," in *The Writings of James Madison, Volume 8,* ed. Gaillard Hunt (New York: G.P. Putnam's Sons, 1908), 192–200.

4.2   Lydia Bacon Enters Fort Detroit (1812)
Biography of Mrs. Lydia B. Bacon (Boston: Massachusetts Sabbath School Society, 1856), 60–70.

4.3   Michel Felice Cornè Portrays the U.S.S. *Constitution* (1812)
"Action between USS *Constitution* and HMS *Guerriére*, 19 August 1812: Oil on canvas, by Michel Felice Cornè," Photo # K-26254, Naval History and Heritage Command, Department of the Navy, Washington, DC. http://www.history.navy.mil/our-collections/photography/numerical-list-of-images/nara-series/80-g-k/80-G-K-20000/80-g-k-26254.html (accessed June 2, 2017).

4.4   Black Hawk Takes the War Path (1813)
Black Hawk, *Autobiography of Ma-ka-tai-me-she-kia-kiak, or Black Hawk,* ed. J. B. Patterson (St. Louis, MO: Continental Printing Co., 1882), 33–39.

4.5   Oliver Hazard Perry Defends Lake Erie (1813)
Herman Allen Fay, ed., *Collection of the Official Accounts, in Detail, of all the Battles Fought by Sea and Land, between the Navy and Army of the United States and the Navy and Army of Great Britain, during the Years 1812, 13, 14, & 15* (New York: Printed by E. Conrad, 1817), 122–125.

4.6   Francis Scott Key Pens "Defence of Fort McHenry" (1814)
"The Star Spangled Banner," in *Report on "The Star-Spangled Banner," "Hail Columbia," "America," "Yankee Doodle,"* comp. Oscar Sonneck (Washington, DC: Library of Congress, 1909), 7–37.

4.7   Andrew Jackson Triumphs at New Orleans (1815)
"General Jackson's Address," in *Official Letters of the Military and Naval Officers of the United States, during the War with Great Britain in the Years 1812, 13, 14, & 15,* ed. John Brannan (Washington, DC: Way & Gideon, 1823), 474–476.

5.1   John C. Calhoun Proposes an Expansible Army (1820)
John C. Calhoun, "Report on the Reduction of the Army, 12 December 1820," *The Works of John C. Calhoun,* Volume 5, ed. by Richard K. Crallé (New York: D. Appleton and Company, 1874), 80–85.

5.2   The National Guard Parades in New York (1825)
Asher Taylor, *Recollections of the Early Days of the National Guard* (New York: J. M. Bradstreet & Son, 1868), 41–45.

5.3   John Downes Sails to Sumatra (1832)
John Downes, "Official Documents," in Jeremiah N. Reynolds, *Voyage of the United States Frigate Potomac* (New York: Harper & Brothers, 1835), 114–120.

5.4   Ethan Allen Hitchcock Patrols in Florida (1836)
Ethan Allen Hitchcock, *Fifty Years in Camp and Field* (London: G. P. Putnam's Sons, 1909), 86–95.

5.5   Juan Seguín Remembers the Alamo (1837)
Juan N. Seguín to Albert Sidney Johnston, 13 March 1837, in *A Revolution Remembered: The Memoirs and Selected Correspondence of Juan N. Seguín*, ed. Jesús F. de la Teja (Austin: Texas State Historical Association, 2002), 161–162. Used with permission of the Texas State Historical Association, Denton.

5.6   Michael H. Garty Serves on the U.S.S. *Somers* (1842)
Proceedings of the Naval Court Martial in the Case of Alexander Slidell Mackenzie, A Commander in the Navy of the United States, &c.: Including the Charges and Specifications of Charges Preferred Against him by the Secretary of the Navy: To Which is Annexed, an Elaborate Review, by James Fennimore [sic] Cooper (New York: Henry G. Langley, 1844), 119–124.

5.7   Henry W. Halleck Lectures on War (1846)
Henry W. Halleck, *Elements of Military Art and Science: Or, Course of Instruction in Strategy, Fortification, Tactics of Battles, Etc.* (New York: D. Appleton and Company, 1846), 121–132.

6.1   James K. Polk Calls for War (1846)
James K. Polk, "Message to the Senate and House, 11 May 1846," in James D. Richardson, ed., *Messages and Papers of the Presidents, 1789–1907*, Volume 4 (New York: Bureau of National Literature and Art, 1908), 437–443.

6.2   James K. Holland Marches into Mexico (1846)
James K. Holland, "Diary of a Texan Volunteer in the Mexican War," *Southwestern Historical Quarterly* 30 (1926): 1–33.

6.3   Zachary Taylor Describes Buena Vista (1847)
Zachary Taylor, "Official Report," in Henry Montgomery, *The Life of Major General Zachary Taylor* (Buffalo: Derby & Hewson Publishers, 1847), 276–294.

6.4   Winfield Scott Lands at Veracruz (1847)
Winfield Scott, *Memoirs of Lieut.-General Scott, LL.D.*, Volume 2 (New York: Sheldon & Company, 1864), 415–432.

6.5   James Walker Views the Storming of Chapultepec (1847)
The Storming of Chapultepec, 1847, Prints and Photographs Division, Library of Congress.

6.6   Matthew C. Perry Steams to Japan (1852)
Matthew C. Perry to the Secretary of the Navy, 14 December 1852, in Francis L. Hawks, *Narrative of the Expedition of an American Squadron to the China Seas and Japan* (New York: D. Appleton and Company, 1856), 105–108.

6.7   Elizabeth C. Smith Petitions for Bounty Land (1853)
Elizabeth C. (Newcom) Smith, Mexican War Service Papers, Collection 995, Item 376, The State Historical Society of Missouri Manuscript Collection.

7.1   Abraham Lincoln Issues Proclamations (1861)
Abraham Lincoln, "Proclamations," in *Life of Abraham Lincoln*, ed. Frank Crosby (Philadelphia: John E. Potter, 1865), 108–113.

7.2   Julia Ward Howe Composes "The Battle Hymn of the Republic" (1862)
Julia Ward Howe, "The Battle Hymn of the Republic," *Atlantic Monthly* 9 (February 1862): 145.

7.3   Samuel Dana Greene Operates an Ironclad (1862)
Lydia Minturn Post, ed., *Soldiers' Letters from Camp, Battle-field and Prison* (New York: Bunce & Huntington, 1865), 106–115.

7.4   Francis Lieber Promulgates Rules for War (1863)
"General Orders No. 100, 24 April 1863," *The Miscellaneous Writings of Francis Lieber*, Volume 2 (Philadelphia: J. B. Lippincott, 1881), 245–253.

7.5   Joshua Lawrence Chamberlain Defends Little Round Top (1863)
Report of Col. Joshua L. Chamberlain, Twentieth Maine Infantry, 6 July 1863, in *War of the Rebellion: A Compilation of the Official Records of the Union and Confederate Armies*, 4 Series, 128 Volumes (Washington, DC: Government Printing Office, 1889), series 1, volume 27, part 1, chapter 39: 622–626.

7.6   Sam R. Watkins Survives Chickamauga (1863)
Sam R. Watkins, *Co. Aytch, Maury Grays, First Tennessee Regiment; or, A Side Show of the Big Show* (Chattanooga, TN: Times Printing Co., 1900), 77–96.

7.7   James Henry Gooding Protests Unequal Pay (1863)
Corporal James Henry Gooding to Abraham Lincoln, 28 September 1863, Letters Received, Series 360, Colored Troops Division, Adjutant General's Office, Record Group 94, National Archives and Records Administration.

7.8   Robert E. Lee Requests Additional Troops (1864)
Robert E. Lee to Jefferson Davis, 2 September 1864, in *Memoirs of Robert E. Lee: His Military and Personal History*, ed. by Armistead L. Long and Marcus J. Wright (New York: J. M. Stoddart and Company, 1887), 658–660.

7.9   Phoebe Yates Pember Nurses at Chimborazo (1864)
Phoebe Yates Pember, *A Southern Woman's Story* (New York: G. W. Carleton & Co., 1879), 120–123, 191–192.

7.10   Ulysses S. Grant Prevails at Appomattox (1865)
Ulysses S. Grant, *Personal Memoirs of U.S. Grant*, Volume 2 (New York: Charles L. Webster and Company, 1885), 488–496.

8.1   William T. Sherman Discusses Indian Policy (1868)
"Report of Lieutenant General William T. Sherman, 1 November 1868," in *Message from the President of the United States to the Two Houses of Congress at the Commencement of the Third Session of the Fortieth Congress*, ed. by Benjamin Perley Poore (Washington, DC: Government Printing Office, 1869), 333–340.

8.2   Elizabeth B. Custer Camps with the Cavalry (1873)
Elizabeth B. Custer, *Boy General: Story of the Life of Major-General George A. Custer*, ed. Mary E. Burt (New York: Charles Scribner's Sons, 1901), 98–105.

8.3   Making Medicine Sketches Warriors and Soldiers (1877)
Detail from U.S. Cavalry and Native American Indians by Making Medicine (Cheyenne), 17.5 x 33.3 cm, Book of Sketches made at Fort Marion, St. Augustine, Fla., ca. 1875–1878, Manuscript collection, Massachusetts Historical Society.

8.4   Emory Upton Evaluates Military Policy (1880)
Emory Upton, *The Military Policy of the United States* (Washington, DC: Government Printing Office, 1904), vii–xv.

8.5   The *Soldier's Handbook* Gives Healthy Advice (1884)
Nathaniel Hershler, ed., *Soldier's Handbook: For the Use of the Enlisted Men of the Army* (Washington, DC: Government Printing Office, 1884), 51–56.

8.6   Henry W. Lawton Pursues the Apache (1886)
"Report of Captain Lawton, 9 September 1886," in *Annual Report of the Secretary of War for the Year 1886*, Volume 1 (Washington, DC: Government Printing Office, 1886), 176–181.

8.7   Nelson A. Miles Remembers Wounded Knee (1890)
Nelson Appleton Miles, *Serving the Republic: Memoirs of the Civil and Military Life of Nelson A. Miles, Lieutenant-General, United States Army* (New York: Harper & Brothers, 1911), 233–247.

9.1   Alfred Thayer Mahan Advocates Sea Power (1890)
Alfred Thayer Mahan, *Influence of Sea Power Upon History, 1660–1783* (Boston: Little, Brown, and Company, 1890), 83–88.

9.2   William McKinley Calls for War (1898)
William McKinley, "Message to the Congress, 11 April 1898," in *Messages and Papers of the Presidents, 1789–1907*, Volume 10, ed. James D. Richardson (New York: Bureau of National Literature and Art, 1908), 56–67.

9.3   Frank W. Pullen Charges in Cuba (1898)
Frank W. Pullen, "The First Battle," in Edward Austin Johnson, ed., *A School History of the Negro Race in America from 1619 to 1890: Combined with the History of the Negro Soldiers in the Spanish-American War*, Rev. Ed. (New York: Isaac Goldmann Company, 1911), 234–242.

9.4   Clara Barton Visits a Field Hospital (1898)
Clara Barton, *The Red Cross: A History of this Remarkable International Movement in the Interest of Humanity* (Washington, DC: American National Red Cross, 1898), 563–573.

9.5   Frederick N. Funston Operates in the Philippines (1901)
Frederick N. Funston, *Memories of Two Wars: Cuban and Philippine Experiences* (New York: Charles Scribner's Sons), 384–426.

9.6   The Committee on Naval Affairs Investigates Submarines (1902)
Hearings Before the Committee on Naval Affairs, House of Representatives, on Submarine Boats (Washington, DC: Government Printing Office, 1902), 2–10.

9.7   Dan Dugal Tours the World (1907–1909)
Dan Dugal, "Journal of a Bluejacket Written at Magdalena Bay," *Overland* 52 (August 1908): 137–143.

10.1   Woodrow Wilson Calls for War (1917)
Woodrow Wilson, "Address to Congress, 2 April 1917," in *President Wilson's State Papers and Addresses*, intro. by Albert Shaw (New York: George H. Doran Company, 1918), 372–383.

10.2   George M. Cohan Composes "Over There" (1917)
George M. Cohan, "Over There," 1917, Notated Music, Library of Congress. https://www.loc.gov/item/ihas.100010516/ (accessed 6 June 2017).

10.3   Congress Passes the Selective Service Act (1917)
Office of the Provost Marshal General, *Selective Service Regulations Prescribed by the President under the Authority Vested in Him by the Terms of the Selective Service Law* (Washington, DC: Government Printing Office, 1917), 222–227.

10.4   John J. Pershing Commands the AEF (1917)
John J. Pershing, *Final Report of General John J. Pershing, Commander in Chief, American Expeditionary Forces* (Washington, DC: Government Printing Office, 1920), 9–19.

10.5   Howard Chandler Christy Publicizes the Navy (1917)
Gee!! I Wish I were a Man, 1917, Prints and Photographs Division, Library of Congress.

10.6   Ida Clyde Clarke Supports the Troops (1918)
Ida Clyde Gallagher Clarke, *American Women and the World War* (New York: D. Appleton and Company, 1918), 85–91.

10.7   Ben Hur Chastaine Reaches the Front (1918)
Ben Hur Chastaine, *Story of the 36th: The Experiences of the 36th Division in the World War* (Oklahoma City: Harlow, 1920), 75–102.

11.1   The American Legion Rallies Veterans (1919)
Resolutions Passed by the St. Louis Caucus, American Legion, 10 May 1919, in George Seay Wheat, *The Story of the American Legion* (New York: G. P. Putnam's Sons, 1919), 199–205.

11.2   George S. Patton Ponders the Next War (1922)
George S. Patton, "What the World War Did for Cavalry," *The Cavalry Journal* 31 (January 1922): 165–169.

11.3   Billy Mitchell Advocates Air Power (1927)
William Mitchell, "Airplanes in National Defense," *Annals of the American Academy of Political and Social Science* 131 (May 1927), 38–42.

11.4   Holland M. Smith Studies Marine Landings (1932)
Holland M. Smith, *Coral and Brass* (1949; rpt. Washington, DC: United States Marine Corps, 1989), 48–60.

11.5   Charles E. Humberger Joins the CCC (1933)
Charles E. Humberger, "The Civilian Conservation Corps in Nebraska: Memoirs of Company 762," *Nebraska History* 75 (1994): 292–300. Used with permission of the Nebraska State Historical Society.

11.6   George C. Marshall Speaks to Historians (1939)
George C. Marshall, "Speech to the American Historical Association," 28 December 1939, in *The Papers of George Catlett Marshall, vol. 2, "We Cannot Delay," July 1, 1939–December 6, 1941*, ed. Larry I. Bland et. al. (Baltimore: The Johns Hopkins University Press, 1986), 123–127. Copyright 1986 The Johns Hopkins University Press. Reprinted with permission of The Johns Hopkins University Press.

11.7   Harold R. Stark Recommends Plan Dog (1940)
Harold R. Stark, Memorandum for the Secretary, 12 November 1940, in Franklin D. Roosevelt, Papers as President: The President's Secretary's File (PSF), 1933–1945, Series 1: Safe File, Box 4, Navy Department, "Plan Dog," Franklin D. Roosevelt Presidential Library and Museum.

12.1   Franklin D. Roosevelt Calls for War (1941)
United States Government Manual (Washington, DC: Government Printing Office, 1942), iii–v.

12.2   Raymond A. Spruance Defends Midway (1942)
Raymond A. Spruance to Chester A. Nimitz, Commander Task Force Sixteen, 16 June 1942, TF 16 Action Report, Navy History and Heritage Command, Department of the Navy. http://www.history.navy.mil/research/archives/digitized-collections/action-reports/wwii-battle-of-midway/tf-16-action-report.html (accessed 16 June 2017).

12.3   Charles C. Winnia Flies in the South Pacific (1943)
Charles C. Winnia, "The Diary of a Corsair Pilot in the Solomons, 1943," ed. Carl S. Richardson. http://www.monongahelabooks.com/winnia.html (accessed 16 June 2017). Used with permission of Carl S. Richardson and Bradley J. Omanson.

12.4   Hiro Higuchi Volunteers for Service (1943)
Wartime Letters of Chaplain Hiro Higuchi, 11 November 1943, Digital Resources, University Archives and Manuscripts Department, University of Hawaii at Manoa Library. https://library.manoa.hawaii.edu/departments/archives/mss/aja/higuchi/hiro.ph (accessed 26 July 2017). Used with permission of the University Archives and Manuscripts Department.

12.5   Dwight D. Eisenhower Invades Normandy (1944)
Dwight D. Eisenhower, *Report by the Supreme Commander to the Combined Chiefs of Staff on the Operations in Europe of the Allied Expeditionary Force, 6 June 1944 to 8 May 1945* (Washington, DC: Government Printing Office, 1946), 21–25.

12.6   Congress Passes the GI Bill (1944)
United States Statutes at Large, 1944, Volume 58, Part 1 (Washington, DC: Government Printing Office, 1945), 287–290.

12.7   Bill Mauldin Draws Willie and Joe (1944)
"Don't hurry for me, son. I like to see young men take an interest in their work," Bill Mauldin Cartoon Collection, 45th Infantry Division Museum, Oklahoma City, Oklahoma. © 1944 Bill Mauldin. Courtesy of Bill Mauldin Estate LLC.

12.8   Melvin E. Bush Crosses the Siegfried Line (1945)
World War II Letters, 1940–1946, Collection 0068, Box 4, Folder 390, The State Historical Society of Missouri Manuscript Collection.

12.9   Jacqueline Cochran Praises the WASPs (1945)
Jacqueline Cochran, WASP Final Report, 1 June 1945, Jacqueline Cochran Papers, WASP Series, Box 12, NAID #12004155, Eisenhower Presidential Library. https://www.eisenhower.archives.gov/research/online_documents/jacqueline_cochran/BinderN.pdf (accessed 18 May 2017).

12.10   B-29s Drop Atomic Bombs on Japan (1945)
United States Strategic Bombing Survey, *Summary Report*, Pacific War (Washington, DC: Government Printing Office, 1946), 22–25.

13.1   James V. Forrestal Manages the Pentagon (1948)
James Forrestal, *First Report of the Secretary of Defense* (Washington, DC: Government Printing Office, 1948), 1–19.

13.2   Omar Bradley Discusses Desegregation (1949)
Statement by General Omar Bradley, 28 March 1949, Record Group 220, Box 10, Records of the President's Committee on Equality of Treatment and Opportunity in the Armed Services, National Archives and Records Administration.

13.3   Harry S. Truman Intervenes in Korea (1950)
Harry S. Truman, "Radio and Television Address to the American People on the Situation in Korea," 19 July 1950, Online by Gerhard Peters and John T. Woolley, The American Presidency Project. http://www.presidency.ucsb.edu/ws/?pid=13561 (accessed 23 May 2017).

13.4   Douglas MacArthur Addresses Congress (1951)
General Douglas MacArthur's "Old Soldiers Never Die" Address to Congress, 19 April 1951, American Memory, Library of Congress. http://memory.loc.gov/cgi-bin/query/r?ammem/mcc:@field(DOCID+@lit(mcc/034)) (accessed 23 May 2017).

13.5   Spike Selmyhr Maneuvers in Korea (1951)
Garlen L. "Spike" Selmyhr Interview, Veteran's Memoirs, Korean War Educator. http://www.koreanwar-educator.org/memoirs/selmyhr_spike/index.htm (accessed 23 May 2017). Used with permission of Garlen L. "Spike" Selmyhr and Lynnita Brown of the Korean War Educator.

13.6   Maxwell D. Taylor Suggests a Flexible Response (1955)
Maxwell D. Taylor, *Officer's Call: The Army in the Atomic Age*, Department of the Army Pamphlet, No. 355-21 (Washington, DC: Government Printing Office, 1955), 3–9.

13.7   Presidential Candidates Debate the Cold War (1960)
"Face-to-Face, Nixon-Kennedy," Vice President Richard M. Nixon and Senator John F. Kennedy Third Joint Television-Radio Broadcast, 13 October 1960, John F. Kennedy Presidential Library and Museum. http://www.jfklibrary.org/Research/Research-Aids/JFK-Speeches/3rd-Nixon-Kennedy-Debate_19601013.aspx (accessed 23 May 2017).

14.1   Herbert L. Ogier Patrols in the Tonkin Gulf (1964)
USS *Maddox* "Report of Action, Gulf of Tonkin, 2 August 1964," Formerly Classified Documents Subsequent to 4 August 1964, Tonkin Gulf Crisis, Navy History and Heritage Command, Department of the Navy. https://www.history.navy.mil/research/

library/online-reading-room/title-list-alphabetically/t/tonkin-gulf-crisis/tonkin-gulf-incidents-of-2-4-aug-1964/uss-maddox-reports-2-4-aug-1964.html#maddox003 (accessed 23 May 2017).

14.2   Lyndon Johnson Escalates the War (1965)
Lyndon B. Johnson, "Address at Johns Hopkins University: Peace without Conquest," 7 April 1965, Online by Gerhard Peters and John T. Woolley, The American Presidency Project. http://www.presidency.ucsb.edu/ws/?pid=26877 (accessed 23 May 2017).

14.3   Sarah L. Blum Encounters Casualties (1967)
Sarah L. Blum, "Sarah, Army Nurse in Vietnam," Women Under Fire. http://women underfire.net/sarah-army-nurse-in-vietnam/ (accessed 22 July 2017).

14.4   William C. Westmoreland Reacts to Tet (1968)
William Westmoreland, Telegram From the Commander, Military Assistance Command, Vietnam, to the Chairman of the Joint Chiefs of Staff and the Commander in Chief, Pacific, 9 February 1968, in *Foreign Relations, 1964–1968*, Volume VI, Vietnam, January–August 1968, Document 63, U.S. Department of State. http://history.state.gov/historicaldocuments/frus1964-68v06/d63 (accessed 23 May 2017).

14.5   George T. Olsen Hunts the Enemy (1969)
"Letter by George T. Olsen" by George T. Olsen, from *Dear America: Letters Home from Vietnam*, ed. Bernard Edelman. © 1985 The Vietnam Veterans Memorial Commission. Used by permission of W. W. Norton & Company, Inc.

14.6   The Gates Commission Proposes an All-Volunteer Force (1970)
Report of the President's Commission on an All-Volunteer Armed Force (Washington, DC: Government Printing Office, 1970), 5–10.

14.7   George J. Eade Assesses the Christmas Bombings (1972)
George J. Eade, "Reflections on Air Power in the Vietnam War," *Air University Review* 24 (November–December 1973), 2–9.

15.1   N. W. Ayer Rebrands the Army (1981)
N. W. Ayer & Son Advertising Records, Archives Center, National Museum of American History, Smithsonian Institution.

15.2   Ronald Reagan Envisions SDI (1983)
Ronald Reagan, "Address to the Nation on Defense and National Security," 23 March 1983, Online by Gerhard Peters and John T. Woolley, The American Presidency Project. http://www.presidency.ucsb.edu/ws/?pid=41093 (accessed 9 June 2017).

15.3   Colin L. Powell Evaluates National Security (1989)
Colin L. Powell, "National Security Challenges in the 1990s: The Future Just Ain't What it Used to Be," *ARMY* 39 (July 1989): 12–14. Reprinted with permission from *ARMY* magazine.

15.4   H. Norman Schwarzkopf Defends the Persian Gulf (1990)
"Desert Shield Boss Talks Issues," *Airman* 34 (November 1990), 24–25.

15.5   Daniel L. Davis Sees Action in Desert Storm (1991)
Daniel L. Davis, "Artillerymen in Action—The 2d ACR at the Battle of 73 Easting," *Field Artillery*, April 1992, 48–53.

15.6   Congress Approves "Don't Ask, Don't Tell" (1993)
United States Statutes at Large, 1993, Volume 107, Part 2 (Washington, DC: Government Printing Office, 1994), 1670–1673.

15.7   Richard I. Thornton Readies the Marines (1999)
House Committee on Armed Services, H.R. 1401, Fiscal Year 2000 National Defense Authorization Act—Military Readiness Issues, Military Readiness Subcommittee Hearing, 106th Congress, 22 March 1999, Serial No. 106–5. http://commdocs.house.gov/committees/security/has081030.000/has081030_0.HTM#0 (accessed 16 June 2017).

16.1   George W. Bush Calls for War (2001)
George W. Bush, "Address Before a Joint Session of the Congress on the United States Response to the Terrorist Attacks of September 11," 20 September 2001, Online by Gerhard Peters and John T. Woolley, The American Presidency Project. http://www.presidency.ucsb.edu/ws/?pid=64731 (accessed 9 June 2017).

16.2   Jessica Lynch Soldiers in Iraq (2003)
House Committee on Oversight and Government Reform, Testimony of Jessica Lynch, Hearing on Misleading Information from the Battlefield, 110th Congress, 24 April 2007, Serial No. 110-54 (Washington, DC: Government Printing Office, 2008), 21–26.

16.3   Craig M. Mullaney Deploys to Afghanistan (2003)
Excerpt from *The Unforgiving Minute: A Soldier's Education* by Craig M. Mullaney, © 2009 by Craig M. Mullaney. Used by permission of Penguin Press, an imprint of Penguin Publishing Group, a division of Penguin Random House LLC. All rights reserved.

16.4   David H. Petraeus Counters an Insurgency (2007)
General David H. Petraeus, Statement to Congress, 11 September 2007, *Iraq: The Crocker-Petraeus Report*, Hearing before the Committee on Foreign Relations, United States Senate, 110th Congress, First Session (Washington, DC: Government Printing Office, 2008), 16–41.

16.5   Sean Householder Shares "The Warrior Song" (2009)
Sean Householder, "The Warrior Song," Echo Sonic Music. http://www.thewarriorsong.com (accessed 30 June 2016). Used with permission of Sean Householder.

16.6   William H. McRaven Commands SEALs (2011)
"We Got Him: Obama, Bin Laden, and The War On Terror," CNN Special, Aired 2 May 2016. http://edition.cnn.com/TRANSCRIPTS/1605/02/se.01.html (accessed 5 July 2016). Courtesy CNN.

16.7   The Pentagon Secures Cyberspace (2015)
Department of Defense, *The DoD Cyber Strategy*, April 2015. http://www.defense.gov/Portals/1/features/2015/0415_cyber-strategy/Final_2015_DoD_CYBER_STRATEGY_for_web.pdf (accessed 25 May 2017).

Index

a

Abrams, Creighton   260
Abu Ghraib   287
Acheson, Dean   238
Adams, John   48–49, 51
Adjusted Service Certificate Act   191
Agent Orange   256
Alamo   86–88
Alexander, Keith   301
All-Volunteer Force (AVF)   3, 262–265, 271, 286
Al-Qaeda   269, 287–289, 292, 295–297, 299, 303
American Expeditionary Forces (AEF) 173, 180–182, 189, 191
American Legion   191–193, 207, 221
American Revolution   23–39, 55, 80, 144, 203
Amherst, Jeffrey   18
Anbar Province   295
Andersonville   130
Annapolis *see* U.S. Naval Academy
Apache Indians   137, 148–150
Appomattox Court House   113, 132
Appomattox Indians   11
Arapaho Indians   138
Armistice Day   173, 217
Army Air Corps   191, 196
Army and Navy Joint Planning Committee   204
Army Nurse Corps   256, 268
Army of the United Colonies   13
Army of the United States   194
Army Reduction Act   77
Army Topographical Corps   77, 95

Arnold, Henry "Hap"   227
atomic weaponry   209, 229–232, 235–236, 238, 245–247, 271–273
Axis powers   191, 204–206, 210, 218

b

Bacon, Elizabeth   11–13
Bacon, Lydia   62–64
Bacon, Nathaniel   7, 11–13
Baker, Newton   177
Barbary piracy   52–54
Barron, Samuel   53
Barton, Clara   162–164
Bataan Death March   209
"The Battle Hymn of the Republic"   116–117
Battle of Antietam   113, 128
Battle of Anzio   209
Battle of Atlanta   113, 128
Battle of Baltimore   59, 71
Battle of Beecher Island   137
Battle of Belleau Wood   173
Battle of Bladensburg   59, 71, 144
Battle of Brandywine   23–24
Battle of Buena Vista   95, 101–103
Battle of Bunker Hill (Breed's Hill)   23
Battle of Camden   23, 33
Battle of Cantigny   173
Battle of Cerro Gordo   95, 105
Battle of Chancellorsville   113, 128
Battle of Chapultepec   95, 105–106
Battle of Chateauguay   59
Battle of Château-Thierry   173
Battle of Chattanooga   113, 123–126
Battle of Chickamauga   113, 123–126
Battle of Chrysler's Farm   59

American Military History: A Documentary Reader, Second Edition. Brad D. Lookingbill.
© 2019 John Wiley & Sons, Inc. Published 2019 by John Wiley & Sons, Inc.

Battle of Churubusco   95, 105
Battle of Cold Harbor   113, 132
Battle of Contreras   95, 105
Battle of Cowpens   23
Battle of Derne   41, 53–55
Battle of El Caney   155, 160–162
Battle of Fallen Timbers   41, 46–48
Battle of First Bull Run   113
Battle of Fredericksburg   113, 128
Battle of Germantown   23–24
Battle of Gettysburg   113, 121–123, 128
Battle of Guadalcanal   209, 214
Battle of Guam   209
Battle of Guilford Courthouse   23
Battle of Ia Drang   251
Battle of Iwo Jima   209, 229
Battle of Kassarine Pass   209
Battle of Khe Sanh   251, 258–259
Battle of King's Mountain   23
Battle of Lake Erie   59, 62, 68–70
Battle of Leyte Gulf   209, 229
Battle of Long Island   24
Battle of Manila Bay   155
Battle of Meuse-Argonne   173, 186–189
Battle of Midway   209, 211–213
Battle of Missionary Ridge   123
Battle of Mogadishu   269, 283
Battle of Molino del Rey   95, 105
Battle of Monmouth   23, 24
Battle of Murfreesboro   113
Battle of New Orleans   59, 72–75
Battle of New York   23–26
Battle of Okinawa   209, 229
Battle of Olustee   126
Battle of Palo Alto   95, 98
Battle of Plattsburgh Bay   59, 71
Battle of Princeton   23, 25
Battle of Queenston Heights   59
Battle of Resaca de la Palma   95, 98
Battle of Rosebud Creek   137
Battle of Sacket's Harbor   59
Battle of Sacramento   95
Battle of San Gabriel   95
Battle of San Jacinto   86–87
Battle of San Pascual   95
Battle of Santiago Bay   155, 160–162
Battle of Saratoga   23, 26
Battle of Second Bull Run   113
Battle of Shiloh   113

Battle of Slim Buttes   137
Battle of Stony Point   23
Battle of the Atlantic   209
Battle of the Bulge   209, 223, 231
Battle of the Coral Sea   209, 211
Battle of the Crater   113
Battle of the Little Bighorn   137, 140, 150
Battle of the Philippine Sea   209
Battle of the Sinkhole   59, 66
Battle of the Thames   59, 68
Battle of the Washita   137, 142
Battle of the White Plains   24–25
Battle of the Wilderness   113, 132
Battle of Tippecanoe   59–60
Battle of Trenton   23–26
Battle of Wake Island   209
Battle of Waxhaws   23
Battle of Wolf Mountains   137, 150
Battle of York   59
Battle of Yorktown   23, 32–34, 36
Battles of Lexington and Concord   20, 23
Bay of Pigs   233
"Be All You Can Be"   269–271
Berkeley, William   11–13
Berlin Airlift   233
Berlin Wall   233, 249, 269, 274
Bill of Rights   41
bin Laden, Osama   287–288, 299–301, 304
Black Hawk   65–68, 74, 77, 93
Bliss, Tasker   177
Blum, Sarah   256–258
Bockscar   229
Bonus March   191–192
Boston Massacre   7
Boxer Rebellion   155
Brace, Jeffrey (Boyrereau Brinch)   28–30
Bradley, Omar   220, 223, 236–238
Bragg, Braxton   99–102, 124
Brock, Isaac   62
Brown, John   116
"buffalo soldiers"   145, 152
Burgoyne, Johnny   26
Burr, Aaron   41, 55
Bush Doctrine   288
Bush, George H.   274, 276, 278–279, 286
Bush, George W.   287–290, 292, 295, 303
Bush, Melvin   224–226
Butler, Benjamin   126

c

Calhoun, John C.   77–80
camp followers   34, 39
Camp Grant   137
Camp Shelby   216–218
Carter, Earl   271
Cass, Lewis   84
CENTCOM   276, 290
Central Intelligence Agency (CIA)   234, 248, 299
Chamberlain, Joshua Lawrence   121–123
Chastaine, Ben Hur   186–189
Cherokee Indians   15–16, 77, 84
Cheyenne Indians   138, 140, 142–143
Chickasaw Indians   15, 84
Choctaw (Choctau) Indians   15, 72, 84
Christy, Howard Chandler   183–184
Church, Benjamin   13–15
Civilian Conservation Corps (CCC)   191, 200–202
civil-military relations   3, 41–45, 111, 114, 119–120, 143, 177, 200, 236, 262, 281
Civil War   1, 91, 113–135, 143, 150, 156, 157, 196, 218, 304
Clarke, Ida Clyde   184–186
Clay, Henry Jr.   101
Clifford, Clark   258
Clinton, Bill   281, 283–284, 286
Cochran, Jacqueline   227–229
Cohan, George   176–177
Cold War   233–250, 265, 274, 286
Comanche Indians   138, 162
Committee on Equality of Treatment and Opportunity in the Armed Services   236
Committee on Public Information   176
Constitutional Convention   41–42
Continental Army   23–24, 26–28, 36, 38–39, 44, 55
Continental Navy   23, 31
Convention of Mortefontaine   41, 49
Cornè, Michel Felice   64–65
Cornwallis, Charles   32–33
counterinsurgency   295–297, 304
Creek Indians   15–16, 72, 75, 77, 84
Cromwell, Samuel   88–90
Crow Indians   138
CSS Virginia see USS Merrimac
Cuban Missile Crisis   233
Custer, Elizabeth   139–142

Custer, George A.   139–142, 153
Cyber Mission Force (CMF)   301–303

d

Daniels, Josephus   183
Davis, Daniel   278–281
Davis, Jefferson   101, 111, 128–129, 135
Dawes Plan   191
D-day   219–221, 223–225
Dearborn, Henry   51
Decatur, Stephen   53
Defense Department   3, 233–236, 274, 292, 301–303
"Don't Ask, Don't Tell"   281–283
Dowdy, Robert   290–291
Downes, John   82–84
Dugal, Dan   169–170
Dulles, John Foster   245

e

Eade, George J.   265–267
Easter Offensive   251, 265–267
Eaton, William   52–55
Eisenhower, Dwight D.   218–221, 223, 224, 228, 245, 248, 249
Emancipation Proclamation   113, 126
Embargo Act of 1807   59
Enola Gay   229
Ericsson, John   118
Espionage Act   176
Evans, Robley   169
Executive Order 9981   233, 236

f

Fahy, Charles   236
Farquhar, Richard   53
Federalist Papers   41–44
Fleet Marine Force (FMF)   198–200
Forrestal, James   233–236, 249
FORSCOM   274
Fort Crook   200
Fort Dearborn   59, 62
Fort Defiance   48
Fort Detroit   18, 59, 62–68
Fort Drum   293
Fort Edward   18
Fort Greenville   46–48
Fort Laramie   137
Fort Leavenworth   109–110

Fort Lee   24
Fort Mackinac   59, 62
Fort Marion   142–143, 153
Fort McHenry   71–72
Fort Meigs   65
Fort Miamis   46–47
Fort Monroe   77, 118
Fort Mystic   9–11
Fort Nassau   7
Fort Recovery   48
Fort San Marcos   16–17
Fort Sill   142
Fort Stephenson   65
Fort Sumter   113–114
Fort Washington   24
Fort Wayne   66
Fourteen Points   173
Fox, Gustavus   119
Franks, Frederick   280
Franks, Tommy   290
Frémont, John C.   96
Frémont Expeditions   95–96
Friedman, Milton   262
Funston, Frederick   165–167

g
Gadsden Purchase   109
Garty, Michael   88–90
Gates, Horatio   26, 33
Gates, Thomas   262
Gates Commission   262–265
Gatewood, Charles   149–150
Geneva Accords of 1954   251
Geneva Conventions   120
Geronimo   137, 148–149, 152
GI Bill (Servicemen's Readjustment Act)
   221–223
Global War on Terror   287–304
Goldwater-Nichols Defense Reorganization
   Act   269, 274
Gooding, James Henry   126–127
Gorbachev, Mikhail   271, 274–275
Gorham, John   14
Grant, Ulysses S.   111, 132–135
Great Sioux War   140
Great War for Empire (French and Indian
   War)   7, 17–22
"Great White Fleet"   155, 169–170
Greene, Nathaniel   33

Greene, Samuel Dana   117–119
Greenspan, Alan   262
Gulf of Tonkin   251–253, 268
Gulf War   268, 276–281, 286
gunboats   53–55, 104

h
Halleck, Henry   90–92
Halsey, William   214
Hamilton, Alexander   41–44, 57
Harrison, William Henry   68, 70
Higuchi, Hiro   216–218
Hiroshima   209, 229–232
Hitchcock, Ethan Allen   84–86
Hitler, Adolf   226
HMS Guerriére   64–65
HMS Serapis   23, 30–32
Ho Chi Minh Trail   254
Holland, James   98–101
Homeland Security Department   287
Householder, Sean   297–299
Houston, Sam   86–88
Howe, Julia Ward   116–117
Hull, Isaac   53, 64
Hull, William   62–63
Humberger, Charles   200–202
Hundred Days Offensive   173, 186–189, 194
Hussein, Saddam   276, 278, 284, 287, 290
Huston, Felix   87

i
Indian Removal Act of 1830   77, 84
intermediate-range nuclear forces   271
International Security Assistance Force
   (ISAF)   292
Iranian Hostage Crisis   269
Iraq Disarmament Crisis   287, 290
Iraq Surge   287, 295–297
ironclads   113, 117–119, 134
Islamic State (ISIS)   295

j
Jackson, Andrew   72–75, 82–84, 93, 101
Jamestown   7–9, 11
Jay's Treaty   41
Jefferson, Thomas   51–53, 57, 59
jihad   288
Johnson, Lyndon B.   252, 254–256,
   258, 268

Joint Chiefs of Staff 241, 254, 260, 268, 274, 281, 295
Joint Special Operations Command (JSOC) 299
Jomini, Antoine Henri 90
Jones, John Paul 23, 30–32, 39

k

Karzai, Hamid 292
Kellogg-Briand Pact 191
Kennedy, John F. 233, 248–249
Kennedy, John P. 107
Key, Francis Scott 71
King George's War 7
King Philip's War 7, 13, 15, 22
King William's War 7
Kiowa Indians 138
Knox, Henry 44–47, 57
Korean War 233, 238–246, 249–250

l

Lawton, Henry 148–150
League of Nations 174–175, 191
Lee, Robert E. 111, 121, 128–130, 132–135
Legion of the United States 49, 52–58
Lejeune, John 198
Lend-Lease Act 191
Liberty Bonds 184
Lieber, Francis 119–121
Lincoln, Abraham 113–115, 119, 126–128, 134–135
Louisiana Purchase 41, 51
Luce, Stephen B. 155
Lusitania 173–175
Lynch, Jessica 290–292

m

MacArthur, Arthur 165–166
MacArthur, Douglas 214, 229, 233, 239–243, 249
Macdonough, Thomas 71
MacKenzie, Alexander Slidell 88–90
Macon's Bill No. 2 59
Madison, James 42, 55, 59–75
Mahan, Alfred Thayer 155–157
Mahan, Denis Hart 90
Making Medicine (David Pendleton Oakerhater) 142–143
Manifest Destiny 68, 110–131

Marine Corps 1, 31, 41, 49, 57, 89, 106, 198–200, 207, 214, 216, 243, 269, 276, 284, 285
Marshall, George 202–204, 207, 218, 233
Mason, John 9–11
Mauldin, Bill 223–224
McKinley, William 157–160, 165
McMaster, H. R. 268, 279–280
McNamara, Robert 254, 268
McRaven, William 299–301
Meade, George 121
Medicine Lodge Treaty of 1867 137
Mexican–American War 95–111, 144
Mexican War Bounty Land Act 109
Miles, Nelson 149–153
Military Assistance Command, Vietnam (MACV) 258
Military Peace Establishment Act 41, 51–52
Militia 3, 9–16, 20–22, 26, 33, 41–47, 53, 57, 62, 72–80, 97, 114–115, 144, 155, 180
Militia Act of 1903 155
Mitchell, William 196–198
Modoc War 137
Mohegan Indians 9
Monroe Doctrine 169, 204
Monroe, James 23–26, 77
Mullaney, Craig 292–294
Munich Agreement 191
My Lai Massacre 251, 258

n

Nagasaki 209, 229–231
Napoleonic Wars 59, 71, 90
National Aeronautics and Space Administration (NASA) 233
National Defense Act 173, 178, 191
National Defense Authorization Act 281
National Guard 1, 77, 80–82, 93, 177, 180, 186, 192, 194, 237, 239, 262, 264, 277
National Security Act 233–235
National Security Council (NSC) 238
Navajo Indians 137, 138
Naval Expansion Act 77
Naval Personnel Act 155
Navy Department 41, 49, 88, 167, 183, 196, 206, 221
Navy Observatory 77
Neutrality Acts 191, 202
Newport, Christopher 7–8
Nez Percé War 137, 150

Niagara Campaign 59, 64, 74
Nimitz, Chester 211–213
Nisei 216–218
Nixon, Richard 248–249, 251, 260, 262, 265
Non-Intercourse Act of 1809 59
North Atlantic Treaty Organization
   (NATO) 233, 234, 248, 274, 287, 292
Nunn, Sam 281
N.W. Ayer & Son 269–271

o

Obama, Barack 299, 301
Odierno, Ray 296–297
Ogier, Herbert 251–253
Oglethorpe, James 15–17
"Old Ironsides" *see USS Constitution*
Olsen, George 260–262
Operation Allied Force 269
Operation Anaconda 287
Operation Big Switch 233
Operation Cedar Falls 251
Operation Chromite 233, 240
Operation Cobra 209, 223
Operation Desert Fox 284
Operation Desert Shield 269, 276–278
Operation Desert Storm 269, 278–281
Operation Dragoon 209
Operation El Dorado Canyon 269
Operation Enduring Freedom 287, 288
Operation Frequent Wind 251
Operation Game Warden 251
Operation Husky 209, 219
Operation Infinite Reach 284
Operation Inherent Resolve 287
Operation Iraqi Freedom 287, 290–292,
   295, 304
Operation Junction City 251
Operation Just Cause 269
Operation Lam Son 719 251
Operation Linebacker I and II 251, 265–267
Operation Little Switch 233
Operation Market Garden 209
Operation Market Time 251
Operation Neptune Spear 287
Operation New Dawn 287
Operation Odyssey Dawn 287
Operation Overlord 209, 218–221
Operation Pointblank 209, 219
Operation Rolling Thunder 251, 254

Operation Sea Dragon 251
Operation Sea Lords 251
Operation Torch 209, 218
Operation Uphold Democracy 283
Operation Urgent Fury 269
"Over There" 176–177

p

Paine, Thomas 23–24
Paiute-Bannock War 137
Pakenham, Edward 72
Paris Peace Accords 251, 265
Patton, George S. 194–195, 207, 223–224
Peace Corps 294
Peace Policy 137–138
Pearl Harbor 201–211
Pember, Phoebe Yates 130–131
Pequot War 7, 9–11, 22
Perry, Matthew 95, 106–109, 111
Perry, Oliver Hazard 68–70
Pershing, John J. 180–182, 186, 189
Petraeus, David 295–297, 304
Philippine–American War 155, 165–167
Pierce, Franklin 109
Piestewa, Lori 290–292
Pinckney's Treaty 41
Polk, James K. 95–98, 111
Powder River War 137
Powell, Colin 274–276, 286
Powhatan 7–9
Pratt, Richard Henry 142
Preble, Edward 53
prisoners of war (POW) 16, 18, 25, 64–67,
   70, 99–100, 103, 105, 119–121, 123, 125,
   130–132, 142–143, 153, 163–165, 225, 233
privateers 17, 30–31
Pullen, Frank 160–162

q

Quasi-War 41, 48–50
Queen Anne's War 7, 13

r

Rangers 16–20
Reagan, Ronald 271–274, 286
Red Cross 162–164, 184
Red River Campaign 113
Red River War 137, 142–143, 150
Reed, Esther DeBerdt 34

Reserve Officer Training Corps (ROTC) 194
Ridgway, Matthew 243
River Raisin Massacre 59, 65
Rogers, Robert 17–20, 22
Roosevelt, Franklin 183, 200–202, 204–207, 210–211, 216, 221–223
Roosevelt, Theodore 155, 158, 160, 169, 171
Roosevelt, Theodore Jr. 191
Rough Riders 160–162, 171

s

Saigon 251–252, 254, 258, 262, 265
Saint Augustine 7, 16–17, 142–143
Sampson, Deborah 34–35, 39
Sampson, William 160
Sand Creek Massacre 137
Santa Anna, Antonio Lopez de 86–87, 101–103, 105–106
Schwarzkopf, H. Norman 276–278
Scott, Hugh 177
Scott, Winfield 103–106, 111
SEALs 299–301
Sedition Act 176
Seguín, Juan 86–88
Selective Service Act 173, 177–180, 193, 237, 239, 262–265
Selmyhr, Garlen "Spike" 243–245
Seminole War 77, 84–86, 93
Shays Rebellion 41
Sherman, William T. 101–102, 111, 128, 135, 137–139
Shuckburgh, Richard 20
Sims, William 183
Single Integrated Operational Plan (SIOP) 248
Sioux Indians 138–140, 150–152
Small, Elisha 88–90
Smith, Bernice 183–184
Smith, Elizabeth C. 109–110
Smith, Holland 198–200, 207
Smith, John 7–9
Society of the Cincinnati 36, 44, 57
Spanish–American War 155–165, 171
Spencer, Philip 88–90
Spruance, Raymond 211–213
Sputnik 233, 248
Stanton, Edwin 116
Stark, Harold 204–207
"Star Spangled Banner" 70–72

Star Wars *see* Strategic Defense Initiative (SDI)
State Department 108, 223, 260
Stoddert, Benjamin 49, 57
Strategic Air Command (SAC) 248, 265
Strategic Defense Initiative (SDI) 271–273, 286
Sumatra 77, 82–84

t

Taliban 287–290, 292–294
Taylor, Maxwell 245–247
Taylor, Zachary 96, 101–104, 110
Tecumseh 68
Teller Amendment 158
Tet Offensive 251, 258–260, 268
Texas Revolution 77, 85–88
Thayer, Sylvanus 90
Thornton, Richard 283–285
Thurman, Maxwell 269–271
Tibbets, Paul 229
Tillman, Pat 291
Tower Commission 269
Trail of Tears 77, 84
Treaty of Ghent 59, 72
Treaty of Guadalupe Hidalgo 95, 106
Treaty of Kanagawa 107
Treaty of Paris (1783) 23, 36
Treaty of Paris (1898) 155, 163
Treaty of Versailles 173, 186
Tripolitan War 41, 52–55
Truman Doctrine 233, 238
Truman, Harry S. 229, 233–245
Truxtun, Thomas 48–50
Tuskegee Airmen 216

u

U2 Incident 233, 248
Underhill, John 10
Uniform Militia Act 41, 44
United Nations (UN) 233, 235, 238–243
Upton, Emory 143–145, 152
U.S. Air Force 1, 196, 234–236, 239, 248, 265, 269, 276, 278, 292
U.S. Army 1, 51–52, 55, 57, 62, 68, 72, 75, 77–80, 93, 109–111, 137–139, 142–148, 150–153, 160–171, 177–189, 194, 200–202, 207, 214, 216, 219, 221–226, 231, 234–238, 240–242, 245–247, 249, 262–265, 268–271, 274–276, 286, 290–292, 304

U.S. Army Air Forces   196–198, 210, 216, 227–232
U.S. Army War College   155
USCYBERCOM   301–303
U.S. Military Academy   51–52, 90–93, 143, 180, 242, 286, 292
U.S. Naval Academy   68, 77, 88, 167
U.S. Naval War College   155, 171, 198–200
U.S. Navy   1, 57, 64–65, 68–70, 74, 77, 82–84, 88–90, 93, 103, 106–109, 117–119, 134, 155–159, 167–171, 180, 183–184, 196, 198–200, 204–207, 209–214, 234–236, 239, 248, 256, 269, 276, 278, 282, 299–301
USS Argus   53–54
USS Ariel   70
USS Bonhomme Richard   31–32
USS Cole   269
USS Congress   118
USS Connecticut   169–170
USS Constitution   59, 64–65
USS C. Turner Joy   252–253
USS Cumberland   118
USS Holland   167–169
USS Lawrence   68–70
USS Maddox   252–253
USS Maine   155, 157–160
USS Merrimac   117–119
USS Minnesota   118–119
USS Missouri   229
USS Monitor   117–119
USS Nautilus   53–54
USS Niagara   68–70
USS Potomac   77, 82–84
USS Princeton   77
USS Pueblo   251
USS Somers   77, 88–90
USS Ticonderoga   252–253
USS Vincennes   77, 82
USS Yorktown   211–213
Ute War   137

v

Valley Forge   26–28
V-E Day   209, 224–226
Verger, Jean Baptiste Antoine de   32–33
Veterans Administration   191–192, 221–223

Viet Cong   251, 258, 261–262, 265
Vietnam War   251–269
Vincent, Strong   121–122
von Steuben, Friederich Wilhelm   26

w

Wainwright, Richard   167–169
Waldo, Albigence   26–28
Walker, James   105–106
Wallis, W. Allen   262
War Department   44–48, 51–52, 72, 77–80, 84, 114, 119–121, 138–139, 142, 145–148, 177–182, 194, 196, 200, 234
War Industries Board   184
War of 1812   57–75, 144
War of Jenkins' Ear *see* King George's War
War Powers Resolution   251
"The Warrior Song"   297–298
War Risk Insurance Act   192–193
Washington, George   21, 23–28, 33, 34, 36–39, 41–42, 44, 48, 57, 101
Watkins, Sam   123–126
Wayne, Anthony   46–48, 57
weapons of mass destruction (WMD)   229–232, 284, 290
Westmoreland, William   258–260, 267
West Point *see* U.S. Military Academy
Whiskey Rebellion   41, 44, 57
Wilkinson, James   55–57
Wilson, Woodrow   173–189
Winnia, Charles   214–216
Women's Air Force Service Pilots (WASP)   227–229, 232
Wool, John   119
World War I   173–189, 191–196, 201, 203
World War II   191, 198, 201, 204–207, 209–232, 248, 254–255, 264, 267, 278, 297
Wounded Knee Massacre   137, 150–152

y

Yamasee War   7
"Yankee Doodle"   20–22
Young Plan   191

z

Zimmerman Telegram   173–175

Printed in the USA
CPSIA information can be obtained
at www.ICGtesting.com
LVHW080044270124
769971LV00008B/1140